AN INTROD BOND MARKETS

Third Edition

The Securities & Investment Institute

Mission Statement:

To set standards of professional excellence and integrity for the investment and securities industry, providing qualifications and promoting the highest level of competence to our members, other individuals and firms.

The Securities and Investment Institute is the UK's leading professional and membership body for practitioners in the securities and investment industry, with more than 16,000 members with an increasing number working outside the UK. It is also the major examining body for the industry, with a full range of qualifications aimed at people entering and working in it. More than 30,000 examinations are taken annually in more than 30 countries.

You can contact us through our website *www.sii.org.uk*

Our membership believes that keeping up to date is central to professional development. We are delighted to endorse the Wiley/SII publishing partnership and recommend this series of books to our members and all those who work in the industry.

Ruth Martin
Managing Director

AN INTRODUCTION TO BOND MARKETS

Third Edition

....

Moorad Choudhry

JOHN WILEY & SONS, LTD

Published in 2006 by John Wiley & Sons Ltd, The Atrium, Southern Gate, Chichester,
West Sussex PO19 8SQ, England

Telephone (+44) 1243 779777

Email (for orders and customer service enquiries): cs-books@wiley.co.uk
Visit our Home Page on www.wiley.com

Other Wiley Editorial Offices

John Wiley & Sons, Inc., 111 River Street, Hoboken, NJ 07030, USA

Jossey-Bass, 989 Market Street, San Francisco, CA 94103-1741, USA

Wiley-VCH Verlag GmbH, Boschstr. 12, D-69469 Weinheim, Germany

John Wiley & Sons Australia Ltd, 42 McDougall Street, Milton, Queensland 4064, Australia

John Wiley & Sons (Asia) Pte Ltd, 2 Clementi Loop #02-01, Jin Xing Distripark, Singapore 129809

John Wiley & Sons Canada Ltd, 22 Worcester Road, Etobicoke, Ontario, Canada M9W 1L1

Wiley also publishes its books in a variety of electronic formats. Some content that appears
in print may not be available in electronic books.

British Library Cataloguing in Publication Data

A catalogue record for this book is available from the British Library

ISBN-13 978-0-470-01758-6 (PB)
ISBN-10 0-470-01758-9 (PB)

Project management by Originator, Gt Yarmouth, Norfolk (typeset in 12/16pt Trump Mediaeval).
Printed and bound in Great Britain by T.J. International Ltd, Padstow, Cornwall.
This book is printed on acid-free paper responsibly manufactured from sustainable forestry
in which at least two trees are planted for each one used for paper production.

For Shareef C
Once were kings ...

CONTENTS

· ·

FOREWORD

Benjamin Franklin must have been delivering advice to an aspiring bond trader when he put forward one of his most memorable quotes "time is money". From present values, through duration and up to maturity the bond markets demonstrate this relationship perfectly because we all know that one Pound tomorrow is worth less than one Pound today.

I learned these basic principles when I first showed an interest in business and had not even begun to grasp how much more I would need to learn to forge a career in the capital markets. What I found is that there is a lot to learn and not many good tutors. I have encountered few people that are willing to share information and even fewer who are able to do so in a clear and concise manner. Moorad therefore falls into that rarest of breeds, a market practitioner and day-to-day trader who finds the time to share his knowledge with others in a way that beginners can understand, while at the same time uncovering topics which offer something new for the experts.

So I will finish up with another quote, this time by Theodor Adorno, "if time is money, it seems moral to save time, above all one's own". I have concluded that his advice to us is why bother learning the hard way – it's all in this book.

Rod Pienaar
Director, Prime Services
UBS AG, London

PREFACE

One hopes that my writing has progressed since the first edition of this book was published in 1999. Certainly the markets themselves have moved on, as the constant dynamic that is the world's fixed income markets results in new products and processes on an almost daily basis. It is a task in itself merely to keep up with new developments in bonds and financial engineering, let alone to write about them in a way that is of value to market practitioners. Still, as the character played by Keifer Sutherland in the 1988 movie *Young Guns* said, "Let's finish out the game!" We began the journey with the first edition, so let us complete it now with this much revised and (we hope!) improved third edition.

The third edition of this book builds on the format established with the first edition, a succinct, accessible description of fixed-income instruments and their analysis. We include related derivative instruments such as interest-rate swaps and futures. We have removed the chapter on repo, as that is a specialized topic worthy of its own book, and replaced it with a general chapter on money markets that includes repo. Other changes are detailed below.

The market in bond market securities, also known as the fixed-income market, is incredibly large and diverse, and one that plays an irreplaceable part in global economic development. The vast majority of securities in the world today are debt instruments, with outstanding volume estimated at over $13 trillion. In this book we provide a concise and accessible description of the main elements of the markets, concentrating on the instruments used and their applications. As it has been designed to be both succinct and concise, the major issues are introduced and described, and where appropriate certain applications are also analysed. There is little or no description of specific markets, exchanges or trading conventions; such topics would result in a very large book and is abundantly covered in existing literature. A very detailed treatment is therefore left out, as required in a book of this size, but interested readers can access the references listed in the Bibliography at the end of most chapters. Where possible, these references are indicated for their level of analysis and technical treatment. All items listed have been read by the author, which serves to make bibliographies relevant and not over-long.

Given the size of the global bond markets, it would never be possible to cover every single instrument and application in a single book. Our intention is to cover the areas most important for beginners. This book is aimed at those with little or no previous understanding of or exposure to the bond markets; however, it also investigates the markets to sufficient depth to be of use to the more experienced practitioner. It is primarily aimed at front-office, middle-office and back-office banking and fund management staff who are involved to some extent with fixed-income securities. Others including corporate and local authority treasurers, bank auditors and consultants, risk managers and legal department staff may also find the contents useful.

The great stride forward in capital markets has been in the synthetic credit markets – namely, structured credit products and credit derivatives. When I was working on the manuscript for the first edition of this book during 1998, the credit derivatives markets were, if not in their infancy, at least still being developed. Now, I would suggest that they represent as liquid and transparent a market for credit as futures and swaps do for interest rates. So, while 8 years ago credit derivatives might be considered to be an arcane, specialist field only worthy of discussion in a specialist book (and still should be, I hasten to add), today one could not think of writing a book on bond markets without discussing credit derivatives. So, this edition includes a chapter on these exciting products.

We continue to emphasise further practical demonstration of main analytical techniques, so, for example, we now make use of Bloomberg screens to demonstrate relative value analysis, asset swap spreads and other yield spreads. We also add a brief word on credit analysis, as the current vogue on ever great risk/return profiles means investors look to ever more credit-risky assets.

Other additions and updates include:

- a revised chapter on approaches to trading reproduced from a book first published in 2002 and edited by Professor Frank Fabozzi;
- a chapter on convertible bonds and warrants;
- a more detailed chapter on Eurobonds;
- a new chapter on securitised products such as asset-backed securities;
- a chapter on index-linked bonds.

We have removed the chapter on the UK gilt market, as my book *The Gilt-Edged Market* (Elsevier 2003), co-written with Graham 'Harry' Cross and James Harrison, is a much better introduction to that subject. Also removed for this edition is the overview chapter on government markets; the original chapter was never really anything more than a random sample of country markets and did not do any of these markets any justice!

A reader emailed me once with his thanks and appreciation, because apparently my books were the first in finance that incorporated Bloomberg, Reuters and other screens as exhibits in the text. I am not so sure myself, I remember seeing a Paul Wilmott book that also had such screens around about the same time as my books were coming out, but irrespective of which authors were the first to adopt this particular idea, I am happy to have been of some small service to people such as he, students and practitioners alike. The global debt markets are far too important, and pivotal in global economic development and progress, for knowledge transfer and dissemination not to be a top priority of everyone that has an interest in them.

As the legendary Professor Emanuel Derman said in the August 2004 issue of *RISK*, "the world is a richer place, in both senses of the word, for the sharing of information."

Amen to that!

Finally, some thanks.

The first edition of this book arose from material put together for the bond markets' course run by the Securities Institute (now the Securities and Investment Institute) in London. My thanks to Zena Deane for giving me the opportunity to teach this course back in 1999.

Big thanks to Anuk Teasdale for assistance with graphics used in the first edition.

And, finally, with only very few exceptions, thanks to everyone I have worked with in the City of London since I first started out there in August 1989 ... yes, this includes you! Whatever we are doing, we are always learning. Good luck, and my best wishes to you all.

Moorad Choudhry
Surrey, England
March 2006

ABOUT THE AUTHOR

Moorad Choudhry is Head of Treasury at KBC Financial Products in London. He is a Visiting Professor at the Department of Economics, London Metropolitan University, a Visiting Research Fellow at the ICMA Centre, University of Reading, a Senior Fellow at the Centre for Mathematical Trading and Finance, Cass Business School and a Fellow of the Securities and Investment Institute.

Do not worry about your difficulties in mathematics. I can assure you mine are still greater.

– Albert Einstein (1879–1955)

Education never ends, Watson. It's a series of lessons, with the greatest for the last.

– *The Adventure of the Red Circle*, His Last Bow
Sir Arthur Conan Doyle (1859–1930)

Chapter

1

INTRODUCTION TO BONDS

Bonds are the basic ingredient of the world's debt-capital markets, which in turn are the cornerstone of the world's economy. Consider how many television news programmes contain a slot during which the newscaster informs viewers where the main stock market indexes closed that day and where key foreign exchange rates ended up. More usefully, the financial sections of most newspapers also indicate at what yield the government long bond closed. This coverage reflects the fact that bond prices are affected directly by economic and political events, and yield levels on certain government bonds are fundamental economic indicators. The yield level on the US Treasury long bond, for instance, mirrors the market's view on US interest rates, inflation, public-sector debt, and economic growth.

The media report the bond yield level because it is so important to the country's economy – as important as the level of the equity market and more relevant as an indicator of the health and direction of the economy. Because of the size and crucial nature of the debt markets, a large number of market participants, ranging from bond issuers to bond investors and associated intermediaries are interested in analysing them. This chapter introduces the building blocks of the analysis.

Bonds are debt instruments that represent cash flows payable during a specified time period. They are a form of debt, much like how a bank loan is a form of debt. The cash flows they represent are the interest payments on the loan and the loan redemption. Unlike commercial bank loans, however, bonds are tradeable in a secondary market. Bonds are commonly referred to as *fixed-income* instruments. This term goes back to a time when bonds paid fixed coupons each year. That is no longer necessarily the case. Asset-backed bonds, for instance, are issued in a number of tranches – related securities from the same issuer – each of which pays a different fixed or floating coupon. Nevertheless, this is still commonly referred to as the fixed-income market.

In the first edition of this book I wrote:

Unlike bank loans however bonds can be **traded** *in a market.*

Actually, the first part of this statement cannot really be said to be accurate anymore. There is a thriving secondary market, certainly for US dollar and pound sterling loans, in bank loans these days. However, it is viewed as a separate market, and is not as liquid as the bond market.[1] We will not discuss it in this book. However, I made this statement originally to highlight the key feature of bonds: they are tradeable after being issued.

A bond is a debt capital market instrument issued by a borrower, who is then required to repay to the lender/investor the amount borrowed plus interest, over a specified period of time. Usually, bonds are considered to be those debt securities with terms to maturity of over 1 year. Debt issued with a maturity of less than 1 year is considered to be *money market* debt. There are many different types of bonds that can be issued. The most common bond is the *conventional* (or *plain vanilla* or *bullet*) *bond*. This is a bond paying a regular (annual or semiannual) fixed interest rate over a fixed period to maturity or redemption, with the return of *principal* (the par or nominal value of the bond) on the maturity date. All other bonds will be variations on this.

There is a wide range of parties involved in the bond markets. We can group them broadly into borrowers and investors, plus the institutions and individuals who are part of the business of bond trading. Borrowers access the bond markets as part of their financing requirements; hence, borrowers can include sovereign governments, local authorities, public-sector organisations and corporates. Virtually all businesses operate with a financing structure that is a mixture of debt and equity finance. The debt finance almost invariably contains a form of bond finance, so it is easy to see what an important part of the global economy the bond markets are. As we shall see in the following chapters, there is a range of types of debt that can be raised to meet the needs of individual borrowers, from short-term paper issued as part of a company's cash flow requirements, to very long-dated bonds that form part of the financing of key projects. An example of the latter was the issue in the summer of 2005 of 50-year bonds by the UK government. The other main category of market participant are investors, those who lend money to borrowers by buying their bonds. Investors range from private individuals to fund managers such as those who manage pensions funds. Often an institution will be active in the markets as both a borrower and an

---

[1] The *secondary* market is the market in which bonds and loans are traded after they have been struck between borrower and lender. The bonds are traded between third parties who generally would not have been party to the initial *primary* market transaction. Liquidity refers to the ease with which bonds can be bought and sold by market participants.

investor. The banks and securities houses that facilitate trading in bonds in both the *primary* and *secondary* markets are also often observed to be both borrowers and investors in bonds. The bond markets in developed countries are large and *liquid*, a term used to describe the ease with which it is possible to buy and sell bonds. In emerging markets a debt market usually develops ahead of an equity market, led by trading in government *bills* and bonds. This reflects the fact that, as in developed economies, government debt is usually the largest in the domestic market and the highest quality paper available.

We look first at some important features of bonds. This is followed by a detailed look at pricing and yield. We conclude this introductory chapter with some spreadsheet illustrations.

DESCRIPTION

Bonds are identified by just one or two key features.

Type of issuer   A key feature of a bond is the nature of the issuer. There are four issuers of bonds: sovereign governments and their agencies, local government authorities, supranational bodies such as the World Bank, and corporations. Within the corporate bond market there is a wide range of issuers, each with differing abilities to satisfy their contractual obligations to investors. An issuer's ability to make these payments is identified by its *credit rating*.

Term to maturity   The *term to maturity* of a bond is the number of years after which the issuer will repay the obligation. During the term the issuer will also make periodic interest payments on the debt. The *maturity* of a bond refers to the date that the debt will cease to exist, at which time the issuer will redeem the bond by paying the principal. The practice in the market is often to refer simply to a bond's 'term' or 'maturity'. The provisions under which a bond is issued may allow either the issuer or investor to alter a bond's term to maturity. The term to maturity is an important consideration in the make-up of a bond. It indicates the time period over which the bondholder can expect to receive the coupon payments and the number of years before the principal will be paid in full. The bond's *yield* also depends on the term to maturity. Finally, the price of a bond will fluctuate over its life as yields in the market change and as it approaches maturity. As we will discover later, the *volatility* of a bond's price is dependent on its maturity; assuming other factors constant, the longer a bond's maturity the greater the price volatility resulting from a change in market yields.

Principal and coupon rate   The *principal* of a bond is the amount that the issuer agrees to repay the bondholder on the maturity date. This amount is also referred to as the *redemption value, maturity value, par value* or *face amount*. The *coupon rate* or *nominal rate* is the interest rate that the issuer agrees to pay each year. The annual amount of the interest payment made is called the *coupon*. The coupon rate multiplied by the principal of the bond provides the cash amount of the *coupon*. For example, a bond with a 7% coupon rate and a principal of £1,000,000 will pay annual interest of £70,000. In the UK, US and Japan the usual practice is for the issuer to pay the coupon in two semi-annual instalments. For bonds issued in European markets and the Eurobond market, coupon payments are made annually. Sometimes one will encounter bonds that pay interest on a quarterly basis.

All bonds make periodic interest payments except for *zero-coupon bonds*. These bonds allow a holder to realise interest by being sold substantially below their principal value. The bonds are redeemed at par, with the interest amount then being the difference between the principal value and the price at which the bond was sold. We will explore zero-coupon bonds in greater detail later.

Another type of bond makes floating-rate interest payments. Such bonds are known as *floating-rate notes* and their coupon rates are reset periodically in line with a predetermined benchmark, such as an interest-rate index.

Embedded options   Some bonds include a provision in their offer particulars that gives either the bondholder and/or the issuer an option to enforce early redemption of the bond. The most common type of option embedded in a bond is a *call feature*. A call provision grants the issuer the right to redeem all or part of the debt before the specified maturity date. An issuing company may wish to include such a feature as it allows it to replace an old bond issue with a lower coupon rate issue if interest rates in the market have declined. As a call feature allows the issuer to change the maturity date of a bond it is considered harmful to the bondholder's interests; therefore, the market price of the bond will reflect this. A call option is included in all asset-backed securities based on mortgages, for obvious reasons (asset-backed bonds are considered in Chapter 10). A bond issue may also include a provision that allows the investor to change the maturity of the bond. This is known as a *put feature* and gives the bondholder the right to sell the bond back to the issuer at par on specified dates. The advantage to the bondholder is that if interest rates rise after the issue date, thus depressing the bond's value, the investor can realise par value by *putting the bond* back to the issuer. A *convertible* bond is an issue giving the bondholder the right to exchange the bond for a specified number of shares (equity) in the issuing company. This feature allows the investor to take advantage of favourable movements in the price of the issuer's shares.

The presence of embedded options in a bond makes valuation more complex compared with plain vanilla bonds, and will be considered separately.

OUTLINE OF MARKET PARTICIPANTS

There is a large variety of players in the bond markets, each trading some or all of the different instruments available to suit their own purposes. We can group the main types of players according to the time horizon of their investment activity.

- *Short-term institutional investors* – these include banks and building societies, money market fund managers, central banks and the treasury desks of some types of corporates. Such bodies are driven by short-term investment views, often subject to close guidelines, and will be driven by the total return available on their investments. Banks will have an additional requirement to maintain *liquidity*, often in fulfilment of regulatory authority rules, by holding a proportion of their assets in the form of easily tradeable short-term instruments.
- *Long-term institutional investors* – typically these types of investors include pension funds and life assurance companies. Their investment horizon is long-term, reflecting the nature of their liabilities; often they will seek to match these liabilities by holding long-dated bonds.
- *Mixed horizon institutional investors* – this is possibly the largest category of investors and will include general insurance companies and most corporate bodies. Like banks and financial sector companies, they are also very active in the primary market, issuing bonds to finance their operations.
- *Market professionals* – this category includes firms that one would not automatically classify as 'investors' although they

will also have an investment objective. Their time horizon will range from 1 day to the very long term. They include the proprietary trading desks of investment banks, as well as bond market makers in securities houses and banks who are providing a service to their customers. Proprietary traders will actively position themselves in the market in order to gain trading profit – for example, in response to their view on where they think interest-rate levels are headed. These participants will trade direct with other market professionals and investors, or via brokers.

Figure 1.1 shows a screen from the Bloomberg news and analytics system, widely used by capital market participants such as investment banks and hedge funds. It is screen DES, which is the description page that can be pulled up for virtually every bond in existence. Our example shows a bond issued by Ford Motor Company, the 2.25% of 2007. We see that all the key identifying features of the bond, such as coupon and maturity date, are listed, together with a confirmation of the bond's credit rating of Baa3 and BB+. This screen was printed in 'December 2005', so the rating may have changed by the time this book is published!

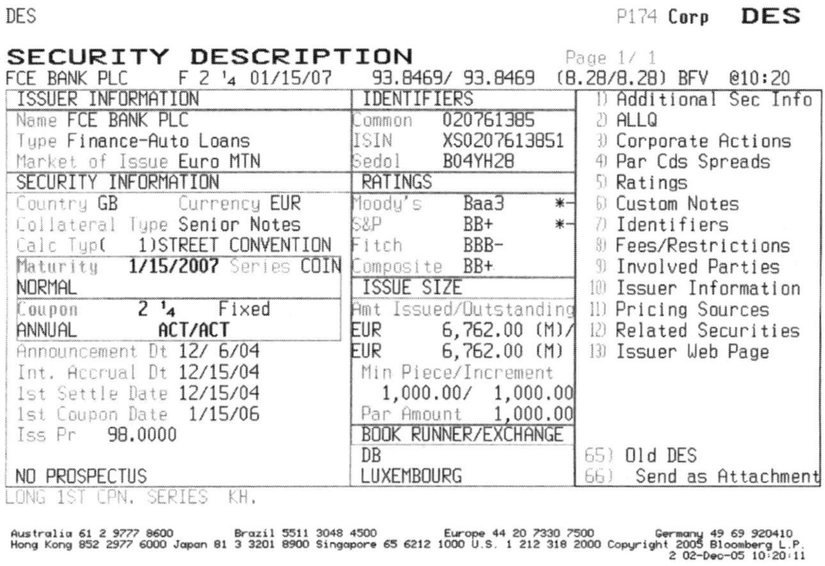

DES   P174 **Corp** **DES**

SECURITY DESCRIPTION   Page 1/ 1
FCE BANK PLC   F 2 ¼ 01/15/07   93.8469/ 93.8469   (8.28/8.28) BFV   @10:20

ISSUER INFORMATION	IDENTIFIERS		1) Additional Sec Info
Name FCE BANK PLC	Common 020761385		2) ALLQ
Type Finance-Auto Loans	ISIN XS0207613851		3) Corporate Actions
Market of Issue Euro MTN	Sedol B04YH28		4) Par Cds Spreads
SECURITY INFORMATION	RATINGS		5) Ratings
Country GB Currency EUR	Moody's Baa3 *–		6) Custom Notes
Collateral Type Senior Notes	S&P BB+ *–		7) Identifiers
Calc Typ(1)STREET CONVENTION	Fitch BBB–		8) Fees/Restrictions
Maturity 1/15/2007 Series COIN	Composite BB+		9) Involved Parties
NORMAL	ISSUE SIZE		10) Issuer Information
Coupon 2 ¼ Fixed	Amt Issued/Outstanding		11) Pricing Sources
ANNUAL ACT/ACT	EUR 6,762.00 (M)/		12) Related Securities
Announcement Dt 12/ 6/04	EUR 6,762.00 (M)		13) Issuer Web Page
Int. Accrual Dt 12/15/04	Min Piece/Increment		
1st Settle Date 12/15/04	1,000.00/ 1,000.00		
1st Coupon Date 1/15/06	Par Amount 1,000.00		
Iss Pr 98.0000	BOOK RUNNER/EXCHANGE		
	DB		65) Old DES
NO PROSPECTUS	LUXEMBOURG		66) Send as Attachment

LONG 1ST CPN. SERIES KH.

Australia 61 2 9777 8600   Brazil 5511 3048 4500   Europe 44 20 7330 7500   Germany 49 69 920410
Hong Kong 852 2977 6000 Japan 81 3 3201 8900 Singapore 65 6212 1000 U.S. 1 212 318 2000 Copyright 2005 Bloomberg L.P.
2 02-Dec-05 10:20:11

Figure 1.1   Bloomberg screen DES for Ford 2.25% 2007 bond.

© Bloomberg L.P. Used with permission. Visit *www.bloomberg.com*

BOND ANALYSIS

In the past, bond analysis was frequently limited to calculating *gross redemption yield*, or *yield to maturity*. Today, basic bond mathematics involves different concepts and calculations. The level of understanding required to master bond pricing is quite high, and beyond the scope of this book. We concentrate instead on the essential elements required for a basic understanding.

In the analysis that follows, bonds are assumed to be *default-free*. This means there is no possibility that the interest payments and principal repayment will not be made. Such an assumption is entirely reasonable for government bonds such as US Treasuries and UK gilt-edged securities. It is less so when you are dealing with the debt of corporate and lower-rated sovereign borrowers. The valuation and analysis of bonds carrying default risk, however, are based on those of default-free government securities. Essentially, the yield investors demand from borrowers whose credit standing is not risk-free is the yield on government securities plus some *credit risk* premium.

Financial arithmetic: The time value of money

Bond prices are expressed 'per 100 nominal' – that is, as a percentage of the bond's face value. (The convention in certain markets is to quote a price per 1,000 nominal, but this is rare.) For example, if the price of a US dollar-denominated bond is quoted as 98.00, this means that for every $100 of the bond's face value, a buyer would pay $98. The principles of pricing in the bond market are the same as those in other financial markets: the price of a financial instrument is equal to the sum of the present values of all the future cash flows from the instrument. The interest rate used to derive the *present values* of the cash flows, known as the *discount rate*, is key, since it reflects where the bond is trading and how its return is perceived by the market. All the factors that identify the bond – including the nature of the issuer, the maturity date, the coupon and the currency in which it was issued – influence the bond's discount rate. Comparable bonds have similar discount rates. The following sections explain the traditional approach to bond pricing for plain-vanilla instruments, making certain assumptions to keep the analysis simple.

Present value and discounting

Since fixed-income instruments are essentially collections of cash flows, it is useful to begin by reviewing two key concepts of cash flow analysis: discounting and present value. Understanding these concepts is essential. In the following discussion, the interest rates cited are assumed to be the market-determined rates.

Financial arithmetic demonstrates that the value of $1 received today is not the same as that of $1 received in the future. Assuming an interest rate of 10% a year, a choice between receiving $1 in a year and receiving the same amount today is really a choice between having $1 a year from now and having $1 plus $0.10 – the interest on $1 for 1 year at 10% per annum.

The notion that money has a time value is basic to the analysis of financial instruments. Money has time value because of the opportunity to invest it at a rate of interest. A loan that makes one interest payment at maturity is accruing *simple interest*. Short-term instruments are usually such loans. Hence, the lenders receive simple interest when the instrument expires. The formula for deriving *terminal*, or *future*, value of an investment with simple interest is shown as (1.1):

$$FV = PV(1 + r) \qquad (1.1)$$

where FV = Future value of the instrument;
   PV = Initial investment, or the present value, of the instrument;
   r = Interest rate.

The market convention is to quote *annualised* interest rates: the rate corresponding to the amount of interest that would be earned if the investment term were 1 year. Consider a 3-month deposit of $100 in a bank earning a rate of 6% a year. The annual interest gain would be $6. The interest earned for the 90 days of the deposit is proportional to that gain, as calculated below:

$$I_{90} = \$6.00 \times \frac{90}{365}$$

$$= \$6.00 \times 0.2465$$

$$= \$1.479$$

The investor will receive $1.479 in interest at the end of the term. The total value of the deposit after the 3 months is therefore $100

plus $1.479. To calculate the terminal value of a short-term invest-
ment – that is, one with a term of less than a year – accruing simple
interest, equation (1.1) is modified as follows:

$$FV = PV\left[1 + r\left(\frac{\text{Days}}{\text{Year}}\right)\right] \tag{1.2}$$

where r = Annualised rate of interest;
     Days = Term of the investment;
     Year = Number of days in the year.

Note that, in the sterling markets, the number of days in the year is
taken to be 365, but most other markets – including the dollar and
euro markets – use a 360-day year. (These conventions are discussed
more fully below.)

Now, consider an investment of $100, again at a fixed rate of 6% a
year, but this time for 3 years. At the end of the first year, the investor
will be credited with interest of $6. Therefore, for the second year the
interest rate of 6% will be accruing on a principal sum of $106.
Accordingly, at the end of year 2, the interest credited will be
$6.36. This illustrates the principle of *compounding*: earning inter-
est on interest. Equation (1.3) computes the future value for a sum
deposited at a compounding rate of interest:

$$FV = PV(1 + r)^n \tag{1.3}$$

where r = Periodic rate of interest (expressed as a decimal);
     n = Number of periods for which the sum is invested.

This computation assumes that the interest payments made during
the investment term are reinvested at an interest rate equal to the
first year's rate. That is why the example above stated that the 6%
rate was *fixed* for 3 years. Compounding obviously results in higher
returns than those earned with simple interest.

Now, consider a deposit of $100 for 1 year, still at a rate of 6% but
compounded quarterly. Again assuming that the interest payments
will be reinvested at the initial interest rate of 6%, the total return at
the end of the year will be:

$$100 \times [(1 + 0.015) \times (1 + 0.015) \times (1 + 0.015) \times (1 + 0.015)]$$
$$= 100 \times [(1 + 0.015)^4]$$
$$= 100 \times 1.6136$$
$$= \$106.136$$

The terminal value for quarterly compounding is thus about 13 cents more than that for annual compounded interest.

In general, if compounding takes place m times per year, then at the end of n years, mn interest payments will have been made, and the future value of the principal is computed using the formula (1.4):

$$FV = PV\left(1 + \frac{r}{m}\right)^{mn} \tag{1.4}$$

As the example above illustrates, more frequent compounding results in higher total returns. In Box 1.1 we show the interest rate factors corresponding to different frequencies of compounding on a base rate of 6% a year:

$$\text{Interest rate factor} = \left(1 + \frac{r}{m}\right)^{m}$$

Box 1.1   Interest rate factors relating to different frequencies of compounding.

Compounding frequency	Interest rate factor for 6%
Annual	$(1 + r) = 1.060\,000$
Semiannual	$\left(1 + \frac{r}{2}\right)^{2} = 1.060\,900$
Quarterly	$\left(1 + \frac{r}{4}\right)^{4} = 1.061\,364$
Monthly	$\left(1 + \frac{r}{12}\right)^{12} = 1.061\,678$
Daily	$\left(1 + \frac{r}{365}\right)^{365} = 1.061\,831$

This shows that the more frequent the compounding, the higher the annualised interest rate. The entire progression indicates that a limit can be defined for continuous compounding – i.e., where $m = $ Infinity. To define the limit, it is useful to rewrite equation

(1.4) as (1.5):

$$FV = PV\left[\left(1 + \frac{r}{m}\right)^{m/r}\right]^{rn}$$

$$= PV\left[\left(1 + \frac{1}{m/r}\right)^{m/r}\right]^{rn}$$

$$= PV\left[\left(1 + \frac{1}{w}\right)^{n}\right]^{rn} \tag{1.5}$$

where $w = m/r$.

As compounding becomes continuous and m and hence w approach infinity, the expression in the square brackets in (1.5) approaches the mathematical constant e (the base of natural logarithmic functions), which is equal to approximately 2.718 281.

Substituting e into (1.5) gives us:

$$FV = PVe^{rn} \tag{1.6}$$

In (1.6) e^{rn} is the *exponential function* of rn. It represents the continuously compounded interest-rate factor. To compute this factor for an interest rate of 6% over a term of 1 year, set r to 6% and n to 1, giving:

$$e^{rn} = e^{0.06 \times 1} = (2.718\,281)^{0.06} = 1.061\,837$$

The convention in both wholesale and personal, or retail, markets is to quote an annual interest rate, whatever the term of the investment, whether it be overnight or 10 years. Lenders wishing to earn interest at the rate quoted have to place their funds on deposit for 1 year. For example, if you open a bank account that pays 3.5% interest and close it after 6 months, the interest you actually earn will be equal to 1.75% of your deposit. The actual return on a 3-year building society bond that pays a 6.75% fixed rate compounded annually is 21.65%. The quoted rate is the annual 1-year equivalent. An overnight deposit in the wholesale, or *interbank*, market is still quoted as an annual rate, even though interest is earned for only 1 day.

Quoting annualised rates allows deposits and loans of different maturities and involving different instruments to be compared. Be careful when comparing interest rates for products that have different payment frequencies. As shown in the earlier examples, the actual interest earned on a deposit paying 6% semiannually will be greater than on one paying 6% annually. The convention in the money markets is to quote the applicable interest rate taking into account payment frequency.

The discussion thus far has involved calculating future value given a known present value and rate of interest. For example, $100 invested today for 1 year at a simple interest rate of 6% will generate $100 \times (1 + 0.06) = \$106$ at the end of the year. The future value of $100 in this case is $106. Conversely, $100 is the present value of $106, given the same term and interest rate. This relationship can be stated formally by rearranging equation (1.3) – i.e., $FV = PV(1 + r)^n$ – as shown in (1.7):

$$PV = \frac{FV}{(1 + r)^n} \qquad (1.7)$$

Equation (1.7) applies to investments earning annual interest payments, giving the present value of a known future sum.

To calculate the present value of an investment, you must prorate the interest that would be earned for a whole year over the number of days in the investment period, as was done in (1.2). The result is equation (1.8):

$$PV = \frac{FV}{\left(1 + r \times \dfrac{\text{Days}}{\text{Year}}\right)} \qquad (1.8)$$

When interest is compounded more than once a year, the formula for calculating present value is modified, as it was in (1.4). The result is shown in equation (1.9):

$$PV = \frac{FV}{\left(1 + \dfrac{r}{m}\right)^{mn}} \qquad (1.9)$$

For example, the present value of $100 to be received at the end of 5 years, assuming an interest rate of 5%, with quarterly compounding is:

$$PV = \frac{100}{\left(1 + \dfrac{0.05}{4}\right)^{(4)(5)}} = \$78.00$$

Interest rates in the money markets are always quoted for standard maturities, such as overnight, 'tom next' (the overnight interest rate starting tomorrow, or 'tomorrow to the next'), 'spot next' (the overnight rate starting 2 days forward), 1 week, 1 month, 2 months and so on, up to 1 year. If a bank or corporate customer wishes to borrow for a nonstandard period, or 'odd date', an interbank desk will calculate the rate chargeable, by interpolating between two standard-period interest rates. Assuming a steady, uniform increase between standard periods, the required rate can be calculated using the formula for *straight line* interpolation, which apportions the difference equally among the stated intervals. This formula is shown as (1.10):

$$r = r_1 + (r_2 - r_1) \times \frac{n - n_1}{n_2 - n_1} \tag{1.10}$$

where $r =$ Required odd-date rate for n days;
             $r_1 =$ Quoted rate for n_1 days;
             $r_2 =$ Quoted rate for n_2 days.

Say the 1-month (30-day) interest rate is 5.25% and the 2-month (60-day) rate is 5.75%. If a customer wishes to borrow money for 40 days, the bank can calculate the required rate using straight line interpolation as follows: the difference between 30 and 40 is one-third that between 30 and 60, so the increase from the 30-day to the 40-day rate is assumed to be one-third the increase between the 30-day and the 60-day rates, giving the following computation:

$$5.25\% + \frac{(5.75\% - 5.25\%)}{3} = 5.4167\%$$

What about the interest rate for a period that is shorter or longer than the two whose rates are known, rather than lying between them? What if the customer in the example above wished to borrow money for 64 days? In this case, the interbank desk would extrapolate from the relationship between the known 1-month and 2-month rates, again assuming a uniform rate of change in the interest rates along the maturity spectrum. So, given the 1-month rate of 5.25% and the 2-month rate of 5.75%, the 64-day rate would be:

$$5.25 + \left[(5.75 - 5.25) \times \frac{34}{30} \right] = 5.8167\%$$

Just as future and present value can be derived from one another, given an investment period and interest rate, so can the interest rate for a period be calculated given a present and a future value. The basic equation is merely rearranged again to solve for r. This, as will be discussed below, is known as the investment's *yield*.

Discount factors

An n-period discount factor is the present value of one unit of currency that is payable at the end of period n. Essentially, it is the present value relationship expressed in terms of \$1. A discount factor for any term is given by (1.11):

$$d_n = \frac{1}{(1+r)^n} \qquad\qquad (1.11)$$

where $n =$ Period of discount.

For instance, the 5-year discount factor for a rate of 6% compounded annually is:

$$d_5 = \frac{1}{(1+0.06)^5} = 0.747\,258$$

The set of discount factors for every period from 1 day to 30 years and longer is termed the *discount function*. Since the following discussion is in terms of PV, discount factors may be used to value any financial instrument that generates future cash flows. For example, the present value of an instrument generating a cash flow of \$103.50 payable at the end of 6 months would be determined as follows, given a 6-month discount factor of 0.987 56:

$$PV = \frac{FV}{(1+r)^n}$$

$$= FV \times d_n$$

$$= \$103.50 \times 0.987\,56$$

$$= \$102.212$$

Discount factors can also be used to calculate the future value of a present investment by inverting the formula. In the example above, the 6-month discount factor of 0.987 56 signifies that \$1 receivable in 6 months has a present value of \$0.987 56. By the same reasoning, \$1 today would in 6 months be worth:

$$\frac{1}{d_{0.5}} = \frac{1}{0.98756}$$

$$= \$1.0126$$

It is possible to derive discount factors from current bond prices. This process can be illustrated using the set of hypothetical bonds, all

Table 1.1 Hypothetical set of bonds and bond prices.

Coupon (%)	Maturity date	Price
7	07-Jun-2001	101.65
8	07-Dec-2001	101.89
6	07-Jun-2002	100.75
6.50	07-Dec-2002	100.37

assumed to have semiannual coupons, that are shown in Table 1.1, together with their prices.

The first bond in Table 1.1 matures in precisely 6 months. Its final cash flow will be $103.50, comprising the final coupon payment of $3.50 and the redemption payment of $100. The price, or present value, of this bond is $101.65. Using this, the 6-month discount factor may be calculated as follows:

$$d_{0.5} = \frac{101.65}{103.50} = 0.982\,13$$

Using this 6-month discount factor, the 1-year factor can be derived from the second bond in Table 1.1, the 8% due 2001. This bond pays a coupon of $4 in 6 months, and in 1 year makes a payment of $104, consisting of another $4 coupon payment plus $100 return of principal.

The price of the 1-year bond is $101.89. As with the 6-month bond, the price is also its present value, equal to the sum of the present values of its total cash flows. This relationship can be expressed in the following equation:

$$101.89 = 4 \times d_{0.5} + 104 \times d_1$$

The value of $d_{0.5}$ is known to be 0.982 13. That leaves d_1 as the only unknown in the equation, which may be rearranged to solve for it:

$$d_1 = \left[\frac{101.89 - 4(0.982\,13)}{104}\right] = \frac{97.961\,48}{104} = 0.941\,94$$

The same procedure can be repeated for the remaining two bonds, using the discount factors derived in the previous steps to derive the set of discount factors in Table 1.2. These factors may also be graphed as a continuous function, as shown in Figure 1.2.

Table 1.2   Discount factors calculated using the bootstrapping technique.

Coupon (%)	Maturity date	Term (years)	Price	$d(n)$
7	07-Jun-2001	0.5	101.65	0.982 13
8	07-Dec-2001	1.0	101.89	0.941 94
6	07-Jun-2002	1.5	100.75	0.922 11
6.50	07-Dec-2002	2.0	100.37	0.882 52

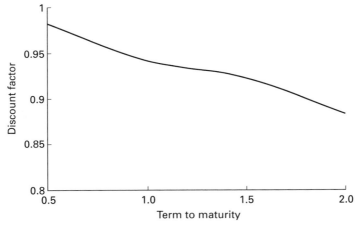

Figure 1.2   Hypothetical discount function.

This technique of calculating discount factors, known as 'bootstrapping', is conceptually neat, but may not work so well in practice. Problems arise when you do not have a set of bonds that mature at precise 6-month intervals. Liquidity issues connected with individual bonds can also cause complications. This is true because the price of the bond, which is still the sum of the present values of the cash flows, may reflect liquidity considerations (e.g., hard to buy or sell the bond, difficult to find) that do not reflect the market as a whole but peculiarities of that specific bond. The approach, however, is still worth knowing.

Note that the discount factors in Figure 1.2 decrease as the bond's maturity increases. This makes intuitive sense, since the present value of something to be received in the future diminishes the farther in the future the date of receipt lies.

BOND PRICING AND YIELD: THE TRADITIONAL APPROACH

The discount rate used to derive the present value of a bond's cash flows is the interest rate that the bondholders require as compensation for the risk of lending their money to the issuer. The yield investors require on a bond depends on a number of political and economic factors, including what other bonds in the same class are yielding. Yield is always quoted as an annualised interest rate. This means that the rate used to discount the cash flows of a bond paying semiannual coupons is exactly half the bond's yield.

Bond pricing

The *fair price* of a bond is the sum of the present values of all its cash flows, including both the coupon payments and the redemption payment. The price of a conventional bond that pays annual coupons can therefore be represented by formula (1.12):

$$P = \frac{C}{(1+r)} + \frac{C}{(1+r)^2} + \frac{C}{(1+r)^3} + \cdots + \frac{C}{(1+r)^N} + \frac{M}{(1+r)^N}$$

$$= \sum_{n=1}^{N} \frac{C}{(1+r)^n} + \frac{M}{(1+r)^N} \qquad (1.12)$$

where
$P =$ Bond's fair price;
$C =$ Annual coupon payment;
$r =$ Discount rate, or required yield;
$N =$ Number of years to maturity, and so the number of interest periods for a bond paying an annual coupon;
$M =$ Maturity payment, or par value, which is usually 100% of face value.

Bonds in the US domestic market – as opposed to international securities denominated in US dollars, such as USD Eurobonds – usually pay semiannual coupons. Such bonds may be priced using the expression in (1.13), which is a modification of (1.12) allowing for twice-yearly discounting:

$$P = \frac{C/2}{(1 + \frac{1}{2}r)} + \frac{C/2}{(1 + \frac{1}{2}r)^2} + \frac{C/2}{(1 + \frac{1}{2}r)^3} + \cdots + \frac{C/2}{(1 + \frac{1}{2}r)^{2N}} + \frac{M}{(1 + \frac{1}{2}r)^{2N}}$$

$$= \sum_{n=1}^{2N} \frac{C/2}{(1 + \frac{1}{2}r)^n} + \frac{M}{(1 + \frac{1}{2}r)^{2N}}$$

$$= \frac{C}{r}\left[1 - \frac{1}{(1 + \frac{1}{2}r)^{2N}}\right] + \frac{M}{(1 + \frac{1}{2}r)^{2N}} \qquad (1.13)$$

Note that $2N$ is now the power to which the discount factor is raised. This is because a bond that pays a semiannual coupon makes two interest payments a year. It might therefore be convenient to replace the number of years to maturity with the number of interest periods, which could be represented by the variable n, resulting in formula (1.14):

$$P = \frac{C}{r}\left[1 - \frac{1}{(1 + \frac{1}{2}r)^n}\right] + \frac{M}{(1 + \frac{1}{2}r)^n} \qquad (1.14)$$

This formula calculates the fair price on a coupon payment date, so there is no *accrued interest* incorporated into the price. Accrued interest is an accounting convention that treats coupon interest as accruing every day a bond is held; this accrued amount is added to the discounted present value of the bond (the *clean price*) to obtain the market value of the bond, known as the *dirty price*. The price calculation is made as of the bond's *settlement date*, the date on which it actually changes hands after being traded. For a new bond issue, the settlement date is the day when the investors take delivery of the bond and the issuer receives payment. The settlement date for a bond traded in the *secondary market* – the market where bonds are bought and sold after they are first issued – is the day the buyer transfers payment to the seller of the bond and the seller transfers the bond to the buyer.

Different markets have different settlement conventions. US Treasuries and UK gilts, for example, normally settle on $T + 1$: one business day after the trade date, T. Eurobonds, on the other hand, settle on $T + 3$. The term *value date* is sometimes used in place of settlement date; however, the two terms are not strictly synonymous. A settlement date can fall only on a business day; a bond traded on a Friday, therefore, will settle on a Monday. A value date, in contrast, can sometimes fall on a non-business day – when accrued interest is being calculated, for example.

Equation (1.14) assumes an even number of coupon payment dates remaining before maturity. If there are an odd number, the formula is modified as shown in (1.15):

$$P = \frac{C}{r}\left[1 - \frac{1}{(1+\frac{1}{2}r)^{2N+1}}\right] + \frac{M}{(1+\frac{1}{2}r)^{2N+1}} \tag{1.15}$$

Another assumption embodied in the standard formula is that the bond is traded for settlement on a day that is precisely one interest period before the next coupon payment. If the trade takes place between coupon dates, the formula is modified. This is done by adjusting the exponent for the discount factor using ratio i, shown in (1.16):

$$i = \frac{\text{Days from value date to next coupon date}}{\text{Days in the interest period}} \tag{1.16}$$

The denominator of this ratio is the number of calendar days between the last coupon date and the next one. This figure depends on the day-count convention (see below) used for that particular bond. Using i, the price formula is modified as (1.17) for annual coupon-paying bonds; for bonds with semiannual coupons, $r/2$ replaces r:

$$P = \frac{C}{(1+r)^i} + \frac{C}{(1+r)^{1+i}} + \frac{C}{(1+r)^{2+i}} + \cdots + \frac{C}{(1+r)^{n-1+i}} + \frac{M}{(1+r)^{n-1+i}} \tag{1.17}$$

where the variables C, M, n and r are as before.

Box 1.2   Example: calculating consideration for a US Treasury bond.

The consideration, or actual cash proceeds paid by a buyer for a bond, is the bond's total cash value together with any costs such as commission. In this example, consideration refers only to the cash value of the bond.

What is the total consideration for £5 million nominal of a Eurobond, where the price is £114.50?

The price of the Eurobond is £114.50 per £100, so the consideration is:

$$1.145 \times 5,000,000 = £5,725,000$$

What consideration is payable for $5 million nominal of a US Treasury, quoted at a price of 99-16?

The US Treasury price is 99-16, which is equal to 99 and 16/32, or 99.50 per $100. The consideration is therefore:

$$0.9950 \times 5,000,000 = \$4,975,000$$

If the price of a bond is below par, the total consideration is below the nominal amount; if it is priced above par, the consideration will be above the nominal amount.

As noted above, the bond market includes securities, known as zero-coupon bonds, or *strips*, that do not pay coupons. These are priced by setting C to 0 in the pricing equation. The only cash flow is the maturity payment, resulting in formula (1.18):

$$P = \frac{M}{(1+r)^N} \tag{1.18}$$

where N = Number of years to maturity.

Note that, even though these bonds pay no actual coupons, their prices and yields must be calculated on the basis of *quasi-coupon* periods, which are based on the interest periods of bonds denominated in the same currency. A US dollar or a sterling 5-year zero-coupon bond, for example, would be assumed to cover ten quasi-coupon periods, and the price equation would accordingly be modified as (1.19):

$$P = \frac{M}{(1+\frac{1}{2}r)^n} \tag{1.19}$$

Box 1.3   Example: zero-coupon bond price.

(a) Calculate the price of a Treasury strip with a maturity of precisely 5 years corresponding to a required yield of 5.40%.

According to these terms, $N = 5$, so $n = 10$, and $r = 0.054$, so $r/2 = 0.027$. $M = 100$, as usual. Plugging these values into the pricing formula gives:

$$P = \frac{100}{(1.027)^{10}} = \$76.611\,782$$

(b) Calculate the price of a French government zero-coupon bond with precisely 5 years to maturity, with the same required yield of 5.40%. Note that French government bonds pay coupon annually:

$$P = \frac{100}{(1.054)^5} = 76.877\,092$$

It is clear from the bond price formula that a bond's yield and its price are closely related. Specifically, the price moves in the opposite direction from the yield. This is because a bond's price is the net present value of its cash flows; if the discount rate – that is, the yield required by investors – increases, the present values of the cash flows decrease. In the same way if the required yield decreases, the price of the bond rises. The stylised relationship between a bond's price and any required yield level is illustrated by the graph in Figure 1.3, which plots the yield against the corresponding price to form a convex curve.

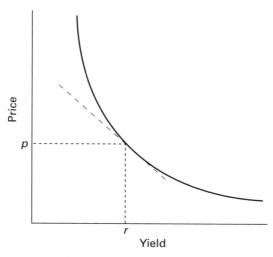

Figure 1.3 The price/yield relationship.

Box 1.4   Summary of the price/yield relationship.

- At issue, if a bond is priced at par, its coupon will equal the yield that the market requires, reflecting factors such as the bond's term to maturity, the issuer's credit rating and the yield on current bonds of comparable quality.
- If the required yield rises above the coupon rate, the bond price will decrease.
- If the required yield goes below the coupon rate, the bond price will increase.

Bond yield

The discussion so far has involved calculating the price of a bond given its yield. This procedure can be reversed to find a bond's yield where its price is known. This is equivalent to calculating the bond's *internal rate of return (IRR)*, also known as its 'yield to maturity' or 'gross redemption yield' (also *yield to workout*). These are among the various measures used in the markets to estimate the return generated from holding a bond.

In most markets, bonds are traded on the basis of their prices. Because different bonds can generate different and complicated cash-flow patterns, however, they are generally compared in terms of their yields. For example, market makers usually quote two-way prices at which they will buy or sell particular bonds, but it is the yield at which the bonds are trading that is important to the market maker's customers. This is because a bond's price does not tell buyers anything useful about what they are getting. Remember that in any market a number of bonds exist with different issuers, coupons and terms to maturity. It is their yields that are compared, not their prices.

The yield on any investment is the discount rate that will make the present value of its cash flows equal its initial cost or price. Mathematically, an investment's yield, represented by r, is the interest rate that satisfies the bond price equation, repeated here as (1.20):

$$P = \sum_{n=1}^{N} \frac{C_n}{(1+r)^n} + \frac{M}{(1+r)^n} \tag{1.20}$$

Other types of yield measure, however, are used in the market for different purposes. The simplest is the *current yield*, also known as the *flat*, *interest* or *running yield*. These are computed by formula (1.21):

$$rc = \frac{C}{P} \times 100 \qquad (1.21)$$

where rc = Current yield.

In this equation the percentage for C is not expressed as a decimal. Current yield ignores any capital gain or loss that might arise from holding and trading a bond and does not consider the time value of money. It calculates the coupon income as a proportion of the price paid for the bond. For this to be an accurate representation of return, the bond would have to be more like an annuity than a fixed-term instrument.

Current yield is useful as a 'rough and ready' interest-rate calculation; it is often used to estimate the cost of or profit from holding a bond for a short-term. For example, if short-term interest rates, such as the 1-week or 3-month, are higher than the current yield, holding the bond is said to involve a *running cost*. This is also known as *negative carry* or *negative funding*. The concept is used by bond traders, market makers and leveraged investors, but it is useful for all market practitioners, since it represents the investor's short-term cost of holding or funding a bond. The yield to maturity (YTM) – or, as it is known in sterling markets, gross redemption yield – is the most frequently used measure of bond return. Yield to maturity takes into account the pattern of coupon payments, the bond's term to maturity and the capital gain (or loss) arising over the remaining life of the bond. The bond price formula shows the relationship between these elements and demonstrates their importance in determining price. The YTM calculation discounts the cash flows to maturity, employing the concept of the time value of money.

As noted above, the formula for calculating YTM is essentially that for calculating the price of a bond, repeated as (1.12). For the YTM of bonds with semiannual coupon, the formula must be modified, as in (1.13). Note, though, that this equation has two variables, the price P and yield r. It cannot, therefore, be rearranged to solve for yield r explicitly. In fact, the only way to solve for the yield is to use numerical iteration. This involves estimating a value for r and calculating the price associated with it. If the calculated price is higher than the bond's current price, the estimate for r is lower than the actual yield, so it must be raised. This process of calculation and adjustment up or down is repeated until the estimates converge on a level that generates the bond's current price.

To differentiate redemption yield from other yield and interest-rate measures described in this book, it will be referred to as rm. Note that this section is concerned with the *gross* redemption yield, the yield that results from payment of coupons without deduction of any withholding tax. The *net redemption yield* is what will be received if the bond is traded in a market where bonds pay coupon *net*, without withholding tax. It is obtained by multiplying the coupon rate C by (1 − Marginal tax rate). The net redemption yield is always lower than the gross redemption yield.

The key assumption behind the YTM calculation has already been discussed: that the redemption yield rm remains stable for the entire life of the bond, so that all coupons are reinvested at this same rate. The assumption is unrealistic, however. It can be predicted with virtual certainty that the interest rates paid by instruments with maturities equal to those of the bond at each coupon date will differ from rm at some point, at least, during the life of the bond. In practice, however, investors require a rate of return that is equivalent to the price that they are paying for a bond, and the redemption yield is as good a measurement as any.

A more accurate approach might be the one used to price interest-rate swaps: to calculate the present values of future cash flows using discount rates determined by the markets' view on where interest rates will be at those points. These expected rates are known as *forward* interest rates. Forward rates, however, are *implied*, and a YTM derived using them is as speculative as one calculated using the conventional formula. This is because the real market interest rate at any time is invariably different from the one implied earlier in the forward markets. So, a YTM calculation made using forward rates would not equal the yield actually realised either. The zero-coupon rate, it will be demonstrated later, is the true interest rate for any term to maturity. Still, despite the limitations imposed by its underlying assumptions, the YTM is the main measure of return used in the markets.

Box 1.5   Example: yield to maturity for semiannual coupon bond.

A bond paying a semiannual coupon has a dirty price of $98.50, an annual coupon of 3% and exactly 1 year before maturity. The bond therefore has three remaining cash flows: two coupon payments of $1.50 each and a redemption payment of $100. Plugging these values into equation (1.13) gives:

$$98.50 = \frac{1.50}{(1 + \frac{1}{2}rm)} + \frac{103.50}{(1 + \frac{1}{2}rm)^2}$$

Note that the equation uses half of the YTM value rm because this is a semiannual paying bond. The expression above is a quadratic equation, which can be rearranged as:

$$98.50x^2 - 1.50x - 103.50 = 0, \quad \text{where } x = 1 + \frac{rm}{2}$$

The equation may now be solved using the standard solution for equations of the form $ax^2 + bx + c = 0$:

$$x = \frac{-b \pm \sqrt{b^2 - 4ac}}{2a}$$

There are two solutions, only one of which gives a positive redemption yield. The positive solution is:

$$\frac{rm}{2} = 0.022\,755 \quad \text{or} \quad rm = 4.551\%$$

YTM can also be calculated using mathematical iteration. Start with a trial value for rm of $r_1 = 4\%$ and plug this into the right-hand side of equation (1.13). This gives a price P_1 of 99.050, which is higher than the dirty market price P_M of 98.50. The trial value for rm was therefore too low.

Next try $r_2 = 5\%$. This generates a price P_2 of 98.114, which is lower than the market price. Because the two trial prices lie on either side of the market value, the correct value for rm must lie between 4 and 5%. Now use the formula for linear interpolation:

$$rm = r_1 + (r_2 - r_1)\frac{P_1 - P_M}{P_1 - P_2}$$

Plugging in the appropriate values gives a linear approximation for the redemption yield of $rm = 4.549\%$, which is near the solution obtained by solving the quadratic equation.

Calculating the redemption yield of bonds that pay semiannual coupons involves the semiannual discounting of those payments. This approach is appropriate for most US bonds and UK gilts. Government bonds in most of continental Europe and most Eurobonds, however, pay annual coupon payments. The appropriate method of calculating their redemption yields is to use annual discounting. The two yield measures are not directly comparable.

It is possible to make a Eurobond directly comparable with a UK gilt by using semiannual discounting of the former's annual coupon payments or using annual discounting of the latter's semiannual payments. The formulas for the semiannual and annual calculations appeared above as (1.13) and (1.12), respectively, and are repeated here as (1.22) and (1.23):

$$P_d = \frac{C}{(1 + \frac{1}{2}rm)^2} + \frac{C}{(1 + \frac{1}{2}rm)^4} + \frac{C}{(1 + \frac{1}{2}rm)^6} + \cdots$$

$$+ \frac{C}{(1 + \frac{1}{2}rm)^{2N}} + \frac{M}{(1 + \frac{1}{2}rm)^{2N}} \tag{1.22}$$

$$P_d = \frac{C/2}{(1 + rm)^{\frac{1}{2}}} + \frac{C/2}{(1 + rm)} + \frac{C/2}{(1 + rm)^{\frac{3}{2}}} + \cdots + \frac{C/2}{(1 + rm)^N} + \frac{M}{(1 + rm)^N} \tag{1.23}$$

Consider a bond with a dirty price – including the accrued interest the seller is entitled to receive – of \$97.89, a coupon of 6% and 5 years to maturity. Table 1.3 shows the gross redemption yields this bond would have under the different yield-calculation conventions.

Table 1.3 Gross redemption yields.

Discounting	Payments	Yield to maturity (%)
Semiannual	Semiannual	6.500
Annual	Annual	6.508
Semiannual	Annual	6.428
Annual	Semiannual	6.605

These figures demonstrate the impact that the coupon-payment and discounting frequencies have on a bond's redemption yield calculation. Specifically, increasing the frequency of discounting lowers the calculated yield, while increasing the frequency of payments raises it. When comparing yields for bonds that trade in markets with different conventions, it is important to convert all the yields to the same calculation basis.

It might seem that doubling a semiannual yield figure would produce the annualised equivalent; the real result, however, is an underestimate of the true annualised yield. This is because of the multiplicative effects of discounting. The correct procedure for converting semiannual and quarterly yields into annualised ones is shown in (1.24).

a. General formula:

$$rm_a = (1 + \text{Interest rate})^m - 1 \qquad (1.24)$$

where m is the number of coupon payments per year.

b. Formulas for converting between semiannual and annual yields:

$$rm_a = (1 + \tfrac{1}{2}rm_s)^2 - 1$$
$$rm_s = \left[(1 + rm_a)^{\frac{1}{2}} - 1\right] \times 2$$

c. Formulas for converting between quarterly and annual yields:

$$rm_a = (1 + \tfrac{1}{4}rm_q)^4 - 1$$
$$rm_q = \left[(1 + rm_a)^{\frac{1}{4}} - 1\right] \times 4$$

where rm_q, rm_s and rm_a are, respectively, the quarterly, semiannually and annually discounted yields to maturity.

Box 1.6   Example: comparing yields to maturity.

A US Treasury paying semiannual coupons, with a maturity of 10 years, has a quoted yield of 4.89%. A Eurodollar government bond with a similar maturity is quoted at a yield of 4.96%. Which bond has the higher yield to maturity in practice?

The effective annual yield of the Treasury is:

$$rm_a = (1 + \tfrac{1}{2} \times 0.0489)^2 - 1 = 4.9498\%$$

Comparing the securities using the same calculation basis reveals that the European government bond does indeed have the higher yield.

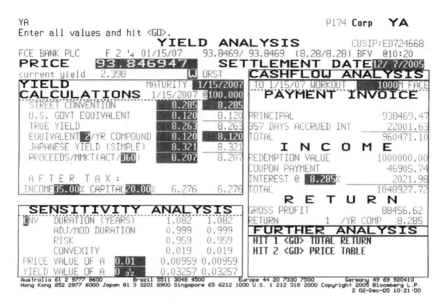

Figure 1.4 Bloomberg page YA for Ford 2.25% 2007 as at 29 November 2005.

The market convention is sometimes simply to double the semi-annual yield to obtain the annualised yields, despite the fact that this produces an inaccurate result. It is only acceptable to do this for rough calculations. An annualised yield obtained in this manner is known as a *bond equivalent yield*. It was noted earlier that the one disadvantage of the YTM measure is that its calculation incorporates the unrealistic assumption that each coupon payment, as it becomes due, is reinvested at the rate *rm*. Another disadvantage is that it does not deal with the situation in which investors do not hold their bonds to maturity. In these cases, the redemption yield will not be as great. Investors might therefore be interested in other measures of return, such as the equivalent zero-coupon yield, which is considered a true yield.

Figure 1.4 shows Bloomberg page YA for the same Ford bond illustrated at Figure 1.1. It shows a number of yield measures for the bond; the principal one for our purposes – the yield to maturity – is the street yield shown as 8.285%.

To review, the redemption yield measure assumes that:

- the bond is held to maturity;
- all coupons during the bond's life are reinvested at the same (redemption yield) rate.

Given these assumptions, the YTM can be viewed as an *expected* or *anticipated* yield. It is closest to reality when an investor buys a bond on first issue at par and holds it to maturity. Even then, however, the actual realised yield at maturity would be different from the YTM because of the unrealistic nature of the second assumption. It is clearly unlikely that all the coupons of any but the shortest-maturity bond will be reinvested at the same rate. As noted earlier, market interest rates are in a state of constant flux, and this would affect money reinvestment rates. Therefore, although YTM is the main market measure of bond levels, it is not a true interest rate. This is an important point.

Another problem with YTM is that it discounts a bond's coupons at the yield specific to that bond. It thus cannot serve as an accurate basis for comparing bonds. Consider a 2-year and a 5-year bond. These securities will invariably have different YTMs. Accordingly, the coupon cash flows they generate in 2 years time will be discounted at different rates (assuming the yield curve is not flat). This is clearly not correct. The present value calculated today of a cash flow occurring in 2 years' time should be the same whether that cash flow is generated by a short- or a long-dated bond.

ACCRUED INTEREST

All bonds except zero-coupon bonds accrue interest on a daily basis that is then paid out on the coupon date. As mentioned earlier, the formulas discussed so far calculate bonds' prices as of a coupon payment date, so that no accrued interest is incorporated in the price. In all major bond markets, the convention is to quote this so-called clean price.

Clean and dirty bond prices

When investors buy a bond in the market, what they pay is the bond's *all-in* price, also known as the dirty, or *gross price*, which is the clean price of a bond plus accrued interest.

Bonds trade either *ex-dividend* or *cum dividend*. The period between when a coupon is announced and when it is paid is the ex-dividend period. If the bond trades during this time, it is the seller, not the buyer, who receives the next coupon payment. Between the coupon payment date and the next ex-dividend date the bond trades cum dividend, so the buyer gets the next coupon payment.

Accrued interest compensates sellers for giving up all the next coupon payment even though they will have held their bonds for part of the period since the last coupon payment. A bond's clean price moves with market interest rates. If the market rates are constant during a coupon period, the clean price will be constant as well. In contrast, the dirty price for the same bond will increase steadily as the coupon interest accrues from one coupon payment date until the next ex-dividend date, when it falls by the present value of the amount of the coupon payment. The dirty price at this point is below the clean price, reflecting the fact that accrued interest is now negative. This is because – if the bond is traded during the ex-dividend period – the seller, not the buyer, receives the next coupon, and the lower price is the buyer's compensation for this loss. On the coupon date, the accrued interest is 0, so the clean and dirty prices are the same.

The net interest accrued since the last ex-dividend date is calculated using formula (1.25):

$$AI = C \times \left[\frac{N_{xt} - N_{xc}}{\text{Day base}}\right] \qquad (1.25)$$

where AI = Next accrued interest;
          C = Bond coupon;
          N_{xc} = Number of days between the *ex-dividend* date and the coupon payment date;
          N_{xt} = Number of days between the *ex-dividend* date and the date for the calculation;
          Day base = Day-count base (see below).

When a bond is traded, accrued interest is calculated from and including the last coupon date up to and excluding the value date, usually the settlement date. Interest does not accrue on bonds whose issuer has defaulted.

As noted earlier, for bonds that are trading ex-dividend, the accrued coupon is negative and is subtracted from the clean price.

The negative accrued interest is calculated using formula (1.26):

$$AI = -C \times \frac{\text{Days to } next \text{ coupon}}{\text{Day base}} \qquad (1.26)$$

Certain classes of bonds – e.g., US Treasuries and Eurobonds – do not have ex-dividend periods and, therefore, trade cum dividend right up to the coupon date.

Day-count conventions

In calculating the accrued interest on a bond, the market uses the day-count convention appropriate to that bond. These conventions govern both the number of days assumed to be in a calendar year and how the days between two dates are figured. We show how the different conventions affect the accrual calculation in Box 1.7.

Box 1.7 Accrual calculation.	
actual/365	$AI = C \times$ Actual days to next coupon payment/365
actual/360	$AI = C \times$ Actual days to next coupon/360
actual/actual	$AI = C \times$ Actual days to next coupon/actual number of days in the interest period
30/360	$AI = C \times$ Days to next coupon, assuming 30 days in a month/360
30E/360	$AI = C \times$ Days to next coupon, assuming 30 days in a month/360

In these conventions, the number of days between two dates includes the first date but not the second. Thus, using actual/365, there are 37 days between August 4 and September 10. The last two conventions assume 30 days in each month, no matter what the calendar says. So, for example, it is assumed that there are 30 days between 10 February and 10 March. Under the 30/360 convention, if the first date is the 31st, it is changed to the 30th; if the second date is the 31st and the first date is either the 30th or the 31st, the second date is changed to the 30th. The 30E/360 convention differs from this in that – if the second date is the 31st – it is changed to the 30th regardless of what the first date is.

ILLUSTRATING BOND YIELD USING EXCEL SPREADSHEETS

In this section we use Microsoft Excel to illustrate bond yield-to-maturity. We do this first by means of function references, then via a real-world illustration of how we can check yields quoted in the market using Excel.

Table 1.4 shows the spreadsheet used to calculate price, yield and duration for a hypothetical bond traded for settlement on 10 December 2005. It has a 5% coupon and matures in July 2012. Given the price we can calculate yield, and given yield we can calculate price and duration. We need to also set the coupon frequency, in this case semiannual, and the accrued interest day-count basis, in this case act/act, in order for the formulae to work.

Table 1.5 is the same spreadsheet but with the actual cell formulae shown.

We can apply the same logic with real-world bond prices and yields. Let us take a corporate bond first, the Ford $7\frac{3}{4}$% of February 2007, traded for settlement on 6 January 2006. This bond accrues interest on a 30/360 basis.

As at the trade date this bond has three more coupons to pay plus its final maturity payment. The time to payment of each cash flow is

Table 1.4   Calculating bond price and yield using Microsoft Excel.

B2	C	D	E
3	11/12/2005	settlement date	
4	11/07/2012	maturity date	
5	5%	coupon	
6	98.95	price	
7	100	par	
8	2	semi annual coupon	
9	1	a/a	
10			
11			
12	YIELD	5.189 5%	0.051 894 9
13			
14	DURATION	5.569 080 372	
15			
16	PRICE	98.950 000 00	

Table 1.5   Table 1.4 showing cell formulae.

B2	C	D	E
3	11/12/2005	settlement date	
4	11/07/2012	maturity date	
5	5%	coupon	
6	98.95	price	
7	100	par	
8	2	semi annual coupon	
9	1	a/a	
10			
11			
12	YIELD	= YIELD(C3,C4,C5,C6,C7,C8,C9)	0.051 329 284
13			
14	DURATION	= DURATION(C3,C4,C5,D12,C8,C9)	
15			
16	PRICE	= PRICE(C3,C4,C5,E12,C7,C8,C9)	

shown in column G of Table 1.6, which is a spreadsheet calculation of its yield. At our trade date, from Bloomberg page YA we see that the bond has a clean price of par and a redemption yield of 7.738%. This is shown at Figure 1.5. Can we check this on Excel?

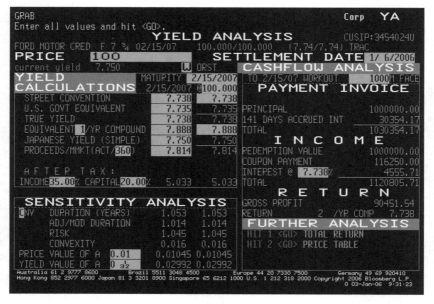

Figure 1.5   Bloomberg page YA for Ford $7\frac{3}{4}$% 2007 bond, 3 Jan 2006.

Table 1.6 Bond yield calculation, Ford and US Treasury securities, 3 January 2006.

C5	D	E	F	G	H	I	J	K
6	Today	03-Jan-06						
7	Settlement Ford	06-Jan-06						
8	Settlement UST	04-Jan-06						
9								
10	**Ford 7.75% 15 Feb 2007 ISIN US345024U26**							
11	semi-annual 30/360							
12	price value 6 Jan 06	100.00						
13	YTM	0.077 38						
14								
15		Date	Payment	Time to payment	n	Discount factor	PV	
16	Coupon date	15-Feb-06	3.875	40 days	0.216 666 667	0.991 808 998	3.843 259 9	
17		15-Aug-06	3.875	221 days	1.216 666 667	0.954 865 261	3.700 102 9	
18		15-Feb-07	3.875	405 days	2.216 666 667	0.919 297 636	3.562 278 3	
19	Maturity date	15-Feb-07	100	405 days	2.216 666 667	0.919 297 636	91.929 764	
20							103.035 4	Price
21							100.00	Clean price
22					less accrued	7.75*0.5(141/360)		
23						3.035 416 667	103.035 4	Dirty price
24								
25								
26								
27	**UST 2.25% 15 Feb 2007 ISIN US912828BY54**							
28	semi-annual act/act							
29	price value 4 Jan 06	97.671 875						
30	YTM	0.044 12						
31								
32		Date	Payment	Time to payment	n	Discount factor	PV	
33	Coupon date	15-Feb-06	1.125	42 days	0.228 260 87	0.995 031 685 6	1.119 410 6	
34		15-Aug-06	1.125	223 days	1.228 260 87	0.973 555 061 0	1.095 249 4	
35		15-Feb-07	1.125	407 days	2.228 260 87	0.952 541 984 8	1.071 609 7	
36	Maturity date	15-Feb-07	100	407 days	2.228 260 87	0.952 541 984 8	95.254 198	
37							98.5405	Price
38							97.671 875	Clean price
39					less accrued	2.25*0.5(142/184)		
40						0.868 206 522	98.540	Dirty price
41								

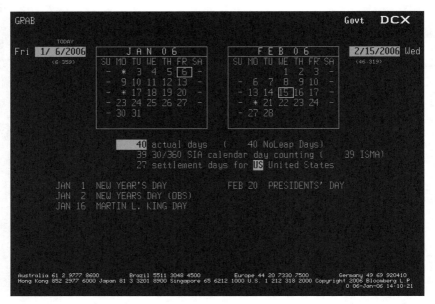

Figure 1.6   Bloomberg page DCX, 3 January 2006, settlement date for Ford bond.

Our confirmation is shown at Table 1.6. It is important to get the day-count fraction for the first coupon payment correct, and the confirm of this is shown at Figure 1.6, which is Bloomberg page DCX with the relevant dates entered. We see that on the 30/360 basis the number of days accrued for the Ford bond for value 6 January 2006 is 39.

The spreadsheet cell formulae are shown at Table 1.7.

We perform a similar exercise for a US Treasury security, the $2\frac{1}{4}\%$ February 2007 bond. This security settles on a $T + 1$ basis, so on our trade date of 3 Januaru 2006 its yield is as at 4 January 2006. Also Treasury bonds accrue interest on an act/act basis. Its yield and price of 4.412% and 97.67, respectively, are given at Figure 1.7, the Bloomberg YA page. The confirm of these is shown at Table 1.6 again.

Table 1.7 Table 1.6 showing cell formulae

C5	D	E	F	G	H	I	J	K
6	Today	03-Jan-06		NOTE for DCX screen				
7	Settlement Ford	06-Jan-06		DCX is for Ford bond, 30/360 days for first coupon				
8	Settlement UST	04-Jan-06						
9				Accrued uses day-count basis, as does discounting days fraction for first coupon				
10	**Ford 7.75% 15 Feb 2007 ISIN US3454024U26**							
11	semi-annual 30/360							
12	price value 6 Jan 06	100.00						
13	YTM	0.077 38						
14								
15		Date	Payment	Time to payment	n	Discount factor	PV	
16	Coupon date	15-Feb-06	3.875	40 days	=39/180	=1/(1+$E$14/2)^H17	=F17*I17	
17		15-Aug-06	3.875	221 days	=219/180	=1/(1+$E$14/2)^H18	=F18*I18	
18		15-Feb-07	3.875	405 days	=399/180	=1/(1+$E$14/2)^H19	=F19*I19	
19	Maturity date	15-Feb-07	100	405 days	=399/180	=1/(1+$E$14/2)^I20	=F20*I20	
20							=SUM(I17:J20)	Price
21				less accrued	7.75*0.5(141/360)		100.00	Clean price
22					=(7.75*0.5)*(141/180)			
23							=J22+I23	Dirty price
24								
25								
26								
27	**UST 2.25% 15 Feb 2007 ISIN US912828BY54**							
28	semi-annual act/act							
29	price value 4 Jan 06	97.671 875						
30	YTM	0.044 12						
31								
32		Date	Payment	Time to payment	n	Discount factor	PV	
33	Coupon date	15-Feb-06	1.125	42 days	=42/184	=1/(1+$E$31/2)^H34	=F34*I34	
34		15-Aug-06	1.125	223 days	=1+H34	=1/(1+$E$31/2)^H35	=F35*I35	
35		15-Feb-07	1.125	407 days	=2+H34	=1/(1+$E$31/2)^H36	=F36*I36	
36	Maturity date	15-Feb-07	100	407 days	=2+H34	=1/(1+$E$31/2)^H37	=F37*I37	
37							=SUM(I34:I37)	Price
38				less accrued	2.25*0.5[142/184]		97.671 875	Clean price
39					=(2.25*0.5)*(142/184)			
40							=J39+I40	Dirty price
41								

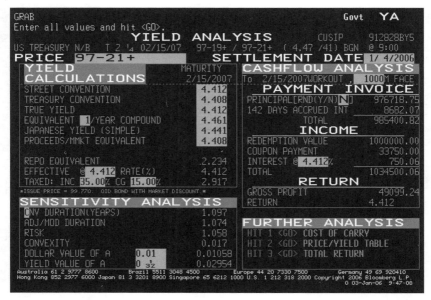

Figure 1.7 Bloomberg page YA for UST $2\frac{1}{4}$% 2007 bond, 3 Jan 2006.

BIBLIOGRAPHY

Crescenzi, A. (2002). *The Strategic Bond Investor*. McGraw-Hill, New York.

Fabozzi, F. (1989). *Bond Markets, Analysis and Strategies* (ch. 2). Prentice Hall, New York.

Fabozzi, F. (1993). *Bond Markets, Analysis and Strategies* (2nd edn). Prentice Hall, New York.

Fabozzi, F. (ed.) (2002). *The Handbook of Fixed Income Securities* (6th edn). McGraw-Hill, Princeton, NJ.

Higson, C. (1995). *Business Finance*. Butterworth, Oxford, UK.

Questa, G. (1999). *Fixed Income Analysis for the Global Financial Market*. John Wiley & Sons, Chichester, UK.

Sundaresan, S. (1997). *Fixed Income Markets and their Derivatives*. South-Western, Cincinnati, OH.

Temple, P. (2002). *First Steps in Bonds*. FT Prentice Hall, London.

Chapter

2

. . . .

THE YIELD CURVE, SPOT AND FORWARD YIELDS

In this chapter we extend the analysis introduced in Chapter 1 with a look at the zero-coupon or spot interest rate and the forward rate. We also look at the yield curve. Investors consider a bond yield and the general market yield curve when undertaking analysis to determine if the bond is worth buying; this is a form of what is known as *relative value* analysis. All investors will have a specific risk/reward profile that they are comfortable with, and a bond's yield relative to its perceived risk will influence the decision to buy (or sell) it.

We consider the different types of yield curve, before considering a specific curve, the zero-coupon or spot yield curve. Yield curve construction itself requires some formidable mathematics and is outside the scope of this book; we consider here the basic techniques only. Interested readers who wish to study the topic further may wish to refer to the author's book *Analysing and Interpreting the Yield Curve.*

THE YIELD CURVE

We have already considered the main measure of return associated with holding bonds, the *yield-to-maturity* or *redemption yield*. Much of the analysis and pricing activity that takes place in the bond markets revolves around the *yield curve*. The yield curve describes the relationship between a particular redemption yield and a bond's maturity. Plotting the yields of bonds along the term structure will give us our yield curve. It is important that only bonds from the same class of issuer or with the same degree of liquidity be used when plotting the yield curve; for example, a curve may be constructed for gilts or for AA-rated sterling Eurobonds, but not a mixture of both.

In this section we will consider the yield-to-maturity yield curve as well as other types of yield curve that may be constructed. Later in this chapter we will consider how to derive spot and forward yields from a current redemption yield curve.

Yield-to-maturity yield curve

The most commonly occurring yield curve is the yield-to-maturity yield curve. The equation used to calculate the yield to maturity was shown in Chapter 1. The curve itself is constructed by plotting the

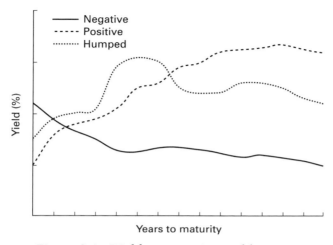

Figure 2.1   Yield-to-maturity yield curves.

yield to maturity against the term to maturity for a group of bonds of the same class. Three different examples are shown at Figure 2.1. Bonds used in constructing the curve will only rarely have an exact number of whole years to redemption; however, it is often common to see yields plotted against whole years on the x-axis. Figure 2.2 shows the Bloomberg page IYC for four government yield curves as at 2 December 2005; these are the US, UK, German and Italian sovereign bond yield curves.

From Figure 2.2 note the yield spread differential between German and Italian bonds. Although both the bonds are denominated in euros and, according to the European Central Bank (*ECB*), are viewed as equivalent for collateral purposes (implying identical credit quality), the higher yield for Italian government bonds proves that the market views them as higher credit risk compared with German government bonds.

The main weakness of the yield-to-maturity yield curve stems from the unrealistic nature of the assumptions behind the yield calculation. This includes the assumption of a constant rate for coupons during the bond's life at the redemption yield level. Since market rates will fluctuate over time, it will not be possible to achieve this (a feature known as *reinvestment risk*). Only zero-coupon bondholders avoid reinvestment risk as no coupon is paid during the life of a zero-coupon bond. Nevertheless, the yield-to-maturity curve is the most commonly encountered in markets.

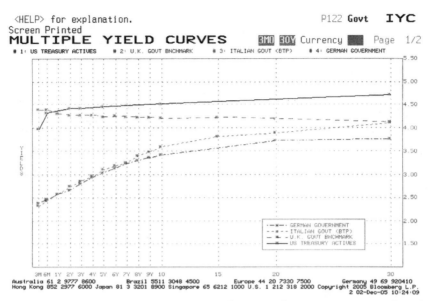

Figure 2.2 Bloomberg page IYC showing four government bond yield curves as at 2 December 2005.

© Bloomberg L.P. Used with permission. Visit *www.bloomberg.com*

For the reasons we have discussed the market often uses other types of yield curve for analysis when the yield-to-maturity yield curve is deemed unsuitable.

The par yield curve

The *par yield curve* is not usually encountered in secondary market trading; however, it is often constructed for use by corporate financiers and others in the new issues or *primary* market. The par yield curve plots yield to maturity against term to maturity for current bonds trading at par. The par yield is therefore equal to the coupon rate for bonds priced at par or near to par, as the yield to maturity for bonds priced exactly at par is equal to the coupon rate. Those involved in the primary market will use a par yield curve to determine the required coupon for a new bond to be issued at par.

As an example, consider that par yields on 1-year, 2-year and 3-year bonds are 5%, 5.25% and 5.75%, respectively. This implies that a new 2-year bond would require a coupon of 5.25% if it were to be issued at par; for a 3-year bond with annual coupons trading at par, the following equality would be true:

$$100 = \frac{5.75}{1.0575} + \frac{5.75}{(1.0575)^2} + \frac{105.75}{(1.0575)^3}$$

This demonstrates that the yield to maturity and the coupon are identical when a bond is priced in the market at par.

The par yield curve can be derived directly from bond yields when bonds are trading at or near par. If bonds in the market are trading substantially away from par then the resulting curve will be distorted. It is then necessary to derive it by iteration from the spot yield curve.

The zero-coupon (or spot) yield curve

The *zero-coupon* (or *spot*) *yield curve* plots zero-coupon yields (or spot yields) against term to maturity. In the first instance, if there is a liquid zero-coupon bond market we can plot the yields from these bonds if we wish to construct this curve. However, it is not necessary to have a set of zero-coupon bonds in order to construct this curve, as we can derive it from a coupon or par yield curve; in fact, in many markets where no zero-coupon bonds are traded, a spot yield curve is derived from the conventional yield-to-maturity yield curve. This of course would be a *theoretical* zero-coupon (spot) yield curve, as opposed to the *market* spot curve that can be constructed from yields of actual zero-coupon bonds trading in the market. The zero-coupon yield curve is also known as the *term structure of interest rates*.

Spot yields must comply with equation (2.1), this equation assumes annual coupon payments and that the calculation is carried out on a coupon date so that accrued interest is 0:

$$P_d = \sum_{t=1}^{T} \frac{C}{(1 + rs_t)^t} + \frac{M}{(1 + rs_T)^T}$$

$$= \sum_{t=1}^{T} C \times D_t + M \times D_T \qquad (2.1)$$

where rs_t = Spot or zero-coupon yield on a bond with t years to maturity;

$D_t \equiv 1/(1 + rs_t)^t$ = Corresponding *discount factor*.

In (2.1), rs_1 is the current 1-year spot yield, rs_2 the current 2-year spot yield and so on. Theoretically, the spot yield for a particular term to maturity is the same as the yield on a zero-coupon bond of the same maturity, which is why spot yields are also known as zero-coupon yields.

This last is an important result. Spot yields can be derived from par yields and the mathematics behind this is considered in the next section.

As with the yield to redemption yield curve the spot yield curve is commonly used in the market. It is viewed as the true term structure of interest rates because there is no reinvestment risk involved; the stated yield is equal to the actual annual return. That is, the yield on a zero-coupon bond of n years maturity is regarded as the true n-year interest rate. Because the observed government bond redemption yield curve is not considered to be the true interest rate, analysts often construct a theoretical spot yield curve. Essentially, this is done by breaking down each coupon bond into a series of zero-coupon issues. For example, £100 nominal of a 10% 2-year bond is considered equivalent to £10 nominal of a 1-year zero-coupon bond and £110 nominal of a 2-year zero-coupon bond.

Let us assume that in the market there are 30 bonds all paying annual coupons. The first bond has a maturity of 1 year, the second bond of 2 years and so on out to 30 years. We know the price of each of these bonds, and we wish to determine what the prices imply about the market's estimate of future interest rates. We naturally expect interest rates to vary over time, but that all payments being made on the same date are valued using the same rate. For the 1-year bond we know its current price and the amount of the payment (comprised of one coupon payment and the redemption proceeds) we will receive at the end of the year; therefore, we can calculate the interest rate for the first year: assume the 1-year bond has a coupon of 10%. If we invest £100 today we will receive £110 in 1 year's time, hence the rate of interest is apparent and is 10%. For the 2-year bond we use this interest rate to calculate the future value of its current price in 1 year's time: *this is how much we would receive if we had invested the same amount in the 1-year bond.* However, the 2-year bond pays a coupon at the end of the first year; if we subtract this amount from the future value of the current price, the net amount is what we should be giving up in 1 year in return for the one remaining payment. From these numbers we can calculate the interest rate in year 2.

Assume that the 2-year bond pays a coupon of 8% and is priced at 95.00. If the 95.00 was invested at the rate we calculated for the 1-year bond (10%), it would accumulate £104.50 in 1 year, made up of the £95 investment and coupon interest of £9.50. On the payment date in 1 year's time, the 1-year bond matures and the 2-year bond pays a coupon of 8%. If everyone expected that at this time the 2-year bond would be priced at more than 96.50 (which is 104.50 minus 8.00), then no investor would buy the 1-year bond, since it would be more advantageous to buy the 2-year bond and sell it after 1 year for a greater return. Similarly, if the price was less than 96.50 no investor would buy the 2-year bond, as it would be cheaper to buy the shorter bond and then buy the longer-dated bond with the proceeds received when the 1-year bond matures. Therefore, the 2-year bond must be priced at exactly 96.50 in 12 months' time. For this £96.50 to grow to £108.00 (the maturity proceeds from the 2-year bond, comprising the redemption payment and coupon interest), the interest rate in year 2 must be 11.92%. We can check this using the present value formula covered earlier. At these two interest rates, the two bonds are said to be in equilibrium.

This is an important result and shows that there can be no arbitrage opportunity along the yield curve; using interest rates available today the return from buying the 2-year bond must equal the return from buying the 1-year bond and rolling over the proceeds (or *re-investing*) for another year. This is the known as the *breakeven principle*.

Using the price and coupon of the 3-year bond we can calculate the interest rate in year 3 in precisely the same way. Using each of the bonds in turn, we can link together the *implied 1-year rates* for each year up to the maturity of the longest-dated bond. The process is known as *boot-strapping*. The 'average' of the rates over a given period is the spot yield for that term: in the example given above, the rate in year 1 is 10%, and in year 2 is 11.92%. An investment of £100 at these rates would grow to £123.11. This gives a total percentage increase of 23.11% over 2 years, or 10.956% per annum (the average rate is not obtained by simply dividing 23.11 by 2, but – using our present value relationship again – by calculating the square root of '1 plus the interest rate' and then subtracting 1 from this number). Thus, the 1-year yield is 10% and the 2-year yield is 10.956%.

In real-world markets it is not necessarily as straightforward as this; for instance, on some dates there may be several bonds maturing, with different coupons, and on some dates there may be no bonds maturing. It is most unlikely that there will be a regular spacing of redemptions exactly 1 year apart. For this reason it is common for practitioners to use a software model to calculate the set of implied forward rates which best fits the market prices of the bonds that do exist in the market. For instance, if there are several 1-year bonds, each of their prices may imply a slightly different rate of interest. We will choose the rate which gives the smallest average price error. In practice, all bonds are used to find the rate in year 1, all bonds with a term longer than 1 year are used to calculate the rate in year 2 and so on. The zero-coupon curve can also be calculated directly from the par yield curve using a method similar to that described above; in this case the bonds would be priced at par (100.00) and their coupons set to the par yield values.

The zero-coupon yield curve is ideal to use when deriving implied forward rates. It is also the best curve to use when determining the relative value, whether cheap or dear, of bonds trading in the market, and when pricing new issues, irrespective of their coupons. However, it is not an accurate indicator of average market yields because most bonds are not zero-coupon bonds.

Zero-coupon curve arithmetic

Having introduced the concept of the zero-coupon curve in the previous paragraph, we can now illustrate the mathematics involved. When deriving spot yields from par yields, one views a conventional bond as being made up of an *annuity*, which is the stream of coupon payments, and a zero-coupon bond, which provides the repayment of principal. To derive the rates we can use (2.1), setting $P_d = M = 100$ and $C = rp_T$, as shown below:

$$100 = rp_T \times \sum_{t=1}^{T} D_t + 100 \times D_T$$

$$= rp_T \times A_T + 100 \times D_T \qquad (2.2)$$

where rp_T is the par yield for a term to maturity of T years, where the discount factor D_T is the fair price of a zero-coupon bond with a par value of £1 and a term to maturity of T years, and where:

$$A_T = \sum_{t=1}^{T} D_t = A_{T-1} + D_T \qquad (2.3)$$

is the fair price of an annuity of £1 per year for T years (with $A_0 = 0$

by convention). Substituting (2.3) into (2.2) and re-arranging will give us the expression below for the T-year discount factor:

$$D_T = \frac{1 - rp_T \times A_{T-1}}{1 + rp_T} \qquad (2.4)$$

In (2.1) we are discounting the t-year cash flow (comprising the coupon payment and/or principal repayment) by the corresponding t-year spot yield. In other words, rs_t is the *time-weighted rate of return* on a t-year bond. Thus, as we said in the previous section, the spot yield curve is the correct method for pricing or valuing any cash flow, including an irregular cash flow, because it uses the appropriate discount factors. This contrasts with the yield-to-maturity procedure discussed earlier, which discounts all cash flows by the same yield to maturity.

THE FORWARD YIELD CURVE

The *forward* (or *forward–forward*) *yield curve* is a plot of forward rates against term to maturity. Forward rates satisfy expression (2.5) below:

$$
\begin{aligned}
P_d &= \frac{C}{(1 + {}_0rf_1)} + \frac{C}{(1 + {}_0rf_1)(1 + {}_1rf_2)} + \cdots + \frac{M}{(1 + {}_0rf_1) \cdots (1 + {}_{T-1}rf_T)} \\
&= \sum_{t=1}^{T} \frac{C}{\prod_{i=1}^{t}(1 + {}_{i-1}rf_i)} + \frac{M}{\prod_{i=1}^{T}(1 + {}_{i-1}rf_i)}
\end{aligned}
\qquad (2.5)
$$

where ${}_{t-1}rf_t$ = Implicit forward rate (or forward–forward rate) on a 1-year bond maturing in year t.

Comparing (2.1) and (2.2) we can see that the spot yield is the *geometric mean* of the forward rates, as shown below:

$$(1 + rs_t)^t = (1 + {}_0rf_1)(1 + {}_1rf_2) \cdots (1 + {}_{t-1}rf_t) \qquad (2.6)$$

This implies the following relationship between spot and forward rates:

$$
\begin{aligned}
(1 + {}_{t-1}rf_t) &= \frac{(1 + rs_t)^t}{(1 + rs_{t-1})^{t-1}} \\
&= \frac{D_{t-1}}{D_t}
\end{aligned}
\qquad (2.7)
$$

Theories of the yield curve

As we can observe by analysing yield curves in different markets at any time, a yield curve can be one of four basic shapes, which are:

- *normal* – in which yields are at 'average' levels and the curve slopes gently upwards as maturity increases;
- *upward sloping* (or *positive* or *rising*) – in which yields are at historically low levels, with long rates substantially greater than short rates;
- *downward sloping* (or *inverted* or *negative*) – in which yield levels are very high by historical standards, but long-term yields are significantly lower than short rates;
- *humped* – where yields are high with the curve rising to a peak in the medium-term maturity area, and then sloping downwards at longer maturities.

Various explanations have been put forward to explain the shape of the yield curve at any one time, which we can now consider.

Unbiased or pure expectations hypothesis

If short-term interest rates are expected to rise, then longer yields should be higher than shorter ones to reflect this. If this were not the case, investors would only buy the shorter-dated bonds and roll over the investment when they matured. Likewise, if rates are expected to fall then longer yields should be lower than short yields. The *expectations hypothesis* states that the long-term interest rate is a geometric average of expected future short-term rates. This was in fact the theory that was used to derive the forward yield curve in (2.5) and (2.6) previously. This gives us:

$$(1 + rs_T)^T = (1 + rs_1)(1 + {}_1rf_2) \cdots (1 + {}_{T-1}rf_T) \qquad (2.8)$$

or

$$(1 + rs_T)^T = (1 + rs_{T-1})^{T-1}(1 + {}_{T-1}rf_T) \qquad (2.9)$$

where rs_T is the spot yield on a T-year bond and ${}_{t-1}rf_t$ is the implied 1-year rate t years ahead. For example, if the current 1-year rate is $rs_1 = 6.5\%$ and the market is expecting the 1-year rate in a year's time to be ${}_1rf_2 = 7.5\%$, then the market is expecting a £100 investment in two 1-year bonds to yield:

$$£100(1.065)(1.075) = £114.49$$

after 2 years. To be equivalent to this an investment in a 2-year bond has to yield the same amount, implying that the current 2-year rate is $rs_2 = 7\%$, as shown below

$$£100(1.07)^2 = £114.49$$

This result must be so to ensure no-arbitrage opportunities exist in the market, and, in fact, we showed as much earlier in the chapter when we considered forward rates.

A rising yield curve is therefore explained by investors expecting short-term interest rates to rise – that is, $_1rf_2 > rs_2$. A falling yield curve is explained by investors expecting short-term rates to be lower in the future. A humped yield curve is explained by investors expecting short-term interest rates to rise and long-term rates to fall. Expectations, or views on the future direction of the market, are a function of the expected rate of inflation. If the market expects inflationary pressures in the future, the yield curve will be positively shaped, while if inflation expectations are inclined towards disinflation, then the yield curve will be negative.

Liquidity preference theory

Intuitively, we can see that longer maturity investments are more risky than shorter ones. An investor lending money for a 5-year term will usually demand a higher rate of interest than if he were to lend the same customer money for a 5-week term. This is because the borrower may not be able to repay the loan over the longer time period as he may, for instance, have gone bankrupt in that period. For this reason longer-dated yields should be higher than short-dated yields.

We can consider this theory in terms of inflation expectations as well. Where inflation is expected to remain roughly stable over time, the market would anticipate a positive yield curve. However, the expectations hypothesis cannot by itself explain this phenomenon, as under stable inflationary conditions one would expect a flat yield curve. The risk inherent in longer-dated investments, or the *liquidity preference theory*, seeks to explain a positive shaped curve. Generally, borrowers prefer to borrow over as long a term as possible, while lenders will wish to lend over as short a term as possible. Therefore, as we first stated, lenders have to be compensated for lending over the longer term; this compensation is considered a premium for a loss in *liquidity* for the lender. The premium is increased the further the investor lends across the term structure, so that the longest-dated investments will, all else being equal, have the highest yield.

Segmentation hypothesis

The capital markets are made up of a wide variety of users, each with different requirements. Certain classes of investors will prefer dealing at the short end of the yield curve, while others will concentrate on the longer end of the market. The *segmented markets* theory suggests that activity is concentrated in certain specific areas of the market, and that there are no inter-relationships between these parts of the market; the relative amounts of funds invested in each of the maturity spectra causes differentials in supply and demand, which results in humps in the yield curve. That is, the shape of the yield curve is determined by supply and demand for certain specific maturity investments, each of which has no reference to any other part of the curve.

For example, banks and building societies concentrate a large part of their activity at the short end of the curve, as part of daily cash management (known as *asset and liability management*) and for regulatory purposes (known as *liquidity* requirements). Fund managers, such as pension funds and insurance companies, however, are active at the long end of the market. Few institutional investors, however, have any preference for medium-dated bonds. This behaviour on the part of investors will lead to high prices (low yields) at both the short and long ends of the yield curve and lower prices (higher yields) in the middle of the term structure.

Further views on the yield curve

As one might expect, there are other factors that affect the shape of the yield curve. For instance, short-term interest rates are greatly influenced by the availability of funds in the money market. The slope of the yield curve (usually defined as the 10-year yield minus the 3-month interest rate) is also a measure of the degree of tightness of government monetary policy. A low, upward sloping curve is often thought to be a sign that an environment of cheap money, due to a more loose monetary policy, is to be followed by a period of higher inflation and higher bond yields. Equally, a high downward sloping curve is taken to mean that a situation of tight credit, due to more strict monetary policy, will result in falling inflation and lower bond yields. Inverted yield curves have often preceded recessions; for instance, *The Economist* in an article from April 1998 remarked that in the US every recession since 1955 bar one has been preceded by a negative yield curve. The analysis is the same: if investors expect a recession they also expect inflation to fall, so the yields on long-term bonds will fall relative to short-term bonds.

There is significant information content in the yield curve, and economists and bond analysts will consider the shape of the curve as part of their policy making and investment advice. The shape of parts of the curve, whether the short end or long end, as well as that of the entire curve, can serve as useful predictors of future market conditions. As part of an analysis it is also worthwhile considering the yield curves across several different markets and currencies. For instance, the interest-rate swap curve, and its position relative to that of the government bond yield curve, is also regularly analysed for its information content. In developed country economies the swap market is invariably as liquid as the government bond market, if not more liquid, and so it is common to see the swap curve analysed when making predictions about, say, the future level of short-term interest rates.

Government policy will influence the shape and level of the yield curve, including policy on public sector borrowing, debt management and open-market operations. The market's perception of the size of public sector debt will influence bond yields; for instance, an increase in the level of debt can lead to an increase in bond yields across the maturity range. Open-market operations, which refers to the daily operation by the Bank of England to control the level of the money supply (to which end the Bank purchases short-term bills and also engages in repo dealing), can have a number of effects. In the short-term it can tilt the yield curve both upwards and downwards; longer term, changes in the level of the base rate will affect yield levels. An anticipated rise in base rates can lead to a drop in prices for short-term bonds, whose yields will be expected to rise; this can lead to a temporary inverted curve. Finally, debt management policy will influence the yield curve. (In the UK this is now the responsibility of the Debt Management Office.) Much government debt is rolled over as it matures, but the maturity of the replacement debt can have a significant influence on the yield curve in the form of humps in the market segment in which the debt is placed, if the debt is priced by the market at a relatively low price and hence high yield.

SPOT RATES

Par, zero-coupon (or spot) and forward rates have a close mathematical relationship. Here we explain and derive these different interest rates and explain their application in the markets.

A *par* yield is the yield to maturity on a bond that is trading at par. From Chapter 1 we know that this means that it is equal to the bond's coupon level. A zero-coupon bond is a bond which has no coupons and, therefore, only one cash flow, the redemption payment on maturity. It is therefore a *discount* instrument, as it is issued at a discount to par and redeemed at par. The yield on a zero-coupon bond can be viewed as a true yield, at the time that it is purchased, if the paper is held to maturity. This is because no reinvestment of coupons is involved and, so, there are no interim cash flows vulnerable to a change in interest rates. Zero-coupon yields are the key determinant of value in the capital markets, and they are calculated and quoted for every major currency. Zero-coupon rates can be used to value any cash flow that occurs at a future date.

Where zero-coupon bonds are traded, the yield on a zero-coupon bond of a particular maturity is the zero-coupon rate for that maturity. Not all debt capital trading environments possess a liquid market in zero-coupon bonds. However, it is not necessary to have zero-coupon bonds in order to calculate zero-coupon rates. It is possible to calculate zero-coupon rates from a range of market rates and prices, including coupon bond yields, interest-rate futures and currency deposits. Why would we wish to do this? Mainly because the zero-coupon rate for any particular maturity term represents that term's true interest rate. The assumptions behind the yield-to-maturity calculation mean that it is not a true interest rate; unless we buy a bond on issue at a price of par and hold it to maturity, and are able to reinvest the coupons at the coupon rate, we will not receive a return on the yield to maturity.[1] So we calculate zero-coupon rates to see what the true interest rate is: investors buying a zero-coupon bond will receive the return of its stated yield.

---

[1] For more detail on the assumptions behind the yield-to-maturity calculation and why it is not a true interest rate, see Chapter 6 in the author's book *The Bond and Money Markets* (Butterworth-Heinemann, 2001).

Discount factors and the discount function

It is possible to determine a set of *discount factors* from market interest rates. A discount factor is a number in the range 0 to 1 which can be used to obtain the present value of some future value. We have:

$$PV_t = d_t \times FV_t \qquad (2.10)$$

where PV_t = Present value of the future cash flow occurring at time t;
    FV_t = Future cash flow occurring at time t;
    d_t = Discount factor for cash flows occurring at time t.

Discount factors can be calculated most easily from zero-coupon rates; equations (2.11) and (2.12) apply to zero-coupon rates for periods up to 1 year and over 1 year, respectively:

$$d_t = \frac{1}{(1 + rs_t T_t)} \qquad (2.11)$$

$$d_t = \frac{1}{(1 + rs_t)^{T_t}} \qquad (2.12)$$

where d_t = Discount factor for cash flows occurring at time t;
    rs_t = Zero-coupon rate for the period to time t;
    T_t = Time from the value date to time t, expressed in years and fractions of a year.

Individual zero-coupon rates allow discount factors to be calculated at specific points along the maturity term structure. As cash flows may occur at any time in the future, and not necessarily at convenient times like in 3 months or 1 year, discount factors often need to be calculated for every possible date in the future. The complete set of discount factors is called the *discount function*.

Implied spot and forward rates[2]

In this section we describe how to obtain zero-coupon and forward rates from the yields available from coupon bonds, using a method

---

[2] This section follows, with permission, the approach used in the book *An Introduction to Option-adjusted Spread Analysis*, by Tom Windas (Bloomberg Publishing, 1993).

Table 2.1 Hypothetical government benchmark bond yields as at
2 January 2000.

Bond	Term of maturity (years)	Coupon (%)	Maturity date	Price	Gross redemption yield (%)
6-month	0.5	4	2 July 2000	100	4
1-year	1	5	2 January 2001	100	5
1.5 year	1.5	6	2 July 2001	100	6
2-year	2	7	2 January 2002	100	7

known as *boot-strapping*. In a government bond market such as
that for US Treasuries or gilts, the bonds are considered to be
default-free. The rates from a government bond yield curve describe
the risk-free rates of return available in the market *today*; however,
they also *imply* (risk-free) rates of return for *future time periods*.
These implied future rates, known as *implied forward rates*, or
simply *forward rates*, can be derived from a given spot yield curve
using boot-strapping. This term reflects the fact that each calculated
spot rate is used to determine the next period spot rate, in successive
steps.

Table 2.1 shows an hypothetical benchmark yield curve for value as
at 2 January 2000. The observed yields of the benchmark bonds that
compose the curve are displayed in the last column. All rates are
annualised and assume semiannual compounding. The bonds all pay
on the same coupon dates of 2 January and 2 July, and as the value
date is a coupon date, there is no accrued interest.

The gross redemption yield or *yield to maturity* of a coupon bond
describes the single rate that present-values each of its future cash
flows to a given price. This yield measure suffers from a fundamental
weakness in that each cash flow is present-valued at the same rate,
an unrealistic assumption in anything other than a flat yield curve
environment. The bonds in Table 2.1 pay semiannual coupons on
2 January and 2 July and have the same time period – 6 months –
between 2 January 2000 (their valuation date) and 2 July 2000 (their
next coupon date). However, since each issue carries a different yield,
the next 6-month coupon payment for each bond is present-valued at
a different rate. In other words, the 6-month bond present-values its
6-month coupon payment at its 4% yield to maturity, the 1-year at
5% and so on.

Because each of these issues uses a different rate to present-value a cash flow occurring at the same future point in time, it is unclear which of the rates should be regarded as the true interest rate or benchmark rate for the 6-month period from 2 January 2000 to 2 July 2000. This problem is repeated for all other maturities. We require a set of true interest rates, however, and so these must be derived from the redemption yields that we can observe from the benchmark bonds trading in the market. These rates we designate as rs_i, where rs_i is the *implied spot rate* or *zero-coupon rate* for the term beginning on 2 January 2000 and ending at the end of period i.

We begin calculating implied spot rates by noting that the 6-month bond contains only one future cash flow, the final coupon payment and the redemption payment on maturity. This means that it is in effect trading as a zero-coupon bond. Since this cash flow's present value, future value and maturity term are known, the unique interest rate that relates these quantities can be solved using the compound interest equation (2.13) below:

$$
\left.
\begin{aligned}
FV &= PV \times \left(1 + \frac{rs_i}{m}\right)^{(nm)} \\[2ex]
rs_i &= m \times \left(\sqrt[(nm)]{\frac{FV}{PV}} - 1\right)
\end{aligned}
\right\}
\qquad (2.13)
$$

where
FV = Future value;
PV = Present value;
rs_i = Implied i-period spot rate;
m = Number of interest periods per year;
n = Number of years in the term.

The first rate to be solved is referred to as the implied 6-month spot rate and is the true interest rate for the 5-month term beginning on 2 January and ending on 2 July 2000.

Equation (2.13) relates a cash flow's present value and future value in terms of an associated interest rate, compounding convention and time period. Of course, if we re-arrange it, we may use it to solve for an implied spot rate. For the 6-month bond the final cash flow on maturity is £102, comprised of the £2 coupon payment and the par redemption amount. So, we have for the first term $i = 1$, $FV = £102$, $PV = £100$, $n = 0.5$ years and $m = 2$. This allows us to calculate the spot rate as follows:

$$
\left.
\begin{aligned}
rs_i &= m \times \left(\sqrt[(nm)]{FV/PV} - 1 \right) \\
rs_1 &= 2 \times \left(\sqrt[(0.5 \times 2)]{£102/£100} - 1 \right) \\
rs_1 &= 0.040\,00 \\
rs_1 &= 4.000\%
\end{aligned}
\right\}
\tag{2.14}
$$

Thus, the implied 6-month spot rate or zero-coupon rate is equal to 4%.[3] We now need to determine the implied 1-year spot rate for the term from 2 January 2000 to 2 January 2001. We note that the 1-year issue has a 5% coupon and contains two future cash flows: a £2.50 6-month coupon payment on 2 July 2000 and a £102.50 1-year coupon and principal payment on 2 January 2001. Since the first cash flow occurs on 2 July – 6 months from now – it must be present-valued at the 4% 6-month spot rate established above. Once this present value is determined, it may be subtracted from the £100 total present value of the 1-year issue to obtain the present value of the 1-year coupon and cash flow. Again we then have a single cash flow with a known present value, future value and term. The rate that equates these quantities is the implied 1-year spot rate. From equation (2.15) the present value of the 6-month £2.50 coupon payment of the 1-year benchmark bond, discounted at the implied 6-month spot rate, is:

$$
PV_{\text{6-month cash flow, 1-year bond}} = £2.50/(1 + 0.04/2)^{(0.5 \times 2)}
$$
$$
= £2.45098
$$

The present value of the 1-year £102.50 coupon and principal payment is found by subtracting the present value of the 6-month cash flow, determined above, from the total present value (current price) of the issue:

$$
PV_{\text{1-year cash flow, 1-year bond}} = £100 - £2.450\,98
$$
$$
= £97.549\,02
$$

The implied 1-year spot rate is then determined by using the £97.549\,02 present value of the 1-year cash flow determined

---

[3] Of course, intuitively we could have concluded that the 6-month spot rate was 4%, without the need to apply the arithmetic, as we had already assumed that the 6-month bond was a quasi-zero-coupon bond.

above:

$$rs_2 = 2 \times \left(\sqrt[(1 \times 2)]{£102.50/£97.549\,02} - 1 \right)$$
$$= 0.050\,125\,6$$
$$= 5.012\,56\%$$

The implied 1.5-year spot rate is solved in the same way:

$$PV_{\text{6-month cash flow, 1.5-year bond}} = £3.00/(1 + 0.04/2)^{(0.5 \times 2)}$$
$$= £2.941\,18$$
$$PV_{\text{1-year cash flow, 1.5-year bond}} = £3.00/(1 + 0.050\,125\,6/2)^{(1 \times 2)}$$
$$= £2.855\,09$$
$$PV_{\text{1.5-year cash flow, 1.5-year bond}} = £100 - £2.941\,18 - £2.855\,09$$
$$= £94.203\,73$$
$$rs_3 = 2 \times \left(\sqrt[(1.5 \times 2)]{£103/£94.203\,73} - 1 \right)$$
$$= 0.060\,407\,1$$
$$= 6.040\,71\%$$

Extending the same process for the 2-year bond, we calculate the implied 2-year spot rate rs_4 to be 7.0906%.

The interest rates rs_1, rs_2, rs_3 and rs_4 describe the true zero-coupon or spot rates for the 6-month, 1-year, 1.5-year and 2-year terms that begin on 2 January 2000 and end on 2 July 2000, 2 January 2001, 2 July 2001 and 2 January 2002, respectively. They are also called 'implied spot rates' because they have been calculated from redemption yields observed in the market from the benchmark government bonds that were listed in Table 2.1.

Note that the 1-, 1.5- and 2-year implied spot rates are progressively greater than the corresponding redemption yields for these terms. This is an important result, and occurs whenever the yield curve is positively sloped. The reason for this is that the present values of a bond's shorter-dated cash flows are discounted at rates that are lower than the redemption yield; this generates higher present values that, when subtracted from the current price of the bond, produce a lower present value for the final cash flow. This lower present value implies a spot rate that is greater than the issue's yield. In an inverted yield curve environment we observe the opposite result: that is, implied rates that lie below the corresponding redemption yields.

If the redemption yield curve is flat, the implied spot rates will be equal to the corresponding redemption yields.

Once we have calculated the spot or zero-coupon rates for the 6-month, 1-year, 1.5-year and 2-year terms, we can determine the rate of return that is implied by the yield curve for the sequence of 6-month periods beginning on 2 January 2000, 2 July 2000, 2 January 2001 and 2 July 2001. These period rates are referred to as *implied forward rates* or *forward–forward rates* and we denote these as rf_i, where rf_i is the implied 6-month forward interest rate today for the ith period.

Since the implied 6-month zero-coupon rate (spot rate) describes the return for a term that coincides precisely with the first of the series of 6-month periods, this rate describes the risk-free rate of return for the first 6-month period. It is therefore equal to the first period spot rate. Thus, we have $rf_1 = rs_1 = 6.0\%$, where rf_1 is the risk-free forward rate for the first 6-month period beginning at period 1. The risk-free rates for the second, third and fourth 6-month periods, designated rf_2, rf_3 and rf_4, respectively, may be solved from the implied spot rates.

The benchmark rate for the second semi-annual period rf_2 is referred to as the one-period forward 6-month rate, because it goes into effect one 6-month period from now ('one-period forward') and remains in effect for 6 months ('6-month rate'). It is therefore the 6-month rate in 6 months' time, and is also referred to as the 6-month forward–forward rate. This rate in conjunction with the rate from the first period rf_1 must provide returns that match those generated by the implied 1-year spot rate for the entire 1-year term. In other words, £1 invested for 6 months from 2 January 2000 to 2 July 2000 at the first period's benchmark rate of 4% and then reinvested for another 6 months from 2 July 2000 to 2 January 2001 at the second period's (as yet unknown) implied *forward* rate must enjoy the same returns as £1 invested for 1 year from 2 January 2000 to 2 January 2001 at the implied 1-year *spot* rate. This reflects the law of no-arbitrage.

A moment's thought will convince us that this must be so. If this were not the case, we might observe an interest-rate environment in which the return over any given term would depend on whether an investment is made at the start period for the entire maturity term or over a succession of periods within the whole term and reinvested. If there were any discrepancies between the returns received from each approach, there would exist an unrealistic arbitrage opportunity, in which investments for a given term carrying a lower return might be sold short against the simultaneous purchase of investments for the same period carrying a higher return, thereby locking in a risk-free, cost-free profit. Therefore, forward interest rates must be calculated so that they are *arbitrage-free*. Excellent mathematical explanations of the no-arbitrage property of interest-rate markets are contained in Ingersoll (1987), Jarrow (1996) and Shiller (1990) among others.

The existence of a no-arbitrage market of course makes it straightforward to calculate forward rates; we know that the return from an investment made over a period must equal the return made from investing in a shorter period and successively reinvesting to a matching term. If we know the return over the shorter period, we are left with only one unknown – the full-period forward rate – which is then easily calculated. In our example, having established the rate for the first 6-month period, the rate for the second 6-month period – the one-period forward 6-month rate – is determined below.

The future value of £1 invested at rf_1, the period 1 forward rate, at the end of the first 6-month period is calculated as follows:

$$FV_1 = £1 \times \left(1 + \frac{rf_1}{2}\right)^{(0.5 \times 2)}$$

$$= £1 \times \left(1 + \frac{0.04}{2}\right)^{1}$$

$$= £1.020\,00$$

The future value of £1 at the end of the 1-year term, invested at the implied benchmark 1-year spot rate, is determined as follows:

$$FV_2 = £1 \times \left(1 + \frac{rs_2}{2}\right)^{(1 \times 2)}$$

$$= £1 \times \left(1 + \frac{0.050\,125\,6}{2}\right)^{2}$$

$$= £1.050\,754$$

The implied benchmark one-period forward rate rf_2 is the rate that equates the value of FV_1 (£1.02) on 2 July 2000 to FV_2 (£1.050 754) on

2 January 2001. From equation (2.13) we have:

$$rf_2 = 2 \times \left(\sqrt[(0.5 \times 2)]{\frac{FV_2}{FV_1}} - 1 \right)$$

$$= 2 \times \left(\frac{£1.050\,754}{£1.02} - 1 \right)$$

$$= 0.060\,302$$

$$= 6.0302\%$$

In other words, £1 invested from 2 January to 2 July at 4.0% (the implied forward rate for the first period) and then reinvested from 2 July to 2 January 2001 at 6.0302% (the implied forward rate for the second period) would accumulate the same returns as £1 invested from 2 January 2000 to 2 January 2001 at 5.012 56% (the implied 1-year spot rate).

The rate for the third 6-month period – the two-period forward 6-month interest rate – may be calculated in the same way:

$$FV_2 = £1.050\,754$$

$$FV_3 = £1 \times (1 + rs_3/2)^{(1.5 \times 2)}$$

$$= £1 \times (1 + 0.060\,407\,1/2)^3$$

$$= £1.093\,375$$

$$rf_3 = 2 \times \left(\sqrt[(0.5 \times 2)]{\frac{FV_3}{FV_4}} - 1 \right)$$

$$= 2 \times \left(\sqrt[1]{\frac{£1.093\,375}{£1.050\,754}} - 1 \right)$$

$$= 0.081\,125$$

$$= 8.1125\%$$

In the same way the three-period forward 6-month rate rf_4 is calculated to be 10.272 47%.

The results of the implied spot (zero-coupon) and forward rate calculations along with the given yield curve are displayed in Table 2.2, and illustrated graphically in Figure 2.3. This methodology can be applied using a spreadsheet for actual market redemption yields, although in practice we will not have a set of bonds with exact

Table 2.2   Calculating spot and forward rates.

Term to maturity (years)	Cash market yield (%)	Implied spot rate (%)	Implied one-period forward rate (%)
0.5	4.000 00	4.000 00	4.000 00
1	5.000 00	5.012 56	6.030 23
1.5	6.000 00	6.040 71	8.112 51
2	7.000 00	7.090 62	10.272 47

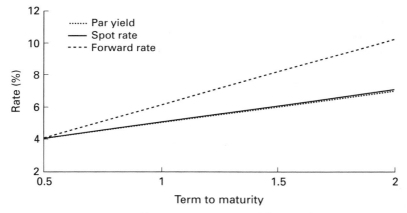

Figure 2.3   Illustrating spot and forward rates.

and/or equal periods to maturity and coupons falling on the same date. In designing a spreadsheet spot rate calculator, therefore, the coupon rate and maturity date are entered as standing data and usually interpolation is used when calculating the spot rates for bonds with uneven maturity dates. A spot curve model that uses this approach in conjunction with the boot-strapping method is available for downloading at *www.yieldcurve.com*

There is a close mathematical relationship between par, zero-coupon and forward rates. We stated that once the discount factors are known any of these rates can be calculated. We also illustrated how the boot-strapping technique could be used to calculate spot and forward rates from bond redemption yields. The relationship between the three rates allows the markets to price interest-rate swap and forward rate agreement (*FRA*) rates, as a swap rate is the weighted arithmetic average of forward rates for the term in question.

Example 2.1

Forward rates: breakeven principle

Consider the following spot yields:

1-year   10%
2-year   12%

Assume that a bank's client wishes to lock in *today* the cost of borrowing 1-year funds in 1 year's time. The solution for the bank (and the mechanism to enable the bank to quote a price to the client) involves raising 1-year funds at 10% and investing the proceeds for 2 years at 12%. As we observed on p. 58, the breakeven principle means that the same return must be generated from both fixed rate and reinvestment strategies.

The breakeven calculation uses the following formula:

$$\left.\begin{array}{c} (1+y_2)^2 = (1+y_1)(1+R) \\[2mm] R = \dfrac{(1+y_2)^2}{(1+y_1)} - 1 \end{array}\right\} \qquad (2.15)$$

In this example, as total funding cost must equal total return on investments (the *breakeven* referred to), the quoted rate minimum is as follows:

$$(1+0.12)^2 = (1+0.10) \times (1+R)$$
$$(1+R) = (1+0.12)^2/(1+0.10)$$
$$(1+R) = 1.140\,36$$
$$r = 14.04\%$$

This rate is the 1-year forward–forward rate, or the implied forward rate.

Example 2.2

If a 1-year AAA Eurobond trading at par yields 10% and a 2-year Eurobond of similar credit quality, also trading at par, yields 8.75%, what should be the price of a 2-year AAA zero-coupon bond? Note that Eurobonds pay coupon annually.

(a)   Cost of 2-year bond (per cent
        nominal)   100

(b) *Less* amount receivable from
     sale of first coupon on this bond
     (i.e., its present value) $= 8.75/1 + 0.10$
                                                   $= 7.95$

(c) *Equals* amount that must be
     received on sale of second
     coupon plus principal in order
     to break even   92.05

(d) Calculate the yield implied in
     the cash flows below (i.e., the
     2-year zero-coupon yield)

     – receive 92.05
     – pay out on maturity 108.75

     Therefore: $92.05 = 108.75/(1 + R)^2$

     Gives R equal to 8.69%

(e) What is the price of a 2-year
     zero-coupon bond with nominal
     value 100, to yield 8.69%? $= (92.05/108.75) \times 100$
                                                   $= 84.64$

Example 2.3

A highly-rated customer asks you to fix a yield at which he could
issue a 2-year zero-coupon USD Eurobond in 3 years' time. At the
time of asking, the US Treasury zero-coupon rates were:

1-year	6.25%
2-year	6.75%
3-year	7.00%
4-year	7.125%
5-year	7.25%

(a) Ignoring borrowing spreads over these benchmark yields, as
     a market maker you could cover the exposure created by
     borrowing funds for 5 years on a zero-coupon basis and
     placing these funds in the market for 3 years before lending

them on to your client. Assume annual interest compounding (even if none is actually paid out during the life of the loans):

Borrowing rate for 5 years $\left[\dfrac{R_5}{100}\right] = 0.0725$

Lending rate for 3 years $\left[\dfrac{R_3}{100}\right] = 0.0700$

(b) The key arbitrage relationship is:

Total cost of funding $=$ Total return on investments

$$(1 + R_5)^5 = (1 + R_3)^3 \times (1 + R_{3\times5})^2$$

Therefore, the breakeven forward yield is:

$$R_{3\times5} = \sqrt[2]{\left[\frac{(1 + R_5)^5}{(1 + R_3)^3}\right]} - 1$$

$$= 7.63\%$$

Example 2.4

Forward rate calculation for money market term

Consider these two positions: a borrowing of £100 million from 5 November 2005 for 30 days at 5.875% and a loan of £100 million from 5 November for 60 days at 6.125%.

The two positions can be viewed as a 30-day forward 30-day interest rate exposure (a 30- versus 60-day forward rate). It is sometimes referred to as a *gap* risk. What forward rate must be used if the trader wished to hedge this exposure?

The 30-day by 60-day forward rate can be calculated using the following formula:

$$R_f = \left[\left(\frac{1 + \left(Lr\% \cdot \dfrac{Ln}{B}\right)}{1 + \left(Sr\% \cdot \dfrac{Sn}{B}\right)}\right) - 1\right] \times \frac{B}{Ln - Sn} \qquad (2.16)$$

where R_f = Forward rate;
$Lr\%$ = Long period rate;
$Sr\%$ = Short period rate;
Ln = Long period days;
Sn = Short period days;
B = Day-count base.

Using this formula we obtain a 30- versus 60-day forward rate of 6.3443%.

This interest rate exposure can be hedged using interest rate futures or FRAs. Either method is an effective hedging mechanism, although the trader must be aware of:

- *basis* risk that exists between repo rates and the forward rates implied by futures and FRAs;
- date mismatch between expiry of futures contracts and the maturity dates of the repo transactions.

Forward rates and compounding

Example 2.1 above is for a forward rate calculation more than 1 year into the future, and therefore the formula used must take compounding of interest into consideration. Example 2.4 is for a forward rate within the next 12 months, with one-period bullet interest payments. A different formula is required to allow for this and is shown in the example.

Graphical illustration

We can illustrate this section on forward rates and the yield curve by reproducing the cash yield curve, implied zero-coupon rate curve and the discount function for the UK gilt market as at July 1997 (shown in Figure 2.4).

Understanding forward rates

Spot and forward rates that are calculated from current market rates follow mathematical principles to establish what the market believes the arbitrage-free rates for dealing *today* at rates that are effective at some point in the future. As such, forward rates are a type of market view on where interest rates will be (or should be!) in the

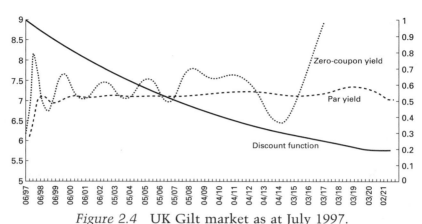

Figure 2.4   UK Gilt market as at July 1997.

Reproduced with permission of Dr Didier Joannas.

future. However, forward rates are not a prediction of future rates. It is important to be aware of this distinction. If we were to plot the forward rate curve for the term structure in 3 months' time, and then compare it in 3 months with the actual term structure prevailing at the time, the curves would almost certainly not match. However, this has no bearing on our earlier statement, that forward rates are the market's expectation of future rates. The main point to bear in mind is that we are not comparing like-for-like when plotting forward rates against actual current rates at a future date. When we calculate forward rates, we use the current term structure. The current term structure incorporates all known information, both economic and political, and reflects the market's views. This is exactly the same as when we say that a company's share price reflects all that is known about the company and all that is expected to happen with regard to the company in the near future, including expected future earnings. The term structure of interest rates reflects everything the market knows about relevant domestic and international factors. It is this information then that goes into the forward rate calculation. In 3 months' time, though, there will be new developments that will alter the market's view and therefore alter the current term structure; these developments and events were (by definition, as we cannot know what lies in the future!) not known at the time we calculated and used the 3-month forward rates. This is why rates actually turn out to be different from what the term structure predicted at an earlier date. However, for dealing today we use today's forward rates, which reflect everything we know about the market today.

THE TERM STRUCTURE OF INTEREST RATES

We describe now a more advanced description of what we have just discussed. It is used to obtain a zero-coupon curve, in the same way as seen previously, but just using more formal mathematics.

Under the following conditions:

- frictionless trading conditions;
- competitive economy;
- discrete time economy;

with discrete trading dates of $\{0, 1, 2, \ldots, \tau\}$, we assume a set of zero-coupon bonds with maturities $\{0, 1, 2, \ldots, \tau\}$. The price of a zero-coupon bond at time t with a nominal value of £1 on maturity at time T (such that $T \geq t$) is denoted with the term $P(t, T)$. The bonds are considered risk-free.

The price of a bond at time t of a bond of maturity T is given by:

$$P(t, T) = \frac{1}{[y(t, T)]^{(T-t)}}$$

where $y(t, T)$ is the yield of a T-maturity bond at time t. Re-arranging the above expression, the yield at time t of a bond of maturity T is given by:

$$y(t, T) = \left[\frac{1}{P(t, T)}\right]^{1/(T-t)}$$

The time t forward rate that applies to the period $[T, T + 1]$ is denoted with $f(t, T)$ and is given in terms of the bond prices by:

$$f(t, T) = \frac{P(t, T)}{P(t, T + 1)}$$

This forward rate is the rate that would be charged at time t for a loan that ran over the period $[T, T + 1]$.

From the above expression we can derive an expression for the price of a bond in terms of the forward rates that run from t to $T - 1$, which is:

$$P(t, T) = \frac{1}{\prod_{j=t}^{T-1} f(t, j)}$$

This expression means:

$$\prod_{j=t}^{T-1} f(t,j) = f(t,t) \cdot f(t,t+1) \cdots f(t,T-1)$$

that is, the result of multiplying the rates that apply to the interest periods in index j that run from t to $T-1$. It means that the price of a bond is equal to £1 received at time T, and has been discounted by the forward rates that apply to the maturity periods up to time $T-1$.

The expression is derived as shown in Box 8.1.

Box 8.1   Expression for a forward rate.

Consider the following expression for the forward rate applicable to the period (t,t):

$$f(t,t) = \frac{P(t,t)}{P(t,t+1)}$$

but, of course, $P(t,t)$ is equal to 1, so therefore:

$$f(t,t) = \frac{1}{P(t,t+1)}$$

which can be re-arranged to give:

$$P(t,t+1) = \frac{1}{f(t,t)}$$

For the next interest period we can set:

$$f(t,t+1) = \frac{P(t,t+1)}{P(t,t+2)}$$

which can be re-arranged to give:

$$P(t,t+2) = \frac{P(t,t+1)}{f(t,t+1)}$$

We can substitute the expression for $f(t,t+1)$ into the above and simplify to give us:

$$P(t,t+2) = \frac{1}{f(t,t)f(t,t+1)}$$

If we then continue for subsequent interest periods $(t,t+3)$ onwards, we obtain:

$$P(t,t+j) = \frac{1}{f(t,t)f(t,t+1)f(t,t+2)\ldots f(t,t+j-1)}$$

which is simplified into our result above.

Given a set of risk-free zero-coupon bond prices, we can calculate the forward rate applicable to a specified period of time that matures up to the point $T - 1$. Alternatively, given the set of forward rates we are able to calculate bond prices.

The zero-coupon or spot rate is defined as the rate applicable at time t on a one-period risk-free loan (such as a one-period zero-coupon bond priced at time t). If the spot rate is defined by $r(t)$ we can state that:

$$r(t) = f(t, t)$$

This spot rate is in fact the return generated by the shortest-maturity bond, shown by:

$$r(t) = y(t, t + 1)$$

We can define forward rates in terms of bond prices, spot rates and spot rate discount factors.

Table 2.3 shows bond prices for zero-coupon bonds of maturity value $1. We can plot a yield curve based on these prices, and we see that we have obtained forward rates based on these bond prices, using the technique described above.

Table 2.3   Zero-coupon bond prices, spot rates and forward rates.

Period	Bond price $[P(0, T)]$	Spot rates	Forward rates
0	1		
1	0.984 225	1.016 027	1.016 027
2	0.967 831	1.016 483	1.016 939
3	0.951 187	1.016 821	1.017 498
4	0.934 518	1.017 075	1.017 836
5	0.917 901	1.017 280	1.018 102
6	0.901 395	1.017 452	1.018 312
7	0.885 052	1.017 597	1.018 465
8	0.868 939	1.017 715	1.018 542
9	0.852 514	1.017 887	1.019 267

BIBLIOGRAPHY

Choudhry, M. (2001). *The Bond and Money Markets*. Butterworth-Heinemann, Oxford, UK.

Choudhry, M. (2004). *Analysing and Interpreting the Yield Curve*. John Wiley & Sons, Singapore.

Ingersoll, J. (1987). *Theory of Financial Decision Making*. Rowman & Littlefield, Lanham, MD.

Jarrow (1996). *Marketing Fixed Income Securities*. McGraw-Hill, New York.

Shiller, R. (1990). *Term Structure of Interest Rates*. McGraw-Hill, New York.

Windas, T. (1993). *An Introduction to Option-adjusted Spread Analysis*. Bloomberg Publishing, Princeton, NJ.

Chapter

3

....

BOND INSTRUMENTS AND INTEREST-RATE RISK

Chapter 1 described the basic concepts of bond pricing. This chapter discusses the sensitivity of bond prices to changes in market interest rates and the key related concepts of duration and convexity.

DURATION, MODIFIED DURATION AND CONVEXITY

Most bonds pay a part of their total return during their lifetimes in the form of coupon interest. Because of this, a bond's term to maturity does not reflect the true period over which its return is earned. Term to maturity also fails to give an accurate picture of the trading characteristics of a bond or to provide a basis for comparing it with other bonds having similar maturities. Clearly, a more accurate measure is needed.

A bond's maturity gives little indication of how much of its return is paid out during its life or of the timing and size of its cash flows. Maturity is thus inadequate as an indicator of the bond's sensitivity to moves in market interest rates. To see why this is so, consider two bonds with the same maturity date but different coupons: the higher-coupon bond generates a larger proportion of its return in the form of coupon payments than does the lower-coupon bond and so pays out its return at a faster rate. Because of this, the higher-coupon bond's price is theoretically less sensitive to fluctuations in interest rates that occur during its lifetime. A better indication of a bond's payment characteristics and interest-rate sensitivity might be the average time to receipt of its cash flows. The cash flows generated during a bond's life differ in value, however. The average time to receipt would be a more accurate measure, therefore, if it were weighted according to the cash flows' present values. The average maturity of a bond's cash flow stream calculated in this manner provides a measure of the speed at which a bond pays out its return, and hence of its price risk relative to other bonds having the same maturity.

The average time until receipt of a bond's cash flows, weighted according to the present values of these cash flows, measured in years, is known as *duration* or *Macaulay's duration*, referring to the man who introduced the concept in 1938 (Macaulay, 1999). Macaulay introduced duration as an alternative for the length of time remaining before a bond reached maturity.

Duration

Duration is a measure of price sensitivity to interest rates – that is, how much a bond's price changes in response to a change in interest rates. In mathematics, change like this is often expressed in terms of differential equations. The price–yield formula for a plain-vanilla bond, introduced in Chapter 1, is repeated as (3.1) below. It assumes complete years to maturity, annual coupon payments and no accrued interest at the calculation date:

$$P = \frac{C}{(1+r)} + \frac{C}{(1+r)^2} + \frac{C}{(1+r)^3} + \cdots + \frac{C}{(1+r)^n} + \frac{M}{(1+r)^n} \qquad (3.1)$$

where $P =$ Bond's fair price;
             $C =$ Annual coupon payment;
             $r =$ Discount rate, or required yield;
             $n =$ Number of years to maturity, and so the number of interest periods for a bond paying an annual coupon;
             $M =$ Maturity payment.

We saw from Chapter 1 that the price and yield of a bond are two sides of the same relationship. Because price P is a function of yield r, we can differentiate the price/yield equation at (3.1), as shown in (3.2). Taking the first derivative of this expression gives (3.2):

$$\frac{dP}{dr} = \frac{(-1)C}{(1+r)^2} + \frac{(-2)C}{(1+r)^3} + \cdots + \frac{(-n)C}{(1+r)^{n+1}} + \frac{(-n)M}{(1+r)^{n+1}} \qquad (3.2)$$

Re-arranging (3.2) gives (3.3). The expression in brackets is the average time to maturity of the cash flows from a bond weighted according to the present value of each cash flow. The whole equation is the formula for calculating the approximate change in price corresponding to a small change in yield:

$$\frac{dP}{dr} = -\frac{1}{(1+r)}\left[\frac{1C}{(1+r)} + \frac{2C}{(1+r)^2} + \cdots + \frac{nC}{(1+r)^n} + \frac{nM}{(1+r)^n}\right] \qquad (3.3)$$

Dividing both sides of (3.3) by P results in expression (3.4):

$$\frac{dP}{dr}\frac{1}{P} = -\frac{1}{(1+r)}\left[\frac{1C}{(1+r)} + \frac{2C}{(1+r)^2} + \cdots + \frac{nC}{(1+r)^n} + \frac{nM}{(1+r)^n}\right]\frac{1}{P} \qquad (3.4)$$

Dividing the bracketed expression by P gives expression (3.5), which is the definition of Macaulay duration, measured in years.

$$D = \frac{\dfrac{1C}{(1+r)} + \dfrac{2C}{(1+r)^2} + \cdots + \dfrac{nC}{(1+r)^n} + \dfrac{nM}{(1+r)^n}}{P} \qquad (3.5)$$

Equation (3.5) can be simplified using $\sum$, as shown in (3.6):

$$D = \frac{\displaystyle\sum_{n=1}^{N} \frac{nC_n}{(1+r)^n}}{P} \qquad (3.6)$$

where C_n represents the bond cash flow at time n.

Box 3.1 Example: calculating the Macaulay duration for the 8% 2009 annual coupon bond.

Issued		30 September 1999	
Maturity		30 September 2009	
Price		$102.497	
Yield		7.634%	

Period (n)	Cash flow	PV at current yield*	$n \times PV$
1	8	7.432 60	7.432 6
2	8	6.905 43	13.810 86
3	8	6.415 66	19.246 98
4	8	5.960 63	23.842 52
5	8	5.537 87	27.689 35
6	8	5.145 09	30.870 54
7	8	4.780 17	33.461 19
8	8	4.441 14	35.529 096
9	8	4.126 15	37.135 35
10	108	51.752 22	517.522 2
Total	102.496 96	746.540 686	

* Calculated as $C/(1+r)^n$.

$$\text{Macaulay duration} = \frac{746.540\,686}{102.497}$$

$$= 7.283\,539\,998 \text{ years}$$

If the expression for Macaulay duration – i.e., (3.5) – is substituted into equation (3.4), which calculates the approximate percentage change in price, (3.7) is obtained. This is the definition of *modified duration*:

$$\frac{dP}{dr}\frac{1}{P} = -\frac{1}{(1+r)}D = \frac{D}{(1+r)}$$

$$= -MD \qquad (3.7)$$

or

$$MD = \frac{D}{(1+r)} \qquad (3.8)$$

Modified duration can be used to demonstrate that small changes in yield produce inverse changes in bond price. This relationship is expressed formally in (3.7), repeated as (3.9):

$$\frac{dP}{dr}\frac{1}{P} = -MD \qquad (3.9)$$

It is possible to shorten the procedure of computing Macaulay duration longhand, by rearranging the bond–price formula (3.1) as shown in (3.10), which, as explained in Chapter 1, calculates price as the sum of the present values of its coupons and its redemption payment. The same assumptions apply as for (3.1):

$$P = C\left[\frac{1 - \frac{1}{(1+r)^n}}{r}\right] + \frac{M}{(1+r)^n} \qquad (3.10)$$

Taking the first derivative of (3.10) and dividing the result by the current bond price, P, produces an alternative formulation for modified duration, shown as (3.11):

$$MD = \frac{\frac{C}{r^2}\left[1 - \frac{1}{(1+r)^n}\right] + \frac{n\left(M - \frac{C}{r}\right)}{(1+r)^{n+1}}}{P} \qquad (3.11)$$

Multiplying (3.11) by $(1+r)$ gives the equation for Macaulay duration. The example in Box 3.2 shows how these shorthand formulas can be used to calculate modified and Macaulay durations.

Box 3.2 Example: calculating the modified and Macaulay durations as of 1999 of a hypothetical bond having an annual coupon of 8% and a maturity date of 2009.

Coupon	8%, paid annually
Yield	7.634%
n	10
Price	$102.497

Plugging these values into the modified-duration equation (3.11) gives:

$$MD = \frac{\dfrac{8}{(0.076\,34^2)}\left[1 - \dfrac{1}{(1.076\,34)^{10}}\right] + \dfrac{10\left(100 - \dfrac{8}{0.076\,34}\right)}{(1.076\,34)^{11}}}{102.497}$$

$MD = 6.766\,95$ years

To obtain the bond's Macaulay duration, this modified duration is multiplied by $(1 + r)$, or 1.076 34, for a value of 7.283 54 years.

Up to this point the discussion has involved plain-vanilla bonds. But, duration applies to all type, even those that have no conventional maturity date – the so-called perpetual, or irredeemable, bonds (also known as annuity bonds) – which pay out interest for an indefinite period. Since these make no redemption payment, the second term on the right-hand side of the duration equation disappears, and since coupon payments can stretch on indefinitely, n approaches infinity. The result is equation (3.12) for Macaulay duration:

$$D = \frac{1}{rc} \qquad (3.12)$$

where $rc = (C/P_d) = $ *Running yield* (or *current yield*) of the bond.

Equation (3.12) represents the limiting value to duration. For bonds trading at or above par, duration increases with maturity, approaching the value given by (3.12), which acts as a ceiling. For bonds trading at a discount to par, duration increases to a maximum of around 20 years and then declines towards the floor given by (3.12). In general, duration increases with maturity, with an upper bound given by (3.12).

Properties of Macaulay duration

Duration varies with maturity, coupon and yield. Broadly, it increases with maturity. A bond's duration is generally shorter than its maturity. This is because the cash flows received in the early years of the bond's life have the greatest present values and therefore are given the greatest weight. That shortens the average time in which cash flows are received. A zero-coupon bond's cash flows are all received at redemption, so there is no present-value weighting. Therefore, a zero-coupon bond's duration is equal to its term to maturity.

Duration increases as coupon and yield decrease. The lower the coupon, the greater the relative weight of the cash flows received on the maturity date, and this causes duration to rise. Among the non-plain-vanilla types of bonds are some whose coupon rate varies according to an index, usually the consumer price index. Index-linked bonds generally have much lower coupons than vanilla bonds with similar maturities. This is true because they are inflation-protected, causing the real yield required to be lower than the nominal yield, but their durations tend to be higher.

Yield's relationship to duration is a function of its role in discounting future cash flows. As yield increases, the present values of all future cash flows fall, but those of the more distant cash flows fall relatively more. This has the effect of increasing the relative weight of the earlier cash flows and hence of reducing duration.

Modified duration

Although newcomers to the market commonly consider duration, much as Macaulay did, a proxy for a bond's time to maturity, this interpretation misses the main point of duration, which is to measure price volatility, or interest-rate risk. Using the Macaulay duration property can derive a measure of a bond's interest-rate price sensitivity – i.e., how sensitive a bond's price is to changes in its yield. This measure is obtained by applying a mathematical property known as a Taylor expansion to the basic equation.

The relationship between price volatility and duration can be made clearer if the bond price equation, viewed as a function of r, is expanded as a Taylor series (see Butler, pp. 112–114 for an accessible explanation of the Taylor expansion). Using the first term of this series, the relationship can be expressed as (3.13):

$$\Delta P = -\left[\frac{1}{(1+r)}\right] \times \text{Macaulay duration} \times \text{Change in yield} \quad (3.13)$$

where r = Yield to maturity of an annual coupon-paying bond.

As stated above, Macaulay duration equals modified duration multiplied by $(1+r)$. The first two components of the right-hand side of (3.13) taken together are therefore equivalent to modified duration, and equation (3.13) expresses the approximate percentage change in price as modified duration multiplied by the change in yield.

Modified duration is a measure of the approximate change in bond price for a 1% change in yield. The relationship between modified duration and bond prices can therefore be expressed as (3.14). A negative is used in this equation because the price movement is inverse to the interest-rate movement, so a rise in yields produces a fall in price, and *vice versa*:

$$\Delta P = -MD \times (\Delta r) \times P \qquad (3.14)$$

The example in Box 3.3 illustrates how the relationships expressed in these equations work.

Box 3.3   Example: applying the duration/price relationships to a hypothetical bond.

Coupon	8%, paid annually
Price	Par
Duration	2.74 years

If yields rise from 8% to 8.50%, the fall in the price of the bond can be computed as follows:

$$\Delta P = -D \times \frac{\Delta(r)}{1+r} \times P$$

$$= -(2.74) \times \left(\frac{0.005}{1.080}\right) \times 100$$

$$= -\$1.2685$$

That is, the price of the bond will fall to $98.7315.

The modified duration of a bond with a duration of 2.74 years and a yield of 8% is:

$$MD = \frac{2.74}{1.08} = 2.537 \text{ years}$$

If a bond has a duration of 4.31 years and a modified duration of 3.99, a 1% move in the yield to maturity produces a move (in the opposite direction) in the price of approximately 3.99%.

Changes in yield are often expressed in terms of *basis points*, which equal hundredths of a percent. For a bond with a modified duration of 3.99, priced at par, an increase in yield of 1 basis point leads to a fall in the bond's price of:

$$\Delta P = \left(\frac{-3.24}{100}\right) \times (+0.01) \times 100.00$$

$$\Delta P = \$0.0399, \text{ or } 3.99 \text{ cents}$$

In this example, 3.99 cents is the *basis point value (BPV)* of the bond – the change in its price given a 1 basis point change in yield. The general formula for deriving the basis point value of a bond is shown in (3.15):

$$BPV = \frac{MD}{100} \times \frac{P}{100} \tag{3.15}$$

Basis point values are used in hedging bond positions. Hedging is done by taking an opposite position – that is, one that will rise in value under the same conditions that will cause the hedged position to fall, and *vice versa*. Say you hold a 10-year bond. You might wish to sell short a similar 10-year bond as a hedge against your long position. Similarly, if you hold a short position in a bond, you might hedge it by buying an equivalent amount of a hedging instrument. A variety of hedging instruments are available, for use both on- and off-balance sheet.

For a hedge to be effective, the price change in the primary instrument should be equal to the price change in the hedging instrument. To calculate how much of a hedging instrument is required to get this type of protection, each bond's BPV is used. This is important because different bonds have different BPVs. To hedge a long position in, say, $1 million nominal of a 30-year bond, therefore, you can't simply sell $1 million of another 30-year bond. There may not be another 30-year bond with the same BPV available. You might have to hedge with a 10-year bond. To calculate how much nominal of the hedging bond is required, you'd use the *hedge ratio* (3.16):

$$\frac{BPV_p}{BPV_h} \times \frac{\text{Change in yield for primary bond position}}{\text{Change in yield for hedge instrument}} \quad (3.16)$$

where BPV_p = Basis point value of the primary bond (the position to be hedged);

BPV_h = Basis point value of the hedging instrument.

The second term in (3.18) is known as the *yield beta*.

Box 3.4   Example: calculating hedge size using basis point value.

Say a trader holds a long position of $1 million of the 8% bond maturing in 2019. The bond's modified duration is 11.146 92, and its price is $129.875 96. Its BPV is therefore 0.144 77. The trader decides to protect the position against a rise in interest rates by hedging it using the zero-coupon bond maturing in 2009, which has a BPV of 0.055 49. Assuming that the yield beta is 1, what nominal value of the zero-coupon bond must the trader sell?

The hedge ratio is:

$$\frac{0.144\,77}{0.055\,49} \times 1 = 2.608\,94$$

To hedge $1 million of the 20-year bond, therefore, the trader must sell short $2,608,940 of the zero-coupon bond. Using the two bonds' BPVs, the loss in the long position produced by a 1 basis point rise in yield is approximately equal to the gain in the hedge position.

Table 3.1 shows how the price of the 8% 2009 bond changes for a selection of yields. For a 1 basis point change in yield, the change in price, indicated as 'price duration for 1 basis point', though not completely accurate because it is a straight line or linear approximation of a non-linear relationship, as illustrated with Figure 3.1 of the price/yield relationship, is a reasonable estimate of the actual change in price. For a large move – say, 200 basis points – the approximation would be significantly off base, and analysts would accordingly not use it.

Note that the price duration figure, calculated from the modified duration measurement, underestimates the change in price resulting

Table 3.1 The modified duration approximation of bond price change at different yields.

Bond	Maturity (years)	Modified duration	Price duration of basis	Yield									
				6.00%	6.50%	7.00%	7.50%	7.99%	8.00%	8.01%	8.50%	9.00%	10.00%
8% 2009	10	6.76695	0.069 36	114.720 17	110.783 25	107.023 58	103.432 04	100.0671	100.000 00	99.932 93	96.719 33	93.582 34	87.710 87

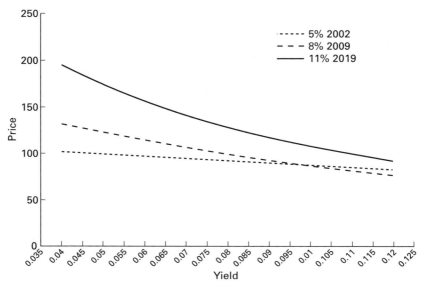

Figure 3.1 Price/yield relationship of three hypothetical bonds.

Table 3.2 Approximation of the bond price
change using modified duration.

Yield change	Price change	Estimate using price duration
Down 1 bp	0.067 13	0.069 36
Up 1 bp	0.067 07	0.069 36
Down 200 bp	14.720 17	13.872
Up 200 bp	12.289 13	13.872

from a fall in yields, but overestimates the change from a rise in
yields. This reflects the convexity of the bond's price–yield relationship; for example, the different convexity profiles of three different
bonds is shown at Figure 3.1. This concept is explained in the next
section.

Convexity

Duration is a first-order measure of interest-rate risk, using first-
order derivatives. If the relationship between price and yield is

plotted on a graph, it forms a curve. Duration indicates the slope of the tangent at any point on this curve. A tangent, however, is a line and, as such, is only an approximation of the actual curve – an approximation that becomes less accurate the farther the bond yield moves from the original point. The magnitude of the error, moreover, depends on the curvature, or convexity, of the curve. This is a serious drawback, and one that applies to modified as well as to Macaulay duration.

Convexity represents an attempt to remedy the drawbacks of duration. A second-order measure of interest-rate risk uses second-order derivatives. It measures the curvature of the price–yield graph and the degree to which this diverges from the straight-line estimation. Convexity can thus be regarded as an indication of the error made when using Macaulay and modified duration. A bond's convexity is positively correlated to the *dispersion* of its cash flows: all else being equal, a bond whose cash flows are more spread out in time – that is, more dispersed – than another's, will have a higher convexity. Convexity is also positively correlated with duration.

The second-order differential of the bond price equation with respect to the redemption yield r is:

$$\frac{\Delta P}{P} = \frac{1}{P}\frac{\Delta P}{\Delta r}(\Delta r) + \frac{1}{2P}\frac{\Delta^2 P}{\Delta r^2}(\Delta r)^2$$

$$= -MD(\Delta r) + \frac{CV}{2}(\Delta r)^2 \qquad (3.17)$$

where CV = Convexity.

Equation (3.17) shows that convexity is the rate at which price sensitivity to yield changes as yield changes. That is, it describes how much a bond's modified duration changes in response to changes in yield. Formula (3.18) expresses this relationship formally. The convexity term can be seen as an 'adjustment' for the error made by duration in approximating the price–yield curve:

$$CV = 10^8\left(\frac{\Delta P'}{P} + \frac{\Delta P''}{P}\right) \qquad (3.18)$$

where $\Delta P'$ = Change in bond price if yield increases by 1 basis point;
          $\Delta P''$ = Change in bond price if yield decreases by 1 basis point.

The unit in which convexity, as defined by (3.18), is measured is the number of interest periods. For annual coupon bonds, this is equal to the number of years; for bonds with different coupon-payment schedules, formula (3.19) can be used to convert the convexity measure from interest periods to years:

$$CV_{years} = \frac{CV}{C^2} \qquad (3.19)$$

The convexity formula for zero-coupon bonds is (3.20):

$$CV = \frac{n(n+1)}{(1+r)^2} \qquad (3.20)$$

Convexity is a second-order approximation of the change in price resulting from a change in yield. This relationship is expressed formally in (3.21):

$$\Delta P = \tfrac{1}{2} \times CV \times (\Delta r)^2 \qquad (3.21)$$

The reason the convexity term is multiplied by one-half is because the second term in the Taylor expansion used to derive the convexity equation contains the coefficient 0.5. The formula is the same for a semiannual-coupon bond.

Note that the value for convexity given by the expressions above will always be positive – that is, the approximate price change due to convexity is positive for both yield increases and decreases, except for certain bonds such as callable bonds.

Box 3.5   Example: calculating the convexity of a bond.

Coupon	5%, paid annually
Maturity	2009, 10 years from present
Price	$96.231 19
Yield	5.50%

If the yield rises to 7.50%, a change of 200 basis points, the percentage price change due to the convexity effect – that is, the convexity adjustment that would be made to the price change calculated using modified duration and equation (3.21) – is:

$$(0.5) \times 96.231\,19 \times (0.02)^2 \times 100 = 1.924\,62\%$$

If the yield fell by 200 basis points, the convexity effect would be the same.

As noted earlier, the price change estimated using modified duration can be quite inaccurate. The convexity measure is the approximation of the size of the inaccuracy. Summing the two values – the price-change estimate using modified duration plus the convexity error adjustment – gives a more accurate picture of the actual magnitude of the price change. The estimated and adjusted values differ significantly, however, only when the change in yield is very large. In Box 3.5, the modified duration of the hypothetical 5% 2009 bond is 7.644 98. For the specified rise in yield of 200 basis points, the approximate price change given by modified duration is:

$$\text{Modified duration} = -7.644\,98 \times 2$$
$$= -15.289\,96$$

Note that the modified duration is given as a negative value, because a rise in yields results in a fall in price. Adjusting the estimate by the convexity of 1.924 62 derived above results in a net percentage price change of 13.365 34. A Hewlett Packard (*HP*) calculator gives the price of the bond at the new yield of 7.50% as \$82.839 80, representing an actual change of 13.92%. So, using the convexity adjustment produces a noticeably more accurate estimate.

Now assume that yields fall just 1.50%, or 150 basis points. The new convexity value is:

$$(0.5) \times 96.231\,19 \times (0.015)^2 \times 100 = 1.0826\%$$

and the price-change estimate based on modified duration is:

$$\text{Modified duration} = 7.644\,98 \times 1.5$$
$$= 11.467\,47$$

Adding the two values together results in an adjusted price-change estimate of 12.550 07%. The actual price change according to the HP calculator is 10.988 43%. In this case, the unadjusted modified duration estimate is closer. This illustrates that the convexity measure is effective for larger yield changes only. Box 3.6 provides an illustration of the greater accuracy produced by combining the modified duration and convexity measures for larger yield shifts.

> *Box 3.6*   Example: convexity adjustment.
>
> Assume that the yield of the hypothetical 5% 2009 bond rises to 8.50%, a change of 300 basis points. The percentage convexity adjustment is:
>
> $$0.5 \times 96.23119 \times (0.03)^2 \times 100 = 4.3304\%$$
>
> The modified duration of the bond at the initial yield, as seen above, is 7.644 98. So, the price-change estimate using modified duration is:
> $$7.644\,98 \times 3.0 = -22.934\,94$$
>
> Adjusting this by the convexity value derived above results in a price change of 18.604 54%. Using an HP calculator, the price of the bond is 77.035 28 for an actual percentage price change of 19.9477%. In this case, the adjusted estimate is closer than that obtained using only the modified duration measure. The continuing error reflects the fact that convexity is a dynamic measure and changes with yield changes; the effect of a large yield movement compounds the inaccuracy of the adjustments.

The convexity measure increases with the square of maturity; it decreases as both coupon and yield rise. It is a function of modified duration; so, index-linked bonds, which have greater duration than conventional bonds of similar maturities, also have greater convexity. For a conventional vanilla bond, convexity is almost always positive. Negative convexity occurs most frequently with callable bonds.

In principle, a bond with greater convexity should fall in price less when yields rise than a less convex one, and rise in price more when yields fall. This is true because convexity is usually positive; so, it lessens the price decline produced by rises in yield and increases the price rise produced by falls in yield. Thus, all else being equal, the higher the convexity of a bond the more desirable it should be to investors. The actual premium attached to higher convexity is a function of current yield levels and market volatility. Remember that modified duration and convexity are both functions of yield level and their effects are magnified at lower yield levels. In addition, the cash effect of convexity is more noticeable for large moves in yield. So, the value investors attach to convexity will vary according to their expectations about the future size of interest-rate changes.

Hence, convexity is more highly valued when market volatility is high.

BIBLIOGRAPHY

Butler, C. (1999). *Mastering Value-at-Risk*. FT Prentice Hall, London.

Macaulay, F. (1999). *Duration and Properties of Bonds*. RISK Classics Library.

Chapter

4

. . . .

REVIEW OF FLOATING-RATE NOTE BOND INSTRUMENTS

In this chapter we describe in generic format some of the more exotic or structured notes that have been introduced into the fixed income market. The motivations behind the development and use of these products are varied, but include the desire for increased yield without additional credit risk, as well as the need to alter, transform or transfer risk exposure and risk–return profiles. Certain structured notes were also developed as hedging instruments. The instruments themselves have been issued by banks, corporate institutions and sovereign authorities. By using certain types of notes, investors can gain access to different markets, sometimes synthetically, that were previously not available to them. For instance, by purchasing a structured note an investor can take on board a position that reflects her views on a particular exchange rate and anticipated changes in yield curve, but in a different market. The investment instrument can be tailored to suit the investor's particular risk profile.

We describe a number of structured notes that are currently available to investors today, although often investors will seek particular features that suit their needs, and so there are invariably detail variations in each note. We stress that this is only the tip of the iceberg, and many different types of notes are available; indeed, if any particular investor or issuer requirement has not been met, it is a relatively straightforward process whereby an investment bank can structure a note that meets one or both specific requirements.

FLOATING-RATE NOTES

Floating-rate notes (*FRNs*) are bonds that have variable rates of interest; the coupon rate is linked to a specified index and changes periodically as the index changes. An FRN is usually issued with a coupon that pays a fixed spread over a reference index; for example, the coupon may be 50 basis points over the 6-month interbank rate. An FRN whose spread over the reference rate is not fixed is known as a *variable rate note*. Since the value for the reference benchmark index is not known, it is not possible to calculate the redemption yield for an FRN. Additional features have been added to FRNs, including *floors* (the coupon cannot fall below a specified minimum rate), *caps* (the coupon cannot rise above a maximum rate) and *callability*. There also exist perpetual FRNs. As in other markets, borrowers frequently issue paper with specific or even esoteric terms in order to meet particular requirements or meet customer demand; for example, Citibank recently issued US dollar-denominated FRNs with interest payments indexed to the euribor rate, and another FRN with its day-count basis linked to a specified London Interbank Offer Rate (*Libor*) range.

Generally, the reference interest rate for FRNs is the Libor rate; the *offered* rate, that is the rate at which a bank will lend funds to another bank is Libor. An FRN will pay interest at Libor plus a quoted margin (or spread). The interest rate is fixed for a 3-month or 6-month period and is reset in line with the Libor *fixing* at the end of the interest period. Hence, at the coupon reset date for a sterling FRN paying 6-month Libor + 0.50%, if the Libor fix is 7.6875%, then the FRN will pay a coupon of 8.1875%. Interest, therefore, will accrue at a daily rate of £0.022 431 5.

On the coupon reset date an FRN will be priced precisely at par. Between reset dates it will trade very close to par because of the way in which the coupon is reset. If market rates rise between reset dates an FRN will trade slightly below par; similarly, if rates fall the paper will trade slightly above. This makes FRNs very similar in behaviour to money market instruments traded on a yield basis, although of course FRNs have much longer maturities. Investors can opt to view FRNs as essentially money market instruments or as alternatives to conventional bonds. For this reason one can use two approaches in analysing FRNs. The first approach is known as the *margin method*. This calculates the difference between the return on an FRN and that on an equivalent money market security. There are two variations on this, simple margin and discounted margin.

The simple margin method is sometimes preferred because it does not require the forecasting of future interest rates and coupon values. *Simple margin* is defined as the average return on an FRN throughout its life compared with the reference interest rate. It has two components: a *quoted margin* either above or below the reference rate, and a capital gain or loss element which is calculated under the assumption that the difference between the current price of the FRN and the maturity value is spread evenly over the remaining life of the bond. Simple margin is given by (4.1):

$$\text{Simple margin} = \frac{(M - P_d)}{(100 \times T)} + M_q \qquad (4.1)$$

where
$P_d = P + AI$, the dirty price;
$M =$ Par value;
$T =$ Number of years from settlement date to maturity;
$M_q =$ Quoted margin.

A quoted margin that is positive reflects yield for an FRN which is offering a higher yield than the comparable money market security.

At certain times the simple margin formula is adjusted to take into account any change in the reference rate since the last coupon reset date. This is done by defining an adjusted price, which is either:

or

$$\left.\begin{array}{l} AP_d = P_d + (re + M) \times \dfrac{N_{sc}}{365} \times 100 - \dfrac{C}{2} \times 100 \\[3ex] AP_d = P_d + (re + M) \times \dfrac{N_{sc}}{365} \times P_d - \dfrac{C}{2} \times 100 \end{array}\right\} \qquad (4.2)$$

where AP_d = Adjusted dirty price;
         re = Current value of the reference interest rate (such as Libor);
         $C/2$ = Next coupon payment (i.e., C is the reference interest rate on the last coupon reset date plus M_q);
         N_{sc} = Number of days between settlement and the next coupon date.

The upper equation in (4.2) above ignores the current yield effect: all payments are assumed to be received on the basis of par, and this understates the value of the coupon for FRNs trading below par and overstates the value when they are trading above par. The lower equation in (4.2) takes account of the current yield effect.

The adjusted price AP_d replaces the current price P_d in (4.1) to give an *adjusted simple margin*. The simple margin method has the disadvantage of amortising the discount or premium on the FRN in a straight line over the remaining life of the bond rather than at a constantly compounded rate. The discounted margin method uses the latter approach. The distinction between simple margin and discounted margin is exactly the same as that between simple yield to maturity and yield to maturity. The discounted margin method does have a disadvantage in that it requires a forecast of the reference interest rate over the remaining life of the bond.

The discounted margin is the solution to equation (4.3) shown below, given for an FRN that pays semiannual coupons.

$$P_d = \left\{ \frac{1}{[1 + \frac{1}{2}(re + DM)]^{days/year}} \right\}$$

$$\times \left\{ \frac{C}{2} + \sum_{t=1}^{N-1} \frac{(re^* + M) \times 100/2}{[1 + \frac{1}{2}(re^* + DM)]^t} + \frac{M}{[1 + \frac{1}{2}(re^* + DM)]^{N-1}} \right\} \quad (4.3)$$

where DM = Discounted margin;
           re = Current value of the reference interest rate;
           re^* = Assumed (or forecast) value of the reference rate over the remaining life of the bond;
           M = Quoted margin;
           N = Number of coupon payments before redemption.

Equation (4.3) may be stated in terms of discount factors instead of the reference rate. The *yield-to-maturity spread* method of evaluating FRNs is designed to allow direct comparison between FRNs and fixed-rate bonds. The yield to maturity on the FRN (rmf) is calculated using (4.3) with both ($re + DM$) and ($re^* + DM$) replaced with rmf. The yield to maturity on a reference bond (rmb) is calculated using (4.4). The yield-to-maturity spread is defined as:

Yield to maturity spread = $rmf - rmb$

If this is positive the FRN offers a higher yield than the reference bond.

In addition to plain vanilla FRNs, some of the other types of floating-rate bonds that have traded in the market are:

- *Collared FRNs* – these offer caps and floors on an instrument, thus establishing a maximum and minimum coupon on the deal. Effectively, these securities contain two embedded options, the issuer buying a cap and selling a floor to the investor.
- *Step-up recovery FRNs* – where coupons are fixed against comparable longer maturity bonds, thus providing investors with the opportunity to maintain exposure to short-term assets while capitalising on a positive sloping yield curve.
- *Corridor FRNs* – these were introduced to capitalise on expectations of comparative interest-rate inactivity. A high-risk/high-reward instrument, it offers investors a very substantial uplift over a chosen reference rate. But rates have to remain within a relatively narrow corridor if the interest payment is not to be forfeited entirely.

- *Flipper bonds* – these have been issued in the USD domestic market, typically by government agencies. They exist in a number of forms. For example, a 2-year flipper bond might have a floating-rate coupon for the first year, and then switch to a fixed-rate coupon for the second year. Investors may wish to buy such a security if they are expecting rates to rise in the near term but then level off after that. This scenario existed in the USD market in the second half of 2005 when the Federal Reserve was more than 1 year into a programme of raising interest rates in 'measured' 25 basis point steps; some analysts suggested that this would tail off by the summer of 2006, making flipper securities look like attractive instruments. An Agency 2-year flipper issued in November 2005 with a call option after 1 year came with a floating coupon of 3-month Libor + 2, with a conversion to 5.50% if not called after 1 year. At the time of issue, the implied forward rate for Agency securities was about 75 basis points below this fixed rate.[1]

INVERSE FLOATING-RATE NOTE

Description

The inverse floating-rate note or *inverse floater* is an instrument that offers enhanced returns to investors that believe the market outlook for bonds generally is positive. An inverse floater pays a coupon that increases as general market rates decline. In other words, it is an instrument for those who have an opposite view to the market consensus. They are suitable in an economic environment of low inflation and a positive yield curve; both these factors would, in a conventional analysis, suggest rising interest rates in the medium term. It is also possible to link the inverse floater's coupon to rates in an environment of a negative yield curve. Such a note would suit an investor who agreed with the market consensus.

The coupon on an inverse floater may be determined in a number of ways. The most common approach involves a formula that quotes a fixed interest rate, minus a variable element that is linked to an index. Coupons are usually set at a floor level, which in the absence of a floor will be 0%.

---

[1] *Source*: JPMorgan fixed income research, 9 November 2005.

Table 4.1 Terms of an inverse floater bond.

Nominal value	£100,000,000
Issue date	5 January 200
Maturity date	5 January 2003
Note coupon	15.75% – (2 × LIBOR)
Day-count basis	Act/365
Index	6-month LIBOR
Current LIBOR rate	5.15%
Rate fixing	Semiannual
Initial coupon	5.45%
Minimum coupon	0%

GBP Libor	Coupon payable
1.00%	14.75%
1.50%	12.75%
2.00%	11.75%
2.50%	10.75%
3.00%	9.75%
3.50%	8.75%
4.00%	7.75%
4.50%	6.75%
5.00%	5.75%
5.50%	4.75%
6.00%	3.75%
6.50%	2.75%
7.00%	1.75%

Issuers of inverse floaters are usually corporates, although special-ised investment vehicles also issue such notes to meet specific client demand.[2]

Table 4.1 illustrates the coupon arrangement on a typical inverse floater, particularly how changes in the Libor rate impact the coupon that is payable on the note.

---

[2] By specialised investment vehicles, we mean funds set up to invest in particular areas or sectors. For example, wholly-owned subsidiaries of Citigroup such as Centauri or Dorada Corporation issue notes, backed by an AAA-rating, specifically to suit investor demand. As such, notes issued by such bodies assume a wide variety of forms, they are often linked with a currency or interest-rate swap element, and in a wide variety of currencies. As they have an ongoing requirement for funds, notes may be issued at any time, especially when a particular investor requirement is identified.

Table 4.2 Duration of 3-year inverse floater note.

Duration of 3-year note with 5.30% coupon	2.218 years
Duration of 3-year inverse floater (×3)	6.654 years

The inverse floater provides investors with a slightly above-market initial coupon in a yield curve environment that is positive. The above-market initial coupon results from the swap bank paying this in return for a Libor income, in a swap structure that matches the maturity of the note. The Libor level will be lower than the longer-term swap rate because we assume a positive sloping yield curve environment. Investors can benefit from an arrangement that provides them with a coupon sensitivity that is twice that of changes in the rate of Libor.

Another interesting feature of inverse floater notes is their high duration, which results from the leveraged arrangement of the coupon. In our hypothetical example, the note has a calendar maturity of 3 years, its modified duration will be much higher. This is shown in Table 4.2. Inverse floaters have the highest duration values of any instrument traded in the fixed income market. This makes them highly interest-rate sensitive products.

A number of variations of the inverse floater described have been introduced. It is straightforward to link the notes of any quoted reference index, which would be of interest to investors who had a particular view of short- or long-term interest rate indices – for example, the central bank repo rate, 10-year swap rates or a government benchmark. The leverage of the notes can also be altered to reflect the investor's risk preference, and the fixed element may be altered for the same reason. Equally, the fixed element can be set to move upwards or downwards as required. As another possibility, investors who have a particular view on a specific foreign interest-rate market, but who (for one reason or another) are not able to invest in that market's securities, can gain an exposure that reflects their views through the purchase of an inverse FRN that is linked to the foreign index but pays coupon in the domestic currency.

Hedging the note

Borrowers often issue notes in a different currency to the currency they require, and will typically swap the proceeds into the required currency by means of a currency swap. An interest-rate swap arrangement is used to hedge the interest-rate exposure on the inverse floater. The issuer will transact the swap structure with a swap bank, usually a high-rated institution. The swap bank will hedge its own exposure as part of its normal operations in the swap markets. The structure that would apply to the hypothetical note above is shown in Figure 4.1.

The swap transacted with the issuer involves:

- paying fixed at the note coupon level;
- receiving Libor.

The other side of this transaction for the swap bank is another swap where it pays floating and receives fixed. This is made up of the following:

- the swap bank pays Libor on the swap;
- it receives 5.30%, which is the 3-year swap rate.

However, the swap bank must also hedge the coupon rate on the note, as this is now his exposure (the issuer being fully hedged by the swap bank and paying Libor, its desired cost of funds). The coupon rate is $15.75\% - (2 \times \text{Libor})$, which in effect means that the note holder is receiving 15.75% and paying $2 \times \text{Libor}$. Therefore, the swap bank in order to hedge this cash flow will pay $2 \times \text{Libor}$ and receive two fixed rates of 5.30%. The three rates for the swap total

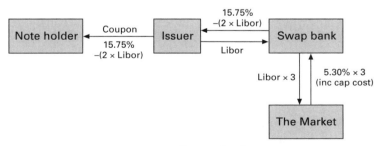

Figure 4.1   Inverse floater hedge structure.

15.90%. This is higher than the fixed component of the coupon in the note by 15 basis points. This difference is the cost of fixing a cap, as detailed below.

The inverse floater has a minimum coupon on 0%, and to hedge this element the swap bank will need to purchase an interest-rate cap on Libor with a strike rate of 7.875%. The strike rate is the note coupon on 15.75% divided by 2. The cap element of the hedge protects the dealer against a rise in Libor over the set rate. The cap has a cost of 15 basis points, which explains the difference over the coupon rate in the swap structure.

INDEXED AMORTISING NOTE

Description

Another type of hybrid note is the Indexed Amortising Note (*IAN*). They were introduced in the US domestic market in the early 1990s at the demand of investors in asset-backed notes known as collateralised mortgage obligations (*CMOs*). IANs are fixed-coupon unsecured notes issued with a nominal value that is not fixed. That is, the nominal amount may reduce in value ahead of the legal maturity according to the levels recorded by a specified reference index such as 6-month Libor. If the reference remains static or its level decreases, the IAN value will amortise in nominal value. The legal maturity of IANs is short- to medium-term, with the 5-year maturity being common. The notes have been issued by banks and corporates, although a large volume has been issued by US government agencies. The yield payable on IANs is typically at a premium above that of similar credit quality conventional debt. The amortisation schedule on an IAN is linked to the movement of the specified reference index, which is easily understood. This is considered an advantage to certain mortgage-backed notes, which amortise in accordance with less clearly defined patterns, such as a *prepayment schedule*.

An issuer of IANS will arrange a hedge that makes the funding obtained more attractive – for example, a straight Libor-type exposure. This is most commonly arranged through a swap arrangement that mirrors the note structure. A diagrammatic representation is shown in Figure 4.2. In fact, it is more common for the swap arrangement to involve a series of options on swaps. The coupon available on an IAN might be attractive to investors when the

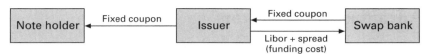

Figure 4.2   IAN hedge arrangement.

volatility on *swaptions* is high and there is a steep positively sloping yield curve; under such an environment the option element of an IAN would confer greatest value.

The terms of an hypothetical IAN issue are given at Table 4.3.

Under the terms of issue of the note summarised in Table 4.3, the coupon payable is the current 2-year government benchmark plus a fixed spread of 1%. The note has a legal maturity of 6 years; however, it will mature in 3 years if the 6-month Libor rate is at a level of 6.00% or below 2 years from the date of issue. If the rate is above 6.00%, the maturity of the note will be extended. The 'lock-out' of 3 years means that the note has a minimum life of 3 years, irrespective of what happens to Libor rates. Amortisation takes place if on sub-sequent rate-fixing dates after the lock-out period the Libor rate rises. The maximum maturity of the note is 6 years. If at any time there is less than 20% of the nominal value in issue, the note is cancelled in full.

Table 4.3   Hypothetical IAN issue

Issuer	Mortgage agency
Nominal value	£250,000,000
Legal maturity	6 years
Coupon	2-year Treasury plus 100 basis points
Interest basis	Monthly
'Lock-out period'	3 years
Reference index	6-month Libor
6 m Libor fixing on issue	5.15%
Minimum level of note	20%

Average life sensitivity

Libor rate (%)	Amortisation rate (%)	Average life (years)
5.15	100	3
6.00	100	3
7.00	21	4.1
8.00	7	5.6
9.00	0.00	6

Advantages to investors

The IAN structure offers advantages to investors under certain conditions. If the credit quality is acceptable, the notes offer a high yield over a relatively low term to maturity. The amortisation structure is easier to understand than that on mortgage-backed securities, which contain prepayment schedules that are based on assumptions that may not apply. This means that investors will know with certainty how the amortisation of the note will proceed, given the level of the reference index at any given time. The lock-out period of a note is usually set at a duration that offers investor comfort, such as 3 years; during this time no amortisation can take place.

As with the other instruments described here, IANs can be tailored to meet individual investor requirements. The legal maturity and lock-out period are features that are most frequently subject to variation, with the yield premium decreasing as the lock-out period becomes closer to the formal maturity. The reference index can be a government benchmark or interbank rate, such as the swap rate. However, the most common reference is the Libor rate.

SYNTHETIC CONVERTIBLE NOTE

Description

Synthetic convertible notes are fixed-coupon securities whose total return is linked to an external source, such as the level of an equity index or the price of a specific security. The fixed-coupon element is typically at a low level, and the investor has greater exposure to the performance of the external index. A common arrangement has the note redeeming at par, but redeemable at a greater amount if the performance of the reference index exceeds a stated minimum. However, the investor has the safety net of redemption at par. Another typical structure is a zero-coupon note, issued at par and redeemable at par, but redeemable at a higher level if a specified equity index performs above a pre-specified level.

Table 4.4 lists the terms of an hypothetical synthetic convertible note issue that is linked to the FTSE 100 equity index. This note will pay par on maturity, but if the level of the FTSE 100 has increased by more than 10% from the level on note issue, the note will be redeemed at par plus this amount. Note, however, that this is an investment suitable only for someone who is very bullish on the

Table 4.4   Terms of a synthetic convertible note issue.

Nominal value	£50,000,000
Term to maturity	2 years
Issue date	17 June 1999
Maturity date	17 June 2001
Issue price	£100
Coupon	0.50%
Interest basis	Semiannual
Redemption proceeds	Min [100, Formula level]
Formula level	$100 + [100 \times R(\mathrm{I}) - (1.1 \times R(\mathrm{II}))/R(\mathrm{II})]$
Index	FTSE 100
$R(\mathrm{I})$	Index level on maturity
$R(\mathrm{II})$	Index level on issue
Hedge terms	
Issuer pays	Libor
Swap bank pays	Redemption proceeds in accordance with formula

prospects for the FTSE 100. If this index does not raise by the minimum level, the investor will have received a coupon of 0.5%, which is roughly five percentage points below the level for 2-year sterling at this time.

Investor benefits

Similarly to a convertible bonds, a synthetic convertible note provides investors with a fixed coupon together with additional market upside potential if the level of the reference index performs above a certain level. Unlike the convertible, however, the payoff is in the form of cash.

The reference can be virtually any publicly quoted source, and notes have been issued whose payout is linked to the exchange rate of two currencies, the days on which Libor falls within a specified range, the performance of a selected basket of stocks (say, 'technology stocks') and so on.

INTEREST DIFFERENTIAL NOTES

Interest differential notes (*IDNs*) are hybrid securities which are aimed at investors who wish to put on a position that reflects their view on the interest-rate differential between rates of two different currencies. Notes in the US market are usually denominated in US dollars, whereas Euromarket notes have been issued in a wide range of global currencies.

There are a number of variations of IDNs. Notes may pay a variable coupon and a fixed redemption amount, or a fixed coupon and a redemption amount that is determined by the level or performance of an external reference index. IDNs have also been issued with payoff profiles that are linked to the differentials in interest rates of two specified currencies, or between one currency across different maturities.

Example of IDN

Here we discuss a 5-year note that is linked to the differential between US dollar Libor and euro-libor.

The return on this note is a function of the spread between the US dollar Libor rate and euro-libor. An increase in the spread results in a higher coupon payable on the note, while a narrowing of the spread results in a lower coupon payable. Such a structure will appeal to an investor who has a particular view on the USD and EUR yield curves. For instance, assume that the USD curve is inverted and the euro curve is positively sloping. A position in an IDN (structured as above) on these two currencies allows an investor to avoid outright yield curve plays in each currency, and instead put on a trade that reflects a view on the relative level of interest rates in each currency. An IDN in this environment would allow an investor to earn a high yield while taking a view that is different from the market consensus.

When analysing an IDN, an investor must regard the note to be the equivalent to a fixed-coupon bond together with a double indexation of an interest-rate differential. The effect of this double indexation on the differential is to create two long positions in a 5-year USD fixed-rate note and two short positions in a EUR fixed-rate note. The short position in the EUR note means that the EUR exchange-rate risk is removed and the investor has an exposure only to the EUR interest-rate risk, which is the desired position.

The issuer of the note hedges the note with a swap structure as with other hybrid securities. The arrangement involves both USD and

Table 4.5 IDN example.

Terms to maturity	5 years
Coupon	$[(2 \times \text{USD Libor}) - (2 \times \text{EUR Libor}) - 0.50\%]$
Current USD Libor	6.15%
Current EUR Libor	3.05%
Rate differential	2.65%
First coupon fix	5.70%
Current 5-year benchmark	4.75%
Yield spread over benchmark	0.95%

Change in Libor spread (basis points p.a.)	Libor spread at rate reset (%)	Spread over benchmark (%)
75	4.78	2.34
50	3.90	1.88
25	3.15	1.21
0	2.65	0.95
−25	1.97	0.56
−50	1.32	0.34
−75	0.89	0.12
−100	0.32	−0.28

EUR interest-rate swaps. The swap bank takes the opposite position in the swaps.

Table 4.5 also illustrates the return profiles possible under different interest-rate scenarios. One possibility shows that the IDN provides a 95 basis point yield premium over the 5-year government benchmark yield; however, this assumes rather unrealistically that the interest differential between the USD and EUR interest rates remains constant through to the final coupon setting date. More significantly though, we see that the yield premium available on the note increases as the spread differential between the two rates increases. In a spread tightening environment, the note offers a premium over the government yield as long as the tightening does not exceed 100 basis points each year.

Benefits to investors

IDN-type instruments allow investors to put on positions that reflect their view on foreign interest-rate direction and/or levels, but without having to expose themselves to currency (exchange-rate) risk at the same time. The notes may also be structured in a way that allows investors to take a view on any maturity point of the yield curve. For instance, the coupon may be set in accordance with the differential between the 10-year government benchmark yields of two specified countries. As another approach, investors can arrange combinations of different maturities in the same currency, which is a straight yield curve or relative value trade in a domestic or foreign currency.

The risk run by a note holder is that the interest-rate differential moves in the opposite direction to that sought, which reduces the coupon payable and may even result in a lower yield than that available on the benchmark bond.

CONVERTIBLE QUANTO NOTE

The index-linked Quanto Note (Figure 4.3) is aimed at investors who wish to gain exposure to a company's equity, but do not wish to invest in assets denominated in the currency of that equity. For example, investors who wish to gain exposure to a Japanese company share but do not wish to hold Yen-denominated assets.

The Note enables investors to gain from upside performance of the selected equity but with no associated foreign exchange (*FX*) risk. For added comfort, investors are protected against any downside performance of the underlying equity by means of the Note structure, which sets a bond floor of a minimum stated return. This is similar to the bond floor in a convertible bond (see Chapter 7). Purchasing the Note is equivalent to purchasing market volatility, in the expectation of higher volatility leading to higher equity prices, whilst retaining an element of downside market protection.

Investors are in effect holding a long position in an option and hence

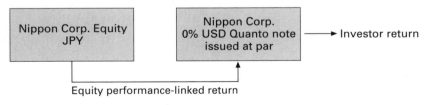

Figure 4.3   The concept behind the Note.

will be exposed to volatility. However, the bond floor protects the investor from downside risk, irrespective of volatility.

Example of Japanese Equity Note

This Note is a USD-denominated bond, issued at par, that pays investors a return, in USD, connected to the share-price performance of a Japanese corporate entity (denominated in JPY). If the underlying equity rises in price (above a specified level, the strike price), the proportionate increase in the share price is paid out on maturity to the Note investor, as a percentage of par. At any time during its life, the price of the Note will reflect (among other things) this increase in underlying share price.

The value of the Note is comprised of two components, the intrinsic value and the option value. On first issue, an equity strike price is set on the Note. This may be at the current underlying share price, or above it. As the underlying share price rises above the Strike price, the Note's intrinsic value will increase proportionally with that of the equity. The option value is an additional value (the premium) above the intrinsic value, and is composed of volatility, time value and the level of USD interest rates. These are standard option pricing parameters.

If the underlying equity falls in price, the investor is protected by the minimum value of the Note, known as the bond floor. This is the minimum price of the Note at any one time; hence, if the equity price falls below a level at which the bond floor kicks in, there is no further downside price risk for the investor.

We can illustrate this with an hypothetical example. Consider the following terms for a USD Quanto Note:

Underlying	Nippon Corp equity (JPY)
Strike	Y1,200
Spot	Y1,150
Note offer	100.00%
Parity	95.83%
Premium	4.35%
Life	3 years
US 3-year rates	3.68%
Bond floor	88.36%
Delta	0.50

The Note is issued at par with a strike of Y1,200.

Consider the following scenarios based on both upside and downside performance of the underlying equity.

If the shares rise to Y1700, a rise of 47.8%, the parity, or intrinsic value would be (1700/1200 * 100) or 141.66%. This is the minimum value of the Note. Hence, a 47.8% gain in the shares has resulted in a minimum 41.66% gain in the Note. Should the underlying equity price fall below the strike price, the note is protected by KBC credit and hence carries a bond floor, currently at 88.36%, accreting to par at maturity. This represents the downside protection for the investor. The option premium above this floor will still reflect the three option components, and because time value is always positive, the total value of the Note will be above this bond floor up to maturity. If the shares fell to Y800, the parity would be 66.66%; however, the minimum value of the Note would still be the bond floor of 88.36%. Therefore, in this instance a fall of 30.4% in the shares has resulted in a maximum 11.6% decline in the Note.

Investors are not exposed to any FX risk because they pay USD for the note, and receive return in USD. However, one of the option value parameters is the level of interest rates, hence investors are exposed to USD interest rates. A call option written on an equity will rise in value if (all other parameters held constant) there is a rise in interest rates, because the cost-of-carry associated with the equity also rises. This sensitivity is carried over in the value of the Note, because the secondary market price of the Note is related to the over-the-counter options market.

A partial measure of the change in the price of an option with respect to a change in the price of the underlying equity is given by the delta of the option, which is:

$$\delta = \frac{\text{Change in Note price}}{\text{Change in underlying price}}$$

For convertible bonds, delta is defined in terms of the sensitivity of the bond's price to changes in its parity. The parity is given from the value of the underlying equity price. The value of this delta can be gauged from Figure 4.4, which illustrates an hypothetical parity and bond floor. The delta is seen from the relationship of the parity and Note price.

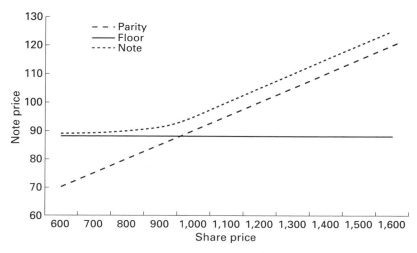

Figure 4.4   Delta value.

In our example the delta is given as 0.5. So, if the Note theoretical price moved from 100 to 100.5 while its parity changed from 95 to 96, the delta would be 0.5.

BIBLIOGRAPHY

Connolly, K. (1998). *Pricing Convertible Bonds*. John Wiley & Sons, Chichester, UK.

Chapter

5

. . . .

THE MONEY
MARKETS

Part of the global debt capital markets, the money markets are a separate market in their own right. Money market securities are defined as debt instruments with an original maturity of less than 1 year, although it is common to find that the maturity profile of banks' money market desks runs out to 2 years.

Money markets exist in every market economy, which is practically every country in the world. They are often the first element of a developing capital market. In every case they are comprised of securities with maturities of up to 12 months. Money market debt is an important part of the global capital markets, and facilitates the smooth running of the banking industry as well as providing working capital for industrial and commercial corporate institutions. The market provides users with a wide range of opportunities and funding possibilities, and the market is characterised by the diverse range of products that can be traded within it. Money market instruments allow issuers, including financial organisations and corporates, to raise funds for short-term periods at relatively low interest rates. These issuers include sovereign governments, who issue Treasury bills, corporates issuing commercial paper and banks issuing bills and certificates of deposit. At the same time, investors are attracted to the market because the instruments are highly liquid and carry relatively low credit risk. The Treasury bill market in any country is that country's lowest-risk instrument, and consequently carries the lowest yield of any debt instrument. Indeed, the first market that develops in any country is usually the Treasury bill market. Investors in the money market include banks, local authorities, corporations, money market investment funds and mutual funds, and individuals.

In addition to cash instruments, the money markets also consist of a wide range of exchange-traded and over-the-counter off-balance sheet derivative instruments. These instruments are used mainly to establish future borrowing and lending rates, and to hedge or change existing interest-rate exposure. This activity is carried out by both banks, central banks and corporates. The main derivatives are short-term interest-rate futures, forward-rate agreements and short-dated interest-rate swaps, such as overnight index swaps.

In this chapter we review the cash instruments traded in the money market. In further chapters we review banking asset and liability management, and the market in repurchase agreements. Finally, we consider the market in money market derivative instruments including interest-rate futures and forward-rate agreements.

INTRODUCTION

The cash instruments traded in money markets include the following:

- time deposits;
- Treasury bills;
- certificates of deposit;
- commercial paper;
- banker's acceptances;
- bills of exchange;
- repo and stock lending.

Treasury bills are used by sovereign governments to raise short-term funds, while certificates of deposit (CDs) are used by banks to raise finance. The other instruments are used by corporates and occasionally banks. Each instrument represents an obligation on the borrower to repay the amount borrowed on the maturity date together with interest if this applies. The instruments above fall into one of two main classes of money market securities: those quoted on a *yield* basis and those quoted on a *discount* basis. These two terms are discussed below. A *repurchase agreement* or 'repo' is also a money market instrument.

The calculation of interest in the money markets often differs from the calculation of accrued interest in the corresponding bond market. Generally, the day-count convention in the money market is the exact number of days that the instrument is held over the number of days in the year. In the UK sterling market the year base is 365 days, so the interest calculation for sterling money market instruments is given by (5.1):

$$i = \frac{n}{365} \tag{5.1}$$

However, the majority of currencies, including the US dollar and the euro, calculate interest on a 360-day base. The process by which an interest rate quoted on one basis is converted to one quoted on the other basis is shown in Appendix 5.1. Those markets that calculate interest based on a 365-day year are also listed at Appendix 5.1.

Dealers will want to know the interest-day base for a currency before dealing in it as foreign exchange (FX) or money markets. Bloomberg

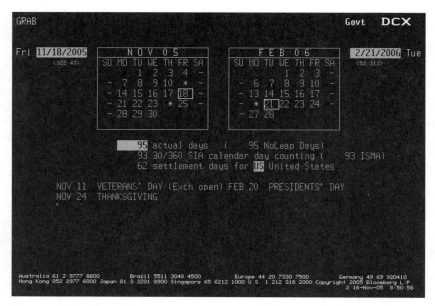

Figure 5.1 Bloomberg screen DCX used for US dollar market, 3-month loan taken out for value 18 November 2005.

© Bloomberg L.P. Used with permission. Visit *www.bloomberg.com*

users can use screen DCX to look up the number of days of an interest period. For instance, Figure 5.1 shows screen DCX for the US dollar market, for a loan taken out on 16 November 2005 for spot value on 18 November 2005 for a straight 3-month period. This matures on 21 February 2006; we see from Figure 5.1 that this is a good day. We see also that 20 February 2006 is a USD holiday. The loan period is actually 95 days, and 93 days under the 30/360-day convention (a bond market accrued interest convention). The number of business days is 62.

For the same loan taken out in Singapore dollars, look at Figure 5.2. This shows that 20 February 2006 is not a public holiday for SGD and so the loan runs for the period 18 December 2005 to 20 February 2006.

Settlement of money market instruments can be for value today (generally only when traded before mid-day), tomorrow or 2 days forward, which is known as *spot*. The latter is most common.

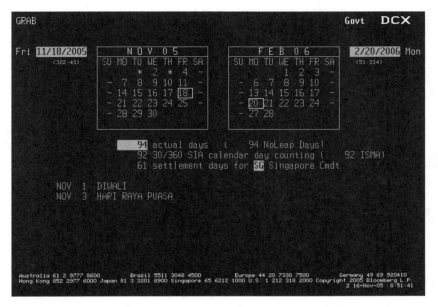

Figure 5.2 Bloomberg screen DCX for Singapore dollar market, 3-month loan taken out for value 18 November 2005.

© Bloomberg L.P. Used with permission. Visit *www.bloomberg.com*

SECURITIES QUOTED ON A YIELD BASIS

Two of the instruments in the list at the top of p. 103 are yield-based instruments.

Money market deposits

These are fixed-interest term deposits of up to 1 year with banks and securities houses. They are also known as *time deposits* or *clean deposits*. They are not negotiable so cannot be liquidated before maturity. The interest rate on the deposit is fixed for the term and related to the London Interbank Offered Rate (*LIBOR*) of the same term. Interest and capital are paid on maturity.

LIBOR

The term LIBOR or 'Libor' comes from London Interbank Offered Rate and is the interest rate at which one London bank offers funds to another London bank of acceptable credit quality in the form of a cash deposit. The rate is 'fixed' by the British Bankers Association at 11 a.m. every business day morning (in practice, the fix is usually about 20 minutes later) by taking the average of the rates supplied by member banks. The term LIBID is the bank's 'bid' rate – that is, the rate at which it pays for funds in the London market. The quote spread for a selected maturity is therefore the difference between LIBOR and LIBID. The convention in London is to quote the two rates as LIBOR–LIBID, thus matching the yield convention for other instruments. In some other markets the quote convention is reversed. EURIBOR is the interbank rate offered for euros as reported by the European Central Bank, fixed in Brussels.

The effective rate on a money market deposit is the annual equivalent interest rate for an instrument with a maturity of less than 1 year.

Example 5.1

A sum of £250,000 is deposited for 270 days, at the end of which the total proceeds are £261,000. What are the simple and effective rates of return on a 365-day basis?

$$\text{Simple rate of return} = \left(\frac{\text{Total proceeds}}{\text{Initial investment}} - 1 \right) \times \frac{M}{n}$$

$$= \left(\frac{261,000}{250,000} - 1 \right) \times \frac{365}{270} = 5.9481\%$$

$$\text{Effective rate of return} = \left(\frac{\text{Total proceeds}}{\text{Initial investment}} \right)^{\frac{M}{n}} - 1$$

$$= \left(\frac{261,000}{250,000} \right)^{\frac{365}{270}} - 1 = 5.9938\%$$

Certificates of Deposit

Certificates of Deposit (*CDs*) are receipts from banks for deposits that have been placed with them. They were first introduced in the sterling market in 1958. The deposits themselves carry a fixed rate of interest related to LIBOR and have a fixed term to maturity, so cannot be withdrawn before maturity. However, the certificates themselves can be traded in a secondary market – that is, they are negotiable.[1] CDs are therefore very similar to negotiable money market deposits, although the yields are about 0.15% below the equivalent deposit rates because of the added benefit of liquidity. Most CDs issued are of between 1 and 3 months' maturity, although they do trade in maturities of 1 to 5 years. Interest is paid on maturity except for CDs lasting longer than 1 year, where interest is paid annually or, occasionally, semiannually.

Banks, merchant banks and building societies issue CDs to raise funds to finance their business activities. A CD will have a stated interest rate and fixed maturity date, and can be issued in any denomination. On issue a CD is sold for face value, so the settlement proceeds of a CD on issue are always equal to its nominal value. The interest is paid, together with the face amount, on maturity. The interest rate is sometimes called the *coupon*, but unless the CD is held to maturity this will not equal the yield, which is of course the current rate available in the market and varies over time. The largest group of CD investors are banks, money market funds, corporates and local authority treasurers.

Unlike coupons on bonds, which are paid in rounded amounts, CD coupon is calculated to the exact day.

CD yields

The coupon quoted on a CD is a function of the credit quality of the issuing bank, its expected liquidity level in the market and, of course, the maturity of the CD, as this will be considered relative to the money market yield curve. As CDs are issued by banks as part of their short-term funding and liquidity requirement, issue volumes are driven by the demand for bank loans and the availability of alternative sources of funds for bank customers. The credit quality

---

[1] A small number of CDs are non-negotiable.

of the issuing bank is the primary consideration, however; in the sterling market the lowest yield is paid by 'clearer' CDs, which are CDs issued by the clearing banks – such as RBS NatWest plc, HSBC and Barclays plc. In the US market 'prime' CDs, issued by highly-rated domestic banks, trade at a lower yield than non-prime CDs. In both markets CDs issued by foreign banks – such as French or Japanese banks – will trade at higher yields.

Euro-CDs, which are CDs issued in a different currency from that of the home currency, also trade at higher yields in the US because of reserve and deposit insurance restrictions.

If the current market price of the CD including accrued interest is P and the current quoted yield is r, the yield can be calculated given the price, using (5.2):

$$r = \left(\frac{M}{P} \times \left(1 + C\left(\frac{N_{im}}{B}\right)\right) - 1\right) \times \left(\frac{B}{N_{sm}}\right) \qquad (5.2)$$

The price can be calculated given the yield using (5.3):

$$P = M \times \left(1 + C\left(\frac{N_{im}}{B}\right)\right) \Big/ 1 + r\left(\frac{N_{sm}}{B}\right)$$

$$= F \Big/ \left(1 + r\left(\frac{N_{sm}}{B}\right)\right) \qquad (5.3)$$

where
C = Quoted coupon on the CD;
M = Face value of the CD;
B = Year day-basis (365 or 360);
F = Maturity value of the CD;
N_{im} = Number of days between issue and maturity;
N_{sm} = Number of days between settlement and maturity;
N_{is} = Number of days between issue and settlement.

After issue a CD can be traded in the secondary market. The secondary market in CDs in the UK is very liquid, and CDs will trade at the rate prevalent at the time, which will invariably be different from the coupon rate on the CD at issue. When a CD is traded in the secondary market, the settlement proceeds will need to take into account interest that has accrued on the paper and the different rate at which the CD has now been dealt. The formula for calculating the settlement figure is given at (5.4) which applies to the sterling market and its 365 day-count basis:

$$\text{Proceeds} = \frac{M \times \text{Tenor} \times C \times 100 + 36{,}500}{\text{Days remaining} \times r \times 100 + 36{,}500} \qquad (5.4)$$

The settlement figure for a new issue CD is, of course, its face value...![2]

The *tenor* of a CD is the life of the CD in days, while *days remaining* is the number of days left to maturity from the time of trade.

The return on holding a CD is given by (5.5):

$$R = \left(\frac{1 + \text{Purchase yield} \times \dfrac{\text{Days from purchase to maturity}}{B}}{1 + \text{Sale yield} \times \dfrac{\text{Days from sale to maturity}}{B}} - 1 \right)$$
$$\times \frac{B}{\text{Days held}} \tag{5.5}$$

Example 5.2

A 3-month CD is issued on 6 September 1999 and matures on 6 December 1999 (maturity of 91 days). It has a face value of £20,000,000 and a coupon of 5.45%. What are the total maturity proceeds?

$$\text{Proceeds} = 20 \text{ millions} \times \left(1 + 0.0545 \times \frac{91}{365}\right)$$
$$= £20,271,753.42.$$

What are the secondary market proceeds on 11 October if the yield for short 60-day paper is 5.60%?

$$P = \frac{20,271,753.42}{\left(1 + 0.056 \times \dfrac{56}{365}\right)} = £20,099,066.64.$$

On 18 November the yield on short 3-week paper is 5.215%. What rate of return is earned from holding the CD for the 38 days from 11 October to 18 November?

$$R = \left(\frac{1 + 0.0560 \times \dfrac{56}{365}}{1 + 0.052\,15 \times \dfrac{38}{365}} - 1 \right) \times \frac{365}{38} = 9.6355\%.$$

---

[2] With thanks to Del Boy during the time he was at Tradition for pointing this out after I'd just bought a sizeable chunk of Japanese bank CDs ...

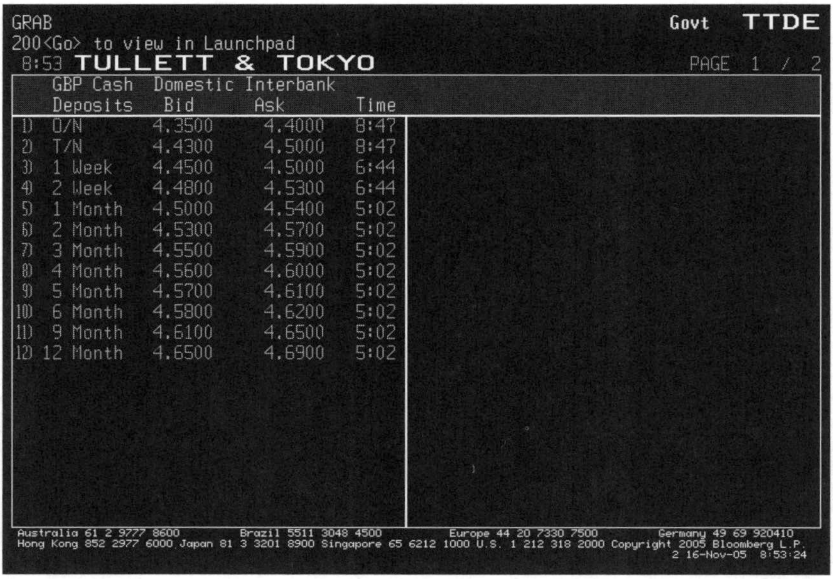

Figure 5.3 Tullett & Tokyo brokers' sterling money markets screen, 18 November 2005.

© Tullett & Tokyo and Bloomberg L.P. Used with permission. Visit *www.bloomberg.com*

An example of the way CDs and time deposits are quoted on screen is shown at Figure 5.3, which shows one of the rates screens displayed by Tullett & Tokyo, money brokers in London, on a Bloomberg screen. Essentially the same screen is displayed on Reuters. The screen has been reproduced with permission from Tullett's and Bloomberg. The screen displays sterling interbank and CD bid and offer rates for maturities up to 1 year as at 18 November 2005. The maturity marked 'O/N' is the overnight rate, which at that time was 4.35–4.40. The maturity marked 'T/N' is 'tom-next', or 'tomorrow-to-the-next', which is the overnight rate for deposits commencing tomorrow. Note that the liquidity of CDs means that they trade at a lower yield to deposits. The bid–offer convention in sterling is that the rate at which the market maker will pay for funds – its borrowing rate – is placed on the left. A 6-month time deposit is lent at 4.62%.

This is a reversal of the sterling market convention of placing the offered rate on the left-hand side, which existed until the end of the 1990s.

US dollar market rates

Treasury bills

The Treasury bill (*T-bill*) market in the US is the most liquid and transparent debt market in the world. Consequently, the bid–offer spread on them is very narrow. The Treasury issues bills at a weekly auction each Monday, made up of 91-day and 182-day bills. Every fourth week the Treasury also issues 52-week bills as well. As a result there are large numbers of T-bills outstanding at any one time. The interest earned on T-bills is not liable to state and local income taxes. T-bill rates are the lowest in the dollar market (as indeed any bill market is in respective domestic environments) and as such represents the corporate financier's *risk-free* interest rate.

Federal funds

Commercial banks in the US are required to keep reserves on deposit at the Federal Reserve. Banks with reserves in excess of required reserves can lend these funds to other banks, and these interbank loans are called *federal funds* or *fed funds* and are usually overnight loans. Through the fed funds market, commercial banks with excess funds are able to lend to banks that are short of reserves, thus facilitating liquidity. The transactions are very large denominations, and are lent at the *fed funds rate*, which can be a relatively volatile interest rate because it fluctuates with market shortages. On average, it trades about 15 basis points or so below the overnight Libor fix. The difference can be gauged by looking at Figures 5.4 and 5.5, which are the graphs for historical USD fed funds and overnight Libor rates, respectively.

Prime rate

The *prime interest rate* in the US is often said to represent the rate at which commercial banks lend to their most creditworthy customers. In practice, many loans are made at rates below the prime rate, so the prime rate is not the best rate at which highly rated firms may borrow. Nevertheless, the prime rate is a benchmark indicator of the level of US money market rates, and is often used as a reference rate for floating-rate instruments. As the market for bank loans is highly competitive, all commercial banks quote a single prime rate, and the rate for all banks changes simultaneously.

Figure 5.4 Bloomberg screen GP showing fed funds rate for period May–November 2005.

Figure 5.5 Bloomberg screen GP showing USD overnight Libor for period May–November 2005.

SECURITIES QUOTED ON A DISCOUNT BASIS

The remaining money market instruments are all quoted on a *discount* basis, and so are known as 'discount' instruments. This means that they are issued on a discount to face value, and are redeemed on maturity at face value. Hence T-bills, bills of exchange, banker's acceptances and commercial paper are examples of money market securities that are quoted on a discount basis – that is, they are sold on the basis of a discount to par. The difference between the price paid at the time of purchase and the redemption value (par) is the interest earned by the holder of the paper. Explicit interest is not paid on discount instruments, rather interest is reflected implicitly in the difference between the discounted issue price and the par value received at maturity.

Treasury bills

Treasury bills (*T-bills*) are short-term government 'IOUs' of short duration, often 3-month maturity. For example, if a bill is issued on 10 January it will mature on 10 April. Bills of 1-month and 6-month maturity are issued in certain markets, but only rarely by the UK Treasury. On maturity the holder of a T-bill receives the par value of the bill by presenting it to the central bank. In the UK most such bills are denominated in sterling but issues are also made in euros. In a capital market, T-bill yields are regarded as the *risk-free* yield, as they represent the yield from short-term government debt. In emerging markets they are often the most liquid instruments available for investors.

A sterling T-bill with £10 million face value issued for 91 days will be redeemed on maturity at £10 million. If the 3-month yield at the time of issue is 5.25%, the price of the bill at issue is:

$$P = \frac{10,000,000}{\left(1 + 0.0525 \times \dfrac{91}{365}\right)}$$

$$= £9,870,800.69$$

In the UK market the interest rate on discount instruments is quoted as a *discount rate* rather than a yield. This is the amount of discount expressed as an annualised percentage of the face value, and not as a percentage of the original amount paid. By definition, the discount rate is always lower than the corresponding yield. If the discount rate on a bill is d, then the amount of discount is given by (5.6):

$$d_{value} = M \times d \times \frac{n}{B} \qquad (5.6)$$

The price P paid for the bill is the face value minus the discount amount, given by (5.7):

$$P = 100 \times \left(\frac{1 - d \times (N_{sm}/365)}{100} \right) \qquad (5.7)$$

If we know the yield on the bill then we can calculate its price at issue by using the simple present value formula, as shown at (5.8):

$$P = \frac{M}{1 + r\dfrac{N_{sm}}{365}} \qquad (5.8)$$

The discount rate d for T-bills is calculated using (5.9):

$$d = (1 - P) \times \frac{B}{n} \qquad (5.9)$$

The relationship between discount rate and true yield is given by (5.10):

$$\left. \begin{array}{l} d = \dfrac{r}{\left(1 + r \times \dfrac{n}{B}\right)} \\[3em] r = \dfrac{d}{1 - d \times \dfrac{n}{B}} \end{array} \right\} \qquad (5.10)$$

Example 5.3

A 91-day £100 T-bill is issued with a yield of 4.75%. What is its issue price?

$$P = £100 \left/ \left(1 + 0.0475 \left(\frac{91}{365} \right) \right) \right.$$

$$= £98.80$$

A UK T-bill with a remaining maturity of 39 days is quoted at a discount of 4.95% What is the equivalent yield?

$$r = \frac{0.0495}{1 - 0.0495 \times \dfrac{39}{365}}$$

$$= 4.976\%$$

If a T-Bill is traded in the secondary market, the settlement proceeds from the trade are calculated using (5.11):

$$\text{Proceeds} = M - \left(\frac{M \times \text{Days remaining} \times d}{B \times 100}\right) \qquad (5.11)$$

Banker's acceptances

A banker's acceptance is a written promise issued by a borrower to a bank to repay borrowed funds. The lending bank lends funds and in return accepts the banker's acceptance. The acceptance is negotiable and can be sold in the secondary market. The investor who buys the acceptance can collect the loan on the day that repayment is due. If the borrower defaults, the investor has legal recourse to the bank that made the first acceptance. Banker's acceptances are also known as *bills of exchange, bank bills, trade bills* or *commercial bills*.

Essentially, banker's acceptances are instruments created to facilitate commercial trade transactions. The instrument is called a *banker's acceptance* because a bank accepts the ultimate responsibility to repay the loan to its holder. The use of banker's acceptances to finance commercial transactions is known as *acceptance financing*. The transactions for which acceptances are created include import and export of goods, the storage and shipping of goods between two overseas countries, where neither the importer nor the exporter is based in the home country,[3] and the storage and shipping of goods between two entities based at home. Acceptances are discount instruments and are purchased by banks, local authorities and money market investment funds.

---

[3] A banker's acceptance created to finance such a transaction is known as a *third-party acceptance*.

The rate that a bank charges a customer for issuing a banker's acceptance is a function of the rate at which the bank thinks it will be able to sell it in the secondary market. A commission is added to this rate. For ineligible banker's acceptances (see below) the issuing bank will add an amount to offset the cost of the additional reserve requirements.

Eligible banker's acceptance

An accepting bank that chooses to retain a banker's acceptance in its portfolio may be able to use it as collateral for a loan obtained from the central bank during open market operations – for example, the Bank of England in the UK and the Federal Reserve in the US. Not all acceptances are eligible to be used as collateral in this way, as they must meet certain criteria set by the central bank. The main requirement for eligibility is that the acceptance must be within a certain maturity band (a maximum of 6 months in the US and 3 months in the UK), and that it must have been created to finance a self-liquidating commercial transaction. In the US eligibility is also important because the Federal Reserve imposes a reserve requirement on funds raised via banker's acceptances that are ineligible. Banker's acceptances sold by an accepting bank are potential liabilities for the bank, but the reserve imposes a limit on the amount of eligible banker's acceptances that a bank may issue. Bills eligible for deposit at a central bank enjoy a finer rate than ineligible bills, and also act as a benchmark for prices in the secondary market.

COMMERCIAL PAPER

Commercial paper (*CP*) is a short-term money market funding instrument issued by corporates. In the UK and US it is a discount instrument. A company's short-term capital and *working* capital requirement is usually sourced directly from banks, in the form of bank loans. An alternative short-term funding instrument is CP, which is available to corporates that have a sufficiently strong credit rating. CP is a short-term unsecured promissory note. The issuer of the note promises to pay its holder a specified amount on a specified maturity date. CP normally has a zero coupon and trades at a *discount* to its face value. The discount represents interest to the investor in the period to maturity. CP is typically issued in bearer form, although some issues are in registered form.

Table 5.1   Comparison of US CP and Eurocommercial CP.

	US CP	Eurocommercial CP
Currency	US dollar	Any euro currency
Maturity	1–270 days	2–365 days
Common maturity	30–180 days	30–90 days
Interest	Zero coupon, issued at discount	Fixed coupon
Quotation	On a discount rate basis	On a yield basis
Settlement	$T + 0$	$T + 2$
Registration	Bearer form	Bearer form
Negotiable	Yes	Yes

In the London market, CP was not introduced until the mid-1980s. In the US, however, the market was developed in the late 19th century, and as early as 1922 there were 2,200 issuers of CP with $700 million outstanding. In 1998 there was just under $1 trillion outstanding. After its introduction in the UK in 1986, CP was subsequently issued in other European countries.

Originally, the CP market was restricted to borrowers with high credit ratings, and although lower-rated borrowers do now issue CP, sometimes by obtaining credit enhancements or setting up collateral arrangements, issuance in the market is still dominated by highly-rated companies. The majority of issues are very short-term, from 30 to 90 days in maturity; it is extremely rare to observe paper with a maturity of more than 270 days or 9 months. This is because of regulatory requirements in the US,[4] which states that debt instruments with a maturity of less than 270 days need not be registered. Companies therefore issue CP with a maturity lower than 9 months and so avoid the administration costs associated with registering issues with the SEC.

There are two major markets, the US dollar market with an out-standing amount in 2005 just under $1 trillion, and the Eurocom-mercial paper market with an outstanding value of $490 billion at the end of 2005.[5] Commercial paper markets are wholesale markets, and transactions are typically very large size. In the US over a third of

---

[4] This is the Securities Act of 1933. Registration is with the Securities and Exchange Commission.
[5] *Source*: BIS.

all CP is purchased by money market unit trusts, known as mutual funds; other investors include pension fund managers, retail or commercial banks, local authorities and corporate treasurers.

Although there is a secondary market in CP, very little trading activity takes place since investors generally hold CP until maturity. This is to be expected because investors purchase CP that matches their specific maturity requirement. When an investor does wish to sell paper, it can be sold back to the dealer or, where the issuer has placed the paper directly in the market (and not via an investment bank), it can be sold back to the issuer.

Commercial paper programmes

The issuers of CP are often divided into two categories of company, banking and financial institutions and non-financial companies. The majority of CP issues are by financial companies. Financial companies include not only banks but also the financing arms of corporates – such as General Motors, Daimler-Chrysler Financial andFord Motor Credit. Most of the issuers have strong credit ratings, but lower-rated borrowers have tapped the market, often after arranging credit support from a higher-rated company, such as a *letter of credit* from a bank, or by arranging collateral for the issue in the form of high-quality assets such as Treasury bonds. CP issued with credit support is known as *credit-supported commercial paper*, while paper backed with assets is known naturally enough as *asset-backed commercial paper*. Paper that is backed by a bank letter of credit is termed *LOC paper*. Although banks charge a fee for issuing letters of credit, borrowers are often happy to arrange for this, since by so doing they are able to tap the CP market. The yield paid on an issue of CP will be lower than that on a commercial bank loan.

Although CP is a short-dated security, typically of 3- to 6-month maturity, it is issued within a longer term programme, usually for 3 to 5 years for euro paper; US CP programmes are often open-ended. For example, a company might arrange a 5-year CP programme with a limit of $100 million. Once the programme is established the company can issue CP up to this amount – say, for maturities of 30 or 60 days. The programme is continuous and new CP can be issued at any time, daily if required. The total amount in issue cannot exceed the limit set for the programme. A CP programme can be used by a company to manage its short-term liquidity – that is, its working capital requirements. New paper can be issued whenever a need for cash arises, and for an appropriate maturity.

Issuers often roll over their funding and use funds from a new issue of CP to redeem a maturing issue. There is a risk that an issuer might be unable to roll over the paper where there is a lack of investor interest in the new issue. To provide protection against this risk issuers often arrange a stand-by line of credit from a bank, normally for all of the CP programme, to draw against in the event that it cannot place a new issue.

There are two methods by which CP is issued, known as *direct-issued* or *direct paper* and *dealer-issued* or *dealer paper*. Direct paper is sold by the issuing firm directly to investors, and no agent bank or securities house is involved. It is common for financial companies to issue CP directly to their customers, often because they have continuous programmes and constantly roll over their paper. It is therefore cost-effective for them to have their own sales arm and sell their CP direct. The treasury arms of certain non-financial companies also issue direct paper; this includes, for example, British Airways plc corporate treasury, which runs a continuous direct CP programme, used to provide short-term working capital for the company. Dealer paper is paper that is sold using a banking or securities house intermediary. In the US, dealer CP is effectively dominated by investment banks, as retail (commercial) banks were until recently forbidden from underwriting commercial paper. This restriction has since been removed and now both investment banks and commercial paper underwrite dealer paper.

Commercial paper yields

CP is a discount instrument. There have been issues of coupon CP in the Euro market, but this is unusual. Thus, CP is sold at a discount to its maturity value, and the difference between this maturity value and the purchase price is the interest earned by the investor. The CP day-count base is 360 days in the US and euro markets, and 365 days in the UK. The paper is quoted on a discount yield basis, in the same manner as T-bills. The yield on CP follows that of other money market instruments and is a function of the short-dated yield curve. The yield on CP is higher than the T-bill rate; this is due to the credit risk that the investor is exposed to when holding CP, for tax reasons (in certain jurisdictions interest earned on T-bills is exempt from income tax) and because of the lower level of liquidity available in the CP market. CP also pays a higher yield than CDs, due to the lower liquidity of the CP market.

Although CP is a discount instrument and trades as such in the US and UK, euro currency Eurocommercial paper trades on a yield basis, similar to a CD. The expressions below illustrate the relationship between true yield and discount rate:

$$P = \frac{M}{1 + r \times \dfrac{\text{Days}}{\text{Year}}} \tag{5.12}$$

$$rd = \frac{r}{1 + r \times \dfrac{\text{Days}}{\text{Year}}} \tag{5.13}$$

$$r = \frac{rd}{1 - rd \times \dfrac{\text{Days}}{\text{Year}}} \tag{5.14}$$

where M is the face value of the instrument, rd is the discount rate and r the true yield.

Example 5.4

1. A 60-day CP note has a nominal value of £100,000. It is issued at a discount of $7\frac{1}{2}\%$ per annum. The discount is calculated as:

$$Dis = \frac{£100,000(0.075 \times 60)}{365}$$

$$= £1,232.88$$

The issue price for the CP is therefore £100,000 – £1,232, or £98,768.

The money market yield on this note at the time of issue is:

$$\left(\frac{365 \times 0.075}{365 - (0.075 \times 60)} \right) \times 100\% = 7.594\%$$

Another way to calculate this yield is to measure the capital gain (the discount) as a percentage of the CP's cost, and convert this from a 60-day yield to a 1-year (365-day) yield, as shown below:

$$r = \frac{1,232}{98,768} \times \frac{365}{60} \times 100\%$$

$$= 7.588\%$$

2. ABC plc wishes to issue CP with 90 days to maturity. The investment bank managing the issue advises that the discount rate should be 9.5%. What should the issue price be, and what is the money market yield for investors?

$$Dis = \frac{100(0.095 \times 90)}{365}$$

$$= 2.342$$

The issue price will be 97.658.

The yield to investors will be:

$$\frac{2.342}{97.658} \times \frac{365}{90} \times 100\% = 9.725\%$$

MONEY MARKET SCREENS ON BLOOMBERG

Market professionals – such as those on the money market trading desks of banks – make extensive use of the Bloomberg system for trading and analytics. In this section we illustrate some of the key Bloomberg screens.

A good overview screen is BTMM. Figures 5.6 and 5.7 show this screen for the US dollar and sterling markets. As we can see, this page is a 'composite' of a number of rates and market sectors – for instance, the US fed funds rate[6] is in the top-left corner, while US Treasury bond yields, swap rates and futures rates are also shown. A slightly different layout is adopted for the UK markets – see Figure 5.7 – which has T-bill rates as well.

---

[6] This is, in effect, the US base interest rate; it is the rate at which the Federal Reserve lends funds to the primary Federal Reserve dealing banks.

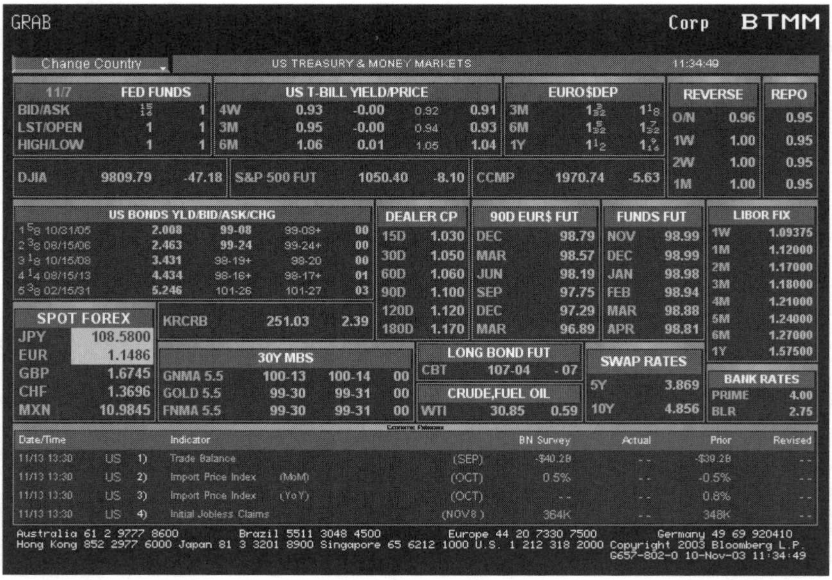

Figure 5.6 Bloomberg screen BTMM US for US dollar rates, 10 November 2003.

© Bloomberg L.P. Used with permission. Visit *www.bloomberg.com*

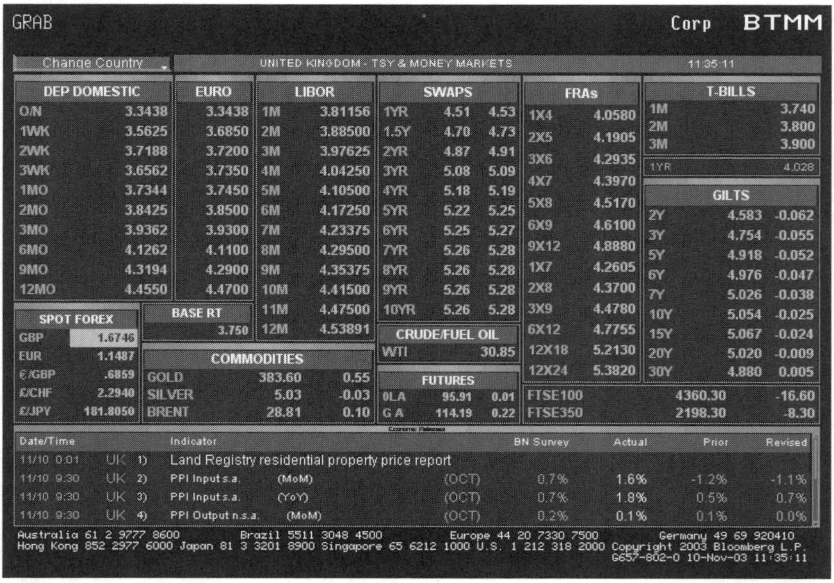

Figure 5.7 Screen BTMM UK for sterling money rates, 10 November 2003.

© Bloomberg L.P. Used with permission. Visit *www.bloomberg.com*

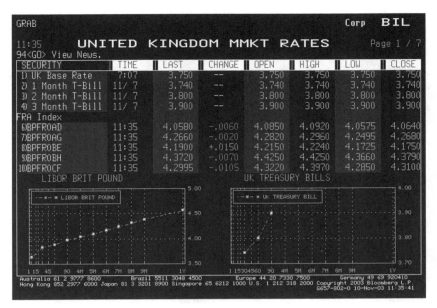

Figure 5.8 MMR Sterling money rates page MMR as at 10 November 2003.

© Bloomberg L.P. Used with permission. Visit *www.bloomberg.com*

A selection of money rates can also be seen using page MMR. Figure 5.8 shows this page for the sterling market. Money market yield curves are accessed from the main MMCV screen. The menu page is shown at Figure 5.9, while the sterling curve is shown at Figure 5.10. This can also be shown as a table, which we illustrate at Figure 5.11.

REPO

The term *repo* is used to cover one of two different transactions, the *classic repo* and the *sell/buy-back*, and sometimes is spoken of in the same context as a similar instrument, the *stock loan*. A fourth instrument is also economically similar in some respects to a repo, known as the *total return swap*, which is now commonly encountered as part of the market in credit derivatives. However, although these transactions differ in terms of their mechanics, legal documentation and accounting treatment, the economic effect of each of them is very similar. The structure of any particular market and the motivations of particular counterparties will determine which transaction is entered into; there is also some crossover between markets and participants.

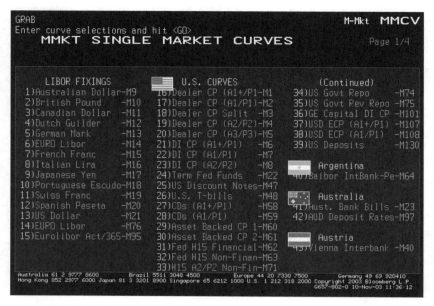

Figure 5.9   MMCV1 main menu page for screen MMCV.

© Bloomberg L.P. Used with permission. Visit *www.bloomberg.com*

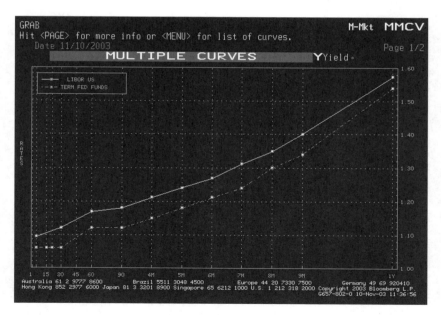

Figure 5.10   MMCV2 UK sterling money market yield curves as at 10 November 2003.

© Bloomberg L.P. Used with permission. Visit *www.bloomberg.com*

```
GRAB                                                    M-Mkt  MMCV
Hit <PAGE> for graph or <MENU> for list of curves.
                                                           Page 2/2
                      MULTIPLE  CURVES
  Date 11/10/2003
                       11:29          11/07
                    LIBOR US      TERM FED FUNDS
                       Yield          Yield          Yield
           1 DAY
           7 DAY    1.09375        1.06000
          15 DAY                   1.06000
          21 DAY                   1.06000
          30 DAY    1.12000        1.06000
          45 DAY
          60 DAY    1.17000        1.12000
          90 DAY    1.18000        1.12000
         4 MONTH    1.21000        1.15000
         5 MONTH    1.24000        1.18000
         6 MONTH    1.27000        1.21000
         7 MONTH    1.31000        1.24000
         8 MONTH    1.35000        1.30000
         9 MONTH    1.40000        1.34000
          1 YEAR    1.57500        1.54000

Australia 61 2 9777 8600      Brazil 5511 3048 4500    Europe 44 20 7330 7500    Germany 49 69 920410
Hong Kong 852 2977 6000 Japan 81 3 3201 8900 Singapore 65 6212 1000 U.S. 1 212 318 2000 Copyright 2003 Bloomberg L.P.
                                                              G657-802-0 10-Nov-03 11:37:19
```

Figure 5.11   MMCV3 UK sterling money market yield curves, table format.

© Bloomberg L.P. Used with permission. Visit *www.bloomberg.com*

Market participants enter into classic repo because they wish to invest cash, for which the transaction is deemed to be *cash-driven*, or because they wish to borrow a certain stock, for which purpose the trade is *stock-driven*. A sell/buy back, which is sometimes referred to as a *buy–sell*, is entered into for similar reasons but the trade itself operates under different mechanics and documentation.[7] A stock loan is just that, a borrowing of stock against a fee. Long-term holders of stock will therefore enter into stock loans simply to enhance their portfolio returns. We will look at the motivations behind the total return swap in a later chapter.

Definition

A repo agreement is a transaction in which one party sells securities to another, and at the same time and as part of the same transaction commits to repurchase identical securities on a specified date at a

---

[7] We shall use the term 'sell/buy-back' throughout this book. A repo is still a repo whether it is cash-driven or stock-driven, and one person's stock-driven trade may well be another's cash-driven one.

specified price. The seller delivers securities and receives cash from the buyer. The cash is supplied at a predetermined rate – *the repo rate* – that remains constant during the term of the trade. On maturity the original seller receives back collateral of equivalent type and quality, and returns the cash plus repo interest. One party to the repo requires either the cash or the securities and provides *collateral* to the other party, as well as some form of compensation for the temporary use of the desired asset. Although legal title to the securities is transferred, the seller retains both the economic benefits and the market risk of owning them. This means that the 'seller' will suffer if the market value of the collateral drops during the term of the repo, as she still retains beneficial ownership of the collateral. The 'buyer' in a repo is not affected in p/l account terms if the value of the collateral drops, although – as we shall see later – there will be other concerns for the buyer if this happens.

We have given here the legal definition of repo. However, the purpose of the transaction as we have described above is to borrow or lend cash, which is why we have used inverted commas when referring to sellers and buyers. The 'seller' of stock is really interested in borrowing cash, on which (s)he will pay interest at a specified interest rate. The 'buyer' requires security or *collateral* against the loan he has advanced, and/or the specific security to borrow for a period of time. The first and most important thing to state is that repo is a secured loan of cash, and would be categorised as a money market yield instrument.[8]

The classic repo

The *classic repo* is the instrument encountered in the US, UK and other markets. In a classic repo one party will enter into a contract to sell securities, simultaneously agreeing to purchase them back at a specified future date and price. The securities can be bonds or equities but also can be money market instruments, such as T-bills. The buyer of the securities is handing over cash, which on the termination of the trade will be returned to him, and on which he will receive interest.

---

[8] That is, a money market instrument quoted on a yield instrument, similar to a bank deposit or a CD. The other class of money market products are *discount* instruments such as T-bills or CP.

The seller in a classic repo is selling or *offering* stock, and therefore receiving cash, whereas the buyer is buying or *bidding* for stock, and consequently paying cash. So, if the 1-week repo interest rate is quoted by a market making bank as '$5\frac{1}{2}$–$5\frac{1}{4}$', this means that the market maker will bid for stock – that is, lend the cash – at 5.50% and offers stock or pays interest on cash at 5.25%.

Illustration of classic repo

There will be two parties to a repo trade, let us say Bank A (the seller of securities) and Bank B (the buyer of securities). On the trade date the two banks enter into an agreement whereby on a set date – the *value or settlement* date – Bank A will sell to Bank B a nominal amount of securities in exchange for cash.[9] The price received for the securities is the market value of the stock on the value date. The agreement also demands that on the termination date Bank B will sell identical stock back to Bank A at the previously agreed price, and, consequently, Bank B will have its cash returned with interest at the agreed repo rate.

In essence, a repo agreement is a secured loan (or *collateralised* loan) in which the repo rate reflects the interest charged.

On the value date, stock and cash change hands. This is known as the start date, *first leg* or *opening leg*, while the termination date is known as the *second leg* or *closing leg*. When the cash is returned to Bank B, it is accompanied by the interest charged on the cash during the term of the trade. This interest is calculated at a specified rate known as the *repo rate*. It is important to remember that although in legal terms the stock is initially 'sold' to Bank B, the economic effects of ownership are retained with Bank A. This means that if the stock falls in price it is Bank A that will suffer a capital loss. Similarly, if the stock involved is a bond and there is a coupon payment during the term of trade, this coupon is to the benefit of Bank A and, although Bank B will have received it on the coupon date, it must be handed over on the same day or immediately after to

---

[9] The two terms are not necessarily synonymous. The value date in a trade is the date on which the transaction acquires value – for example, the date from which accrued interest is calculated. As such it may fall on a non-business day – such as a weekend or public holiday. The settlement date is the day on which the transaction settles or *clears*, and so can only fall on a working day.

Figure 5.12 Classic repo transaction.

Bank A. This reflects the fact that, although legal title to the collateral passes to the repo buyer, economic costs and benefits of the collateral remain with the seller.

A classic repo transaction is subject to a legal contract signed in advance by both parties. A standard document will suffice; it is not necessary to sign a legal agreement prior to each transaction.

Note that, although we have called the two parties in this case 'Bank A' and 'Bank B', it is not only banks that get involved in repo transactions – we have used these terms for the purposes of illustration only.

The basic mechanism is illustrated in Figure 5.12.

A seller in a repo transaction is entering into a repo, whereas a buyer is entering into a *reverse repo*. In Figure 5.12 the repo counterparty is Bank A, while Bank B is entering into a reverse repo. That is, a reverse repo is a purchase of securities that are sold back on termination. As is evident from Figure 5.12, every repo is a reverse repo, and the name given is dependent on from whose viewpoint one is looking at the transaction.[10]

---

[10] Note that the guidelines to the syllabus for the Chartered Financial Analyst examination, which is set by the Association for Investment Management and Research, defines repo and reverse repo slightly differently. Essentially, a 'repo' is conducted by a bank counterparty and a 'reverse repo' is conducted by an investment counterparty or non-financial counterparty. Another definition states that a 'repo' is any trade where the bank counterparty is offering stock (borrowing cash) and a 'reverse repo' is any trade where the non-bank counterparty is borrowing cash.

Examples of classic repo

The basic principle is illustrated with the following example. This considers a *specific* repo – that is, one in which the collateral supplied is specified as a particular stock – as opposed to a *general collateral* (GC) trade in which a basket of collateral can be supplied, of any particular issue, as long as it is of the required type and credit quality.

We consider first a classic repo in the UK gilt market between two market counterparties, in the 5.75% Treasury 2012 gilt stock as at 2 December 2005. The terms of the trade are given in Table 5.2 and it is illustrated at Figure 5.13.

The repo counterparty delivers to the reverse repo counterparty £10 million nominal of the stock, and in return receives the purchase proceeds. In this example no margin has been taken, so the start proceeds are equal to the market value of the stock which is £10,539,928. It is common for a rounded sum to be transferred on the opening leg. The repo interest is 4.50%, so the repo interest charged for the trade is:

$$10{,}539{,}928 \times 4.50\% \times \frac{7}{365}$$

Table 5.2 Terms of classic repo trade.

Trade date	2 December 2005
Value date	5 December 2005
Repo term	1 month
Termination date	5 January 2006
Collateral (stock)	UKT 5% 2012
Nominal amount	£10,000,000
Price	104.17
Accrued interest (89 days)	1.229 281 8
Dirty price	105.3993
Haircut	0%
Settlement proceeds (*wired amount*)	£10,539,928.18
Repo rate	4.50%
Repo interest	£40,282.74
Termination proceeds	£10,580,210.92

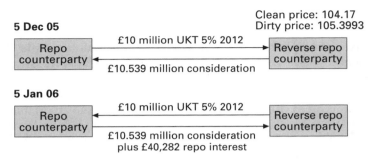

Figure 5.13   Classic repo trade.

or £40,282.74. The sterling market day-count basis is actual/365, so the repo interest is based on a 7-day repo rate of 4.50%. Repo rates are agreed at the time of the trade and are quoted, like all interest rates, on an annualised basis. The settlement price (dirty price) is used because it is the market value of the bonds on the particular trade date and therefore indicates the cash value of the gilts. By doing this, the cash investor minimises credit exposure by equating the value of the cash and the collateral.

On termination the repo counterparty receives back its stock, for which it hands over the original proceeds plus the repo interest calculated above.

Market participants who are familiar with the Bloomberg LP trading system will use screen RRRA for a classic repo transaction. For this example the relevant screen entries are shown at Figure 5.14. This screen is used in conjunction with a specific stock, so in this case it would be called up by entering:

UKT 5 12 <GOVT> RRRA <GO>

where 'UKT' is the ticker for UK gilts. Note that the date format for Bloomberg screens is mm/dd/yy. The screen inputs are relatively self-explanatory, with the user entering the terms of the trade that are detailed in Table 5.2. There is also a field for calculating margin, labelled 'collateral' on the screen. As no margin is involved in this example, it is left at its default value of 100.00%. The bottom of the screen shows the opening leg cash proceeds or 'wired amount', the repo interest and the termination proceeds.

The repo rate for the trade is the 1-month rate of 4.50%, as shown in Figure 5.15, which is the HBOS repo rates screen as at 29 November 2005.

· ·

<HELP> for explanation.   P174 Corp   **RRRA**
Enter <1><GO> to send screen via <MESSAGE> System.
REPO/REVERSE REPO ANALYSIS

TREASURY   UKT 5 03/07/12   104.1700/104.2300   (4.23/4.22) BGN @13:31
BOND IS CUM-DIVIDEND AT SETTLEMENT   CUSIP: EC3919569

SETTLEMENT DATE   12/ 5/05   RATE (365)   4.5000%
<SETTLEMENT PRICE> <MARKET PRICE>   COLLATERAL: 100.0000% OF MONEY
PRICE   104.1700000   104.170000   Y/N, HOLD COLLATERAL PERCENT CONSTANT?   Y
YIELD   4.2329041   4.2329041 Y/N, BUMP ALL DATES FOR WEEKENDS/HOLIDAYS? Y
ACCRUED   1.2292818   1.2292818
FOR 89 DAYS   ROUNDING 1   1 = NOT ROUNDED
TOTAL   105.3992818   105.399282   2 = ROUND TO NEAREST 1/ 8
BOND IS CUM-DIVIDEND AT TERMINATION

FACE AMT   10000000   <OR>   SETTLEMENT MONEY   10539928.18
<OR> To solve for PRICE: Enter NUMBER of BONDS, SETTLEMENT MONEY & COLLATERAL
TERMINATION DATE   1/ 5/06   <OR>   TERM (IN DAYS)   31
ACCRUED 1.657459 FOR 120 DAYS.

MONEY AT TERMINATION
WIRED AMOUNT	10,539,928.18
REPO INTEREST	40,282.74
TERMINATION MONEY	10,580,210.92
NOTES:

Australia 61 2 9777 8600   Brazil 5511 3048 4500   Europe 44 20 7330 7500   Germany 49 69 920410
Hong Kong 852 2977 6000 Japan 81 3 3201 8900 Singapore 65 6212 1000 U.S. 1 212 318 2000 Copyright 2005 Bloomberg L.P.
                                                                                        2 02-Dec-05 13:33:25

Figure 5.14 Bloomberg screen RRRA for classic repo.

© Bloomberg L.P. Used with permission. Visit *www.bloomberg.com*

200<GO>to view this page in Launchpad   P122 a **Govt   HBOS**
HBOS Treasury Services

                                                                    Page 1 of 1
                                                                     13:31 GMT
	EUR			GBP		02-Dec-05
	Bid	Offer		Bid	Offer	
TN	2.09	2.04	1W	4.55	4.45	
SN	2.34	2.30	2W	4.50	4.40	
SW	2.32	2.29	3W	4.50	4.40	
1MTH	2.33	2.30	1M	4.50	4.40	
2MTH	2.32	2.29	2M	4.50	4.40	
3MTH	2.35	2.32	3M	4.48	4.38	
4MTH	2.38	2.35	4M	4.47	4.37	
5MTH	2.42	2.39	5M	4.45	4.35	
6MTH	2.45	2.42	6M	4.43	4.33	
7MTH	2.49	2.46	9M	4.40	4.30	
8MTH	2.52	2.49	1Y	4.38	4.28	
9MTH	2.55	2.52				
10MTH	2.57	2.54				
11MTH	2.59	2.56				
YR	2.61	2.58				

Australia 61 2 9777 8600   Brazil 5511 3048 4500   Europe 44 20 7330 7500   Germany 49 69 920410
Hong Kong 852 2977 6000 Japan 81 3 3201 8900 Singapore 65 6212 1000 U.S. 1 212 318 2000 Copyright 2005 Bloomberg L.P.
                                                                                        3 02-Dec-05 13:33:17

Figure 5.15 HBOS repo rates screen as at 2 December 2005.

© Bloomberg L.P. Used with permission. Visit *www.bloomberg.com*

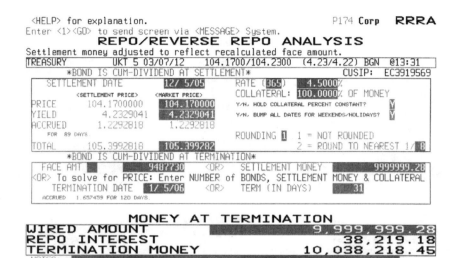

<HELP> for explanation.   P174 Corp   **RRRA**
Enter <1><GO> to send screen via <MESSAGE> System.
              REPO/REVERSE REPO ANALYSIS
Settlement money adjusted to reflect recalculated face amount.
TREASURY   UKT 5 03/07/12   104.1700/104.2300   (4.23/4.22) BGN @13:31
          BOND IS CUM-DIVIDEND AT SETTLEMENT   CUSIP: EC3919569
    SETTLEMENT DATE   12/ 5/05   RATE (365)   4.5000%
          <SETTLEMENT PRICE>   <MARKET PRICE>   COLLATERAL: 100.0000% OF MONEY
    PRICE   104.1700000   104.170000   Y/N, HOLD COLLATERAL PERCENT CONSTANT?   Y
    YIELD   4.2329041   4.2329041   Y/N, BUMP ALL DATES FOR WEEKENDS/HOLIDAYS? Y
    ACCRUED   1.2292818   1.2292818
       FOR 89 DAYS   ROUNDING 1   1 = NOT ROUNDED
    TOTAL   105.3992818   105.399282   2 = ROUND TO NEAREST 1/ 8
          BOND IS CUM-DIVIDEND AT TERMINATION
    FACE AMT   9487730   <OR>   SETTLEMENT MONEY   9999999.28
    <OR> To solve for PRICE: Enter NUMBER of BONDS, SETTLEMENT MONEY & COLLATERAL
       TERMINATION DATE 1/ 5/06   <OR>   TERM (IN DAYS)   31
       ACCRUED 1.657459 FOR 120 DAYS.

                    MONEY AT TERMINATION
    WIRED AMOUNT   9,999,999.28
    REPO INTEREST   38,219.18
    TERMINATION MONEY   10,038,218.45
    NOTES:

Australia 61 2 9777 8600   Brazil 5511 3048 4500   Europe 44 20 7330 7500   Germany 49 69 920410
Hong Kong 852 2977 6000 Japan 81 3 3201 8900 Singapore 65 6212 1000 U.S. 1 212 318 2000 Copyright 2005 Bloomberg L.P.
                                                                      2 02-Dec-05 13:35:17

Figure 5.16   Bloomberg screen for classic repo trade described on
this page.
© Bloomberg L.P. Used with permission. Visit *www.bloomberg.com*

What if a counterparty is interested in investing £10 million against
gilt collateral? Let us assume that a corporate treasury function with
surplus cash wishes to invest this amount in repo for a 1-week term.
It invests this cash with a bank that deals in gilt repo. We can use
Bloomberg screen RRRA to calculate the nominal amount of collateral required. Figure 5.16 shows the screen for this trade, again
against the 5.75% Treasury 2012 stock as collateral. We see from
Figure 5.16 that the terms of the trade are identical to that in Table
5.2, including the term of the trade and the repo rate; however, the
opening leg wired amount is entered as £10 million, which is the
cash being invested. Therefore, the nominal value of the gilt collateral required will be different, as we now require a market value of
this stock of £10 million. From the screen we see that this is
£9,487,773.00. The cash amount is different from the example at
Figure 5.14, so of course the repo interest charged is different and is
£38,219.18 for the 1-month term.

The diagram at Figure 5.17 illustrates the transaction.

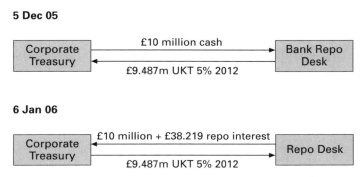

Figure 5.17 Corporate treasury classic repo, as illustrated in Figure 5.16.

The sell/buy-back

In addition to classic repo, there exists *sell/buy-back*. A sell/buy-back is defined as an outright sale of a bond on the value date, and an outright repurchase of that bond for value on a *forward* date. The cash flows therefore become a sale of the bond at a *spot* price, followed by repurchase of the bond at the *forward* price. The forward price calculated includes the interest on the repo, and is therefore a different price to the spot price. That is, repo interest is realised as the difference between the spot price and forward price of the collateral at the start and termination of the trade. The sell/buy-back is entered into for the same considerations as a classic repo, but was developed initially in markets where no legal agreement to cover repo transactions, and where the settlement and IT systems of individual counterparties were not equipped to deal with repo. Over time sell/buy-backs have become the convention in certain markets, most notably Italy, and so the mechanism is still retained. In many markets, therefore, sell/buy-backs are not covered by a legal agreement, although the standard legal agreement used in classic repo now includes a section that describes them.[11]

A sell/buy-back is a spot sale and forward repurchase of bonds transacted simultaneously, and the repo rate is not explicit, but is implied in the forward price. Any coupon payments during the

---

[11] This is the PSA/ISMA Global Master Repurchase Agreement, which is reviewed in the author's book *Introduction to Repo Markets*, 3rd edition, part of this series by John Wiley & Sons.

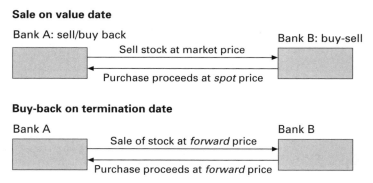

Figure 5.18   Sell/buy-back transaction.

term are paid to the seller; however, this is done through incorporation into the forward price, so the seller will not receive it immediately, but on termination. This is a disadvantage when compared with classic repo. However, there will be compensation payable if a coupon is not handed over straight away, usually at the repo rate implied in the sell/buy-back. As sell/buy-backs are not subject to a legal agreement in most cases, in effect the seller has no legal right to any coupon, and there is no provision for marking-to-market and *variation margin*. This makes the sell/buy-back a higher risk transaction when compared with classic repo, even more so in volatile markets.

A general diagram for the sell/buy-back is given at Figure 5.18.

Examples of sell/buy-back

We use the same terms of trade given in the previous section, but this time the trade is a sell/buy-back.[12] In a sell/buy-back we require the forward price on termination, and the difference between the spot and forward price incorporates the effects of repo interest. It is

---

[12] The Bank of England discourages sell/buy-backs in the gilt repo and it is unusual, if not unheard of, to observe them in this market. However, we use these terms of trade for comparison purposes with the classic repo example given in the previous section.

important to note that this forward price has nothing to with the actual market price of the collateral at the time of forward trade. It is simply a way of allowing for the repo interest that is the key factor in the trade. Thus, in sell/buy-back the repo rate is not explicit (although it is the key consideration in the trade), rather it is implicit in the forward price.

In this example, one counterparty sells £10 million nominal of the UKT 5% 2012 at the spot price of 104.17, this being the market price of the bond at the time. The consideration for this trade is the market value of the stock, which is £10,539,928.18 as before. Repo interest is calculated on this amount at the rate of 4.50% for 1 month, and from this the termination proceeds are calculated. The termination proceeds are divided by the nominal amount of stock to obtain the forward dirty price of the bond on the termination date. For various reasons – the main one being that settlement systems deal in clean prices, we require the forward clean price, which is obtained by subtracting from the forward dirty price the accrued interest on the bond on the termination date. At the start of the trade, the 5% 2012 had 89 days' accrued interest, therefore on termination this figure will be 89 + 31 or 120 days.

Bloomberg users access a different screen for sell/buy-backs, which is BSR. This is shown at Figure 5.19. Entering in the terms of the trade, we see from Figure 5.19 that the forward price is 104.144. However, the fundamental element of this transaction is evident from the bottom part of the screen: the settlement amount ('wired amount'), repo interest and termination amount are identical to the classic repo trade described earlier. This is not surprising; the sell/buy-back is a loan of £10.539 million for 1 month at an interest rate of 4.50%. The mechanics of the trade do not impact on this key point.

Screen BSR on Bloomberg has a second page, which is shown at Figure 5.20. This screen summarises the cash proceeds of the trade at start and termination. Note how the repo interest is termed 'funding cost'. This is because the trade is deemed to have been entered into by a bond trader who is funding his book. This will be considered later, but we can see from the screen details that during the 1 month of the trade the bond position has accrued interest of £165,745.00. This compares favourably with the repo funding cost of £122,928.18. The funding cost is therefore below the accrued interest gained on the bondholding, as shown in the screen.

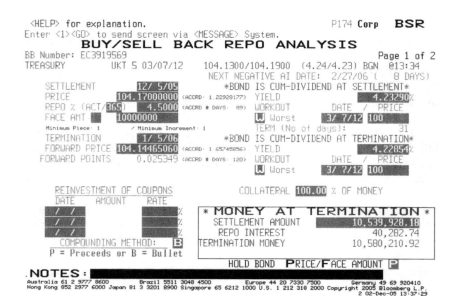

<HELP> for explanation.   P174 Corp BSR
Enter <1><GO> to send screen via <MESSAGE> System.
        BUY/SELL BACK REPO ANALYSIS
BB Number: EC3919569   Page 1 of 2
TREASURY   UKT 5 03/07/12   104.1300/104.1900 (4.24/4.23) BGN @13:34
                          NEXT NEGATIVE AI DATE: 2/27/06 (8 DAYS)
      SETTLEMENT   12/ 5/05   *BOND IS CUM-DIVIDEND AT SETTLEMENT*
      PRICE   104.17000000 (ACCRD: 1.22928177) YIELD   4.23290%
      REPO % (ACT/365)   4.5000 (ACCRD # DAYS: 89) WORKOUT   DATE / PRICE
      FACE AMT   10000000   W Worst   3/ 7/12 100
      Minimum Piece: 1   / Minimum Increment: 1   TERM (No of days):   31
      TERMINATION   1/ 5/06   *BOND IS CUM-DIVIDEND AT TERMINATION*
      FORWARD PRICE 104.14465060 (ACCRD: 1.65745856) YIELD   4.22854%
      FORWARD POINTS   0.025349 (ACCRD # DAYS: 120) WORKOUT   DATE / PRICE
                                                  W Worst   3/ 7/12 100

      REINVESTMENT OF COUPONS   COLLATERAL 100.00 % OF MONEY
       DATE   AMOUNT   RATE
        / /   %.   * MONEY AT TERMINATION *
        / /   %.   SETTLEMENT AMOUNT   10,539,928.18
        / /   %.   REPO INTEREST   40,282.74
      COMPOUNDING METHOD: B   TERMINATION MONEY   10,580,210.92
      P = Proceeds or B = Bullet
                                   HOLD BOND PRICE/FACE AMOUNT P
.NOTES :
Australia 61 2 9777 8600   Brazil 5511 3048 4500   Europe 44 20 7330 7500   Germany 49 69 920410
Hong Kong 852 2977 6000 Japan 81 3 3201 8900 Singapore 65 6212 1000 U.S. 1 212 318 2000 Copyright 2005 Bloomberg L.P.
                                                                            2 02-Dec-05 13:37:29

Figure 5.19 Bloomberg screen BSR for sell/buy-back trade in 5% 2012.

© Bloomberg L.P. Used with permission. Visit *www.bloomberg.com*

<HELP> for explanation.   P174 Corp BSR
Enter <1><GO> to send screen via <MESSAGE> System.
        BUY/SELL BACK REPO ANALYSIS
BB Number: EC3919569   Page 2 of 2
TREASURY   UKT 5 03/07/12   104.1300/104.1900 (4.24/4.23) BGN @13:34

        BOND INCOME   FUNDING COST

AT SETTLEMENT DATE: 12/ 5/05
PRINCIPAL   10,417,000.00
  ACCRUED INTEREST   122,928.18   --->   10,539,928.18 @   4.5000
TOTAL: 10,539,928.18   for 31 day(s)

AT TERMINATION DATE: 1/ 5/06
PRINCIPAL   10,417,000.00
COUPON(S)   0.00
  ACCRUED INTEREST   165,745.86
  INTEREST ON CPNS   0.00
TOTAL: 10,582,745.86

     NET INCOME: 42,817.68   COST: 40,282.74

DIFFERENCE   2,534.94 TERMINATION
PER 100 NOM: 0.02534936 AMOUNT   10,414,465.06
Australia 61 2 9777 8600   Brazil 5511 3048 4500   Europe 44 20 7330 7500   Germany 49 69 920410
Hong Kong 852 2977 6000 Japan 81 3 3201 8900 Singapore 65 6212 1000 U.S. 1 212 318 2000 Copyright 2005 Bloomberg L.P.
                                                                            2 02-Dec-05 13:37:34

Figure 5.20 Bloomberg screen BSR page 2 for sell/buy-back trade in 5.75% 2009.

© Bloomberg L.P. Used with permission. Visit *www.bloomberg.com*

If there is a coupon payment during a sell/buy-back trade and it is not paid over to the seller until termination, a compensating amount is also payable on the coupon amount, usually at the trade's repo rate. When calculating the forward price on a sell/buy-back where a coupon will be paid during the trade, we must subtract the coupon amount from the forward price. Note also that sell/buy-backs are not possible on an open basis, as no forward price can be calculated unless a termination date is known.

Repo collateral

The collateral in a repo trade is the security passed to the lender of cash by the borrower of cash. It is not always secondary to the transaction; in stock-driven transactions the requirement for specific collateral is the motivation behind the trade. However, in a classic repo or sell/buy-back, the collateral is always the security handed over against cash.[13] In a stock loan transaction, the collateral against stock lent can be either securities or cash. Collateral is used in repo to provide security against default by the cash borrower. Therefore, it is protection against counterparty risk or *credit risk*, the risk that the cash borrowing counterparty defaults on the loan. A secured or *collateralised* loan is theoretically lower credit risk exposure for a cash lender compared with an unsecured loan.

The most commonly encountered collateral is government bonds, and the repo market in government bonds is the largest one in the world. Other forms of collateral include Eurobonds, other forms of corporate and supranational debt, asset-backed bonds, mortgage-backed bonds, money market securities such as T-bills, and equities.

In any market where there is a defined class of collateral of identical credit quality, this is known as *general collateral* (*GC*). So, for example, in the UK gilt market a GC repo is one where any gilt will be acceptable as repo collateral. Another form of GC might be 'AA-rated sterling Eurobonds'. In the US market the term *stock collateral* is sometimes used to refer to GC securities. In equity repo it is more problematic to define GC and by definition almost all trades are specifics; however, it is becoming more common for counterparties to specify any equity being acceptable if it is in an established index – for example, a FTSE 100 or a CAC 40 stock – and this is perhaps the equity market equivalent of GC. If a specific

---

[13] So that even in a stock-driven reverse repo the collateral is the security handed over against the borrowing of cash by the repo seller.

security is required in a reverse repo or as the other side of a sell/buy-back, this is known as a *specific* or *specific collateral*. A specific stock that is in high demand in the market, such that the repo rate against it is significantly different from the GC rate, is known as a *special*.

Where a coupon payment is received on collateral during the term of a repo, it is to the benefit of the repo seller. Under the standard repo legal agreement, legal title to collateral is transferred to the buyer during the term of the repo, but it is accepted that the economic benefits remain with the seller. For this reason, coupon is returned to the seller. In classic repo (and in stock lending) the coupon is returned to the seller on the dividend date, or in some cases on the following date. In a sell/buy-back the effect of the coupon is incorporated into the repurchase price. This includes interest on the coupon amount that is payable by the buyer during the period from the coupon date to the buy-back date.

Legal treatment

Classic repo is carried out under a legal agreement that defines the transaction as a full transfer of the title to the stock. The standard legal agreement is the PSA/ISMA GRMA, which we review in the sister book in this series, *An Introduction to Repo Markets*. It is now possible to trade sell/buy-backs under this agreement as well. This agreement was based on the PSA standard legal agreement used in the US domestic market, and was compiled because certain financial institutions were not allowed to legally borrow or lend securities. By transacting repo under the PSA agreement, these institutions were defined as legally buying and selling securities rather than borrowing or lending them.

Margin

To reduce the level of risk exposure in a repo transaction, it is common for the lender of cash to ask for a margin, which is where the market value of collateral is higher than the cash value of cash lent out in the repo. This is a form of protection, should the cash borrowing counterparty default on the loan. Another term for margin is *overcollateralisation* or *haircut*. There are two types of margin, an *initial margin* taken at the start of the trade and *variation margin* which is called if required during the term of the trade.

Initial margin

The cash proceeds in a repo are typically no more than the market value of the collateral. This minimises credit exposure by equating the value of the cash to that of the collateral. The market value of the collateral is calculated at its *dirty* price, not *clean* price – that is, including accrued interest. This is referred to as *accrual pricing*. To calculate the accrued interest on the (bond) collateral we require the day-count basis for the particular bond.

The start proceeds of a repo can be less than the market value of the collateral by an agreed amount or percentage. This is known as the *initial margin* or *haircut*. The initial margin protects the buyer against:

- a sudden fall in the market value of the collateral;
- illiquidity of collateral;
- other sources of volatility of value (e.g., approaching maturity);
- counterparty risk.

The margin level of repo varies from 0%–2% for collateral such as UK gilts to 5% for cross-currency and equity repo, to 10%–35% for emerging market debt repo.

In both classic repo and sell/buy-back, any initial margin is given to the supplier of cash in the transaction. This remains the case in the case of specific repo. For initial margin the market value of the bond collateral is reduced (or given a *haircut*) by the percentage of the initial margin and the nominal value determined from this reduced amount. In a stock loan transaction the lender of stock will ask for margin.

There are two methods for calculating the margin; for a 2% margin this could be one of the following:

- the dirty price of the bonds × 0.98;
- the dirty price of the bonds ÷ 1.02.

The two methods do not give the same value! The RRRA repo page on Bloomberg uses the second method for its calculations, and this method is turning into something of a convention.

For a 2% margin level the PSA/ISMA GRMA defines a 'margin ratio' as:

$$\frac{\text{Collateral value}}{\text{Cash}} = 102\%$$

The size of margin required in any particular transaction is a function of the following:

- the credit quality of the counterparty supplying the collateral – for example, a central bank counterparty, interbank counterparty and corporate will all suggest different margin levels;
- the term of the repo – an overnight repo is inherently lower risk than a 1-year repo;
- the duration (price volatility) of the collateral – for example, a T-bill against the long bond;
- the existence or absence of a legal agreement – a repo traded under a standard agreement is considered lower risk.

However, in the final analysis, margin is required to guard against market risk, the risk that the value of collateral will drop during the course of the repo. Therefore, the margin call must reflect the risks prevalent in the market at the time; extremely volatile market conditions may call for large increases in initial margin.

Variation margin

The market value of the collateral is maintained through the use of *variation margin*. So, if the market value of the collateral falls, the buyer calls for extra cash or collateral. If the market value of the collateral rises, the seller calls for extra cash or collateral. In order to reduce the administrative burden, margin calls can be limited to changes in the market value of the collateral in excess of an agreed amount or percentage, which is called a *margin maintenance limit*.

The standard market documentation that exists for the three structures covered so far includes clauses that allow parties to a transaction to call for variation margin during the term of a repo. This can be in the form of extra collateral, if the value of the collateral has dropped in relation to the asset exchanged, or a return of collateral, if the value has risen. If the cash borrowing counterparty is unable to supply more collateral where required, he will have to return a portion of the cash loan. Both parties have an interest in making and meeting margin calls, although there is no obligation. The level at which variation margin is triggered is often agreed beforehand in the legal agreement put in place between individual counterparties. Although primarily viewed as an instrument used by the supplier of cash against a fall in the value of the collateral, variation margin can

of course also be called by the repo seller if the value of the collateral
has risen in value.

Appendix 5.A   CURRENCIES USING MONEY MARKET YEAR BASE OF 365 DAYS

- Sterling;
- Hong Kong dollar;
- Malaysian ringgit;
- Singapore dollar;
- South African rand;
- Taiwan dollar;
- Thai baht.

In addition, the domestic markets, but not the international markets,
of the following currencies also use a 365-day base:

- Australian dollar;
- Canadian dollar;
- Japanese yen;
- New Zealand dollar.

To convert an interest rate i quoted on a 365-day basis to one quoted
on a 360-day basis (i^*) use the expressions given at (5.22):

$$\left.\begin{array}{l} i = i^* \times \dfrac{365}{360} \\[2mm] i^* = i \times \dfrac{360}{365} \end{array}\right\} \tag{5.22}$$

Chapter

6

....

THE EUROBOND MARKET

The Eurobond market is an important source of funds for many banks and corporates, as well as central governments. The Eurobond market has benefited from many of the advances in financial engineering, and has undergone some innovative changes in the debt capital markets. It continues to develop new structures, in response to the varying demands and requirements of specific groups of investors. The range of innovations have customised the market to a certain extent, and often the market is the only opening for certain types of government and corporate finance. Investors also often look to the Eurobond market due to constraints in their domestic market, and Euro securities have been designed to reproduce the features of instruments that certain investors may be prohibited from investing in in their domestic arena. Other instruments are designed for investors in order to provide tax advantages. The traditional image of the Eurobond investor – the so-called 'Belgian dentist' – has changed and the investor base is both varied and geographically dispersed worldwide.

The key feature of Eurobonds, which are also known as *international securities*, is the way they are issued, internationally across borders and by an international underwriting syndicate. The method of issuing Eurobonds reflects the cross-border nature of the transaction, and unlike government markets where the auction is the primary issue method, Eurobonds are typically issued under a 'fixed price re-offer' method or a 'bought deal'. There is also a regulatory distinction as no one central authority is responsible for regulating the market and overseeing its structure.

This chapter reviews the Eurobond market in terms of the structure of the market, the nature of the instruments themselves, the market players, the issuing process and technical aspects – such as taxation and swap arrangements.

EUROBONDS

A Eurobond is a debt capital market instrument issued in a 'Eurocurrency' through a syndicate of issuing banks and securities houses, and distributed internationally when issued – that is, sold in more than one country of issue and subsequently traded by market participants in several international financial centres. The Eurobond market is divided into sectors depending on the currency in which the issue is denominated. For example, US dollar Eurobonds are often referred to as *Eurodollar* bonds, similar sterling issues are called

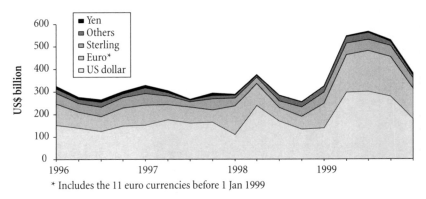

* Includes the 11 euro currencies before 1 Jan 1999

Figure 6.1   Non-government international bond issuance, 1996–1999.

Source: Bank of England.

Eurosterling bonds. The prefix 'Euro' was first used to refer to deposits of US dollars in continental Europe in the 1960s. The Euro-deposit now refers to any deposit of a currency outside the country of issue of that currency, and is not limited to Europe. For historical reasons and also due to the importance of the US economy and investor base, the major currency in which Eurobonds are denominated has always been US dollars. The volume of non-sovereign Eurobond issues from 1996 to 1999 is shown at Figure 6.1.

The first ever Eurobond is generally considered to be the issue of $15 million nominal of 10-year 5½% bonds by Autostrada, the Italian state highway authority, in July 1963.[1] The bonds were denominated in US dollars and paid an annual coupon in July each year. This coincides with the imposition in the US of the Interest Equalisation Tax, a withholding tax on domestic corporate bonds, which is often quoted as being a prime reason behind the establishment of overseas deposits of US dollars. Table 6.1 shows the diversity of the market with a selection of Eurobond issues in June 2005.

---

[1] Decovny (1998) states that the first Eurobond issue was in 1957, but its identity is not apparent.

Table 6.1 Selected Eurobond issues in first half of June 2005.

Issuer	Moody's/S&P rating	Coupon	Maturity	Issue size	Launch speed to benchmark (bps)
Daimler Chrysler NA	A3/BBB	4.875%	15 June 2010	USD 1,000 million	130
Development Bank of Japan	Aaa/AAA	4.25%	9 June 2015	USD 700 million	38.8
Federal Home Loan Bank	AAA	3.625%	20 June 2007	USD 4,000 million	17
GE Capital	Aaa/AAA	4.75%	15 June 2011	GBP 250 million	52
General Electric Capital Corp.	Aaa/AAA	4.00%	15 June 2009	USD 500 million	48
If Skadeforsakring AB	Baa2/BBB	4.943%	Perpetual/Callable	EUR 150 million	179.8; fixed coupon to June 2015, thereafter, 3-month Euribor + 265
ING Group N.V.	A2/A–	4.176%	Perpetual/Callable	EUR 500 million	95.3; fixed coupon to June 2015, thereafter, 3-month Euribor + 180
Kingdom of Belgium	Aa1/AA+	3.000%	28 March 2010	EUR 6,145 million	9
Korea Exchange Bank	Baa3/BB+	5.00%	10 June 2015	USD 300 million	151
Lambay Capital Securities	Baa1	FRN	Perpetual	GBP 300 million	3-month Libor + 166. Coupon step-up after 2015
LB Baden-Wuerttemberg	Aaa/AAA	6.50%	26 November 2007	NZD 50 million	23
Legal & General Group	A2/A	4.00%	8 June 2025	EUR 600 million	85.1
Portugal Telecom	A3/A–	4.50%	16 June 2025	EUR 500 million	137
Republic of El Salvador	Baa2/BB+	7.65%	15 June 2035	USD 375 million	345
Republic of Turkey	B1/BB–	7.00%	5 June 2020	USD 1,250 million	332.4
Zurich Finance (USA) Inc.	Baa2/BBB+	4.50%	15 June 2025	EUR 500 million	135.00 to June 2015; thereafter, 3-month Euribor + 220

FOREIGN BONDS

At this stage it is important to identify 'foreign bonds' and distinguish them from Eurobonds. Foreign bonds are debt capital market instruments that are issued by foreign borrowers in the domestic bond market of another country. As such, they trade in a similar fashion to the bond instruments of the domestic market in which they are issued. They are usually underwritten by a single bank or a syndicate of domestic banks, and are denominated in the currency of the market in which they are issued. For those familiar with the sterling markets, the best example of a foreign bond is a *Bulldog* bond, which is a sterling bond issued in the UK by a non-UK domiciled borrower. Other examples are *Yankee* bonds in the US, *Samurai* bonds in Japan, *Rembrandt* bonds in the Netherlands, *Matador* bonds in Spain, and so on. Hence, a US company issuing a bond in the UK, denominated in sterling and underwritten by a domestic bank would be issuing a Bulldog bond, which would trade

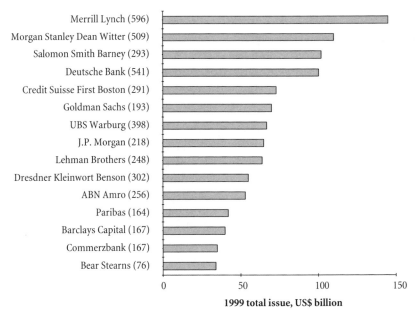

Figure 6.2   International Bond Issues in 1999, with leading book-runners (the number in parentheses is the number of issues). Note the disappearance of some of these names as at January 2006!
Source: The Economist.

as a gilt, except with an element of credit risk attached. In today's integrated global markets, however, the distinction is becoming more and more fine. Many foreign bonds pay gross coupons and are issued by a syndicate of international banks, so the difference between them and Eurobonds may be completely eroded in the near future.

The most important domestic market for foreign bond issues has been the US dollar market, followed by euros, Swiss francs and Japanese yen. There are also important markets in Canadian and Australian dollars, and minor markets in currencies such as Hong Kong dollars, Kuwaiti dinars and Saudi Arabian riyals.

EUROBOND INSTRUMENTS

There is a wide range of instruments issued in the Eurobond market, designed to meet the needs of borrowers and investors. We review the main types in this section.

Conventional bonds

The most common type of instrument issued in the Euromarkets is the conventional vanilla bond, with fixed coupon and maturity date. Coupon frequency is on an annual basis. The typical face value of such Eurobonds is $1,000, €1,000, £1,000 and so on. The bond is unsecured, and therefore depends on the credit quality of its issuer in order to attract investors. Eurobonds have a typical maturity of 5–10 years, although many high-quality corporates have issued bonds with maturities of 30 years or even longer. The largest Eurobond market is in US dollars, followed by issues in euros, Japanese yen, sterling and a range of other currencies such as Australian, New Zealand and Canadian dollars, South African rand and so on. Issuers will denominate bonds in a currency that is attractive to particular investors at the time, and it is common for bonds to be issued in more 'exotic' currencies, such as East European, Latin American and Asian currencies.

Eurobonds are not regulated by the country in whose currency the bonds are issued. They are typically registered on a national stock exchange, usually London or Luxembourg. Listing of the bonds enables certain institutional investors, who are prohibited from holding assets that are not listed on an exchange, to purchase them. The volume of trading on a registered stock exchange is negligible, however; virtually all trading is on an over-the-counter (*OTC*) basis directly between market participants.

Interest payments on Eurobonds are paid gross and are free of any withholding or other taxes. This is one of the main features of Eurobonds, as is the fact that they are 'bearer' bonds – that is, there is no central register. Historically, this meant that the bond certificates were bearer certificates with coupons attached; these days bonds are still designated 'bearer' instruments but are held in a central depository to facilitate electronic settlement.

Floating rate notes

An early innovation in the Eurobond market was the floating rate note (*FRN*). They are usually short- to medium-dated issues, with interest quoted as a spread to a reference rate. The reference rate is usually the London interbank offered rate (*Libor*), or the Singapore interbank offered rate for issues in Asia (*Sibor*). The euro interbank rate (*Euribor*) is also now commonly quoted. The spread over the reference rate is a function of the credit quality of the issuer, and can range from 10 to 150 basis points over the reference rate or even higher. Bonds typically pay a semiannual coupon, although quarterly coupon bonds are also issued. The first FRN issue was by ENEL, an Italian utility company, in 1970. The majority of issuers are financial institutions – such as banks and securities houses.

There are also perpetual, or undated, FRNs, the first issue of which was by National Westminster Bank plc in 1984. They are essentially similar to regular FRNs except that they have no maturity date and are therefore 'perpetual'. Most perpetual FRNs are issued by banks, for whom they are attractive because they are a means of raising capital, similar to equity but with the tax advantages associated with debt. They also match the payment characteristics of the bank's assets. Traditionally, the yield on perpetuals is higher than both conventional bonds and fixed-term FRNs.

Zero-coupon bonds

An innovation in the market from the late 1980s was the zero-coupon bond, or *pure discount* bond, which makes no interest payments. Like zero-coupon bonds initially in government markets, the main attraction of these bonds for investors was that, as no interest was payable, the return could be declared entirely as capital gain, thus allowing the bondholder to avoid income tax. Most jurisdictions including the US and UK have adjusted their tax legislation so that the return on zero-coupon bonds now counts as income and not capital gain.

Convertible bonds[2]

Another instrument that is common in the Eurobond market is the convertible bond. A Eurobond is convertible if it may be exchanged at some point for another instrument, usually the ordinary shares (equity) of the issuing company. The decision to elect to convert is at the discretion of the bondholder. Convertibles are analysed as a structure comprised of a conventional bond and an embedded option.

The most common conversion feature is an *equity convertible*, which is a conventional bond that is convertible into the equity of the issuer. The conversion feature allows the bondholder to convert the Eurobond, on maturity or at specified times during the bond's life, into a specified number of shares of the issuing company at a set price. In some cases the bond is convertible into the shares of the company that is guaranteeing the bond. The issuing company must release new shares in the event of conversion. The price at which the bond is convertible into shares, known as the 'exercise price', is usually set at a premium above the market price of the ordinary shares in the market on the day the bond is issued. Investors will exercise their conversion rights only if the market price has risen sufficiently that a gain will be realised by converting. The incorporation of a conversion feature in a bond is designed to make the bond more attractive to investors, as it allows them to gain from a rise in the issuing company's share price. The conversion feature also acts as a floor for the bond price.

The advantages of convertibles for borrowers include the following:

- as the bond incorporates an added attraction in the form of the conversion feature, the coupon payable on the bond is lower than it otherwise would be – this enables the borrower to save on interest costs;

---

[2] Convertible bonds are reviewed in Chapter 7.

- issuing convertibles is one method by which companies can broaden the geographical base of their equity holders;
- companies are usually able to raise a higher amount at one issue if the bond is convertible, compared with a conventional bond.

Against these factors must be weighed certain disadvantages associated with convertibles, which include the following:

- the investor's insurance against the volatility of share price movements – an attraction of the convertible – is gained at the cost of a lower coupon than would be obtained from a conventional bond;
- convertibles are often issued by companies that would have greater difficulty placing conventional paper. Convertibles are usually subordinated and are often viewed more as equity rather than debt. The credit and interest-rate risk associated with them is consequently higher than for conventional bonds.

Currency convertibles are bonds that are issued in one currency and are redeemed in another currency or currencies. Often this is at the discretion of the bondholder; other currency convertibles pay their coupon in a different currency to the one they are denominated in. In certain respects, currency convertibles possess similar characteristics to a conventional bond issued in conjunction with a forward contract. The conversion rate is specified at the time of issue, and may be either a fixed-rate option or a floating-rate option. With a fixed-rate option the exchange rate between the currencies is fixed for the entire maturity of the bond at the time it is issued; with a floating-rate option the exchange rate is not fixed and is the rate prevailing in the market at the time the conversion is exercised. Initially, most currency convertibles offered a fixed-rate option, so that the foreign exchange risk resided entirely with the issuer. Floating-rate options were introduced in the 1970s when exchange rates began to experience greater volatility.

THE ISSUE PROCESS: MARKET PARTICIPANTS

When a company raises a bond issue its main concerns will be the success of the issue, and the interest rate that must be paid for the funds borrowed. An issue is handled by an international syndicate of banks. A company wishing to make a bond issue will invite a number of investment banks and securities houses to bid for the role of lead manager. The bidding banks will indicate the price at which they believe they can get the issue away to investors, and the size of their fees. The company's choice of lead manager will be based not only on the bids, but also the reputation and standing of the bank in the market. The lead manager when appointed will assemble a syndicate of other banks to help with the issue. This syndicate will often be made up of banks from several different countries. The lead manager has essentially agreed to underwrite the issue, which means that he guarantees to take the paper off the issuer's hands (in return for a fee). If there is an insufficient level of investor demand for the bonds the lead manager will be left holding ('wearing') the issue, which in addition to being costly will not help its name in the market. When we referred to an issuer assessing the reputation of potential lead managers, this included the company's view on the 'placing power' of the bank, its perceived ability to get the entire issue away. The borrowing company would prefer the issue to be over-subscribed, which is when demand outstrips supply.

In many cases the primary issue involves a *fixed price re-offer* scheme. The lead manager will form the syndicate which will agree on a fixed issue price, a fixed commission and the distribution amongst themselves of the quantity of bonds they agreed to take as part of the syndicate. The banks then re-offer the bonds that they have been allotted to the market, at the agreed price. This technique gives the lead manager greater control over a Eurobond issue. It sets the price at which other underwriters in the syndicate can initially sell the bonds to investors. The fixed price re-offer mechanism is designed to prevent underwriters from selling the bonds back to the lead manager at a discount to the original issue price – that is, 'dumping' the bonds.

Before the bond issue is made, but after its basic details have been announced, it is traded for a time in the *grey market*. This is a term used to describe trading in the bonds before they officially come to the market – i.e., mainly market makers selling the bond short to other market players or investors. Activity in the grey market serves as useful market intelligence to the lead manager, who can gauge the level of demand that exists in the market for the issue. A final decision on the offer price is often delayed until dealing in the grey market indicates the best price at which the issue can be got away.

Let us now consider the primary market participants in greater detail.

The borrowing parties

The range of borrowers in the Euromarket is very diverse. From virtually the inception of the market, borrowers representing corporates, sovereign and local governments, nationalised corporations, supranational institutions and financial institutions have raised finance in the international markets. The majority of borrowing has been by governments, regional governments and public agencies of developed countries, although the Eurobond market is increasingly a source of finance for developing country governments and corporates.

Governments and institutions access the Euromarket for a number of reasons. Under certain circumstances it is more advantageous for a borrower to raise funds outside its domestic market, due to the effects of tax or regulatory rules. The international markets are very competitive in terms of using intermediaries, and a borrower may well be able to raise cheaper funds in them. Other reasons why borrowers access Eurobond markets include:

- a desire to diversify sources of long-term funding. A bond issue is often placed with a wide range of institutional and private investors, rather than the more restricted investor base that may prevail in a domestic market. This gives the borrower access to a wider range of lenders, and for corporate borrowers this also enhances the international profile of the company;
- for both corporates and emerging country governments, the prestige associated with an issue of bonds in the international market;
- the flexibility of a Eurobond issue compared with a domestic bond issue or bank loan, illustrated by the different types of Eurobond instruments available.

Against this are balanced the potential downsides of a Eurobond issue, which include the following:

- for all but the largest and most creditworthy of borrowers, the rigid nature of the issue procedure becomes significant during times of interest and exchange-rate volatility, reducing the funds available for borrowers;
- issuing debt in currencies other than those in which a company holds matching assets, or in which there are no prospects of earnings, exposes the issuer to foreign exchange risk.

Generally though, the Euromarket remains an efficient and attractive market in which a company can raise finance for a wide range of maturities.

The nature of the Eurobond market is such that the ability of governments and corporates to access it varies greatly. Access to the market for a first-time borrower has historically been difficult, and has been a function of global debt market conditions. There is a general set of criteria, first presented by van Agtmael (1983), that must be fulfilled initially, which for corporates includes the following:

- the company should ideally be domiciled in a country that is familiar to Eurobond issuers, usually as a result of previous offerings by the country's government or a government agency. This suggests that it is difficult for a corporate to access the market ahead of a first issue by the country's government;
- the borrowing company must benefit from a level of name recognition or, failing this, a sufficient quality credit rating;
- the company ideally must have a track record of success, and needs to have published financial statements over a sufficient period of time, audited by a recognised and respected firm, and the company's management must make sufficient financial data available at the time of the issue;
- the company's requirement for medium-term or long-term finance, represented by the bond issue, must be seen to fit into a formal strategic plan.

Generally, Eurobond issuers are investment-grade rated, and only a small number, less than 5%,[3] are not rated at all.

The underwriting lead manager

Issuers of debt in the Eurobond market select an investment bank to manage the bond issue for them. This bank is known as the underwriter because in return for a fee it takes on the risk of placing the bond amongst investors. If the bond cannot be placed in total, the underwriting bank will take on the paper itself. The issuer will pick an investment bank with whom it already has an existing relationship, or it may invite a number of banks to bid for the mandate. In the event of a competitive bid, the bank will be selected on the basis of the prospective coupon that can be offered, the fees and other

---

[3] *Source*: IMF.

expenses that it will charge, the willingness of the bank to support the issue in the secondary market, the track record of the bank in placing similar issues and the reach of the bank's client base. Often it is a combination of a bank's existing relationship with the issuer and its reputation in the market for placing paper that will determine whether or not it wins the mandate for the issue.

After the mandate has been granted, and the investment bank is satisfied that the issuer meets its own requirements on counterparty and reputational risk, both parties will prepare a detailed financing proposal for the bond issue. This will cover topics such as the specific type of financing, the size and timing of the issue, approximate pricing, fees and so on. The responsibilities of the lead manager include the following:

- analysing the prospects of the bond issue being accepted by the market – this is a function of both the credit quality of the issuer and the market's capacity to absorb the issue;
- forming the *syndicate* of banks to share responsibility for placing the issue – these banks are co-lead managers and syndicate banks;
- assisting the borrower with the prospectus, which details the bond issue and also holds financial and other information on the issuing company;
- assuming responsibility for the legal issues involved in the transaction, for which the bank's in-house legal team and/or external legal counsel will be employed;
- preparing the documentation associated with the issue;
- taking responsibility for the handling of the fiduciary services associated with the issue, which is usually handled by a specialised agent bank;
- if deemed necessary, establishing a pool of funds that can be used to stabilise the price of the issue in the *grey market*, used to buy (or sell) bonds if required.

These duties are usually undertaken jointly with other members of the syndicate. For first-time borrowers the prospectus is a very important document, as it is the main communication media used to advertise the borrower to investors. In a corporate issue, the prospectus may include the analysis of the company by the underwriters, financial indicators and balance sheet data, a detailed description of the issue specifications, the members of the underwriting syndicate and details of placement strategies. In a sovereign issue, the prospectus may cover a general description of the country's economy, including key economic indicators such as balance of payments figures and export and import levels, the state of the national accounts and budget, a description of the political situation (with an eye on the stability of the country), current economic activity, and a statement of the current external and public debt position of the country.

The co-lead manager

The function of the co-lead manager in Eurobond issues developed as a consequence of the distribution of placing ability across geographic markets. For example, as the Eurobond market developed, underwriters who were mainly US or UK banks did not have significant client bases in, say, the continental European market, and so banking houses that had a customer base there would be invited to take on some of the issue. For a long time the ability to place $500,000 nominal of a new Eurobond issue was taken as the benchmark against a potential co-lead manager.

The decision by a lead manager to invite other banks to participate will depend on the type and size of the issue. Global issues such as those by the World Bank, which have nominal sizes of $1 billion or more, have a fairly large syndicate. The lead manager will assess whether it can place all the paper or, in order to achieve geographic spread (which may have been stipulated by the issuer), it needs to form a syndicate. It is common for small issues to be placed entirely by a single lead manager.

Investors

The structure of the Eurobond market, compared with domestic markets, lends a certain degree of anonymity, if such is desired, to end-investors. This is relevant essentially in the case of private investors. The institutional holders of investors are identical to those in the domestic bond markets, and include institutional investors such as insurance companies, pension funds, investment trusts, commercial banks and corporations. Other investors include central banks and government agencies; for example, the Kuwait Investment Office and the Saudi Arabian Monetary Agency both have large Eurobond holdings. In the UK, banks and securities houses are keen holders of FRN Eurobonds, usually issued by other financial institutions.

FEES, EXPENSES AND PRICING
Fees

The fee structure for placing and underwriting a Eurobond issue
are relatively identical for most issues. The general rule is that
fees increase with maturity and decreasing credit quality of the
issuer, and decrease with nominal size. Fees are not paid directly
but are obtained by adjusting the final price paid to the issuer – that
is, taken out of the sale proceeds of the issue. The allocation of fees
within a syndicate can be slightly more complex, and in the form of
an *underwriting allowance*. This is usually paid out by the lead
manager.

Typical fees will vary according to the type of issue and issuer, and
also whether the bond itself is plain vanilla or more exotic. Fees
range from 0.25% to 0.75% of the nominal of an issue. Higher fees
may be charged for small issues.

Expenses

The expenses associated with the launch of a Eurobond issue vary
greatly. Table 6.2 illustrates the costs associated with a typical
Eurobond transaction. Not every bond issue will incur every
expense; however, these elements are common.

The expense items in Table 6.2 do not include the issuer's own
expenses with regard to financial accounting and marketing. The
reimbursement for underwriters is intended to cover such items as
legal expenses, travel, delivery of bonds and other business expenses.

In general, Eurobonds are listed on either the London or Luxembourg
Stock Exchanges. Certain issues in the Asian markets are listed on
the Singapore Exchange. To enable listing to take place an issuer will
need to employ a listing agent, although this is usually arranged by

Table 6.2   Expense elements, Eurobond issue.

Printing (prospectus, certificates, etc.)	Clearing and bond issuance
Legal counsel (issuer and investment bank)	Paying agent
Stock exchange listing fee	Trustee
Promotion	Custodian
Underwriter's expenses	Common depositary

the lead manager. The function of the listing agent is to (i) provide a professional opinion on the prospectus, (ii) prepare the documentation for submission to the stock exchange and (iii) make a formal application and conduct negotiations on behalf of the issuer.

Pricing

One of the primary tasks of the lead manager is the pricing of the new issue. The lead manager faces an inherent conflict of interest between its need to maximise its returns from the syndication process and its obligation to secure the best possible deal for the issuer, its client. An inflated issue price invariably causes the yield spread on the bond to rise as soon as the bond trades in the secondary market. This would result in a negative impression being associated with the issuer, which would affect its next offering. On the other hand, too low a price can permanently damage a lead manager's relationship with the client.

For Eurobonds that are conventional vanilla fixed-income instruments, pricing does not present too many problems in theory. The determinants of the price of a new issue are the same as those for a domestic bond offering, and include the credit quality of the borrower, the maturity of the issue, the total nominal value, the presence of any option feature, and the prevailing level and volatility of market interest rates. Eurobonds are perhaps more heavily influenced by the target market's ability to absorb the issue, and this is gauged by the lead manager in its preliminary offering discussions with investors. The credit rating of a borrower is often similar to that granted to it for borrowings in its domestic market, although in many cases a corporate will have a different rating for its foreign currency debt compared with its domestic currency debt.

In the grey market the lead manager will attempt to gauge the yield spread over the reference pricing bond at which investors will be happy to bid for the paper. The reference bond is the benchmark for the maturity that is equivalent to the maturity of the Eurobond. It is commonly observed that Eurobonds have the same maturity date as the benchmark bond that is used to price the issue. As lead managers often hedge their issue using the benchmark bond, an identical maturity date helps to reduce basis risk.

ISSUING THE BOND

The three key dates in a new issue of Eurobonds are the announcement date, the offering day and the closing day. Prior to the announcement date the borrower and the lead manager (and co-lead managers if applicable) will have had preliminary discussions to confirm the issue specifications, such as its total nominal size, the target coupon and the offer price. These details are provisional and may well be different at the time of the closing date. At these preliminary meetings the lead manager will appoint a fiscal agent or trustee, and a principal paying agent. The lead manager will appoint other members of the syndicate group, and the legal documentation and prospectus will be prepared.

On the announcement date the new issue is formally announced, usually via a press release. The announcement includes the maturity of the issuer and a coupon rate or range in which the coupon is expected to fall. A telex is also sent by the lead manager to each prospective underwriter, which is a formal invitation to participate in the syndicate. These banks will also receive the preliminary offering circular, a timetable of relevant dates for the issue and documentation that discloses the legal obligations that they are expected to follow should they decide to participate in the issue. The decision to join is mainly, but not wholly, a function of the bank's clients' interest in the issue, which the bank needs to sound out.

The *pricing day* signals the end of the subscription period, the point at which the final terms and conditions of the issue are agreed between the borrower and the syndicate group. If there has been a significant change in market conditions, the specifications of the bond issue will change. Otherwise, any required final adjustment of the price is usually undertaken by a change in the price of the bond relative to par. The ability of the lead manager to assess market conditions accurately at this time is vital to the successful pricing of the issue.

Once the final specifications have been determined, members of the syndicate have roughly 24 hours to accept or reject the negotiated terms; the bonds are then formally offered on the *offering day*, the day after the pricing day, when the issuer and the managing group sign the subscription or underwriting agreement containing the final specifications of the issue. The underwriting syndicate then enters into a legal commitment to purchase the bonds from the issuer at the price announced on the pricing day. A final offering circular is then produced, and the lead manager informs the syndicate of the amount of their allotments. The lead manager may wish to either over-allocate or under-allocate the number of available bonds, depending on its view on future levels and direction of interest rates. There then begins the *stabilisation period*, when the bonds begin to trade in the secondary period, where Eurobonds trade in an over-the-counter market. About 14 days after the offering day, the *closing day* occurs. This is when syndicate members pay for bonds they have purchased, usually by depositing funds into a bank account opened and run by the lead manager on behalf of the issuer. The bond itself is usually represented by a *global note*, held in Euroclear or Clearstream, initially issued in temporary form. The temporary note is later changed to a *permanent* global note. Tranches of an issue targeted at US investors may be held in the Depositary Trust Corporation as a registered note.

The grey market

The subscription period of a new Eurobond issue is characterised by uncertainty about potential changes in market conditions. After the announcement of the issue, but before the bonds have been formally issued, the bonds trade in the *grey market*. The grey market is where bonds are bought and sold pre-issue for settlement on the first settlement date after the offering day. Grey market trading enables the lead manager to gauge the extent of investor appetite for the issue, and make any adjustment to coupon if required. A grey market that functions efficiently will at any time reflect the market's view on where the bond should trade, and what yield the bond should be offered. It enables investors to trade in the primary market possessing information as to the likely price of the issue in the secondary market.

Another principal task of the lead manager is to stabilise the price of the bond issue for a short period after the bond has started trading in the secondary market. This is known as the stabilisation period, and the process is undertaken by the lead manager in concert with some or all of the syndicate members. A previously established pool of funds may be used for this purpose. The price at which stabilisation occurs is known as the *syndicate bid*.

Alternative issue procedures

In addition to the traditional issue procedure where a lead manager and syndicate offer bonds to investors based on a price set on pricing day, based on a yield over the benchmark bond, there are a number of other issue procedures that are used. One of these methods includes the *bought deal*, where a lead manager or a managing group approaches the issuer with a firm bid, specifying issue price, amount, coupon and yield. Only a few hours are allowed for the borrower to accept or reject the terms. If the bid is accepted, the lead manager purchases the entire bond issue from the borrower. The lead manager then has the option of selling part of the issue to other banks for distribution to investors, or doing so itself. In a volatile market the lead manager will probably parcel some of the issue to other banks for placement. However, it is at this time that the risk of banks dumping bonds on the secondary market is highest; in this respect lead managers will usually pre-place the bonds with institutional investors before the bid is made. The bought deal is focused primarily on institutional rather than private investors. As the syndicate process is not used, the bought deal requires a lead manager with sufficient capital and placement power to enable the entire issue to be placed.

In a *pre-priced offering* the lead manager's bid is contingent on its ability to form a selling group for the issue. Any alterations in the bid required for the formation of the group must be approved by the borrower. The period allocated for the formation of the group is usually 2–4 days, and after the group has been formed the process is identical to that for the bought deal.

Yet another approach is the *auction issue*, under which the issuer will announce the maturity and coupon of a prospective issue and invite interested investors to submit bids. The bids are submitted by banks, securities houses and brokers, and include both price and amount. The advantages of the auction process are that it avoids the management fees and costs associated with a syndicate issue. However, the issuer does not have the use of a lead manager's marketing and placement expertise, which means it is a method that can only be employed by very high quality, well-known borrowers.

COVENANTS

Eurobonds are unsecured and, as such, the yield demanded by the market for any particular bond will depend on the credit rating of the issuer. Until the early 1980s Eurobonds were generally issued without covenants, due to the high quality of most issuers. Nowadays it is common for covenants to be given with Eurobond issues. Three covenants in particular are frequently demanded by investors:

- a negative pledge;
- an 'event risk' clause;
- a gearing ratio covenant.

Negative pledge

A negative pledge is one that restricts the borrowings of the group which ranks in priority ahead of the debt represented by the Eurobond. In the case of an unsecured Eurobond issue this covenant restricts new secured borrowings by the issuer, as well as new unsecured borrowings by any of the issuer's subsidiaries, since these would rank ahead of the unsecured borrowings by the parent company in the event of the whole group going into receivership.

Disposal of assets covenant

This sets a limit on the number of assets that can be disposed of by the borrower during the tenor (term to maturity) of the debt. The limit on disposals could be, typically, a cumulative total of 30% of the gross assets of the company. This covenant is intended to prevent a break-up of the company without reference to the Eurobond investors.

Gearing ratio covenant

This places a restriction on the total borrowings of the company during the tenor of the bond. The restriction is set as a maximum percentage – say, 150–175% of the company's or group's net worth (share capital and reserves).

TRUST SERVICES

A Eurobond issue requires an agent bank to service it during its life. The range of activities required are detailed below.

Depositary

The depositary for a Eurobond issue is responsible for the safekeeping of securities. In the Euromarket well over 90% of investors are institutions, and so as a result issues are made in dematerialised form and are represented by a global note. Trading and settlement is in computerised book-entry form via the two main international clearing systems, Euroclear and Clearstream. Both these institutions have appointed a group of banks to act on their behalf as depositaries for book-entry securities; this is known as *common depositaries*, because the appointment is common to both Euroclear and Clearstream. Both clearing firms have appointed separately a network of banks to act as specialised depositaries, which handle securities that have been issued in printed note or *definitive* form.

As at February 2005 there were 20 banks that acted as common depositaries on behalf of Euroclear and Clearstream, although the majority of the trading volume was handled by just three banks, Citibank NA, JPMorgan Chase and Deutsche Bank. The common depositary is responsible for:

- representing Euroclear and Clearstream and facilitating delivery-versus-payment of the primary market issue by collecting funds from the investors, taking possession of the temporary global note (which allows securities to be released to investors) and making a single payment of funds to the issuer;
- holding the temporary global note in safe custody, until it is exchanged for definitive notes or a permanent global note;
- making adjustments to the nominal value of the global note that occur after the exercise of any options or after conversions, in line with instructions from Euroclear or Clearstream and the fiscal agent;
- surrendering the cancelled temporary global note to the fiscal agent after the exchange into definitive certificates or a permanent global note, or on maturity of the permanent global note.

A specialised depositary will hold definitive notes representing aggregate investor positions held in a particular issue; on coupon and maturity dates it presents the coupons or bond to the paying agent and passes the proceeds on to the clearing system.

Paying agent

Debt issuance in the Euromarkets requires a fiscal or principal paying agent, or in the case of a programme of issuance (e.g., a Euro-MTN programme) an issuing and paying agent. The responsibility of the paying agent is to provide administrative support to the issuer throughout the lifetime of the issue. The duties of a paying agent include:

- issuing securities upon demand in the case of a debt programme;
- authenticating definitive notes;
- collecting funds from the issuer and paying these out to investors as coupon and redemption payments;
- in the case of global notes, acting on behalf of the issuer to supervise payments of interest and principal to investors via the clearing systems, and in the case of definitive notes, paying out interest and coupon on presentation by the investor of the relevant coupon or bond to the paying agent;
- transferring funds to sub-paying agents, where these have been appointed – a security that has been listed in Luxembourg must have a local sub-paying agent appointed for it;
- maintaining an account of the cash flows paid out on the bond;
- arranging the cancellation and subsequent payment of coupons, matured bonds and global notes, and sending destroyed certificates to the issuer.

A paying agent will act solely on behalf of the issuer, unlike a trustee who has an obligation to look after the interests of investors. For larger bond issues there may be a number of paying agents appointed, of which the *principal paying agent* is the coordinator. A number of *sub-paying agents* may be appointed to ensure that bondholders in different country locations may receive their coupon and redemption payments without delay. The term *fiscal agent* is used to describe a paying agent for a bond issue for which no trustee has been appointed.

Registrar

The role of the registrar is essentially administrative; it is responsible for keeping accurate records of bond ownership for registered securities. As most Eurobonds are issued in bearer form, there is not a great deal of work for registrars in the Euromarket, and the number of holders of registered notes is normally quite low.

The responsibilities of the registrar include:

- maintaining a register of all bondholders and records of all transfers of ownership;
- coordinating the registration, transfer or exchange of bonds;
- issuing and authenticating new bonds should any transfer or exchange take place;
- maintaining a record of the outstanding principal value of the bond;
- undertaking administrative functions relating to any special transfers.

Trustee

An issuer may appoint a trustee to represent the interests of investors. In the event of default, the trustee is required to discharge its duties on behalf of bondholders. In certain markets a trustee is required by law – for instance, in the US a trustee has been a legal requirement since 1939. In other markets an issuer may appoint a trustee in order to make the bond issue more attractive to investors, as it means that there is an independent body to help look after their interests. This is particularly important for a secured issue, where the trustee sometimes holds collateral for the benefit of investors. Assets that are held by the trustee can be protected from the creditors of the issuer in the event of bankruptcy. A trustee has a variety of powers and discretion, which are stated formally in the issue trust deed, and these include its duties in relation to the monitoring of covenants and duties to bondholders.

Custodian

A custodian provides safekeeping services for securities belonging to a client. The client may be an institutional investor, such as a pension fund, that requires a portfolio of securities in many locations to be kept in secure custody on their behalf. As well as holding securities, the custodian usually manages corporate actions such as dividend payments.

FORM OF THE BOND

Eurobonds are issued in temporary global form or permanent global form. If issued in temporary form, the note is subsequently changed into either permanent global form or *definitive* form, which may be either a bearer note or registered.

Temporary global form

On issue the majority of Eurobonds are in the form of a single document known as a temporary global bond. This document represents the entire issue, executed by an officer of the issuer and certified by the fiscal agent or principal paying agent. After a period of time the temporary global bond, as its name suggests, is exchanged for either a permanent global bond or bonds in definitive form, which are separate certificates representing each bondholding.

The main reason bonds are issued in temporary form is because of time constraints between the launch of issue, when the offer is announced to the market, and closing, when the bonds are actually issued. This period differs according to the type of issue and instrument – for example, for a plain-vanilla issue it can be as little as 2 weeks whereas for more exotic issues (such as a securitisation) it can be a matter of months. The borrower will be keen to have the periods as short as possible, as the financing is usually required quickly. As this results in there being insufficient time to complete the security printing and authentication of the certificates, which represent the final definitive form, a temporary bond is issued to enable the offering to be closed and placed in a clearing system, while the final certificates are produced. Bonds are also issued in temporary form to comply with certain domestic selling regulations and restrictions. For example, there is a US regulation that definitive bonds cannot be delivered for a 40-day period after issue. This is known as the *lock-up* period.

Permanent global bond

Like the temporary bond the permanent global bond is a word-processed document and not a security-printed certificate, issued on the closing date. It represents the entire issue and is compiled by the underwriter's legal representatives. In most cases it is actually held for safekeeping on behalf of Euroclear and Clearstream by the trust or clearing arm of a bank, known as the *common depositary*. Borrowers often prefer to issue notes in permanent global form because this carries lower costs compared with definitive notes, which are security-printed.

Definitive form

Under any circumstances where it is required that investors have legal ownership of the debt obligation represented by a bond issue they have purchased, a borrower is obliged to issue the bond in definitive form. The situations under which this becomes necessary are listed on the permanent global bond document, and include the following:

- where an investor requires a definitive bond to prove legal entitlement to the bond (s)he has purchased, in the case of any legal proceedings undertaken concerning the bond issue;
- in the event of default, or if investors believe default to have occurred;
- where for any reason the bonds can no longer be cleared through a clearing system, in which case they must be physically delivered in the form of certificates.

Bonds issued in definitive form may be either *bearer* or *registered* securities. A bearer security has similar characteristics to cash money, in that the certificates are documents of value and the holder is considered to be the beneficiary and legal owner of the bond. The bond certificate is security-printed and the nature of the debt obligation is detailed on the certificate. Transfer of a bearer security is by physical delivery. Some of the features of traditional bearer securities include:

- *coupons*, attached to the side of the certificate, and which represent each interest payment for the life of the bond. The holder is required to detach each coupon as it becomes due and send it to the issuer's paying agent;[4]

---

[4] This is the origin of the term 'coupon' when referring to the periodic interest payments of a bond. There is a marvellous line in the film *Mission Impossible* when the character played by Tom Cruise, discussing terms in the back of a car with the character played by Vanessa Redgrave, demands payment in the form of US Treasury securities 'with coupons attached'. This is wonderfully out-of-date, but no less good fun for it!

- a *promise to pay*, much like a bank note, which confirms that the issuer will pay the bearer the face value of the bond on the specified maturity date;
- in some cases, a *talon* – this is the right for the bondholder to claim a further set of coupons once the existing set has been used (this only applies to bonds that have more than 27 interest payments during their lifetime, as IPMA rules prohibit the attachment of more than 27 coupons to a bond on issue).

The administrative burdens associated with bearer securities is the main reason why the procedures associated with them are carried out via the clearing systems and paying agents, rather than individually by each investor.

Registered bonds

Bonds issued in registered form are transferred by an entry on a *register* held by the issuer or its agent; the promise to pay is made to those names that appear on the register. Most Eurobonds are issued in bearer form for ease in clearing. Issues that are placed wholly or partly in the US do, however, include an option allowing investors to take the bonds in registered form. This is done as most issues in the US are sold under *private placement*, in order to be exempt from SEC selling restrictions, and private placement in that country requires that the bonds are in registered form. In such cases the issuer will appoint a New York *registrar* for the issuer, usually the trust arm of a bank.

Fiscal agent

A Eurobond issuer will appoint either a fiscal agent or a trustee; both perform similar roles but under differing legal arrangements. The fiscal agent is appointed by and is the representative of the issuer, so unlike a trustee it does not represent the bondholders. The main responsibilities of the fiscal agent are to pay the principal and interest payments, and it performs a number of administrative roles as well, such as the publication of financial information and notices to investors.

Listing agent

Issuers must appoint a listing agent if they wish to list the bond on the London or Luxembourg Stock Exchanges, as this is a requirement of the rules of the exchange. The listing agent communicates with the exchange on behalf of the issuer, and lodges the required documentation with it. In the UK the listing agent must be authorised under financial regulatory legislation (at the time of writing, the Financial Services Act 1986, although this is in the process of being updated with new legislation covering the new Financial Services Authority regulatory body). The listing agent is usually the lead manager for the issue, although it is also common for a fiduciary service provider to be appointed to this role.

CLEARING SYSTEMS

The development of the international bond market has taken place alongside the introduction of specialised clearing systems, which are responsible (among other things) for the settlement and safekeeping of Eurobonds. The two main clearing systems are Euroclear and Clearstream.[5]

Euroclear was created by the Morgan Guaranty Trust Company of New York in 1968. Ultimately, ownership passed to a consortium of banks. It is now run by Euroclear Clearance Systems plc, and operated by a cooperative company in Brussels.

The original Cedel was created in 1970 in Luxembourg and is owned by a consortium of around 100 banks, no one of which may hold more than 5% of the company. The two clearing systems do not restrict their operations to the settlement and custody of Eurobonds.

Both clearing systems exist to avoid the physical handling of bearer instruments, both on issue and in the secondary market. This means that on issue the actual bond certificates, which may be in *definitive bearer* or *global* form are passed on to a 'trust' bank, known as the *depositary* for safekeeping. The clearing system will track holdings via a book entry. To participate in the clearing system set-up, an investor must have two accounts with it, which may be its own accounts or accounts held by their bank who will act as a nominee on

---

[5] Clearstream was previously known as Cedel Bank.

their behalf; these are a *securities clearance* account, to which a security is credited, and a *cash* account, through which cash is received or paid out.

The clearing system will allocate a unique identification code, known as the International Securities Identification Number (*ISIN*) to each Eurobond issue, and a 'Common Code' is derived from the ISIN. The Common Code is essentially the identification used for each bond issue whenever an instruction is sent to the clearing agent to deal in it. The ISIN will be in addition to any number issued by a domestic clearing agent – for example, the Stock Exchange number (*SEDOL*) for London-listed securities. Both clearing systems have specific roles in both the primary and secondary markets. In the primary market they accept a new issue of Eurobonds, and on *closing* the required number of bonds are credited to the securities clearance account of the banks that are part of the issue syndicate. Securities are then transferred (electronic book entry) to the securities accounts of investors.

The clearance systems keep a record on the coupon payment and redemption dates for each bond, and 'present' the bonds for payment on each appropriate date. Investors therefore do not need to present any coupons or certificates themselves, which is why the system is now paperless.

MARKET ASSOCIATIONS

International Capital Market Association

The International Capital Market Association (*ICMA*) is a self-regulatory body based in Zurich whose membership (from over 60 countries) consists of firms dealing in the international securities markets. It was previously known as the International Securities Market Association, and prior to that as the Association of International Bond Dealers. The body provides a regulatory framework for the international markets and has established uniform practices that govern nearly all transactions in Eurobonds between members. ICMA has also:

- introduced a standard method of calculating yields for Eurobonds;

- contributed towards the harmonisation of procedures for settling market transactions, and cooperation between the two main settlement institutions, Euroclear and Cedel;
- introduced TRAX, a computerised system for matching and reporting transactions in the market.

Dealers in the international markets must cooperate with national governments and ensure that market practice is consistent with national laws. ICMA provides a point of contact between the markets and government bodies. The ICMA Centre at the University of Reading in England has also established itself as a leading research body, concentrating on the financial and securities markets, as well as offering master's degrees in a range of capital markets subjects.

BLOOMBERG SCREENS

Eurobonds can be analysed using all the Bloomberg screens available for bonds generally. Figure 6.3 shows Bloomberg screen NIM which is the new issues monitor. It shows all new and recent issues in the market, in this case as at 13 August 2003. Issues that were placed on preceding days are also shown. We see that on the day in question seven bonds were placed in the market, another two were announced or were beginning to be placed by their underwriters.

Figure 6.4 shows a screen that can be obtained from the FMC menu page on Bloomberg, which stands for 'fair market curve'. Using this page a user can select the yield curve for a number of market sectors; our example shows AAA-, A- and BBB-rated euro-denominated Eurobond curves as at 13 August 2003. The curves are labelled 'composite' because they take Eurobonds of the required rating from a number of different sectors, such as telecoms, utilities, industrials and so on.

SECONDARY MARKET

Most Eurobonds are tradeable, although the liquidity of individual issues is variable. Although in theory transfer is by physical delivery, because the bonds are bearer instruments the great majority of bonds will settle by the Euroclear or Clearstream International

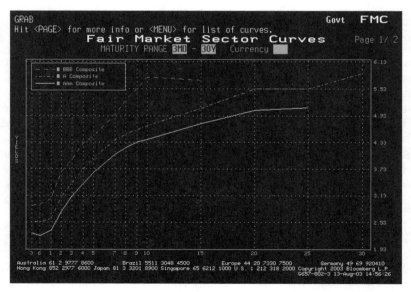

```
GRAB                                              Pfd    NIM
Enter # <GO> for DES.                           Page 1 / 22
New Issues: Euro Market - All             Phone: 44-20-7330-7333
                   Cpn    Mty     Sprd  Outstand   Book Mgr
     Issuer        (%)   (M/D/Y)  (BP)  Amt (Mil)  (*=group)  Note
               -------- WEDNESDAY, AUGUST 13 --------
 1) VOLKSWAGEN FIN  2⁷₈   08/29/05       EUR 50     DZBK-sole
 2) Standard Life Bank Begins Selling Floating-Rate Bonds in Euros
 3) ABN AMRO BOUWFON 3.65 08/22/08       EUR 40     DRES
 4) FREDDIE MAC     2³₄   08/15/06  +38  USD 5B     DB,ML,MS    PXD @ 99.923
 5) STANDARD LIFE   WI    08/26/05       EUR 250    DB,UBS      TO BE PRICED
 6) RABOBANK        1¹₄   04/30/07       CHF 200    CSFB,DB     INC BY 50MM
 7) EUROHYPO SA LUX 3¹₂   12/28/07 +116  USD 500    JOINT LEADS
 8) ERSTE EUROPAEISC FRN  09/19/05       CHF 200    UBS-sole    3ML FLAT
 9) Daimler to Sell $1.27 Bln in Asset-Backed Securities (Update2)
               -------- TUESDAY, AUGUST 12 --------
10) FANNIE MAE      4     09/02/08  +75  USD 1B     C,LEH,ML    PXD @ 99.935
11) BANCO BRADES CI 6³₄   08/20/10 +365  USD 200    ABN-sole
12) BANCO BRADES CI FRN   08/20/10       USD 200    ABN-sole    3ML +6B
13) SPIRIT FUNDING  FRN   03/28/18       GBP 66     GS          FUNGIBLE
14) SPIRIT FUNDING  FRN   12/28/31       GBP 41.5   GS          3ML +350
15) SPIRIT FUNDING  FRN   09/28/29       GBP 25     GS          FUNGIBLE
16) FHLMC Launches Sale of $5 Bln 3-Yr Reference Notes
17) GATX CORP       5     08/15/23       USD 115    C,DB,JPM    CVT-NC5
18) AUSTRIAN T-BILL ZERO  09/15/03       EUR 10                 1MO
Australia 61 2 9777 8600      Brazil 5511 3048 4500      Europe 44 20 7330 7500      Germany 49 69 920410
Hong Kong 852 2977 6000 Japan 81 3 3201 8900 Singapore 65 6212 1000 U.S. 1 212 318 2000 Copyright 2003 Bloomberg L.P.
                                                        G657-802-3 13-Aug-03 15:21:51
```

Figure 6.3   Bloomberg new issues monitor screen, as at 13 August 2005.

© Bloomberg L.P. Used with permission. Visit *www.bloomberg.com*

Figure 6.4   Fair market curves on Bloomberg screen FMC.

© Bloomberg L.P. Used with permission. Visit *www.bloomberg.com*

('Clearstream') settlement systems.[6] Liquidity in the market varies over time and for individual issues will be a function of:

• size of issue;
• level of investor demand for the paper;
• commitment of market makers to support the issue.

A large number of Eurobonds are illiquid and market makers will quote a bid price only. No offer price is made because the market maker (unless he actually owns some of the issue) will be unable to find bonds to deliver to the buyer if it is illiquid. Many Eurobonds issued in the second-tier currencies, such as Greek drachma, will have been issued and then immediately asset-swapped, and hence there will be no paper available to trade. (Many large issuers will issue Eurobonds in a currency other than that which they require, in order to meet a specific customer demand for paper in that currency; after issue the proceeds are swapped into the desired currency. In the meantime the bonds will be held to maturity by the investors and usually not traded in the secondary market.)

High-quality Eurobond issues will trade almost as government paper. For example, issues by the World Bank or the European Investment Bank (*EIB*) trade at very low spreads above the same currency government bonds and are highly liquid. At times EIB sterling Eurobonds have traded at only 7–9 basis points above the same maturity gilt.

SETTLEMENT

Settlement of Eurobond transactions takes place within 28 days for primary market issues and $T + 3$ days for secondary market trades. Virtually all trades settle within the two main clearing systems, Euroclear and Clearstream. Euroclear was established in Brussels in 1968 by an international group of banks, the original entity known as Cedel was established in Luxembourg in 1970. Both clearing systems will settle in $T + 3$ days; however, the facility exists to settle trades in $T + 1$ if both parties to a trade wish it.

In the Euroclear system bonds are placed in the custody of the clearing system through a Europe-wide network of depository

---

[6] In 1999 Cedel Bank and Deutsche Terminbörse merged their operations, and the resulting entity was named Clearstream International or simply Clearstream. Cedel Bank had originally been known as Cedel.

banks. The transfer of bonds on settlement is undertaken by means of a computer book entry. This was the basic concept behind the introduction of Euroclear, the substitution of book entries for the physical movement of bonds. The actual physical securities to which a trading party has title are not identified in the majority of transactions made through Euroclear. The clearing system is made possible because the terms and conditions of any Eurobond issue are objectively specified, so that all bonds of a particular issue are standardised, and so fungible for one another. There is no requirement to assign a specific bond serial number to an individual holder, which occurs with registered bonds. Clearstream operates on much the same basis. Participants in either system must be institutions with their own account (they may have an agent settle for them). Settlement takes place through the simultaneous exchange of bonds for cash on the books of the system. An 'electronic bridge' connecting the two systems allows transfer of securities from one to the other.

BIBLIOGRAPHY

Andersen, T. (1982). How the grey market became respectable. *Euromoney*, May.

Crawford, A. (1987). Stabilization brings the jitters. *Euromoney*, April, p. 277.

Decovny, S. (1998). *Swaps*, FT Prentice Hall, London, p. 68.

Kerr, I. (1984). *A History of the Eurobond Market*. Euromoney Publications, London.

Van Agtmael, A. (1983). Issuance of Eurobonds: Syndication and underwriting techniques and costs. In: A. George and I. Giddy (eds), *International Financial Handbook*. John Wiley & Sons, Chichester, UK, §5.2.

Chapter

7

....

CONVERTIBLE BONDS, MTNs AND WARRANTS

A significant segment of the Eurobond market is that of convertible bonds. Convertibles (and warrants) are instruments that have option features attached to them, issued primarily by corporates but also sometimes by governments. The option attachments act as a further inducement for investors, and which serve to make the instrument easier to sell than a plain-vanilla bond issued by the same company.

DESCRIPTION

A *convertible* bond is a bond that can be converted at the option of the holder into the ordinary shares of the issuing company. Once converted into ordinary shares, the shares cannot be exchanged back into bonds. The ratio of exchange between the convertible bond and the ordinary shares can be stated either in terms of a *conversion price* or a *conversion ratio*. For example, ABC plc's 10% convertible bonds, with a face value of £1,000, may have a conversion price of £8.50, which means that each bond is convertible into 117.64 ordinary shares. To obtain this figure we have simply divided the face value of the bond by the conversion price to obtain the conversion ratio, which is £1,000/£8.50 = 117.64 shares. The conversion privilege can be stated in terms of either the conversion price or the conversion ratio. Conversion terms for a convertible do not necessarily remain constant over time. In certain cases convertible issues will provide for increases or *step-ups* in the conversion price at periodic intervals. A £1,000 denomination face value bond may be issued with a conversion price of, say, £8.50 a share for the first 3 years, £10 a share for the next 3 years and £12 for the next 5 years and so on. Under this arrangement the bond will convert to fewer ordinary shares over time which, given that the share price is expected to rise during this period, is a logical arrangement. The conversion price is also adjusted for any corporate actions that occur after the convertibles have been issued, such as rights issues or stock dividends. For example, if there was a 2 for 1 rights issue, the conversion price would be halved. This provision protects the convertible bondholders and is known as an *anti-dilution* clause.

Analysis

We have already referred to the conversion ratio, which defines the number of shares of common stock that is received when the bond is converted; and the conversion price is the price paid for the shares when conversion takes place.

$$\text{Conversion price} = \frac{\text{Par value of bond}}{\text{Conversion ratio}} \qquad (7.1)$$

The *percentage conversion premium* is the percentage by which the conversion price exceeds the current share price. Let us assume a convertible with a conversion ratio of 20 (i.e., 20 shares are received in return for the bond with a par value of £100) and therefore a conversion price of £5.00. If the current price of the share is £3.70, then we have:

$$\text{Percentage conversion premium} = \frac{\text{Conversion price} - \text{Share price}}{\text{Share price}}$$

$$= \frac{£5 - £3.70}{£3.70}$$

$$= 35.14\% \qquad (7.2)$$

The *conversion value* of the bond is given by:

$$\text{Conversion value} = \text{Share price} \times \text{Conversion ratio}$$

This shows the current value of the shares received in exchange for the bond. If we say that the current share price is again £3.70, then the current conversion value is given by:

$$\text{Conversion value} = £3.70 \times 20$$

$$= £74.00$$

If the bond is trading at 82.50 (per 100), then the *percentage conversion price premium*, or the percentage by which the current bond price exceeds the current conversion value, is given by (7.3):

$$\text{Percentage conversion price premium} = \frac{\text{Price of bond} - \text{Conversion value}}{\text{Conversion value}} \qquad (7.3)$$

In our example:

$$\text{Premium value} = \frac{82.50 - 74.00}{74.00}$$

$$= 11.49\%$$

A convertible can be viewed as a conventional bond with a warrant attached to it. Its fair price will therefore be related to the price of a vanilla bond and the price of a call option, taking into account both the dilution effect of the new shares that are issued and the coupon payments that are saved as a result of conversion.

The proportionate increase in the number of shares outstanding if all the bonds are converted, referred to as q, is given by (7.4):

$$q = \frac{\text{Number of convertible bonds} \times \text{Conversion ratio}}{\text{Number of shares outstanding before conversion}} \quad (7.4)$$

The fair price of the convertible is given by (7.5):

$$\text{Price of convertible} = \text{Price of vanilla bond} + \frac{P^C}{1+q} \times \text{Conversion ratio}$$

$$(7.5)$$

where P^C = Value of an American call option with an exercise price equal to the conversion price and an expiry date equal to the maturity of the bond.

The price of the vanilla bond is calculated in exactly the same way as a standard bond in the same risk class.

Expression (7.5) will give us the fair price of a convertible if the bond is not callable. However, some convertibles are callable at the issuer's option prior to the final maturity date. The issuer can therefore force conversion when the share price has risen to the point where the value of the shares received on conversion equals the call price of the bond. Since the firm has a clear incentive to call the bond when this occurs, the call price puts an effective ceiling on the price of the convertible given in (7.5).

It is possible to calculate the likely call date for a callable convertible by using the expression at (7.6):

$$\text{Call price} = \text{Current share price} \times (1+g)^t \times \text{Conversion ratio} \quad (7.6)$$

where g = Expected growth rate in the share price;
          t = Time in years.

Let us then assume that the call price of the bond is £110 (i.e., £10 over par or face value), the conversion ratio is 20 and the current share price is £3.70 and is growing at 8.25% per year. Given that the right-hand side of expression (7.6) is the conversion value of the convertible in t years' time, it can be seen using (7.6) that the conversion value will equal the call price in 5 years. Therefore, the bond is likely to be called in 5 years' time.

If we look again at (7.5), and using our assumed terms and values, we can see that the price of the convertible depends on the price of a vanilla bond with 5 years to maturity (and a terminal value of £110) and a call option with 5 years to expiry. If we say that the vanilla bond has a fair price of 63.30, the call option has a premium of £1.20, and the proportionate increase in the number of shares is 25%, then the fair price of the convertible is shown below:

$$\text{Price of convertible} = £63.30 + \frac{£1.20}{1.25} \times 20$$

$$= £82.50$$

VALUE AND PREMIUM ISSUES

The attraction of a convertible for a bondholder lies in its structure being one of a combined vanilla bond and option. As we shall see in our introductory discussion of options, option valuation theory tells us that the value of an option increases with the price variance of the underlying asset. However, bond valuation theory implies that the value of a bond decreases with the price variance of the issuer's shares, because the probability of default is increased. Therefore, attaching an option to a bond will act as a kind of hedge against excessive downside price movement, while simultaneously preserving the upside potential if the firm is successful, since the bondholder has the right to convert to equity. Due to this element of downside protection, convertible bonds frequently sell at a premium over both their bond value and conversion value, resulting in the premium over conversion value that we referred to earlier. The conversion feature also leads to convertibles generally trading at a premium over bond value as well; the higher the market price of the ordinary share relative to the conversion price, the greater the resulting premium.

Example 7.1   Consider the following euro convertible bond currently trading at 104.80.

Denomination:	£1,000
Coupon:	4.50%
Maturity:	15 years
Conversion price:	£25 per share

The issuer's shares are currently trading at £19.50.

(a) Number of shares into which the bond is convertible:

$$\text{Conversion ratio} = \frac{\text{£1,000}}{25}$$

$$= 40$$

(b) Parity or conversion value:

$$\frac{\text{Current share price}}{\text{Conversion price}} \times 100 = 78\%$$

(c) Effective conversion price:

$$\frac{\text{Price of convertible}}{\text{Conversion ratio}} = 2.62$$

(i.e., £26.20 per £1,000).

(d) Conversion premium:

$$\frac{((c) - \text{Current share price})}{\text{Current share price}} \times 100\% = 34.36\%$$

(e) Conversion premium – alternative formula:

$$\text{Convertible price/Parity} = 34.36\%$$

(f) What do the following represent in terms of intrinsic value and time value?

Parity: parity value reflects the equity value of the bond.

Premium: the ratio of the bond price divided by parity value; this includes a measure of time value.

WARRANTS

A warrant is an option issued by a firm to purchase a given number of shares in that firm (*equity warrant*) or more of the firm's bonds (*bond warrant*), at a given exercise price at any time before the warrant expires. If the warrant is exercised, the firm issues new shares (or bonds) at the exercise price and so raises additional finance. Warrants generally have longer maturities than conventional options – 5 years or longer, although these days it is not difficult to trade very long-dated over-the-counter (*OTC*) equity options – and some warrants are perpetual.

Warrants are usually attached to bonds (*host bond*) to start with; in most cases such warrants are detachable and can be traded separately. Equity warrants do not carry any shareholder's rights until they are exercised – for example, they pay no dividends and have no voting rights. Bond warrants can either be exercised into the same class of bonds as the host bond or into a different class of bond. In valuing a warrant it is important to recognise that exercising the warrant (unlike exercising an ordinary call option) will increase the number of shares outstanding. This will have the effect of diluting earnings per share and hence reducing the share price. Hence, an equity warrant can be valued in the same way as an American call option, but also taking into account this dilution effect.

As with ordinary options the value of a warrant has two components, an intrinsic value (which in warrant terminology is called the *formula value*) and a time value (*premium* over formula value). The formula value is determined by equation (7.7):

Formula value = (Share price – Exercise price)

$$\times \text{ Number of new shares issued on exercise} \quad (7.7)$$

If the exercise price exceeds the share price, the formula value is 0 and the warrant is said to be 'out-of-the-money'. If the share price exceeds the exercise price the warrant is in-the-money and the formula value is positive. The time value is always positive up until expiry of the warrant. As with options the time value declines as the expiry date approaches, and on the expiry date itself the time value is 0.

The fair price of a warrant is given by (7.8):

$$\text{Warrant value} = \frac{P^C}{1+q} \times \frac{\text{Number of new shares issued}}{\text{if warrant is exercised}} \quad (7.8)$$

where q = Proportionate increase in the number of shares outstanding if all the warrants were exercised;

P^C = Value of an American call option with the same exercise price and expiry date as the warrant.

A warrant is attractive to investors because if the firm is successful and its share price rises accordingly, the warrant can be exercised and the holder can receive higher-value shares at the lower exercise price. Virtually all warrants are issued by corporations and are equity warrants. In the late 1980s the Bank of England introduced *gilt warrants* which could be exercised into gilts; however, none is in existence at present. It is of course possible to trade in OTC call options on gilts with any number of banks.

MEDIUM-TERM NOTES

Medium-term notes (*MTNs*) are corporate debt securities ranging in maturity from 9 months to 30 years. As with vanilla bonds the issuer promises to pay the noteholder a specified sum (usually par) at maturity. The unique characteristic of MTNs is that they are offered to investors continually over a period of time by an agent of the issuer. Notes can be issued either as *bearer* securities or *registered* securities. The market originated in the US (where the first issue was introduced by Merrill Lynch in 1981 for Ford Motor Credit) to close the funding gap between *commercial paper* and long-term bonds.

A Euromarket in MTNs developed in the mid-1980s. Euro MTNs (*EMTNs*) trade in a similar fashion to Eurobonds; they are debt securities issued for distribution across markets internationally. After initial liquidity problems the market grew in size considerably and is now fairly liquid.

MTN programme

Issues of MTNs are arranged within a programme. A continuous MTN programme is established with a specified issue limit, and sizes can vary from $100 million to $2,000 million or more. Within the programme, MTNs can be issued at any time, daily if required. The programme is similar to a revolving loan facility; as maturing notes are redeemed, new notes can be issued. The issuer usually specifies the maturity of each note issue within a programme, but cannot exceed the total limit of the programme.

Example 7.2   ABC plc.

ABC plc establishes a 5-year $200 million MTN programme and immediately issues the following notes:

$50 million of notes with a 1-year maturity
$70 million of notes with a 5-year maturity

> ABC plc can still issue a further $80 million of notes; however, in 1 year's time when $50 million of notes mature, it will be able to issues a further $50 million if required. The total amount in issue at any one time never rises above $200 million.

Interest on MTNs is paid on a 30/360-day basis, the same arrangement for Eurobonds. Within the MTN market there is a variety of structures on offer, including floating-rate MTNs, amortising MTNs and multi-currency MTNs.

Shelf registration

Under regulations in the US, any corporate debt issued with a maturity of more than 270 days must be registered with the Securities and Exchange Commission (*SEC*). In 1982 the SEC adopted Rule 415 which permitted shelf registration of new corporate debt issues. A continuous MTN programme can be registered in this way. The issuer must file with the SEC details on (i) historical and current financial information and (ii) the type and number of securities it plans to issue under the programme. This is known as 'filing a shelf'. The adoption of Rule 415 made the administration of continuously offered notes relatively straightforward for the issuer.

Credit rating

MTNs are unsecured debt. A would-be issuer of MTNs will usually seek a credit rating for its issue from one or more of the main rating agencies, such as Moody's or Standard & Poor's. The rating is given by the agency for a specific amount of possible new debt; should the issuer decide to increase the total amount of MTNs in issue it will need to seek a review of its credit rating. Because MTNs are unsecured, only the higher rated issuers, with an 'investment grade' rating for their debt, are usually able to embark on a revolving facility. There is no liquid market in 'junk'-rated MTNs.

Secondary market

A liquid secondary market in MTNs was first established in the US market by Merrill Lynch which undertook to quote bid prices to any investor wishing to sell MTNs before maturity, provided that the investor had originally bought the notes through Merrill Lynch. In other words, Merrill's was guaranteeing a secondary market to issuers that sold notes through it. This undertaking was repeated by other banks, resulting in a market that is now both large and liquid. That said, MTNs are not actively traded and market makers do not quote real-time prices on dealing screens. The relatively low volume of secondary market trading stems from a disinclination of investors to sell notes they have bought, rather than a lack of market liquidity.

Issuers and investors

The main issuers of MTNs in the US market are:

- general finance companies;
- banks, both domestic and foreign;
- governments and government agencies;
- supranational bodies such as the World Bank;
- domestic, industrial and commercial companies;
- savings and loan institutions.

There is a large investor demand in the US for high-quality corporate paper, much more so than in Europe where the majority of bonds are issued by financial companies. This demand is particularly great at the short- to medium-term maturity end. Because the market has a large number of issuers, investors are able to select issues that meet precisely their requirements for maturity and credit rating. The main investors are:

- investment companies;
- insurance companies;
- banks;
- savings and loan institutions;
- corporates;
- state institutions.

It can be seen that the investor base is very similar to the issuer base!

All the main US investment banks make markets in MTNs, including Merrill Lynch, Goldman Sachs, Morgan Stanley, Credit Suisse and Citigroup. In the UK active market makers in MTNs include RBoS and Barclays Capital.

MTNs and corporate bonds

A company wishing to raise a quantity of medium-term or long-term capital over a period of time can have the choice of issuing MTNs or long-dated bonds. An MTN programme is a series of issues over time, matching the issuer's funding requirement, and therefore should be preferred over a bond by companies that do not need all the funding at once, nor for the full duration of the programme. Corporate bonds are preferred where funds are required immediately. They are also a better choice for issuers that expect interest rates to rise in the near future and wish to lock in a fixed borrowing rate for all the funds required.

Example 7.3   Reverse FRN with swap.

A subsidiary of Citibank that engages in investment activity requires US dollar funding. A proportion of its funds are raised as part of a $5 billion EMTN programme. Due to demand for sterling assets, they issue a 5-year, pounds sterling, reverse floating rate MTN as part of the MTN programme, with the following details:

Issue size	£15 million
Issue date	20 January 1998
Maturity	21 January 2003
Rate payable	9% from 20/1/98 to 20/7/98
	19% − (2 × LIBOR6mo)
	thereafter to maturity
Price at issue	98.92
Proceeds	£14,838,000

As the issuer requires US dollar funding, it swaps the proceeds into dollars in the market in a cross-currency swap, and pays US dollar 3-month Libor for this funding. On termination the original currencies are swapped back and the note redeemed. This is shown in Figure 7.1 (overleaf).

Start 21/07/98

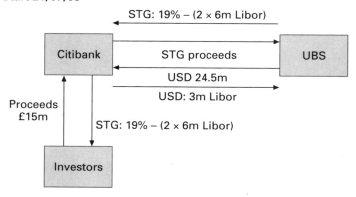

Termination 21/01/03

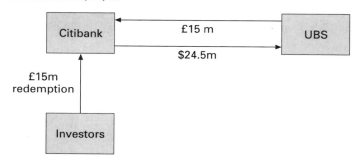

Figure 7.1   Reverse FRN with swap.

Chapter

8

....

CREDIT RATINGS

The risks associated with holding a fixed-interest debt instrument are closely connected with the ability of the issuer to maintain the regular coupon payments as well as redeem the debt on maturity. Essentially, *credit risk* is the main risk of holding a bond. Only the highest quality government debt, and a small number of supranational issues, may be considered to be entirely free of credit risk. Therefore, at any time the yield on a bond reflects investors' views on the ability of the issuer to meet its liabilities as set out in the bond's terms and conditions. A delay in paying a cash liability as it becomes due is known as technical default and is a cause for extreme concern for investors; failure to pay will result in the matter being placed in the hands of the legal court as investors seek to recover their funds. To judge the ability of an issue to meet its obligations for a particular debt issue, for the entire life of the issue, requires judgemental analysis of the issuer's financial strength and business prospects. There are a number of factors that must be considered, and larger banks, fund managers and corporates carry out their own *credit analysis* of individual borrowers' bond issues. The market also makes a considerable use of formal *credit ratings* that are assigned to individual bond issues by a formal credit rating agency. In the international markets arguably the two influential ratings agencies are Standard & Poor's Corporation (*S&P*) and Moody's Investors Service, Inc. (*Moody's*), based in the US. Fitch Investors Service, Inc. (*Fitch*) also has a high profile.[1]

The specific factors that are considered by a ratings agency, and the methodology used in conducting the analysis, differ slightly amongst the individual ratings agencies. Although in many cases the ratings assigned to a particular issue by different agencies are the same, they occasionally differ, and in these instances investors usually seek to determine what aspect of an issuer is given more weight in an analysis by which individual agency. Note that a credit rating is not a recommendation to buy (or, equally, sell) a particular bond, nor is it a comment on market expectations. Credit analysis does take into account general market and economic conditions; the overall purpose of credit analysis is to consider the financial health of the issuer and its ability to meet the obligations of the specific issue being rated. Credit ratings play a large part in the decision-making of

---

[1] Fitch and IBCA previously merged to become FitchIBCA and subsequently Fitch Investors Service, usually referred to simply as 'Fitch'.

investors, and also have a significant impact on the interest rates payable by borrowers.

CREDIT RATINGS

A credit rating is a formal opinion given by a rating agency, of the *credit risk* for investors in a particular issue of debt securities. Ratings are given to public issues of debt securities by any type of entity, including governments, banks and corporates. They are also given to short-term debt such as commercial paper as well as bonds and medium-term notes.

Purpose of credit ratings

Investors in securities accept the risk that the issuer will default on coupon payments or fail to repay the principal in full on the maturity date. Generally, credit risk is greater for securities with a long maturity, as there is a longer period for the issuer potentially to default. For example, if a company issues 10-year bonds, investors cannot be certain that the company will still exist in 10 years' time. It may have failed and gone into liquidation some time before that. That said, there is also risk attached to short-dated debt securities; indeed, there have been instances of default by issuers of commercial paper, which is a very short-term instrument.

The prospectus or offer document for an issue provides investors with some information about the issuer so that some credit analysis can be performed on the issuer before the bonds are placed. The information in the offer documents enables investors themselves to perform their own credit analysis by studying this information before deciding whether or not to invest. Credit assessments take up time, however, and also require the specialist skills of credit analysts. Large institutional investors do in fact employ such specialists to carry out credit analysis; however, often it is too costly and time-consuming to assess every issuer in every debt market. Therefore, investors commonly employ two other methods when making a decision on the credit risk of debt securities:

- name recognition;
- formal credit ratings.

Name recognition is when the investor relies on the good name and reputation of the issuer and accepts that the issuer is of such good financial standing, or sufficient financial standing, that a default on interest and principal payments is highly unlikely. An investor may feel this way about, say, Microsoft or British Petroleum plc. However, the experience of Barings in 1995 suggested to many investors that it may not be wise to rely on name recognition alone in today's market place. The tradition and reputation behind the Barings name allowed the bank to borrow at the London Interbank Offer Rate (*Libor*) and occasionally at sub-Libor interest rates in the money markets, which put it on a par with the highest-quality clearing banks in terms of credit rating. However, name recognition needs to be augmented by other methods to reduce the risk against unforeseen events, as happened with Barings. Credit ratings are a formal assessment, for a given issue of debt securities, of the likelihood that the interest and principal will be paid in full and on schedule. They are increasingly used to make investment decisions about corporate or lesser-developed government debt.

Formal credit ratings

Credit ratings are provided by the specialist agencies, including S&P's, Fitch and Moody's.[2] There are other agencies both in the US and other countries. On receipt of a formal request the credit rating agencies will carry out a rating exercise on a specific issue of debt capital. The request for a rating comes from the organisation planning the issue of bonds. Although ratings are provided for the benefit of investors, the issuer must bear the cost. However, it is in the issuer's interest to request a rating as it raises the profile of the bonds, and investors may refuse to buy paper that is not accompanied with a recognised rating. Although the rating exercise involves a credit analysis of the issuer, the rating is applied to a specific debt issue. This means that, in theory, the credit rating is applied not to an organisation itself, but to specific debt securities that the organisation has issued or is planning to issue. In practice, it is common for the market to refer to the creditworthiness of organisations themselves in terms of the rating of their debt. A highly-rated company such as Commerzbank is therefore referred to as a 'triple-A rated' company, although it is the bank's debt issues that are rated as triple-A.

---

[2] The first ever credit rating was published by John Moody in the US in 1909, in a document that rated US Railway bonds.

The rating for an issue is kept constantly under review, and if the credit quality of the issuer declines or improves the rating will be changed accordingly. An agency may announce in advance that it is reviewing a particular credit rating, and may go further and state that the review is a precursor to a possible downgrade or upgrade. This announcement is referred to as putting the issue under *credit watch*. The outcome of a credit watch is in most cases likely to be a rating downgrade; however, the review may re-affirm the current rating or possibly upgrade it. During the credit watch phase the agency will advise investors to use the current rating with caution. When an agency announces that an issue is under credit watch, the price of the bonds will fall in the market as investors look to sell out of their holdings. This upward movement in yield will be more pronounced if an actual downgrade results. For example, in October 1992 the government of Canada was placed under credit watch and subsequently lost its AAA credit rating; as a result, there was an immediate and sharp sell-off in Canadian government Eurobonds, before the rating agencies had announced the actual results of their credit review.

Credit ratings vary between agencies. Separate categories are used by each agency for short-term debt (with original maturity of 12 months or less) and long-term debt of over 1 year original maturity. It is also usual to distinguish between higher 'investment grade' ratings where the credit risk is low and lower quality 'speculative grade' ratings, where the credit risk is greater. High-yield bonds are speculative-grade bonds and are generally rated no higher than double-B, although some issuers have been upgraded to triple-B in recent years and a triple-B rating is still occasionally awarded to a high-yield bond. A summary of long-term ratings is shown at Table 8.1 (overleaf).

Ratings can be accessed on the Bloomberg system. Composite pages are shown at Figures 8.1 and 8.2 (see p. 193) – Bloomberg screen RATD.

Table 8.1 Summary of credit rating agency bond ratings.

Fitch	Moody's	S&P	Summary description
Investment grade – high credit quality			
AAA	Aaa	AAA	Gilt edged, prime, lowest risk, risk-free
AA+	Aa1	AA+	⎫
AA	Aa2	AA	⎬ High-grade, high credit quality
AA−	Aa3	AA−	⎭
A+	A1	A+	⎫
A	A2	A	⎬ Upper-medium grade
A−	A3	A−	⎭
BBB+	Baa1	BBB+	⎫
BBB	Baa2	BBB	⎬ Lower-medium grade
BBB−	Baa3	BBB−	⎭
Speculative – lower credit quality			
BB+	Ba1	BB+	⎫
BB	Ba2	BB	⎬ Low grade; speculative
BB−	Ba3	BB−	⎭
B+	B1	B+	⎫
B	B2	B	⎬ Highly speculative
B−	B3	B−	⎭
Highly speculative, substantial risk or in default			
		CCC+	⎫
CCC	Caa	CCC	⎬ Considerable risk, in poor standing
		CCC−	⎭
CC	Ca	CC	May already be in default, very speculative
C	C	C	Extremely speculative
		CI	Income bonds – no interest being paid
DDD			⎫
DD			⎬ Default
D		D	⎭

Source: Rating agencies.

LONG-TERM RATING SCALES COMPARISON — Page 1/2

MOODY'S	Aaa	Aa1	Aa2	Aa3	A1	A2	A3	Baa1	Baa2	Baa3
S&P	AAA	AA+	AA	AA-	A+	A	A-	BBB+	BBB	BBB-
COMP	AAA	AA+	AA	AA-	A+	A	A-	BBB+	BBB	BBB-
TBW	AAA	AA+	AA	AA-	A+	A	A-	BBB+	BBB	BBB-
FITCH	AAA	AA+	AA	AA-	A+	A	A-	BBB+	BBB	BBB-
CBRS	AAA	AA+	AA	AA-	A+	A	A-	BBB+	BBB	BBB-
DOMINION	AAA	AAH	AA	AAL	AH	A	AL	BBBH	BBB	BBBL
R&I	AAA	AA+	AA	AA-	A+	A	A-	BBB+	BBB	BBB-
JCR	AAA	AA+	AA	AA-	A+	A	A-	BBB+	BBB	BBB-
MI	AAA		AA			A			BBB	

Note: white = investment grade, yellow = non-investment grade

Australia 61 2 9777 8600   Brazil 5511 3048 4500   Europe 44 20 7330 7500   Germany 49 69 920410
Hong Kong 852 2977 6000 Japan 81 3 3201 8900 Singapore 65 6212 1000 U.S. 1 212 318 2000 Copyright 2005 Bloomberg L.P.
G479-793-0 29-Mar-05 7:50:48

Figure 8.1   Bloomberg screen RATD showing rating agency investment grade ratings scale.

© Bloomberg L.P. Used with permission. Visit *www.bloomberg.com*

LONG-TERM RATING SCALES COMPARISON — Page 2/2

MOODY'S	Ba1	Ba2	Ba3	B1	B2	B3	Caa1	Caa2	Caa3	Ca	C	
S&P	BB+	BB	BB-	B+	B	B-	CCC+	CCC	CCC-	CC	C	D
COMP	BB+	BB	BB-	B+	B	B-	CCC+	CCC	CCC-	CC	C	DDD
TBW	BB+	BB	BB-	CCC+	CCC	CCC-	CC+	CC	CC-			D
FITCH	BB+	BB	BB-	B+	B	B-	CCC+	CCC	CCC-	CC	C	D
CBRS	BB+	BB	BB-	B+	B	B-					C	D
DOMINION	BBH	BB	BBL	BH	B	BL	CCCH	CCC	CCCL	CC	C	D
R&I	BB+	BB	BB-	B+	B	B-	CCC+	CCC	CCC-	CC+	CC	CC-
JCR	BB+	BB	BB-	B+	B	B-		CCC		CC	C	D
MI		BB			B		CCC		CC			DDD

Note: white = investment grade, yellow = non-investment grade

Australia 61 2 9777 8600   Brazil 5511 3048 4500   Europe 44 20 7330 7500   Germany 49 69 920410
Hong Kong 852 2977 6000 Japan 81 3 3201 8900 Singapore 65 6212 1000 U.S. 1 212 318 2000 Copyright 2005 Bloomberg L.P.
G479-793-0 29-Mar-05 7:51:33

Figure 8.2   Bloomberg screen RATD showing rating agency sub-investment grade ratings scale.

© Bloomberg L.P. Used with permission. Visit *www.bloomberg.com*

Chapter

9

....

INFLATION-LINKED BONDS

Certain countries have markets in bonds whose coupon or final redemption payment, or both, are linked to their consumer price indexes. Generally, the most liquid markets in these *inflation-indexed*, or *index-linked*, debt instruments are the ones for government issues. Investors' experiences with the bonds differ, since the securities were introduced at different times in different markets and so are designed differently. In some markets, for instance, only the coupon payment, and not the redemption value, is index-linked. This makes comparisons in terms of factors such as yield difficult and has in the past hindered arbitrageurs seeking to exploit real yield differences. This chapter highlights the basic concepts behind indexed bonds and how their structures may differ from market to market.

BASIC CONCEPTS

The features considered in the design of index-linked bonds are the type of index, the indexation lag, the coupon frequency and the type of indexation.

Choice of index

In principle, bonds can be linked to almost any variable, including various price indexes, earnings measures, GDP output, specific commodities and the exchange rate of foreign currencies against another currency. Ideally, the chosen index should reflect the hedging requirements of both parties – i.e., the issuer and the investor. Their needs, however, may not coincide. For instance, retail investors overwhelmingly favour indexation to consumer prices, to hedge against inflation, which erodes bond earnings. Pension funds, on the other hand, prefer linking to earnings levels, to offset their earnings-linked pension liabilities. In practice, most bonds have been tied to inflation indexes, since these are usually widely circulated, well-understood and issued on a regular basis. US Treasury inflation-indexed securities (*TIIS*) or Treasury inflation-protected securities (*TIPS*), for instance, are linked to the US Consumer Price Index (*CPI-U*), the non-seasonally adjusted average of prices for urban consumers. The securities' daily interest accrual is based on straight-line interpolation, and there is a 3-month lag. So, for example, the October 2003 index level is used to determine the adjustment for 1 January 2004. Figure 9.1 is the Bloomberg DES

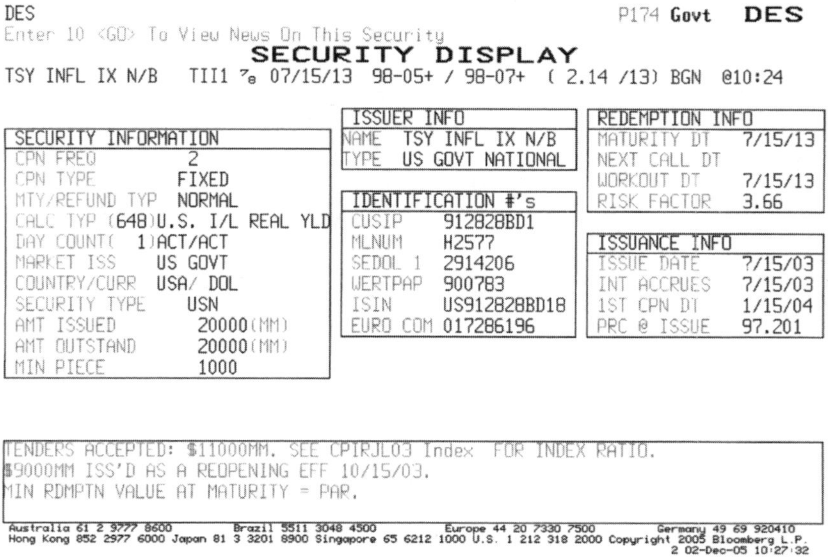

• •

```
DES                                              P174 Govt   DES
Enter 10 <GO> To View News On This Security
                  SECURITY DISPLAY
TSY INFL IX N/B   TII1 ⅞ 07/15/13  98-05+ / 98-07+  ( 2.14 /13) BGN  @10:24
```

SECURITY INFORMATION		ISSUER INFO		REDEMPTION INFO	
CPN FREQ	2	NAME TSY INFL IX N/B		MATURITY DT	7/15/13
CPN TYPE	FIXED	TYPE US GOVT NATIONAL		NEXT CALL DT	
MTY/REFUND TYP	NORMAL			WORKOUT DT	7/15/13
CALC TYP (648)U.S. I/L REAL YLD		IDENTIFICATION #'s		RISK FACTOR	3.66
DAY COUNT(1)ACT/ACT		CUSIP	912828BD1		
MARKET ISS	US GOVT	MLNUM	H2577	ISSUANCE INFO	
COUNTRY/CURR	USA/ DOL	SEDOL 1	2914206	ISSUE DATE	7/15/03
SECURITY TYPE	USN	WERTPAP	900783	INT ACCRUES	7/15/03
AMT ISSUED	20000(MM)	ISIN	US912828BD18	1ST CPN DT	1/15/04
AMT OUTSTAND	20000(MM)	EURO COM	017286196	PRC @ ISSUE	97.201
MIN PIECE	1000				

```
TENDERS ACCEPTED: $11000MM. SEE CPIRJL03 Index FOR INDEX RATIO.
$9000MM ISS'D AS A REOPENING EFF 10/15/03.
MIN RDMPTN VALUE AT MATURITY = PAR.
```

Australia 61 2 9777 8600   Brazil 5511 3048 4500   Europe 44 20 7330 7500   Germany 49 69 920410
Hong Kong 852 2977 6000 Japan 81 3 3201 8900 Singapore 65 6212 1000 U.S. 1 212 318 2000 Copyright 2005 Bloomberg L.P.
                                                                          2 02-Dec-05 10:27:32

Figure 9.1   Bloomberg DES Screen for the July 2013 TIPS.

© Bloomberg L.P. Used with permission. Visit *www.bloomberg.com*

('description') screen for the TIPS maturing in July 2013. Figure 9.2 shows the yield analysis page for this bond as at 2 December 2005.

Figure 9.3 is the DES screen for the CPI index in July 2003, which was the base month for this security when it was issued.

Indexation lag

To provide precise protection against inflation, interest payments for a given period would need to be corrected for actual inflation over the same period. Lags, however, exist between the movements in the price index and the adjustment to the bond cash flows. According to Deacon and Derry (1998), such lags are unavoidable for two reasons. First, inflation statistics for 1 month are usually not known until well into the following month and are published some time after that. This causes a lag of at least 1 month. Second, in some markets the size of a coupon payment must be known before the start of the coupon period in order to calculate the accrued interest. There is thus a delay – between the date the coupon amount is fixed and the

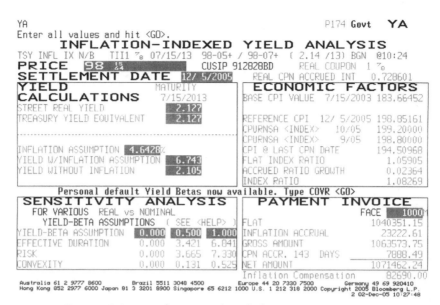

Figure 9.2 YA for same bond shown in Figure 9.1.

© Bloomberg L.P. Used with permission. Visit *www.bloomberg.com*

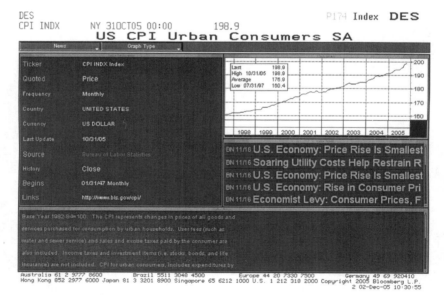

Figure 9.3 Bloomberg DES screen for the July 2003 Consumer Price Index.

© Bloomberg L.P. Used with permission. Visit *www.bloomberg.com*

time the inflation rate for the period affecting that payment is known – that is equal to the length of time between coupon payments. Deacon and Derry (1998) also note that the lag can be minimised – for example, by basing the accrued interest calculation on cumulative movements in the consumer price index since the last coupon date, as is done for Canadian Real Return Bonds.

Coupon frequency

Index-linked bonds often pay interest semiannually. Certain long-dated investors, such as fund managers whose liabilities include inflation-indexed annuities, may be interested in indexed bonds that pay on a quarterly or even monthly basis.

Type of indexation

There are five basic methods of linking the cash flows from a bond to an inflation index: interest indexation, capital indexation, zero-coupon indexation, annuity indexation and current pay. Which method is chosen depends on the requirements of the issuers and of the investors they wish to attract. The principal factors considered in making this choice, according to Deacon and Derry (1998), are duration, reinvestment risk and tax treatment.

Interest indexation Interest-indexed bonds have been issued in Australia, although not since 1987. They pay a coupon fixed rate at a real – inflation-adjusted – interest rate. They also pay a principal adjustment (equal to the percentage change in the CPI from the issue date times the principal amount) every period. The inflation adjustment is thus fully paid out as it occurs, and no adjustment to the principal repayment at maturity is needed.

Capital indexation Capital-indexed bonds have been issued in the US, Australia, Canada, New Zealand and the UK. Their coupon rates are specified in real terms, meaning that the coupon paid guarantees the real amount. For example, if the coupon is stated as 2%, what the buyer really gets is 2% after adjustment for inflation. Each period this rate is applied to the inflation-adjusted principal amount to produce the coupon payment amount. At maturity the principal repayment is the product of the bond's nominal value times the cumulative change in the index since issuance. Compared with interest-indexed bonds of similar maturity, these bonds have longer durations and lower reinvestment risk.

Zero-coupon indexation   Zero-coupon indexed bonds have been issued in Sweden. As their name implies, they pay no coupons; the entire inflation adjustment occurs at maturity, applied to their redemption value. These bonds have the longest duration of all indexed securities and no reinvestment risk.

In the US, Canada and New Zealand, indexed bonds can be stripped, allowing coupon and principal cash flows to be traded separately. This obviates the need for specific issues of zero-coupon indexed securities, since the market can create products such as deferred-payment indexed bonds in response to specific investor demand. In markets allowing stripping of indexed government bonds, a strip is simply a single cash flow with an inflation adjustment. An exception to this is in New Zealand, where the cash flows are separated into three components: the principal, the principal inflation adjustment and the inflation-linked coupons – the latter being an indexed annuity.

Annuity indexation   Indexed-annuity bonds have been issued in Australia, although not by the central government. They pay a fixed annuity payment plus a varying element that compensates for inflation. These bonds have the shortest duration and highest reinvestment risk of all index-linked debt securities.

Current pay   Current-pay bonds have been issued in Turkey. They are similar to interest-indexed bonds in that their redemption payments at maturity are not adjusted for inflation. They differ, however, in their term cash flows. Current-pay bonds pay an inflation-adjusted coupon plus an indexed amount that is related to the principal. In effect, they are inflation-indexed floating-rate notes.

Duration   Duration measures something slightly different for an indexed bond than it does for a conventional bond, indicating price sensitivity to changes in real, inflation-adjusted interest rates, instead of in nominal, unadjusted ones. As with conventional bonds, however, the duration of zero-coupon indexed bonds is longer than that of equivalent coupon bonds. As noted above, indexed annuities will have the shortest duration of the inflation-linked securities.

Investors with long-dated liabilities should theoretically prefer hedging instruments with long durations.

Reinvestment risk   Like holders of a conventional bond, investors in a coupon indexed bond are exposed to reinvestment risk: because they cannot know in advance what rates will be in effect when the bond's coupon payments are made, investors cannot be sure when they purchase their bond what yield they will earn by holding it to maturity. Bonds, such as indexed annuities, that pay more of their return in the form of coupons carry more reinvestment risk. Indexed zero-coupon bonds, like their conventional counterparts, carry none.

Tax treatment   Tax treatment differs from market to market and from product to product. Some jurisdictions, for example, treat the yearly capital gain on zero-coupon bonds as current income for tax purposes. This is a serious drawback, since the actual gain is not available until maturity, and it reduces institutional demand for these instruments.

INDEX-LINKED BOND CASH FLOWS AND YIELDS

As noted above, index bonds differ in whether their principal payments or their coupons, or both, are linked to the index. When the principal alone is linked, each coupon and the final principal payment are determined by the ratio of two values of the relevant index. US TIPS' coupon payments, for instance, are calculated using an accretion factor based on the ratio between two CPI-U levels, defined by equation (9.1):

$$IR_{Set\ date} = \frac{CPI_{Settlement}}{CPI_{Issue}} \qquad (9.1)$$

where

$IR_{Set\ date}$ = Index ratio;
$Settlement$ = Bond's settlement date
$Issue$ = Bond's issue date;
CPI_{M-3} = CPI level 3 months before the bond's redemption date;
$CPI_{Settlement}$ and CPI_{Issue} = Consumer price index levels recorded 3 months before the relevant dates.

For a settlement or issue date of 1 May, for instance, the relevant CPI level would be the one recorded on 1 February. For a settlement or

issue occurring on any day besides the first of the month, linear
interpolation is used to calculate the appropriate CPI level. This
is done by subtracting the reference month's CPI-U level from the
following month's level, then dividing the difference by the number
of days between the readings and multiplying the result by the
number of days in the month leading up to the reference date. As
an illustration, consider an issue date of 7 April. The relevant index
level would be the one for 7 January. Say the 1 January CPI-U level is
160.5 and the 1 February level 160.6. The difference between these
two values is:

$$160.6 - 160.5 = 0.10.$$

Dividing this difference by the number of days between 1 January
and 1 February gives:

$$\frac{0.10}{31} = 0.003\,225\,81$$

and multiplying the result by the number of days in January before
the reference date gives:

$$0.003\,225\,81 \times 6 = 0.193\,55$$

So, the CPI-U for January 7 is $160.5 + 0.19$, or 160.69.

TIPS cash flow calculations

TIPS periodic coupon payments and their final redemption payments
are both calculated using an inflation adjustment. Known as the
inflation compensation, or IC, this is defined as in expression (9.2):

$$IC_{Set\ date} = (P \times IR_{Set\ date}) - P \qquad (9.2)$$

where $P =$ Bond's principal.

The semiannual coupon payment, or interest, on a particular dividend date is calculated using equation (9.3):

$$Interest_{Div\ date} = \frac{C}{2} \times (P + IC_{Div\ date}) \qquad (9.3)$$

where $C =$ Annual coupon rate.

The principal repayment is computed as in expression (9.4). Note
that the redemption value of a TIPS is guaranteed by the Treasury to

be a minimum of \$100 – i.e., 100% of the face value.

$$\text{Principal repayment} = 100 \times \frac{CPI_{M-3}}{CPI_0} \qquad (9.4)$$

where $CPI_0 = Base$ CPI level – that is, the level 3months before the bond's issue date.

TIPS price and yield calculations

The price of a TIPS comprises its real price plus any accrued interest, both of which are adjusted for inflation by multiplying them times the index ratio for the settlement date. The bond's unadjusted accrued interest, as explained in Chapter 1, is calculated using expression (9.5):

$$\frac{C}{2} \times \frac{(d-f)}{d} \qquad (9.5)$$

where $f =$ Number of days from the settlement date to the next coupon date;

$d =$ Number of days in the regular semiannual coupon period ending on the next coupon date;

$C =$ Unadjusted coupon payment.

The TIPS real price is given by equation (9.6):

$$\text{Real price} = \left[\frac{1}{1+\frac{f}{d}\frac{r}{2}}\right]\left(\frac{C}{2}+\frac{C}{2}\sum_{j=1}^{n}\phi^{j}+100\phi^{n}\right) - RAI \quad (9.6)$$

where $\phi = \left(\dfrac{1}{1+\dfrac{r}{2}}\right)$;

$r =$ TIPS real annual yield;

$RAI =$ Unadjusted accrued interest;

$n =$ Number of full semiannual coupon periods between the next coupon date and the maturity date.

Example 9.1   TIPS coupon and redemption payment calculation.

Consider a TIPS issued on 15 January 1998, with coupon of 3.625% and a maturity date of 15 January 2008. The base CPI-U level for the bond is the one registered in October 1997. Say this is 150.30. Assume that the CPI for October 2007, the relevant computing level for the January 2008 cash flows, is 160.5. Using these values, the final coupon payment and principal repayment per $100 face value will be:

$$\text{Coupon payment} = \frac{3.625}{2} \times \frac{160.5}{150.3} = \$1.9355$$

$$\text{Principal repayment} = 100 \times \frac{160.5}{150.3} = \$106.786$$

The markets use two main yield measures for all index-linked bonds: the *money*, or *nominal yield*, and the *real yield*. Both are varieties of yield to maturity.

To calculate a money yield for an indexed bond, it is necessary to forecast all its future cash flows. This requires forecasting all the relevant future CPI-U levels. The market convention is to take the latest available CPI reading and assume a constant future inflation rate, usually 2.5% or 5%. The first relevant future CPI level is computed using equation (9.7):

$$CPI_1 = CPI_0 \times (1 + \tau)^{m/12} \qquad (9.7)$$

where $CPI_1 =$ Forecast CPI level;
        $CPI_0 =$ Latest available CPI;
        $\tau =$ Assumed future annual inflation rate;
        $m =$ Number of months between CPI_0 and CPI_1.

Consider an indexed bond that pays coupons every June and December. To compute its yield, it is necessary to forecast the CPI levels registered 3 months before June and 8 months before December – that is, the October and April levels. Say this computation takes place in February. The first CPI level that must be forecast is thus next April's. This means that in equation (9.7), $m = 2$. Say the February CPI is 163.7. Assuming an annual inflation rate of 2.5%, the CPI for the following April is computed as follows:

$$CPI_1 = 163.7 \times (1.025)^{2/12}$$

$$= 164.4$$

Equation (9.8) is used to forecast the subsequent relevant CPI levels:

$$CPI_{j+1} = CPI_1 \times (1 + \tau)^{(j+1)/2} \qquad (9.8)$$

where $j =$ Number of semiannual forecasts after CPI_1.

The forecast CPI level for the following October is calculated as follows:

$$CPI_2 = 164.4 \times (1.025)^{1/2}$$

$$= 168.5$$

Once the CPIs have been forecast, the bond's yield can be calculated. Assuming that the analysis is carried out on a coupon date so that accrued interest is 0, the money yield of a bond paying semiannual coupons is calculated by solving equation (9.9) for r_i:

$$P_d = \frac{\left(\frac{C}{2}\right)\left(\frac{CPI_1}{CPI_0}\right)}{\left(1+\frac{1}{2}r_i\right)} + \frac{\left(\frac{C}{2}\right)\left(\frac{CPI_2}{CPI_0}\right)}{\left(1+\frac{1}{2}r_i\right)^2} + \cdots + \frac{\left(\left[\frac{C}{2}\right]+M\right)\left(\frac{CPI_N}{CPI_0}\right)}{\left(1+\frac{1}{2}r_i\right)^N} \quad (9.9)$$

where $\quad r_i =$ Semiannual money yield;
$\quad\quad\quad N =$ Number of coupon payments (interest periods) up to maturity;
$\quad\quad\quad M =$ Bond principal;
$\quad\quad\quad C =$ Unadjusted coupon payment.

The equation for indexed bonds paying annual coupons is (9.10):

$$P_d = \frac{C\left(\frac{CPI_1}{CPI_0}\right)}{(1+r_i)} + \frac{C\left(\frac{CPI_2}{CPI_0}\right)}{(1+r_i)^2} + \cdots + \frac{(C+M)\left(\frac{CPI_N}{CPI_0}\right)}{(1+r_i)^N} \quad (9.10)$$

The real yield, ry, first described by Fisher in *Theory of Interest* (1930), is related to the money yield through equation (9.11) – for bonds paying semiannual coupons:

$$(1+\tfrac{1}{2}ry) = (1+\tfrac{1}{2}ri)/(1+\tau)^{\frac{1}{2}} \quad (9.11)$$

To illustrate this relationship, say the money yield is 5.5% and the forecast inflation rate is 2.5%. The real yield would then be:

$$ry = \left\{ \frac{[1+\frac{1}{2}(0.055)]}{[1+(0.025)]^{\frac{1}{2}}} - 1 \right\} \times 2 = 0.0297 \quad \text{or } 2.97\%$$

Re-arranging equation (9.11) to express ri in terms of ry and substituting the resulting expression for ri in equation (9.9) gives equation (9.12), which can be solved to give the real yield, calculated on a coupon date, of index bonds paying semiannual coupons:

$$P_d = \frac{CPI_a}{CPI_0} \left[\frac{\left(\frac{C}{2}\right)(1+\tau)^{\frac{1}{2}}}{\left(1+\frac{1}{2}ri\right)} + \frac{\left(\frac{C}{2}\right)(1+\tau)}{\left(1+\frac{1}{2}ri\right)^2} + \cdots + \frac{\left(\left\{\frac{C}{2}\right\}+M\right)(1+\tau)^{\frac{N}{2}}}{\left(1+\frac{1}{2}ri\right)^N} \right]$$

$$= \frac{CPI_a}{CPI_0} \left[\frac{\left(\frac{C}{2}\right)}{\left(1+\frac{1}{2}ry\right)} + \cdots + \frac{\left(\frac{C}{2}\right)+M}{\left(1+\frac{1}{2}ry\right)^N} \right] \tag{9.12}$$

where $CPI_a = \dfrac{CPI_1}{(1+\tau)^{\frac{1}{2}}}$;

CPI_0 = Base index level;

$\dfrac{CPI_a}{CPI_0}$ = Rate of inflation between the bond's issue date and the date the yield calculation is carried out.

The equations for money yield and real yield can be interpreted as indicating what redemption yield to employ as the discount rate in calculating the present value of an index bond's future cash flows. From this perspective, equation (9.9) shows that the money yield is the appropriate rate for discounting money or nominal cash flows. Equation (9.12) shows that the real yield is the appropriate rate for discounting real cash flows.

Assessing yields on index-linked bonds

Index-linked bonds do not offer complete protection against a fall in the real value of an investment. These bonds, including TIPS, do not have guaranteed real returns, despite having their cash flows linked to a price index such as the CPI. The reason for this is the lag in indexation, which for TIPS is 3 months. The time lag means that an indexed bond is not protected against inflation for the last interest period of its life. Any inflation occurring during the final interest period will not be reflected in the bond's cash flows and will reduce the real value of the redemption payment and hence the bond's real yield. This may not be a major consideration when the inflation rate is low, but it can be a worry for investors when the rate is high. The only way to effectively eliminate inflation risk is to reduce the time lag in indexation of payments to 1 or 2 months.

Bond analysts frequently compare the yields on index-linked bonds with those on conventional bonds of the same maturity to determine the market's expectation with regard to inflation rates. Of course, many factors can influence the gap between conventional and indexed bond yields, including supply and demand, and liquidity (conventional bonds are generally more liquid than indexed ones). A large part of the difference, however, is the inflation *premium*, which reflects the market's expectations about inflation during the life of the bond. To determine the implied expectation, analysts calculate the *break-even inflation rate*: the rate for which the money yield on an index-linked bond equals the redemption yield on a conventional bond of the same maturity.

Which to hold: indexed or conventional bonds?

Accepting that developed, liquid markets, such as that for Treasuries, are efficient, with near-perfect information available to most if not all participants, then the inflation expectation is built into the conventional treasury yield. If the inflation premium understates what certain market participants expect, investors will start buying more of the index-linked bond in preference to the conventional bond. This activity will force the indexed yield down (or the conventional yield up). If, on the other hand, investors think that the implied inflation rate overstates expectations, they will buy more of the conventional bond.

The higher yields of the conventional bonds compared with those of the index-linked bonds represent compensation for the effects of inflation. Bondholders will choose to hold index-linked bonds instead of conventional ones if they are worried about unexpected inflation. An individual's view on future inflation will depend on several factors, including the current macroeconomic environment and the credibility of the monetary authorities, be they the central bank or the government. Fund managers take their views of inflation, among other factors, into account in deciding how much of the TIPS and how much of the conventional Treasury to hold. Investment managers often hold indexed bonds in a portfolio against specific index-linked liabilities, such as pension contracts that increase their payouts in line with inflation each year.

In certain countries, such as the UK and New Zealand, the central bank has explicit inflation targets, and investors may believe that over the long-term those targets will be met. If the monetary authorities have good track records, investors may further believe that inflation is not a significant issue. In such situations, the case for holding index-linked bonds is weakened.

Indexed bonds' real yields in other markets are also a factor in investors' decisions. The integration of markets around the world in the past 20 years has increased global capital mobility, enabling investors to shun markets where inflation is high. Over time, therefore, expected returns should be roughly equal around the world, at least in developed and liquid markets, and so should real yields. Accordingly, index-linked bonds should have roughly similar real yields, whatever market they are traded in.

The yields on indexed bonds in the US, for example, should be close to those in the UK indexed market. In May 1999, however, long-dated indexed bonds in the US were trading at a real yield of 3.8%, compared with just 2% for long-dated index-linked gilts. Analysts interpreted this difference as a reflection of the fact that international capital was not as mobile as had been thought and that productivity gains and technological progress in the US had boosted demand for capital there to such an extent that the real yield had had to rise.

BIBLIOGRAPHY

Deacon and Derry (1998). *Inflation-linked Securities*. FT Prentice Hall, London.
Fisher (1930). *Theory of Interest*. Oxford University Press, Oxford, UK.

Chapter

10

....

AN INTRODUCTION TO SECURITISED BONDS[1]

---

[1] This chapter was co-authored with Anuk Teasdale of YieldCurve.com.

There is a large group of bond instruments that trade under the overall heading of *asset-backed bonds*. These are created by bundling together a set of non-marketable assets – such as bank loans, mortgages, credit-card loans or other assets – and issuing bonds that are backed by this pool of assets. This process is known as *securitisation*, when an institution's loan (assets) are removed from its balance sheet and packaged together as one large loan, and then 'sold' on to an investor, or series of investors, who then receive the interest payments due on the assets until they are redeemed. The purchasers of the securitised assets often have no recourse to the original borrowers; in fact, the original borrowers are not usually involved in the transaction or any of its processes.

Securitisation was introduced in the US market, and this market remains the largest for asset-backed bonds. The earliest examples of such bonds were in the US mortgage market, where residential mortgage loans made by a *thrift* (building society) were packaged together and sold on to investors who received the interest and principal payments made by the borrowers of the original loans. The process benefited the original lender in a number of ways. One key benefit was that removing assets from the balance sheet reduced risk exposure for the bank and enhanced its liquidity position.

The effect of these benefits is increased with the maturity of the original loans. For example, in the case of mortgage loans, the term to maturity can be up to 25 years, perhaps longer. The bulk of these loans are financed out of deposits that can be withdrawn on demand, or at relatively short notice. In addition, it is often the case that, as a result of securitisation, the packaged loans are funded at a lower rate than that charged by the original lending institution. This implies that the bundled loans can be sold off at a higher value than the level at which the lending institution valued them. Put another way, securitising loans adds value to the loan book and it is the original lender that receives this value. Another benefit is that, as a result of securitisation, the total funding available to the lending institution may well increase due to its access to capital markets; in other words, the firm becomes less dependent on its traditional deposit base. And, finally, by reducing the level of debt on the lending institution's balance sheet, it will improve the firm's gearing ratio.

The main advantage to the investor of securitisation is that it offers a marketable asset-backed instrument to invest in. Often the instrument offers two levels of protection, the original assets and *credit enhancement*. The original assets will provide good security if they are well-diversified and equivalent in terms of quality, terms and conditions (e.g., the repayment structure and maturity of assets). A diversified asset base reduces the risk of a single drastic failure, while homogeneous assets make it more straightforward to analyse the loan base. If there is little or no liquidity in the original loans (no secondary market) then investors will often require credit enhancement in the form of an insurance contract, letters of credit, subordination of a second tranche which absorbs losses first, over-collateralisation (having more underlying assets than is represented by the amount of bonds issued) or a reserve fund, for the instrument to be sold at a price acceptable to the original lender. Ironically, by implementing one or more of the protection features described, securitisation provides a better credit risk for the investor than the loans represented to the original lender.

Securitisation began in the US housing market in 1970 after the Government National Mortgage Association (*GNMA* or 'Ginnie Mae') began issuing *mortgage pass-through certificates*. A pass-through is a security representing ownership in a pool of mortgages. The mortgages themselves are sold through a grantor trust and the certificates are sold in the capital markets. As with standard mortgages the interest and amortised principal are paid monthly. Later on, *mortgage-backed bonds* were issued with semiannual payments and maturities of up to 15 years, which were terms familiar to domestic bondholders. In 1983 *collateralised mortgage obligations* were issued, the collateral provided by mortgages issued by the Federal Home Loans Mortgage Corporation. Being government agencies, the bonds that they issue are guaranteed and, as such, carry little additional risk compared with US Treasury securities. They can therefore be priced on the same basis as Treasuries. However, they present an additional type of risk, that of *pre-payment risk*. This is the risk that mortgages will be paid off early, ahead of their term, a risk that increases when mortgages have been taken out at high fixed-interest rates and rates have subsequently fallen. The existence of this risk therefore dictates that these bonds pay a higher return than corresponding Treasury bonds. The term *average life* is used to describe the years to maturity for asset-backed bonds that have an element of pre-payment risk about them, and is obviously an estimate used by bond analysts.

Securitisation was introduced in the UK market in 1985. A number of institutions were established for the purpose of securitising mortgages and other assets such as car loans and credit-card debt. These included National Home Loans Corporation, Mortgage Funding Corporation and First Mortgage Securities.

In this chapter we introduce the basic concepts of securitisation and look at the motivation behind their use, as well as their economic impact. We illustrate the process with a brief hypothetical case study.

THE CONCEPT OF SECURITISATION

Securitisation is a well-established practice in the global debt capital markets. It refers to the sale of assets, which generate cash flows, from the institution that owns them, to another company that has been specifically set up for the purpose, and the issuing of notes by this second company. These notes are backed by the cash flows from the original assets. The technique was introduced initially as a means of funding for US mortgage banks. Subsequently, the technique was applied to other assets such as credit-card payments and leasing receivables. It has also been employed as part of asset/liability management, as a means of managing balance sheet risk.

Securitisation allows institutions such as banks and corporates to convert assets that are not readily marketable – such as residential mortgages or car loans – into rated securities that are tradeable in the secondary market. The investors that buy these securities gain an exposure to these types of original assets that they would not otherwise have access to. The technique is well-established and was first introduced by mortgage banks in the US during the 1970s. The later synthetic securitisation market is much more recent, dating from 1997. The key difference between cash and synthetic securitisation is that in the former, as we have noted, the assets in question are actually sold to a separate legal company known as a special purpose vehicle (SPV).[2] This does not occur in a synthetic transaction, as we shall see.

Sundaresan (1997) defines securitisation as:

.... *a framework in which some illiquid assets of a corporation or a financial institution are transformed into a package of*

---

[2] An SPV is also referred to as a special purpose entity (SPE) or a special purpose company (SPC).

*securities backed by these assets, through careful packaging,
credit enhancements, liquidity enhancements and structuring*

(p. 359)

The process of securitisation creates asset-backed bonds. These are
debt instruments that have been created from a package of loan
assets on which interest is payable, usually on a floating basis. The
asset-backed market is a large, diverse market containing a wide
range of instruments. Techniques employed by investment banks
today enable an entity to create a bond structure from any type of
cash flow; assets that have been securitised include loans such as
residential mortgages, car loans and credit-card loans. The loans
form assets on a bank or finance house balance sheet, which are
packaged together and used as backing for an issue of bonds. The
interest payments on the original loans form the cash flows used to
service the new bond issue. Traditionally, mortgage-backed bonds
are grouped in their own right as mortgage-backed securities (*MBSs*)
while all other securitisation issues are known as asset-backed
securities (*ABS*).

Reasons for undertaking securitisation

The driving force behind securitisation has been the need for banks to
realise value from the assets on their balance sheet. Typically, these
assets are residential mortgages, corporate loans and retail loans
such as credit-card debt. Let us consider the factors that might
lead a financial institution to securitise a part of its balance sheet.
These might be for the following reasons:

- if revenues received from assets remain roughly unchanged but
  the size of assets has decreased, this will lead to an increase in the
  return on equity ratio;
- the level of capital required to support the balance sheet will
  be reduced, which again can lead to cost savings or allows the
  institution to allocate the capital to other, perhaps more profitable, business;
- to obtain cheaper funding – frequently, the interest payable on
  ABS is considerably below the level payable on the underlying
  loans. This creates a cash surplus for the originating entity.

In other words, the main reasons that a bank will securitise part of its balance sheet is for one or all of the following reasons:

- funding the assets it owns;
- balance sheet capital management;
- risk management and credit risk transfer.

We consider each of these in turn.

Funding

Banks can use securitisation to (i) support rapid asset growth, (ii) diversify their funding mix and reduce cost of funding, and (iii) reduce maturity mis-matches. The market for ABS is large, with an estimated size of US$1,000 billion invested in ABS issues worldwide annually, of which US$150 billion is in the European market alone.[3] Access to this source of funding will enable a bank to grow its loan books at a faster pace than if they were reliant on traditional funding sources alone. For example, in the UK a former building society-turned-bank, Northern Rock plc, has taken advantage of securitisation to back its growing share of the UK residential mortgage market. Securitising assets also allows a bank to diversify its funding mix. Banks will not wish to be reliant on only a single or a few sources of funding, as this can be high-risk in times of market difficulty. Banks aim to optimise their funding between a mix of retail, interbank and wholesale sources. Securitisation has a key role to play in this mix. It also enables a bank to reduce its funding costs. This is because the securitisation process de-links the credit rating of the originating institution from the credit rating of the issued notes. Typically, most of the notes issued by SPVs will be higher-rated than the bonds issued direct by the originating bank itself. While the liquidity of the secondary market in ABS is frequently lower than that of the corporate bond market, and this adds to the yield payable by an ABS, it is frequently the case that the cost to the originating institution of issuing debt is still lower in the ABS market because of the latter's higher rating. Finally, there is the issue of maturity mis-matches. The business of bank asset-liability management (ALM) is inherently one of maturity mis-match, since a bank often funds long-term assets – such as residential mortgages –

---

[3] Source: CSFB, Credit Risk Transfer, 2 May 2003.

with short-asset liabilities – such as bank account deposits or inter-bank funding. This can be removed via securitisation, as the originating bank receives funding from the sale of the assets, and the economic maturity of the issued notes frequently matches that of the assets.

Balance sheet capital management

Banks use securitisation to improve balance sheet capital management. This provides (i) regulatory capital relief, (ii) economic capital relief and (iii) diversified sources of capital. As stipulated in the Bank for International Settlements (BIS) capital rules,[4] also known as the Basel rules, banks must maintain a minimum capital level for their assets, in relation to the risk of these assets. Under Basel I, for every $100 of risk-weighted assets a bank must hold at least $8 of capital; however, the designation of each asset's risk-weighting is restrictive. For example, with the exception of mortgages, customer loans are 100% risk-weighted regardless of the underlying rating of the borrower or the quality of the security held. The anomalies that this raises, which need not concern us here, is being addressed by the Basel II rules which become effective from 2007. However, the Basel I rules, which have been in place since 1988 (and effective from 1992), are another driver of securitisation. As an SPV is not a bank, it is not subject to Basel rules and need only such capital that is economically required by the nature of the assets they contain. This is not a set amount, but is significantly below the 8% level required by banks in all cases. Although an originating bank does not obtain 100% regulatory capital relief when it sells assets off its balance sheet to an SPV, because it will have retained a 'first-loss' piece out of the issued notes, its regulatory capital charge will be significantly reduced after the securitisation.[5]

To the extent that securitisation provides regulatory capital relief, it can be thought of as an alternative to capital raising, compared with the traditional sources of Tier 1 (equity), preferred shares, and perpetual loan notes with step-up coupon features. By reducing the amount of capital that has to be used to support the asset pool, a bank can also improve its return-on-equity (ROE) value. This will be received favourably by shareholders.

---

[4] For further information on this see Choudhry (2001).
[5] We discuss first-loss later on.

Risk management

Once assets have been securitised, the credit risk exposure on these assets for the originating bank is reduced considerably and, if the bank does not retain a first-loss capital piece (the most junior of the issued notes), it is removed entirely. This is because assets have been sold to the SPV. Securitisation can also be used to remove non-performing assets from banks' balance sheets. This has the dual advantage of removing credit risk and a potentially negative sentiment from the balance sheet, as well as freeing up regulatory capital as before. Further, there is a potential upside from securitising such assets: if any of them start performing again, or there is a recovery value obtained from defaulted assets, the originator will receive any surplus profit made by the SPV.

Benefits of securitisation to investors

Investor interest in the ABS market has been considerable from the market's inception. This is because investors perceive ABS as possessing a number of benefits. Investors can:

- diversify sectors of interest;
- access different (and sometimes superior) risk–reward profiles;
- access sectors that are otherwise not open to them.

A key benefit of securitisation notes is the ability to tailor risk–return profiles. For example, if there is a lack of assets of any specific credit rating, these can be created via securitisation. Securitised notes frequently offer better risk–reward performance than corporate bonds of the same rating and maturity. While this might seem peculiar (why should one AA-rated bond perform better in terms of credit performance than another just because it is asset-backed?), this often occurs because the originator holds the first-loss piece in the structure.

A holding in an ABS also diversifies the risk exposure. For example, rather than invest $100 million in an AA-rated corporate bond and be exposed to 'event risk' associated with the issuer, investors can gain exposure to, for instance, 100 pooled assets. These pooled assets will clearly have lower concentration risk.

THE PROCESS OF SECURITISATION

We look now at the process of securitisation, the nature of the SPV structure and issues such as credit enhancements and the cash flow waterfall.

Securitisation process

The securitisation process involves a number of participants. In the first instance is the *originator*, the firm whose assets are being securitised. The most common process involves an *issuer* acquiring the assets from the originator. The issuer is usually a company that has been specially set up for the purpose of the securitisation, which is the SPV. The SPV is a legal entity but is essentially a brass plate; it is usually domiciled offshore. The creation of an SPV ensures that the underlying asset pool is held separate from the other assets of the originator. This is done so that in the event that the originator is declared bankrupt or insolvent the assets that have been transferred to the SPV will not be affected. This is known as being bankruptcy-remote. Conversely, if the underlying assets begin to deteriorate in quality and are subject to a ratings downgrade, investors have no recourse to the originator.

By holding the assets within an SPV framework, defined in formal legal terms, the financial status and credit rating of the originator becomes almost irrelevant to the bondholders. The process of securitisation often involves *credit enhancements*, in which a third-party guarantee of credit quality is obtained, so that notes issued under the securitisation are often rated at investment grade and up to AAA-grade.

The process of structuring a securitisation deal ensures that the liability side of the SPV – the issued notes – carries lower cost than the asset side of the SPV. This enables the originator to secure lower cost funding that it would not otherwise be able to obtain in the unsecured market. This is a tremendous benefit for institutions with lower credit ratings. Figure 10.1 illustrates the process of securitisation in simple fashion.

Mechanics of securitisation

Securitisation involves a 'true sale' of the underlying assets from the balance sheet of the originator. This is why a separate legal

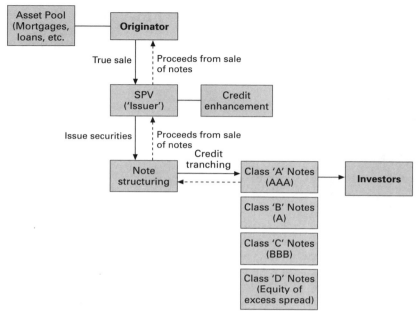

Figure 10.1   The securitisation process.

entity, the SPV, is created to act as the issuer of the notes. The assets being securitised are sold onto the balance sheet of the SPV. The process involves:

- undertaking 'due diligence' on the quality and future prospects of the assets;
- setting up the SPV and then effecting the transfer of assets to it;
- underwriting of loans for credit quality and servicing;
- determining the structure of the notes, including how many tranches are to be issued, in accordance to originator and investor requirements;
- the notes being rated by one or more credit rating agencies;
- placing of notes in the capital markets.

The sale of assets to the SPV needs to be undertaken so that it is recognised as a true legal transfer. The originator will need to hire legal counsel to advise it in such matters. The credit rating process will consider the character and quality of the assets, and also whether any enhancements have been made to the assets that will raise their credit quality. This can include *over-collateralisation*, which is when the principal value of notes issued is lower than the principal value of assets, and a liquidity facility provided by a bank.

A key consideration for the originator is the choice of the under-writing bank, which structures the deal and places the notes. The originator will award the mandate for its deal to an investment bank on the basis of fee levels, marketing ability and track record with assets being securitised.

SPV structures

There are essentially two main securitisation structures, amortising (pass-through) and revolving. A third type, the master trust, is used by frequent issuers.

Amortising structures

Amortising structures pay principal and interest to investors on a coupon-by-coupon basis throughout the life of the security, as illustrated in Figure 10.2. They are priced and traded based on expected maturity and weighted-average life (*WAL*), which is the time-weighted period during which principal is outstanding. A WAL approach incorporates various pre-payment assumptions, and any change in this pre-payment speed will increase or decrease the rate at which principal is repaid to investors. Pass-through structures are

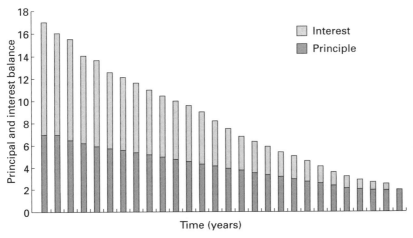

Figure 10.2 Amortising structure.

commonly used in residential and commercial MBS deals, and consumer loan ABS.

Revolving structures

Revolving structures revolve the principal of the assets; that is, during the revolving period, principal collections are used to purchase new receivables which fulfil the necessary criteria. The structure is used for short-dated assets with a relatively high pre-payment speed, such as credit-card debt and auto loans. During the amortisation period, principal payments are paid to investors either in a series of equal instalments (*controlled amortisation*) or principal is 'trapped' in a separate account until the expected maturity date and then paid in a single lump sum to investors (*soft bullet*).

Master trust

Frequent issuers under US and UK law use *master trust* structures, which allow multiple securitisations to be issued from the same SPV. Under such schemes, the originator transfers assets to the master trust SPV. Notes are then issued out of the asset pool based on investor demand. Master trusts have been used by MBS and credit-card ABS originators.

Securitisation note tranching

As illustrated in Figure 10.1, in a securitisation the issued notes are structured to reflect the specified risk areas of the asset pool, and thus are rated differently. The senior tranche is usually rated AAA. The lower-rated notes usually have an element of *over-collateralisation* and are thus capable of absorbing losses. The most junior note is the lowest-rated or non-rated. It is often referred to as the *first-loss piece*, because it is impacted by losses in the underlying asset pool first. The first-loss piece is sometimes called the *equity piece* or *equity note* (even though it is a bond) and is usually held by the originator.

Credit enhancement

Credit enhancement refers to the group of measures that can be instituted as part of the securitisation process for ABS and MBS issues, so that the credit rating of the issued notes meets investor requirements. The lower the quality of the assets being securitised, the greater the need for credit enhancement. This is usually by one of the following methods:

- *Over-collateralisation* – where the nominal value of the assets in the pool are in excess of the nominal value of issued securities.
- *Pool insurance* – an insurance policy provided by a composite insurance company to cover the risk of principal loss in the collateral pool. The claims paying rating of the insurance company is important in determining the overall rating of the issue.
- *Senior/Junior note classes* – credit enhancement is provided by subordinating a class of notes ('class B' notes) to the senior class notes ('class A' notes). The class B note's right to its proportional share of cash flows is subordinated to the rights of the senior noteholders. Class B notes do not receive payments of principal until certain rating agency requirements have been met, specifically satisfactory performance of the collateral pool over a predetermined period, or in many cases until all of the senior note classes have been redeemed in full.
- *Margin step-up* – a number of ABS issues incorporate a step-up feature in the coupon structure, which typically coincides with a call date. Although the issuer is usually under no obligation to redeem the notes at this point, the step-up feature was introduced as an added incentive for investors, to convince them from the outset that the economic cost of paying a higher coupon would be unacceptable and that the issuer would seek to refinance by exercising its call option.
- *Excess spread* – this is the difference between the return on the underlying assets and the interest rate payable on the issued notes (liabilities). The monthly excess spread is used to cover expenses and any losses. If any surplus is left over, it is held in a reserve account to cover against future losses or (if not required for that), as a benefit to the originator. In the meantime the reserve account is a credit enhancement for investors.
- *Substitution* – this feature enables the issuer to utilise principal cash flows from redemptions to purchase new collateral from the originator. This has the effect of lengthening the effective life of the transaction as the principal would otherwise have been used to redeem the notes. The issuer is usually under no obligation to substitute and it is an option granted by the investor.

All securitisation structures incorporate a *cash waterfall* process, whereby all the cash that is generated by the asset pool is paid in order of payment priority. Only when senior obligations have been

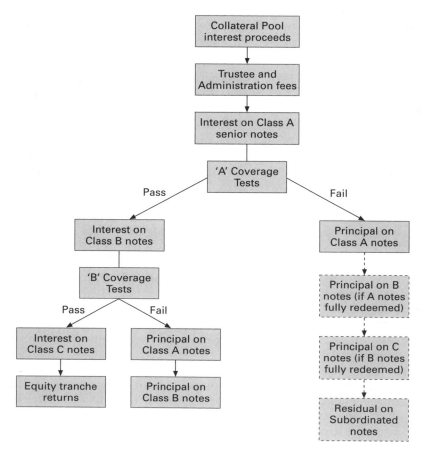

Figure 10.3 Cashflow waterfall (priority of payments).

met can more junior obligations be paid. An independent third-party agent is usually employed to run 'tests' on the vehicle to confirm that there is sufficient cash available to pay all obligations. If a test is failed, then the vehicle will start to pay off the notes, starting from the senior notes. The waterfall process is illustrated in Figure 10.3.

Impact on balance sheet

Figure 10.4 illustrates – by an hypothetical example – the effect on the liability side of an originating bank's balance sheet from a

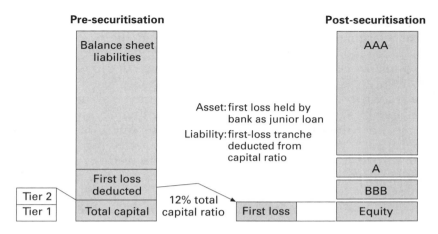

Figure 10.4   Regulatory capital impact of securitisation.

securitisation transaction. Following the process, selected assets have been removed from the balance sheet, although the originating bank will usually have retained the first-loss piece. With regard to the regulatory capital impact, this first-loss amount is deducted from the bank's total capital position. For example, assume a bank has $100 million of risk-weighted assets and a target Basel ratio of 12%,[6] and securitises all $100 million of these assets. It retains the first-loss tranche which forms 1.5% of the total issue. The remaining 98.5% will be sold on to the market. The bank will still have to set aside 1.5% of capital as a buffer against future losses, but it has been able to free itself of the remaining 10.5% of capital.

Credit rating

In the sterling market all public MBSs and ABS are explicitly rated by one or both of two of the largest credit-rating agencies, Moody's and S&P's. In structured financings it is normal for the rating of the paper to be investment grade, with most issues at launch being rated Aaa and/or AAA. We can briefly touch on the issues involved in rating such paper. The rating of the issue is derived from a

---

[6] The minimum is 8% but many banks prefer to set aside an amount well in excess of this minimum required level.

combination of factors. Insofar as it cannot generally be expected that investors will be sufficiently protected by the performance of the collateral alone, the rating agencies look to minimise the risk of principal default and ensure timely payment of interest coupons by requiring additional enhancement. The percentage of additional enhancement is determined by analysing the 'riskiness' of the collateral under a range of stress-tested environments which seek to quantify the effect of various interest-rate, foreclosure and loss scenarios, which are largely based on the expected performance of the collateral base in a recession. Much of the analysis is based on performance in the US markets, and the rating agencies try to establish criteria for each market and collateral type that is rated. The amount of enhancement required depends on the rating required at launch; for instance, less is required for a lower rated issue. In many cases issues will be backed by a larger nominal value of collateral; for example, an issue size of £100 million is formed out of assets composed of, say, £110 million.

Enhancement levels are also determined by the agencies reviewing the legal risks in the transaction. The legal analysis examines the competing rights and interests in the assets, including those of the bondholders and various third parties. MBSs and ABS are typically issued out of low-capitalised SPV companies, established solely for the purpose of issuing the securities. The rating agencies need to be assured that there is no risk to the bondholders in the event of the originator – that is, the seller of the assets to the SPV – becoming insolvent, and to be certain that a receiver or administrator cannot seize the assets or obtain rights to the SPV's cash flows. In the same way the agencies need to be satisfied that the SPV will be able to meet its obligations to its investors in circumstances where the service body (the entity responsible for administering the collateral, usually the originator) becomes insolvent. Consequently, significant emphasis is placed on ensuring that all primary and supporting documentation preserves the rights of investors in the security. An independent trustee is appointed to represent the interests of investors.

A change in rating for an ABS or MBS issue may be due to deterioration in performance of the collateral, heavy utilisation of credit enhancement or downgrade of a supporting rating – for example, an insurance company that was underwriting insurance on the pool of the assets.

Redemption mechanism

ABS and MBS issue terms incorporate one of two main methods through which redeeming principal can be passed back to investors:

- *Drawing by lot* – the available principal from the relevant interest period is repaid to investors by the international clearing agencies, Euroclear and Clearstream, drawing notes, at random, for cancellation. Notes will therefore trade at their nominal value.
- *Pro rata* – the available principal for the interest period is distributed among all investors, dependent upon their holding in the security. A *pool factor* is calculated, which is the remaining principal balance of the note expressed as a factor of 1. For instance, if the pool factor is 0.625 57, this means that for each note of £10,000 nominal, £3,744.30 of principal has been repaid to date. A pool factor value is useful to investors since early repayment of, say, mortgages reduces the level of asset backing available for an issue; the outstanding value of such an issue is reduced on a pro-rata basis, like early redemption, by a set percentage so that the remaining amount outstanding is adequately securitised.

Average life

Some ABS structures will incorporate a *call option* feature. In some cases the terms of the issue prevent a call being exercised until a certain percentage of the issue remains outstanding, usually 10%, and a certain date has been passed.

It is common for ABS issues to have an *average life* quoted for them. This says that, based on the most recent principal balance for the security, it is assumed that a redemption rate is applied such that the resultant average life equals the number of months left from the last interest payment date until 50% of the principal balance remains. Some issuers will announce the expected average life of their paper, and yield calculations are based on this average life.

It is necessary to allow for the particular characteristics of ABS and MBS bonds. Reinvestment risk, the risk that the coupon payments are reinvested at a lower rate than the redemption yields, is more acute for ABS bonds because often payments are received as frequently as every month. The yield calculation, or *cash flow yield*, is dependent on realisation of the projected cash flow according to a set pre-payment rate. If actual pre-payments differ from that set by the pre-payment rate, the cash flow yield will not be realised.

At the time that an investor purchases an MBS, it is not possible to calculate an exact yield; this will depend on the actual pre-payments of mortgages in the pool. The convention in the market is to quote the yield as a spread over a comparable government bond. The repayment of principal over time makes it inaccurate to compare the yield of an MBS with a gilt or Treasury of a stated maturity. Market participants instead use two measures: Macaulay duration and *average life*. The average life is the average time to receipt of principal payments (projected scheduled principal payments and projected principal repayments), weighted by the amount of principal expected and divided by the total principal to be repaid. We can represent this using equation (10.1):

$$\text{Average life} = \frac{1}{12} \sum_{t=1}^{n} \frac{t(\text{Principal expected at time } t)}{\text{Total principal}} \quad (10.1)$$

where n is the number of months remaining.

ILLUSTRATING THE PROCESS OF SECURITISATION

To illustrate the process of securitisation, we consider an hypothetical airline ticket receivables transaction, being originated by the fictitious ABC Airways plc and arranged by the equally fictitious XYZ Securities Limited. We show the kind of issues that will be considered by the investment bank that is structuring the deal.

Case study.	
Originator	ABC Airways plc
Issuer	'Airways No 1 Ltd'
Transaction	Ticket receivables airline future flow securitisation bonds €200m three-tranche floating rate notes, legal maturity 2010 Average life 4.1 years

Tranches	Class 'A' note (AA), Libor plus [ ] bps
	Class 'B' note (A), Libor plus [ ] bps
	Class 'E' note (BBB), Libor plus [ ] bps

Arranger   XYZ Securities plc

Due diligence

XYZ Securities will undertake due diligence on the assets to be securitised. For this case, it will examine the airline performance figures over the last 5 years, as well as model future projected figures, including:

- total passenger sales;
- total ticket sales;
- total credit-card receivables;
- geographical split of ticket sales.

It is the future flow of receivables, in this case credit-card purchases of airline tickets, that is being securitised. This is a higher-risk asset class than, say, residential mortgages, because the airline industry has a tradition of greater volatility of earnings than, say, mortgage banks.

Marketing approach

The present and all future credit-card ticket receivables generated by the airline will be transferred to an SPV. The investment bank's syndication desk will seek to place the notes with institutional investors across Europe. The notes are first given an indicative pricing ahead of the issue, to gauge investor sentiment. Given the nature of the asset class, during November 2002 the notes would be marketed at around 3-month Libor plus 70–80 basis points (AA note), 120–130 basis points (A note) and 260–270 basis points (BBB note). The notes are 'benchmarked' against recent issues with similar asset classes, as well as the spread level in the unsecured market of comparable issuer names.

Deal structure

The deal structure is shown at Figure 10.5.

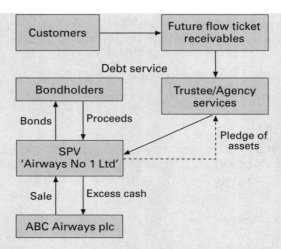

Figure 10.5   Airways No 1 Ltd deal structure.

The process leading to issue of notes is as follows:

- ABC Airways plc sells its future flow ticket receivables to an offshore SPV set up for this deal, incorporated as Airways No 1 Ltd;
- the SPV issues notes in order to fund its purchase of the receivables;
- the SPV pledges its right to the receivables to a fiduciary agent, the Security Trustee, for the benefit of the bondholders;
- the Trustee accumulates funds as they are received by the SPV;
- the bondholders receive interest and principal payments, in the order of priority of the notes, on a quarterly basis.

In the event of default, the Trustee will act on behalf of the bondholders to safeguard their interests.

Financial guarantors

The investment bank will consider if an insurance company, known as a monoline insurer, should be approached to 'wrap' the deal by providing a guarantee of backing for the SPV in the event of default. This insurance is provided in return for a fee.

Financial modelling

XYZ Securities will construct a cash flow model to estimate the size of the issued notes. The model will consider historical sales values, any seasonal factors in sales, credit-card cash flows and so on. Certain assumptions will be made when constructing the model – for example, growth projections, inflation levels, tax levels and so on. The model will consider a number of different scenarios, and also calculate the minimum asset coverage levels required to service the issued debt. A key indicator in the model will be the debt service coverage ratio (*DSCR*). The more conservative the DSCR, the more comfort there will be for investors in the notes. For a residential mortgage deal, this ratio might be approximately 2.5–3.0; however, for an airline ticket receivables deal, the DSCR would be unlikely to be lower than 4.0. The model will therefore calculate the amount of notes that can be issued against the assets, whilst maintaining the minimum DSCR.

Credit rating

It is common for securitisation deals to be rated by one or more of the formal credit ratings agencies such as Moody's, Fitch or S&P's. A formal credit rating will make it easier for XYZ Securities to place the notes with investors. The methodology employed by the ratings agencies takes into account both qualitative and quantitative factors, and will differ according to the asset class being securitised. The main issues in a deal such as our hypothetical Airways No 1 deal would be expected to include:

- *corporate credit quality* – these are risks associated with the originator, and are factors that affect its ability to continue operations, meet its financial obligations and provide a stable foundation for generating future receivables. This might be analysed according to the following: (i) ABC Airways' historical financial performance, including its liquidity and debt structure; (ii) its status within its domicile country (e.g., whether it is state-owned); (iii) the general economic conditions for industry and for airlines and (iv) the historical record and current state of the airline (e.g., its safety record and age of its aeroplanes);
- *the competition and industry trends* – ABC Airways' market share, the competition on its network;

- *regulatory issues* – such as need for ABC Airways to comply with forthcoming legislation that would impact its cash flows;
- *legal structure of the SPV and transfer of assets*;
- *cash flow analysis.*

Based on the findings of the ratings agency, the arranger may re-design some aspect of the deal structure so that the issued notes are rated at the required level.

This is a selection of the key issues involved in the process of securitisation. Depending on investor sentiment, market conditions and legal issues, the process from inception to closure of the deal may take anything from 3 to 12 months or more. After the notes have been issued, the arranging bank will no longer have anything to do with the issue; however, the bonds themselves require a number of agency services for their remaining life until they mature or are paid off. These agency services include paying agent, cash manager and custodian.

BLOOMBERG SCREENS

We conclude this chapter with a selection of Bloomberg screens illustrating features of ABS and MBSs.

The transaction under consideration is the GMAC Mortgage Corporation Loan Trust, a Master Trust vehicle. This deal, an MBS issue, had a large number of tranches, shown at Figure 10.6. The specific tranche we look at using other screens is the GMAC 2005-J1 A2 note.

Figure 10.6 shows the list of tranches for the deal. Figure 10.7 shows page DES for the A2 note. Note the pool factor of 1.000 000 00, this being the number we multiply the nominal amount by when calculating the market value of a holding of the bond. At this stage of the note's life there had been no pay-down of principal, so the pool factor was still 1.00.

Figure 10.8 shows the yield table for the same bond, with the various assumed pre-payment rates 'PSA' shown that can be selected by the user. Figure 10.9 is the quick yield analysis page CFG.

Figure 10.10 shows the weighted average life for the A2 note, as at 2 December 2005, under the different assumed pre-payment scenarios. The different PSA rates are plotted along the x-axis.

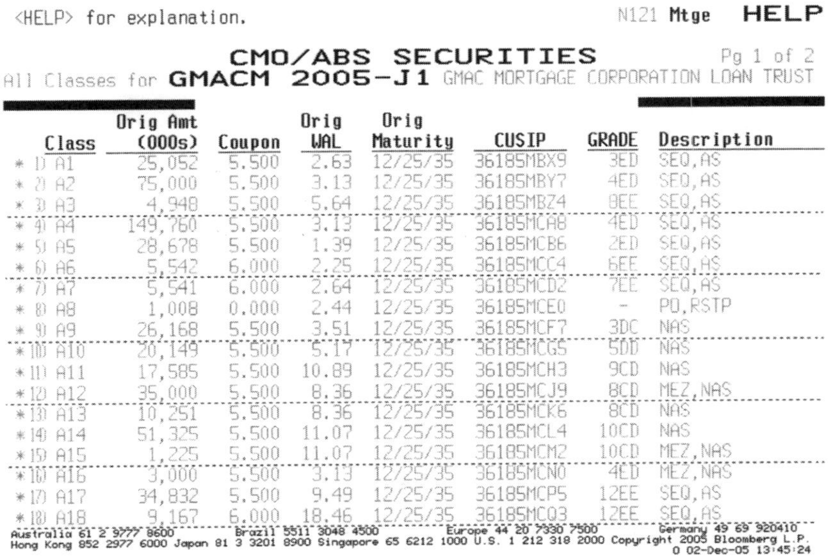

Figure 10.6 Bloomberg screen for GMAC MBS transaction.

© Bloomberg L.P. Used with permission. Visit *www.bloomberg.com*

Figure 10.7 Bloomberg screen DES for GMAC 2005-J1 A2 note as at 2 December 2005, GMAC transaction.

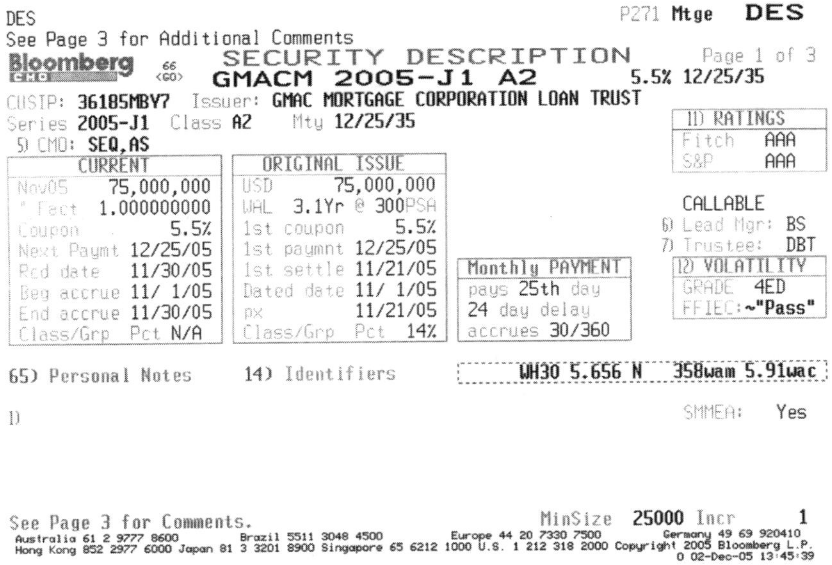

© Bloomberg L.P. Used with permission. Visit *www.bloomberg.com*

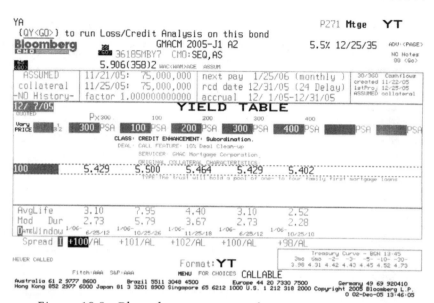

Figure 10.8 Bloomberg screen YT for GMAC 2005-J1 A2.

© Bloomberg L.P. Used with permission. Visit *www.bloomberg.com*

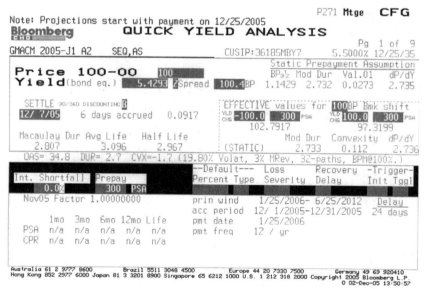

Figure 10.9 Bloomberg screen CFG for GMAC 2005-J1 A2.

© Bloomberg L.P. Used with permission. Visit *www.bloomberg.com*

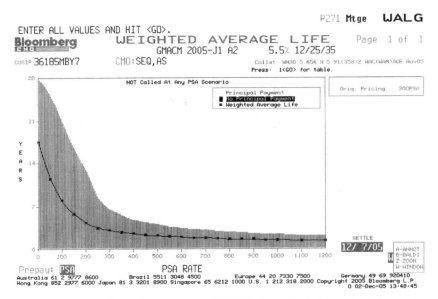

Figure 10.10 Bloomberg screen WALG for GMAC 2005-J1 A2 note.

© Bloomberg L.P. Used with permission. Visit *www.bloomberg.com*

```
                                                    P271 Mtge   CFG
Note: Projections start with payment on 12/25/2005
Bloomberg  PROJECTED  CASH  FLOWS              Pg  3 of  9
           5.5000% 12/25/35 GMACM 2005-J1 A2    SEQ,AS
                                               Final Pmt  6/25/2012
  Price  100       Accrued  0.0917 for   6 days  Interest  Pmt 12/yr  24 Delay
  Yield  5.4293                         shortfall Acc Date  12/ 1/2005
  Settle 12/ 7/05    300  PSA  QUOTED        0.0% Pmt Date  1/25/2006
                                               Nov05 Factor 1.0000000000
                                         Total Org Face    75,000,000.00
                                          Your Org Face    75,000,000.00
 Payment Period      First prin. pmt.  1/25/06  Prev. Bal.= 74,716,980
 No.   Date    Coupon    Interest   Principal    Cashflow    Balance
   1  1/25/06   5.500     342,453    340,469      682,922    74,376,511
   2  2/25/06n  5.500     340,892    397,724      738,616    73,978,787
   3  3/25/06n  5.500     339,069    454,718      793,787    73,524,069
   4  4/25/06   5.500     336,985    511,364      848,349    73,012,705
   5  5/25/06   5.500     334,642    567,572      902,214    72,445,133
   6  6/25/06n  5.500     332,040    623,255      955,295    71,821,878
   7  7/25/06   5.500     329,184    678,328    1,007,512    71,143,550
   8  8/25/06   5.500     326,075    732,701    1,058,776    70,410,849
   9  9/25/06   5.500     322,716    786,289    1,109,005    69,624,560
  10 10/25/06   5.500     319,113    839,008    1,158,121    68,785,552
  11 11/25/06n  5.500     315,267    890,776    1,206,043    67,894,776
  12 12/25/06n  5.500     311,184    941,507    1,252,691    66,953,269
Australia 61 2 9777 8600    Brazil 5511 3048 4500   Europe 44 20 7330 7500   Germany 49 69 920410
Hong Kong 852 2977 6000 Japan 81 3 3201 8900 Singapore 65 6212 1000 U.S. 1 212 318 2000 Copyright 2005 Bloomberg L.P.
                                                                       0 02-Dec-05 13:52:05
```

Figure 10.11 GMAC 2005-J1 A2 note projected cashflows.

© Bloomberg L.P. Used with permission. Visit *www.bloomberg.com*

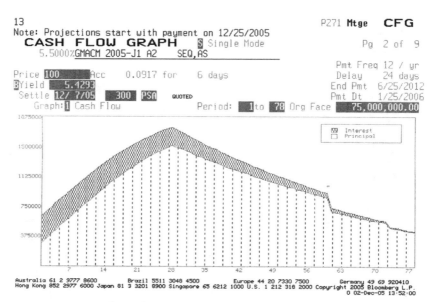

Figure 10.12 Bloomberg screen CFG for GMAC 2005-J1 A2 note.

© Bloomberg L.P. Used with permission. Visit *www.bloomberg.com*

The weighted average life falls for a higher PSA number – as expected, because a higher PSA means a faster speed of pre-payment.

The projected cash flows for the A2 note are shown at Figure 10.11, and these can be viewed in graphical form using screen CFG, which is shown at Figure 10.12.

BIBLIOGRAPHY

Bhattacharya, A. and Fabozzi, F. (eds) (1996). *Asset-Backed Securities*, FJF Associates, New Hope, PA.

Choudhry, M. (2001). *The Bond and Money Markets: Strategy, Trading, Analysis.* Butterworth-Heinemann, Oxford, UK.

CSFB (2003), *Credit Risk Transfer.* CSFB, London.

Hayre, L. (ed.) (2001). *The Salomon Smith Barney Guide to Mortgage-Backed and Asset-Backed Securities.* John Wiley & Sons, Chichester, UK.

Martellini, L., Priaulet, P. and Priaulet, S. (2003). *Fixed Income Securities*, John Wiley & Sons, Chichester, UK.

Morris, D. (1990). *Asset Securitisation: Principles and Practices*, Executive Enterprise, London.

Sundaresan, S. (1997). *Fixed Income Markets and Their Derivatives.* South-Western Publishing, Southwestern University, IL, ch. 9.

Chapter

11

....

INTRODUCTION TO DERIVATIVE INSTRUMENTS

One of the success stories of the global capital markets is the growth in the use of derivatives, or off-balance sheet instruments. The products now traded by virtually all participants in financial markets include forward contracts, futures, swaps and options. These instruments are used as tools in their own right, as well as to form the building blocks of more complex structures or *structured products*. Derivative instruments are often tailored by a bank to meet the specific requirements of a particular customer, so-called *over-the-counter* (*OTC*) products. The range of uses to which derivatives are put is as varied as the types of instrument available; as we might expect, the subject area is a large one, and a great deal has been written about the use of derivatives. Because these instruments are widely used and an integral part of the operations of the debt capital markets, it is worthwhile to consider them here. The subject matter is large; so, even though this is an introduction, the chapter is a large one.

We will look at the various types of off-balance sheet (*OBS*) instruments that are traded as part of the operations of a bond desk within a bank. This will include descriptions of the instruments, as well as a brief look at pricing, trading and some uses. We can of course only touch upon the issue, which is a huge subject in its own right. There are a large number of uses for derivatives, due to their flexibility and versatility, and the liquid market that exists for them. Banks use them to manage their risk and that of their clients, and as speculative trading instruments. While it is appropriate only to take an introductory look at these instruments here, interested readers may wish to consult some of the large number of texts available that cover this area, including those listed in the bibliography on p. 298.

INTEREST-RATE SWAPS

The growth in the swaps market (see Figure 11.1) illustrates perfectly the flexibility and application of financial engineering in the capital markets. The market is large and liquid and has a variety of applications; at the time of writing, for interest-rate (*IR*) swaps the notional principal outstanding exceeded $5,000 billion. *Swaps* are synthetic securities involving combinations of two or more basic building blocks. Most swaps currently traded in the market involve combinations of cash market securities; for example, a fixed IR security combined with a floating IR security, possibly also combined with a currency transaction. However, the market has also seen swaps that involve a futures or forward component, as well as swaps that involve an option component. The first example of a swap is often said to be that set up between IBM and the World Bank in 1981 – since when the swap market has grown considerably. The market in, say, dollar and sterling IR swaps is very large and very liquid. The main types of swap are IR swaps, asset swaps, basis swaps, fixed-rate currency swaps and currency coupon swaps. The market for swaps is organised by the International Swap Dealers Association (*ISDA*).

IR swaps are the most important type of swap in terms of volume of transactions. They are commonly used to manage and hedge IR risk and exposure, while market makers will also take positions in swaps reflecting their view on the direction of interest rates. An IR swap is an agreement between two counterparties to make periodic interest payments to one another during the life of the swap, on a predetermined set of dates, based on a *notional* principal amount. One party is the fixed-rate payer, and this rate is agreed at the time of trade of the swap; the other party is the floating-rate payer, the floating rate being determined during the life of the swap by reference to a specific market index. The principal or notional amount is never physically exchanged (hence the term 'off-balance sheet') but is used merely to calculate the interest payments. The fixed-rate payer receives floating-rate interest and is said to be 'long' or to have 'bought' the swap. The long side has conceptually purchased a floating-rate note (because it receives floating-rate interest) and issued a fixed-coupon bond (because it pays out fixed interest at intervals) – that is, it has in principle borrowed funds. The floating-rate payer is said to be 'short' or to have 'sold' the swap. The short side has conceptually purchased a coupon bond (because it receives fixed-rate interest) and issued a floating-rate note (because it pays floating-rate interest). So an IR swap is:

- an agreement between two parties to exchange a stream of cash flows;
- calculated as a percentage of a *notional* sum and calculated on different bases.

For example, in a trade between Bank A and Bank B, Bank A may agree to pay fixed semiannual coupons of 10% on a notional principal sum of £1 million, in return for receiving from Bank B the prevailing 6-month sterling London Interbank Offered Rate (*Libor*) on the same amount. The known cash flow is the fixed payment of £50,000 every 6 months by Bank A to Bank B.

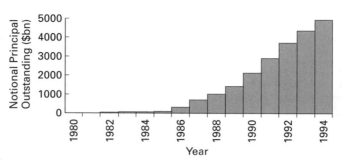

Figure 11.1   Growth of interest-rate swap market.

Source: ISDA.

Characteristics of IR swaps

Like other financial instruments, IR swaps trade in a secondary market. The value of a swap moves in line with market interest rates, in exactly the same fashion as bonds. If a 5-year IR swap is transacted today at a rate of 5%, and 5-year interest rates subsequently fall to 4.75%, the swap will have decreased in value to the fixed-rate payer, and correspondingly increased in value to the floating-rate payer, who has now seen the level of interest payments fall. The opposite would be true if 5-year rates moved to 5.25%. Why is this? Consider the fixed-rate payer in an IR swap to be a borrower of funds; if she fixes the interest rate payable on a loan for 5 years, and then this interest rate decreases shortly afterwards, is she better off? No, because she is now paying above the market rate for the funds borrowed. For this reason a swap contract decreases in value to the fixed-rate payer if there is a fall in rates. Equally, a floating-rate payer gains if there is a fall in rates, as he can take advantage of the new rates and pay a lower level of interest; hence, the value of a swap increases to the floating-rate payer if there is a fall in rates. We can summarise the profit/loss (*p/l*) profile of a swap position, as shown in Table 11.1.

A bank's swap desk will have an overall net IR position arising from all the swaps it has traded that are currently on the book. This

Table 11.1   P/L profile of an IR swap.

	Fall in rates	**Rise in rates**
Fixed-rate payer	Loss	Profit
Floating-rate payer	Profit	Loss

position is an IR exposure at all points along the term structure, out to the maturity of the longest-dated swap. At the close of business each day all the swaps on the book will be *marked-to-market* at the IR quote for that day, and the resulting p/l for the book will be in line with the profile shown in Table 11.1.

A swap can be viewed in two ways, either as a bundle of forward or futures contracts, or as a bundle of cash flows arising from the 'sale' and 'purchase' of cash market instruments. If we imagine a strip of futures contracts, maturing every 3 or 6 months out to 3 years, we can see how this is conceptually similar to a 3-year IR swap. However, it is probably better to visualise a swap as being a bundle of cash flows arising from cash instruments.

Let us imagine we have only two positions on our book:

- a long position in £100 million of a 3-year floating-rate note (*FRN*) that pays 6-month Libor semiannually, and is trading at par;
- a short position in £100 million of a 3-year gilt with coupon of 6% that is also trading at par.

Being short a bond is the equivalent to being a borrower of funds. Assuming this position is kept to maturity, the resulting cash flows are shown in Table 11.2.

There is no net outflow or inflow at the start of these trades, as the £100 purchase of the FRN is netted with receipt of £100 million

Table 11.2   3-year cash flows – cash flows resulting from a long position in FRNs and a short position in gilts.

Period (6-month)	FRN	Gilt	Net cash flow
0	−£100m	+£100m	£0
1	+(Libor × 100)/2	−3	+(Libor × 100)/2–3.0
2	+(Libor × 100)/2	−3	+(Libor × 100)/2–3.0
3	+(Libor × 100)/2	−3	+(Libor × 100)/2–3.0
4	+(Libor × 100)/2	−3	+(Libor × 100)/2–3.0
5	+(Libor × 100)/2	−3	+(Libor × 100)/2–3.0
6	+[(Libor × 100)/2] + 100	−103	+(Libor × 100)/2–3.0

The Libor rate is the 6-month rate prevailing at the time of the setting – for instance, the Libor rate at period 4 will be the rate actually prevailing at period 4.

from the sale of the gilt. The resulting cash flows over the 3-year period are shown in the last column of Table 11.2. This net position is exactly the same as that of a fixed-rate payer in an IR swap. As we had at the start of the trade, there is no cash inflow or outflow on maturity. For a floating-rate payer, the cash flow would mirror exactly a long position in a fixed-rate bond and a short position in an FRN.

Therefore, the fixed-rate payer in a swap is said to be short in the bond market – that is, a borrower of funds; the floating-rate payer in a swap is said to be long the bond market.

The cash flows resulting from a vanilla IR swap are illustrated in Figure 11.2, using the normal convention where cash inflows are shown as an arrow pointing up, while cash outflows are shown as an arrow pointing down. In a swap contract the *trade date* is the date on which the two parties agree to swap their contractual commitments. ISDA has drawn up a standard legal agreement and standard documentation for swap contracts and virtually all swaps traded will use this agreement and documentation. The points unique about each swap traded are agreed at the time of trade; these are the fixed rate at which the fixed-rate payments are calculated (the *swap rate*), and the

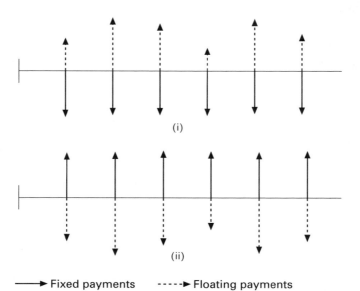

(i)

(ii)

⟶ Fixed payments ----▶ Floating payments

Figure 11.2 Cash flows for typical IR swap: (i) cash flows for fixed-rate payer and (ii) cash flows for floating-rate payer.

frequency and basis for both the fixed-rate and floating-rate interest payments. Payments are usually annual or semiannual, or occasionally quarterly. There is no requirement for the fixed- and floating-rate payments to have matching frequency or day-count basis. The trade date is usually also the first *setting date*, when the floating rate for the next period is determined. Most swaps use Libor as the market rate for the floating leg. The *effective date* is the date when interest starts to accrue on both legs of the swap, usually two business days after the trade date (unless it is a *forward starting swap*). The first payment date is at the end of the first swap period, when one party will be a net creditor while the other will be a net debtor. In the market only the net difference between the two payments is handed over, rather than both payments being passed between the two parties. Payments continue until the maturity date of the swap.

Swap spreads and the swap yield curve

In the market, banks will quote two-way swap rates, on screens and on the telephone or via a dealing system such as Reuters. Brokers will also be active in relaying prices in the market. The convention in the market is for the swap market maker to set the floating leg at Libor and then quote the fixed rate that is payable for that maturity. So, for a 5-year swap a bank's swap desk might be willing to quote the following:

- *Floating-rate payer*: Pay 6-month Libor
  Receive fixed rate of 5.19%.

- *Fixed-rate payer*: Pay fixed rate of 5.25%
  Receive 6-month Libor.

In this case the bank is quoting an offer rate of 5.25%, which the fixed-rate payer will pay, in return for receiving Libor flat. The bid price quote is 5.19% which is what a floating-rate payer will receive fixed. The bid–offer spread in this case is therefore 6 basis points. The fixed-rate quotes are always at a spread above the government bond yield curve. Let us assume that the 5-year gilt is yielding 4.88%; in this case then the 5-year swap bid rate is 31 basis points above this yield. So, the bank's swap trader could quote the swap rates as a spread above the benchmark bond yield curve – say, 37–31 – which is her swap spread quote. This means that the bank is happy to enter into a swap paying fixed 31 basis points above the benchmark yield and receiving Libor, and receiving fixed 37 basis points above the

Table 11.3   Swap quotes.

1 year	4.50	4.45	+17
2 year	4.69	4.62	+25
3 year	4.88	4.80	+23
4 year	5.15	5.05	+29
5 year	5.25	5.19	+31
10 years	5.50	5.40	+35

yield curve and paying Libor. The bank's screen on, say, Bloomberg or Reuters might look something like Table 11.3, which quotes the swap rates as well as the current spread over the government bond benchmark.

The swap spread is a function of the same factors that influence the spread over government bonds for other instruments. For shorter duration swaps – say, up to 3 years – there are other yield curves that can be used in comparison, such as the cash market curve or a curve derived from futures prices. For longer-dated swaps the spread is determined mainly by the credit spreads that prevail in the corporate bond market. Because a swap is viewed as a package of long and short positions in fixed- and floating-rate bonds, it is the credit spreads in these two markets that will determine the swap spread. This is logical; essentially, it is the premium for greater credit risk involved in lending to corporates that dictates that a swap rate will be higher than the same maturity government bond yield. Technical factors will be responsible for day-to-day fluctuations in swap rates, such as the supply of corporate bonds and the level of demand for swaps, plus the cost to swap traders of hedging their swap positions.

We can summarise by saying that swap spreads over government bonds reflect the supply and demand conditions of both swaps and government bonds, as well as the market's view on the credit quality of swap counterparties. There is considerable information content in the swap yield curve, much like that in the government bond yield curve. During times of credit concerns in the market, such as the corrections in Asian and Latin American markets in summer 1998, and the possibility of default by the Russian government regarding its long-dated US dollar bonds, the swap spread will increase, more so at higher maturities. To illustrate this, let us consider the sterling swap spread in 1998/99. The UK swap spread widened from the second half of 1998 onwards, a reaction to market turmoil around the world. At such times investors embark on a 'flight to quality' that

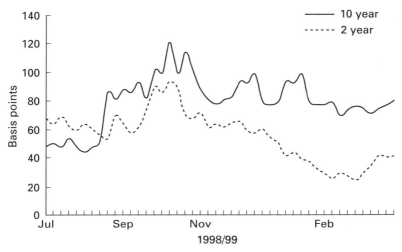

Figure 11.3   Sterling 2-year and 10-year swap spreads 1998/99.
Source: BoE.

results in yield spreads widening. In the swap market, the spread between 2-year and 10-year swaps also increased, reflecting market concern with credit and counterparty risk. The spreads narrowed in the first quarter 1999, as credit concerns brought about by market corrections in 1998 declined. The change in swap spreads is shown in Figure 11.3.

In Chapter 2 we discussed the interpretation of yield curves and their information content, in the context of government bond yield curves. In certain circumstances it is more relevant to use the swap curve for market analysis and as an information and IR predictor. This is usually the case where a liquid market in IR swaps exists out to long-dated maturities. A situation under which the swap curve should be examined is when it is a different shape to the government bond yield curve; usually, the swap curve will mirror the shape of the government curve, but at a higher yield level due to the swap spread. In the UK market the government curve has been inverted (negative) since July 1997, and the swap curve has been slightly inverted or flat. However, in the last quarter on 1998 the swap curve became slightly upward sloping, whereas the gilt curve remained inverted. This suggested that the market was predicting higher future short-term interest rates, and had priced this into swap rates, while the gilt curve remained unchanged.

Swap duration

We have seen how – exactly as with bonds – the value of a swap contract will move in line with interest rates. As duration is a measure of the IR sensitivity of a bond (see Chapter 2) it will apply to swaps as well. For the fixed-rate payer in a swap we have shown that the position is equivalent to holding a floating-rate bond and being short a fixed-rate bond. To measure the duration of the swap from the fixed-rate payer's point of view, we can take the difference in duration between the two 'bonds' that make up this position. That is:

$$\text{Duration of swap} = \text{Duration of floating-rate bond}$$
$$- \text{Duration of fixed-rate bond}$$

The duration of an FRN is relatively low as it will be lower than the time to the next reset date; therefore, for a bond that paid semi-annually the duration would never be higher than 6 months. The IR sensitivity for a swap will therefore be made up almost exclusively of the fixed-rate element. It is the fixed-rate element that is also considered when pricing swaps.

Summary of IR swap

Let us summarise the chief characteristics of swaps. A plain-vanilla swap has the following characteristics:

- one leg of the swap is fixed-rate interest, while the other will be floating-rate, usually a standard index;
- the fixed rate is just that – fixed through the entire life of the swap;
- the floating rate is set in advance of each period (quarterly, semiannually or annually) and paid in arrears;
- both legs have the same payment frequency;
- the maturity can be standard whole years up to 30 years, or set to match customer requirements;
- the notional principal remains constant during the life of the swap.

Of course, to meet customer demand banks can set up swaps that have variations on any or all of the above standard points.

Non-standard swaps

The swap market is very flexible and instruments can be tailor-made to fit the requirements of individual customers. A variety of swap contracts can be traded and we briefly describe some of them in this section:

- *Accreting and amortising swaps* – in a plain-vanilla swap the notional principal remains unchanged during the life of the swap. However, it is possible to trade a swap where the notional principal varies during its life. An accreting (or *step-up*) swap is one in which the principal starts off at one level and then increases in amount over time. The opposite, an amortising swap (see Figure 11.4), is one in which the notional reduces in size over time. An accreting swap would be useful where, for instance, a funding liability that is being hedged increases over time. The amortising swap might be employed by a borrower hedging a bond issue that featured sinking fund payments, where a part of the notional amount outstanding is paid off at set points during the life of the bond.
- *Zero-coupon swap* – a zero-coupon swap replaces the stream of fixed-rate payments with a single payment at the end of the swap's life or, more unusually, at the beginning. The floating-rate payments are made in the normal way. Such a swap exposes the floating-rate payer to some credit risk because it makes regular payments but does not receive any payment until the termination date of the swap.

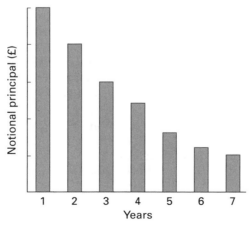

Figure 11.4 Amortising swap.

- *Libor-in-arrears swap* – in this type of swap (also known as a *back-set swap*) the setting date is just before the end of the accrual period for the floating-rate setting and not just before the start. Such a swap would be attractive to a counterparty who had a different view on interest rates compared with the market consensus. For instance, in a rising yield curve environment, forward rates will be higher than current market rates, and this will be reflected in the pricing of a swap. A Libor-in-arrears swap would be priced higher than a conventional swap. If the floating-rate payer believed that interest rates would in fact rise more slowly than forward rates (and the market) were suggesting, she may wish to enter into an arrears swap as opposed to a conventional swap.

- *Basis swap* – in a conventional swap one leg comprises fixed-rate payments and the other floating-rate payments. In a basis swap both legs are floating-rate, but linked to different money market indices. One leg is normally linked to Libor, while the other might be linked to the CD rate, say, or the commercial paper rate. This type of swap would be used by a bank in the US that had made loans that paid at the prime rate, and financed its loans at Libor. A basis swap would eliminate the *basis risk* between the bank's income and expense cash flows. Other basis swaps have been traded where both legs are linked to Libor, but at different maturities; for instance, one leg might be at 3-month Libor and the other at 6-month Libor. In such a swap the basis is different and so is the payment frequency: one leg pays out semiannually while the other would be paying quarterly.

- *Margin swap* – it is common to encounter swaps where there is a margin above or below Libor on the floating leg, as opposed to a floating leg of Libor flat. If a bank's borrowing is financed at Libor + 25 basis points, it may wish to receive Libor + 25 basis points in the swap so that its cash flows match exactly. The fixed-rate quote for a swap must be adjusted correspondingly to allow for the margin on the floating side; so, in our example if the fixed-rate quote is, say, 6.00%, it would be adjusted to around 6.25%; differences in the margin quoted on the fixed leg might arise if the day-count convention or payment frequency were to differ between fixed and floating legs.

- *Forward-start swaps* – a forward-start swap is one where the *effective date* is not the usual 1 or 2 days after the trade date but a considerable time afterwards – for instance, 6 months after trade date. Such a swap might be entered into where one counterparty wanted to fix a hedge or cost of borrowing now, but for a start point some time in the future. Typically, this would be because the party considered that interest rates would rise or the cost of hedging would rise.

Using swaps

Swaps are part of the OTC market and so they can be tailored to suit the particular requirements of the user. It is common for swaps to be structured so that they match particular payment dates, payment frequencies and Libor margins, which may characterise the underlying exposure of the customer. As the market in IR swaps is so large, liquid and competitive, banks are willing to quote rates and structure swaps for virtually all customers. In the sterling market, for example, the large clearing banks are reluctant to quote rates for swaps of below £10 million or £5 million notional value; however, customers such as small building societies can readily obtain quotes for swaps as small as £1 million nominal from other institutions (the author has personal experience of dealing with such customers!).

Swap applications can be viewed as being one of two main types, asset-linked swaps and liability-linked swaps. Asset-linked swaps are created when the swap is linked to an asset such as a bond in order to change the characteristics of the income stream for investors. Liability-linked swaps are traded when borrowers of funds wish to change the pattern of their cash flows.

A straightforward application of an IR swap is when a borrower wishes to convert a floating-rate liability into a fixed-rate one, usually in order to remove the exposure to upward moves in interest rates. For instance, a company may wish to fix its financing costs. Let us assume a company currently borrowing money at a floating rate – say, 6-month Libor + 100 basis points – fears that interest rates may rise in the remaining 3 years of its loan. It enters into a 3-year semiannual IR swap with a bank, as the fixed-rate payer, paying, say, 6.75% against receiving 6-month Libor. This fixes the company's borrowing costs for 3 years at 7.75% (7.99% effective annual rate). This is shown in Figure 11.5.

Figure 11.5 Converting floating-rate to fixed-rate liability.

It is less common for borrowers to enter into swap contracts in order to switch from fixed-rate to floating-rate liability, but this does occur. An example would be where a bank or corporate had issued bonds of, say, 10-year maturity at a coupon of 8%, only for interest rates to fall shortly after issue of the debt. The company may wish to switch to floating-rate liability by receiving fixed in a swap, reducing the level of its fixed-rate borrowing. In such a scenario, however, the borrower is now exposed to rising rates, and so switching liabilities in this fashion is to imply that the company does not expect the yield curve to rise substantially over the medium term. If rates did then move up again the borrower may switch liabilities again by entering into a second swap.

Example 11.1　　Liability-linked swap, fixed- to floating- to fixed-rate exposure.

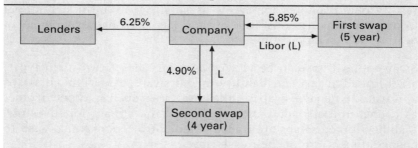

Figure 11.6　　Liability-linked swap.

A corporate borrows for 5 years at a rate of $6\frac{1}{4}\%$ and shortly after enters into a swap paying floating rate, so that its net borrowing cost is Libor + 40 basis points. After 1 year, swap rates have fallen such that the company is quoted 4-year swap rates as 4.90–84%. The company decides to switch back into fixed-rate liability in order to take advantage of the lower IR environment. It enters into a second swap paying fixed at 4.90% and receiving Libor. The net borrowing cost is now 5.30%. The arrangement is illustrated in Figure 11.6. The company has saved 95 basis points on its original borrowing cost, which is the difference between the two swap rates.

Asset-linked swap structures might be required when, for example, investors require a fixed-interest security when floating-rate assets

Figure 11.7   Fixed- to floating-rate swap.

are available. Borrowers often issue FRNs, the holders of which may prefer to switch the income stream into fixed coupons. As an example, consider a local authority pension fund holding 2-year floating-rate gilts. This is an asset of the highest quality paying Libid − 12.5 basis points. The pension fund wishes to swap the cash flows to create a fixed-interest asset. It obtains a quote for a tailor-made swap where the floating leg pays Libid, the quote being 5.55–5.50%. By entering into this swap the pension fund has in place a structure that pays a fixed coupon of 5.375%. This is shown in Figure 11.7.

Cancelling a swap

Where companies have entered into swap contracts to hedge IR liabilities, the swap will be kept in place until expiry. However, circumstances may change or, as we have seen, a company may alter its view on interest rates, and so it may be necessary to terminate the swap. The most straightforward option is for the company to take out a second contract that negates the first. This allows the first swap to remain in place, but there may be residual cash flows unless the two swaps cancel each other out precisely. The terms for the second swap, being non-standard (and unlikely to be exactly whole years to maturity, unless traded on the anniversary of the first), may also result in it being more expensive than a vanilla swap. As it is unlikely that the second swap will have the same rate, the two fixed legs will not net to 0. And if the second swap is not traded on an anniversary, payment dates will not match.

For these reasons the company may wish to cancel the swap entirely. To do this it will ask a swap market maker for a quotation on a cancellation fee. The bank will obtain the cancellation fee by calculating the net present value of the remaining cash flows in the swap, using the discount factor that pertains to each future cash flow. In practice, just the fixed leg will be present-valued, and then netted with Libor. The net present value of all the cash flows is the fair price for cancelling the swap. The valuation principles we established earlier on will apply; that is, if the fixed-rate payer is asking to cancel the swap when interest rates have fallen, he will pay the cancellation fee, and *vice versa* if rates have risen.

Zero-coupon swap pricing

So far we have discussed how vanilla swap prices are often quoted as a spread over the benchmark government bond yield in that currency, and how this swap spread is mainly a function of the credit spread required by the market over the government (risk-free) rate. This method is convenient and also logical because banks use government bonds as the main instrument when hedging their swap books. However, because much bank swap trading is now conducted in non-standard, tailor-made swaps, this method can sometimes be unwieldy as each swap needs to have its spread calculated to suit its particular characteristics. Therefore, banks use a standard pricing method for all swaps known as *zero-coupon* swap pricing.

In earlier chapters we referred to zero-coupon bonds and zero-coupon interest rates. A bond that has only one cash flow, its redemption payment on maturity, has no coupons and consequently offers no *reinvestment risk* to the bondholder. If a zero-coupon bond – such as a gilt strip – is purchased at a particular yield, and held to maturity, the return for the strip holder will be exactly the yield that applied at the time of purchase. Zero-coupon rates, or *spot rates*, are therefore true interest rates for their particular term to maturity. In zero-coupon swap pricing, a bank will view all swaps, even the most complex, as a series of cash flows. The zero-coupon rates that apply now for each of the cash flows in a swap can be used to value these cash flows. Therefore, to value and price a swap, each of the swap's cash flows is present-valued using known spot rates; the sum of these present values is the value of the swap.

In a swap the fixed-rate payments are known in advance and so it is straightforward to present-value them. The present value of the floating-rate payments is usually estimated in two stages. First, the implied forward rates can be calculated using (11.1):

$$f_i = \left(\frac{d_i}{d_{i+1}} - 1 \right) F \qquad (11.1)$$

where f_i = Forward rate;
             i = Total number of coupons (generic bond);
             d = Discount factor for the relevant cash flow date;
             F = Number of times per year that coupons are paid.

Once the size of the floating-rate payments have been estimated, these can also be valued by using the spot rates. The total value of the fixed and floating legs is the sum of all the present values, so the value of the total swap is the net of the present values of the fixed and floating legs.

Earlier in this chapter we illustrated how cash flows in a vanilla interest-rate swap, where the party is paying floating, are conceptually the same as that from a long position in a fixed IR bond and a short position in an FRN. Such a swap would also be identical to a long position in a bond that was financed by borrowings at Libor. As the resulting cash flows are identical whatever position is put on, we can say that the fixed rate on a vanilla IR swap is the same as the yield (and coupon) on a bond that is trading at par. (Par because such a bond is priced at 100. If we wish to replicate the conditions of a swap, the initial cash flows need to be identical. At par, the cash flows from buying £100 million of the bond and financing with borrowing of £100 million at Libor is identical to that resulting from £100 million of a swap where the party is paying the floating leg.) So, if we wish to determine the correct rate for the fixed leg of a vanilla swap we need to calculate the correct coupon for a bond of the same maturity that we wish to issue at par. In fact, the swap rate is the weighted arithmetic average of the forward rates up to the swap's maturity. For example, the 5-year swap rate is the weighted average of the strip of five 1-year forward rates. We calculated forward rates in Chapter 3, and using these principles we can calculate swap rates.

To recap, we have stated that the first step in swap pricing is to derive the spot rates up to the maturity required. These spot rates are then used to value all the cash flows in a swap. This technique is used for both pricing and valuing the swap. The market convention is to use the term *pricing* when trying to find the correct fixed rate for a new swap such that its net present value is 0. *Valuing* is the term used to describe the process of finding the net present value of an existing swap for which the fixed rate has already been set.

Hedging using bonds and swaps

A swap book can be hedged using other swaps, futures contracts or bonds. A bond book can similarly be hedged using futures, swaps and other bonds. In some of the larger banks an integrated risk management technique is used, whereby the bank's overall net risk exposure, arising from its entire position in all instruments including swaps, FRAs and futures, is managed as a whole. This results in cheaper hedging. However, it is still common for individual books to be hedged separately. If an integrated method is used, the bank must identify all the points along the term structure where it has an IR exposure, and then calculate the present value of a basis point (*PVBP*) at each of these points. That is, it must calculate the change in value of its positions along each maturity bucket (or *grid point* – see Chapter 14) that would result from a 1-basis-point change in that maturity's IR. The bank's daily risk report will also list the bank's aggregate risk along the entire yield curve.

Let us now consider some of the points involved in hedging a swap book. When hedging a position we will want to put on another position of the same *basis point value* (*BPV*) and in the opposite direction. Assume we have only one position on the book, a 5-year sterling swap of £5 million notional, in which we pay fixed- and receive floating-rate interest. This is conceptually similar to borrowing money. As the maturity of the swap is longer than that of the longest IR futures contract – which is 3 years – we decide to hedge the position using a gilt. As we have 'borrowed' funds, the hedge action must be to 'lend' funds. Therefore, we need to buy a gilt to hedge the swap. In summary:

- *Swap position*:   Pay fixed
                       Receive fixed (buy bond).

- *Hedge*:   Receive fixed
               Pay fixed (sell bond).

In normal situations we will probably wish to put on the hedge using the 5-year benchmark gilt. We need to establish the hedge ratio to enable us to decide how much nominal of the gilt to buy, which is done using each instrument's BPV. The BPV of a swap is another term for PVBP, the change in value of a swap resulting from a 1-basis-point move in interest rates. To establish the nominal amount of the gilt required, the basic calculation is:

$$\frac{\text{BPV swap}}{\text{BPV gilt}} \times 10,000$$

In our example we would need to calculate the BPV for the 5-year swap. One way to do this is to view the swap as a strip of futures contracts, whose BPV is known with certainty. The short sterling future traded on the London International Financial Futures Exchange (*LIFFE*) is a standardised contract with a BPV or 'tick value' of £12.50. (In fact, short sterling futures move in minimum units of 0.005, so that a tick value is actually £6.25. However, this is exactly half of a basis point.) As our swap is a sterling swap it will pay semiannually, while short sterling futures mature every quarter. The calculations are given in Table 11.4.

Table 11.4 Calculating the BPV for a 5-year swap.

Convert swap nominal to futures	5m × 2	=	£10m
Futures periods	4 × 5 years	=	20 contracts
Less 'fixing' of first period of swap (if a quarterly paying swap is −1)	−2	=	18 contracts
BPV	18 × 12.5 × 10	=	£2,250

The BPV of the gilt is a simple function of its modified duration (see Chapter 3) and is straightforward to calculate, although in practice will be obtained direct from a spreadsheet model or Bloomberg.

A bond trading book will often be hedged using swaps, although it is more usual for desks to use futures. The same principles will apply as we have mentioned above. Swaps are more commonly used to hedge a new issue of bonds or as asset swaps to change an IR basis from fixed to floating or *vice versa*. Two examples of swaps traded simultaneously with a purchase or issue of bonds are shown in Examples 11.2 and 11.3.

Example 11.2

A subsidiary of a leading US bank conducts investment business in the US and wishes both its income and interest payments to be on a floating-rate basis.

Purchase of Deutsche Bank 6.7% 2006 USD bond, swapped with swap counterparty, resulting in floating-rate income.

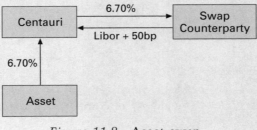

Figure 11.8 Asset swap.

The company also raises finance in the debt markets, and wishes its interest payments to be on a floating-rate basis. It issues a 1-year medium-term note (*MTN*), £15m, paying 5.3%. The bank simultaneously enters into a swap with terms on the same basis, coupon (for the fixed-rate leg) and coupon dates as the MTN, with the result that its IR liability is floating-rate.

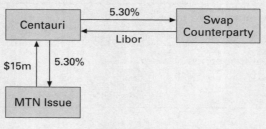

Figure 11.9   Liability swap.

Example 11.3   IR swap structure.

Consider two companies borrowing costs for a 5-year loan of £50m.

Company A: fixed 8.75%; floating Libor – desired basis is floating.

Company B: fixed 10%; floating Libor + 100 basis points – desired basis is fixed.

Without a swap:

- Company A borrows floating and pays Libor.
- Company B borrows fixed and pays 10%.

The two companies (directly, or more usually via an intermediary) decide to enter into a swap (see Figure 11.10), whereby Company A borrows fixed at 8.7% and receives fixed from Company B, who has

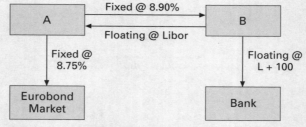

Figure 11.10   The theory of comparative advantage.

borrowed at Libor + 100 basis points and receives Libor in the swap. Company A pays floating, and company B pays fixed at the 5-year swap rate of 8.90%. The fixed leg rate is the swap rate, quoted by the bank intermediary.

With a swap:

- A pays 8.75% + Libor − 8.90% = Libor − 15 basis points.
- B pays Libor + 100 basis points + 8.90% − Libor = 9.90%.

Company A saves 15 basis points (pays Libor − 15 basis points rather than Libor flat) and B saves 10 basis points (pays 9.90% rather than 10%).

Both parties benefit from a *comparative advantage* of A in the fixed-rate market and B in the floating-rate market (spread of B over A is 125 basis points in the fixed-rate market but 100 basis points in the floating-rate market).

Swaptions

A bank or corporate may enter into an option on a swap, which is known as a *swaption*. The buyer of a swaption has the right but not the obligation to enter into an IR swap agreement during the life of the option. The terms of the swaption will specify whether the buyer is the fixed- or floating-rate payer; the seller of the options (the *writer*) becomes the counterparty to the swap if the option is exercised. In the market the convention is that if the buyer has the right to exercise the option as the fixed-rate payer, he has traded a *call swaption*, while if – by exercising the option – the buyer of the swaption becomes the floating-rate payer he has bought a *put swaption*. The writer of the swaption is the party to the other leg.

Swaptions are up to a point similar to forward start swaps, but the buyer has the *option* of whether or not to commence payments on the effective date. A bank may purchase a call swaption if it expects interest rates to rise, and will exercise the option if indeed rates do rise as the bank has expected. This is shown in the payout profiles in Figure 11.11.

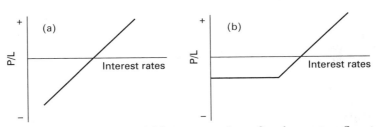

Figure 11.11 Swaptions: (a) long swap (pay fixed, receive floating);
(b) long call swaption to pay fixed and receive floating.

CROSS-CURRENCY SWAPS

So far we have discussed swap contracts where the interest payments are both in the same currency. A *cross-currency* swap is similar to an interest-rate swap, except that the currencies of the two legs are different. Like interest-rate swaps, the legs are usually fixed- and floating-rate, although again it is common to come across both fixed-rate or both floating-rate legs in a currency swap. On maturity of the swap there is an exchange of principals, and usually (but not always) there is an exchange of principals at the start of the swap. Where currencies are exchanged at the start of the swap, at the prevailing spot exchange rate for the two currencies, the exact amounts are exchanged back on maturity. During the time of the swap, the parties make interest payments in the currency that they have *received* where principals are exchanged. It may seem that exchanging the same amount on maturity gives rise to some sort of currency risk; in fact, it is this feature that removes any element of currency risk from the swap transaction.

It is probably helpful if we illustrate currency swaps with an example. In Example 11.2 we referred to a subsidiary of a US bank that invested in projects in the US. The company's requirement is for US dollars; however, it is active in issuing bonds in various currencies, according to where the most favourable conditions can be obtained and to meet investor demand. When an issue of debt is made in a currency other than dollars, the proceeds must be swapped into dollars for use in the US. To facilitate this the issuer will enter into a currency swap. One of the bank's issues was a Swiss franc step-up bond, part of the company's global MTN programme; the details of the bond are summarised below:

- *Issue date*:   March 1998
- *Maturity*:   March 2003
- *Size*:   CHF 15 million
- *Coupon*:   2.40% to 25/3/99

2.80% to 25/3/00
3.80% to 25/3/01
4.80% to 25/3/02

The bond was also callable on each anniversary from March 1999 onwards, and in fact was called by the issuer at the earliest opportunity. The issuing bank entered into a currency swap that resulted in the exchange of principals and the Swiss franc interest payments being made by the swap counterparty; in return, it paid US dollar 3-month Libor during the life of the swap. At the prevailing spot rate on the effective date, CHF 15 million was exchanged for $10.304 million; these exact same amounts would be exchanged back on the maturity of the swap. When the issue was called the swap was cancelled and the swap counterparty paid a cancellation fee. The interest payment dates on the fixed leg of the swap matched the coupon dates of the bond exactly, as shown above. The floating leg of the swap paid USD Libor on a quarterly basis, as required by the bond issuer.

The structure is shown in Figure 11.12. A currency swap structure enables a bank or corporate to borrow money in virtually any

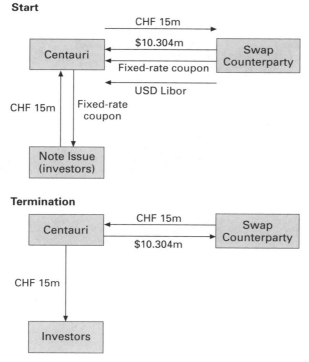

Figure 11.12 MTN issue with currency swap structure.

currency in which a liquid swap market exists, and swap this into a currency that is required. In our example the US bank was able to issue a bond that was attractive to investors. The swap mechanism also hedged the IR exposure on the Swiss franc note. The liability remaining for the issuer was quarterly floating-rate interest on US dollars as part of the swap transaction.

Bloomberg screens

There are a large number of Bloomberg screens that traders and investors can use for swaps analysis. We illustrate some of these here.

Figure 11.13 shows page SWPM which is the swap calculator. This presents the cash flow and other details for a swap of the following terms:

- USD 10 million notional;
- 5-year term;

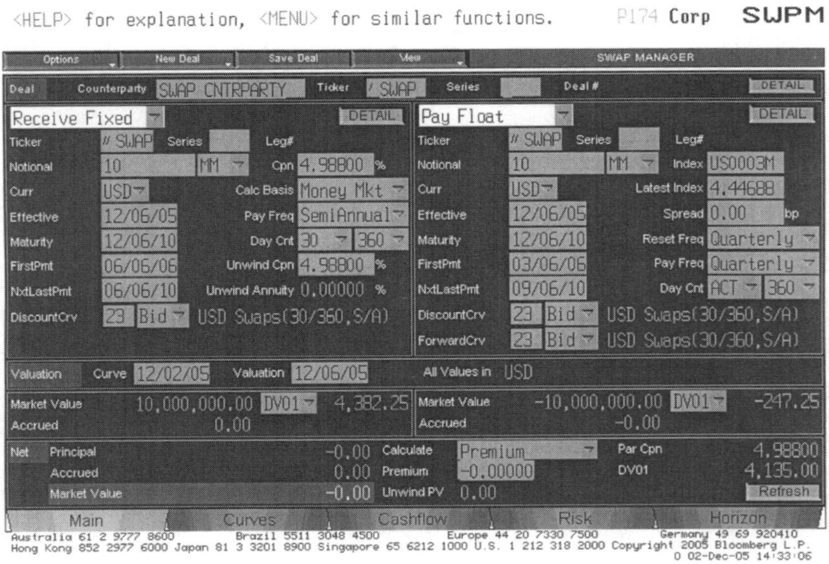

Figure 11.13 Bloomberg page SWPM, swap calculator for hypothetical USD 10 million interest-rate swap, 5-year maturity, pay floating receive fixed.

© Bloomberg L.P. Used with permission. Visit www.bloomberg.com

- pay floating, receive fixed;
- floating leg 3-month USD Libor;
- fixed rate 4.988%, semiannual.

Figure 11.14 is the term structure for the swap, showing the zero-coupon rates for each period. This is page 2 of the same screen. Figure 11.15 shows the interest-rate risk for the swap, most notably the DV01 value of $4,382. This is of course the equivalent of the basis point value (BPV) for a bond, derived from the instrument's modified duration value. Figure 11.16 shows the swap cash flows as at each payment date.

Figure 11.17 is screen SWCV which is the current swap curve as at any time; here the USD curve is shown for 2 December 2005. This screen can be updated by the user with his own inputs – for example, from the swap rules screen for a broker. These include TTIS and ICAU for Tullett and ICAP, respectively.

Figure 11.14 Bloomberg page SWPM, swap calculator page 2.

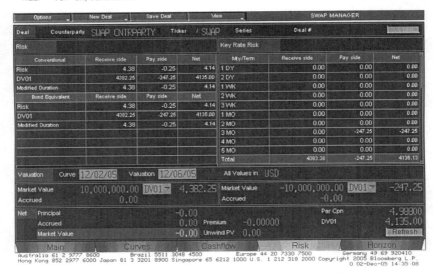

Figure 11.15 Bloomberg page SWPM, swap calculator page 3.

© Bloomberg L.P. Used with permission. Visit *www.bloomberg.com*

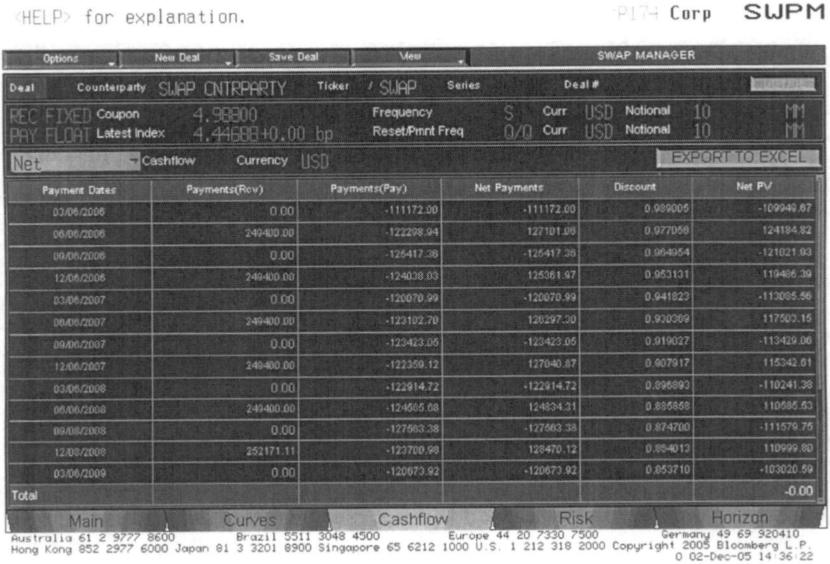

Figure 11.16 Bloomberg page SWPM, swap calculator page 4.

© Bloomberg L.P. Used with permission. Visit *www.bloomberg.com*

```
<HELP> for explanation, <MENU> for similar functions.    P174 Corp  SWCV
ENTER ALL VALUES AND HIT <GO>.
                    SWAP  CURVE  UPDATE
                       US  Curve
```

Mty/Term	Rate	Spot	Mty/Term	Rate	Spot	Mty/Term	Rate	Spot
12/ 5/05	4.0000	4.000	12/ 4/06	4.8500	4.850			
12/ 6/05	4.0300	4.030	12/ 3/07	4.8890	4.891			
12/ 9/05	4.1400	4.140	12/ 2/08	4.9180	4.921			
12/16/05	4.2000	4.200	12/ 2/09	4.9560	4.961			
12/23/05	4.2300	4.230	12/ 2/10	4.9910	4.999			
1/ 3/06	4.3200	4.320	12/ 2/11	5.0170	5.027			
2/ 2/06	4.3888	4.389	12/ 3/12	5.0400	5.053			
3/ 2/06	4.4469	4.447	12/ 2/13	5.0610	5.076			
4/ 3/06	4.5088	4.509	12/ 2/14	5.0860	5.106			
5/ 2/06	4.5719	4.572	12/ 2/15	5.1110	5.136			
6/ 2/06	4.6450	4.645	12/ 2/16	5.1360	5.166			
7/ 3/06	4.6913	4.691	12/ 4/17	5.1590	5.195			
8/ 2/06	4.7313	4.731	12/ 2/20	5.2150	5.266			
9/ 5/06	4.7719	4.772	12/ 2/25	5.2680	5.334			
10/ 2/06	4.7994	4.799	12/ 2/30	5.2920	5.363			
11/ 2/06	4.8250	4.825	12/ 3/35	5.3000	5.367			

```
                          Legend
 Shift all  |      MMkt: ACT/360
   rates    |      Swap: 30/360 , Semi                 |■|  to return to
    bp      |                                          |    calculator
Australia 61 2 9777 8600       Brazil 5511 3048 4500         Europe 44 20 7330 7500      Germany 49 69 920410
Hong Kong 852 2977 6000 Japan 81 3 3201 8900 Singapore 65 6212 1000 U.S. 1 212 318 2000 Copyright 2005 Bloomberg L.P.
                                                                          2 02-Dec-05 14:32:54
```

Figure 11.17 Bloomberg page SWCV, USD swap curve as at 2 December 2005.

FUTURES CONTRACTS

Description

A *futures contract* is an agreement between two counterparties that fixes the terms of an exchange that will take place between them at some future date. They are standardised agreements as opposed to OTC ones – when traded on an exchange – so they are also referred to as *exchange-traded futures*. In the UK financial futures are traded on LIFFE, which opened in 1982. LIFFE is the biggest financial futures exchange in Europe in terms of volume of contracts traded. There are four classes of contract traded on LIFFE: short-term IR contracts, long-term IR contracts (bond futures), currency contracts and stock index contracts. In this section we will look at bond futures contracts, which are an important part of the bond markets; they are used for hedging and speculative purposes. Most futures contracts on exchanges around the world trade at 3-month maturity intervals, with maturity dates fixed at March, June, September and December each year. This includes the contracts traded on LIFFE. Therefore, at pre-set times during the year a contract for each of these months will *expire*, and a final *settlement* price is determined for it. The further out one goes the less liquid the trading is in that contract. It is normal to see liquid trading only in the *front month* contract (the current contract, so that if we are trading in April 1999 the front month is the June 1999 future), and possibly one or two of the next contracts, for most bond futures contracts. The liquidity of contracts diminishes the further one trades out in the maturity range.

When a party establishes a position in a futures contract, it can either run this position to maturity or close out the position between trade date and maturity. If a position is closed out the party will have either a profit or loss to book. If a position is held until maturity, the party who is long the future will take delivery of the underlying asset (bond) at the settlement price; the party who is short futures will deliver the underlying asset. This is referred to as *cash settlement*.

There is no counterparty risk associated with trading exchange-traded futures, because of the role of a *clearing house* – such as the London Clearing House (*LCH*). This is the body through which contracts are settled. A clearing house acts as the buyer to all contracts sold on the exchange, and the seller to all contracts that are bought. So, in the London market the LCH acts as the counterparty to all transactions, so that settlement is effectively guaranteed. The LCH requires all exchange participants to deposit *margin* with it, a cash sum that is the cost of conducting business (plus broker's commissions). The size of the margin depends on the size of a party's net *open* position in contracts (an open position is a position in a contract that is held overnight and not closed out). There are two types of margin, *maintenance margin* and *variation margin*. Maintenance margin is the minimum level required to be held at the clearing house; the level is set by the exchange. Variation margin is the additional amount that must be deposited to cover any trading losses as the size of net open positions increases. Note that this is not like margin in, say, a repo transaction. Margin in repo is a safeguard against a drop in value of collateral that has been supplied against a loan of cash. The margin deposited at a futures exchange clearing house acts essentially as 'good faith' funds, required to provide comfort to the exchange that the futures trader is able to satisfy the obligations of the futures contract.

Bond futures contracts

We have noted that futures contracts traded on an exchange are standardised. This means that each contract represents exactly the same commodity, and it cannot be tailored to meet individual customer requirements. In this section we describe two very liquid and commonly traded contracts, starting with the US T-bond contract traded on the Chicago Board of Trade (*CBOT*). The details of this contract are given at Table 11.5.

Figure 11.18 shows Bloomberg page DES for the 'front month' long-bond futures contract as at December 2005, which was the March 2006 or H6 contract.

The terms of this contract relate to a US Treasury bond with a minimum maturity of 15 years and a notional coupon of 6%. Yet again, we've come across this term 'notional'. A futures contract specifies a notional coupon to prevent delivery and liquidity problems that would arise if there was shortage of bonds with exactly the coupon required, or if one market participant purchased a large proportion of all the bonds in issue with the required coupon.

Table 11.5 CBOT US T-bond futures contract.

Unit of trading	US Treasury bond with notional value of $100,000 and a coupon of 6%
Deliverable grades	US T-bonds with a minimum maturity of 15 years from first day of delivery month
Delivery months	March, June, September, December
Delivery date	Any business day during the delivery month
Last trading day	12:00 noon, seventh business day before last business day of delivery month
Quotation	Percent of par expressed as points and thirty-seconds of a point – e.g., 108-16 is 108 16/32 or 108.50
Minimum price movement	1/32
Tick value	$31.25
Trading hours	07:20–14:00 (trading pit) 17:20–20:05 22:30–06:00 hours (screen trading)

```
DES                                                          P174 Comdty DES
Type # <GO> For Related Function
        Futures  Contract  Description                          Page 1/2
┌─Exchange (CBT) Chicago Board of Trade ──┬─────Related Functions─────────┐
│ Name          US LONG BOND(CBT) Mar06   │ 1) CT   Contract Table         │
│ Ticker        USH6      <CMDTY>          │ 2) FHG  Futures History Graph  │
│ Notional      US 20yr 6%                 │ 3) EXS  Expiration Schedule    │
│ Contract Size  USD 100,000               │ 4) DLV  Cheapest to Deliver    │
│ Value of 1.0 pt  $  1,000                │ 5) ECO  US Economic Releases   │
│ Tick Size        0-01    (32nds)         ├──────Margin Limits────────────┤
│ Tick Value     $  31.25                  │             Speculator  Hedger │
│ Current Price  111-22   points           │ Initial        1553     1150   │
│ Contract Value $  111,687.5  @ 14:18:58  │ Secondary      1150     1150   │
│ Cycle  --- --- Mar --- --- Jun --- --- Sep --- --- Dec                    │
├──────Trading Hours──────────┬─U.S. Treasury bonds that, if callable, are not│
│ Chicago         Local       │ callable for at least 15 years from the first day│
│ 18:00-16:00   00:00-22:00   │ of the delivery month or, if not callable, have a│
│ 07:20-14:00   13:20-20:00   │ maturity of at least 15 years from the first day │
│                             │ of the delivery month.                         │
│                             │ Please see EUSA <comdty> for e-CBOT platform.  │
├─────────────────────────────┼────────────────────┬───────────────────────┤
│ First Delivery  Wed Mar  1, 2006 │ Life High  118-19 │ Generics Available   │
│ Last Delivery   Fri Mar 31, 2006 │ Life Low   108-24 │ US1   <CMDTY>        │
│ Last Trade      Wed Mar 22, 2006 │                   │     Through          │
│ First Notice    Tue Feb 28, 2006 │                   │ US5   <CMDTY>        │
│ First Trade     Tue Dec 21, 2004 │                   │                      │
└──────────────────────────────────────────────────────────────────────────┘
Australia 61 2 9777 8600      Brazil 5511 3048 4500    Europe 44 20 7330 7500    Germany 49 69 920410
Hong Kong 852 2977 6000 Japan 81 3 3201 8900 Singapore 65 6212 1000 U.S. 1 212 318 2000 Copyright 2005 Bloomberg L.P.
                                                                    0 02-Dec-05 14:19:21
```

Figure 11.18 Bloomberg page DES for March 2006 ('H6') Treasury long-bond contract.

© Bloomberg L.P. Used with permission. Visit *www.bloomberg.com*

For exchange-traded futures, a short future can deliver any bond that fits the maturity criteria specified in the contract terms. Of course, a long future would like to be delivered a high-coupon bond with significant accrued interest, while the short future would want to deliver a low-coupon bond with a low amount of interest accrued. In fact, this issue does not arise because of the way the *invoice amount* (the amount paid by the long future to purchase the bond) is calculated. The invoice amount on the expiry date is given at (11.2):

$$Inv_{amt} = P_{fut} \times CF + AI \qquad (11.2)$$

where $Inv_{amt} =$ Invoice amount;
$P_{fut} =$ Futures price;
$CF =$ Conversion factor;
$AI =$ Bond accrued interest.

Any bond that meets the maturity specifications of the futures contract is said to be in the *delivery basket*, the group of bonds that are eligible to be delivered into the futures contract. Every bond in the delivery basket will have its own *conversion factor*, which is used to equalise coupon and the accrued interest differences of all the delivery bonds. The exchange will announce the conversion factor for each bond before trading in a contract begins; the conversion factor for a bond will change over time. If a contract specifies a bond with a notional coupon of 7%, like the gilt future, then the conversion factor will be less than 1.0 for bonds with a coupon lower than 7% and higher than 1.0 for bonds with a coupon higher than 7%. A formal definition of conversion factor is given below.

Conversion factor

The conversion factor (or price factor) gives the price of an individual cash bond such that its yield to maturity on the delivery day of the futures contract is equal to the notional coupon of the contract. The product of the conversion factor and the futures price is the forward price available in the futures market for that cash bond (plus the cost of funding, referred to as the gross basis).

Although conversion factors equalise the yield on bonds, bonds in the delivery basket will trade at different yields, and for this reason they are not 'equal' at the time of delivery. Certain bonds will be cheaper than others, and one bond will be the *cheapest-to-deliver* (*CTD*) bond. The CTD bond is the one that gives the greatest return from a strategy of buying a bond and simultaneously selling the futures contract, and then closing out positions on the expiry of the contract. This so-called *cash-and-carry trading* is actively pursued by proprietary trading desks in banks. If a contract is purchased and then held to maturity the buyer will receive, via the exchange's clearing house, the CTD gilt. Traders sometimes try to exploit arbitrage price differentials between the future and the CTD gilt, known as *basis trading*. This is discussed in the author's book *The Futures Bond Basis*, the second edition of which is part of the same John Wiley & Sons series as this book.

Figure 11.19 shows page DLV, which is the delivery basket for the Mar06 Treasury long-bond contract, the same contract whose terms were shown at Figure 11.18. We see that the CTD bond as at 2 December 2005 is the 8.125% 2021 Treasury bond. There are a large number of eligible securities in this basket.

We summarise the contract specification of the long gilt futures contract traded on LIFFE at Table 11.6. There is also a medium gilt contract on LIFFE, which was introduced in 1998 (having been

● ●

```
<HELP> for explanation, <MENU> for similar functions.        P174 Comdty DLV
Hit (NUMBER) <GO> to view Historical Basis/Repo
Cheapest  to  Deliver          Trade 12/ 2/05 Dlv 3/31/06 p.1 / 2
   US LONG BOND(CBT) Mar06  USH6  111-20    Set 12/ 5/05 Cheapest IRP= 3.98
                                          <32NDS>  116 Days Act/360  <32NDS>
PRICES AS DECIMALS N      (Mid)         Conv.       Gross Implied  Actual  Net
     Order DR re-sort? Y  Price Source Yield C.Factor Basis Repo%    Repo% Basis
             MASTER=                                                 4.12
  1) T 8 ⅛ 05/15/21    135-23+ BGN  4.818 1.2083   27.5  3.98       4.12   2.0
  2) T 8 ⅛ 08/15/21    136-00+ BGN  4.825 1.2102   29.7  3.74       4.12   5.4
  3) T 8   11/15/21    135-00  BGN  4.827 1.2000   33.6  3.47       4.12   9.1
  4) T 7 ¼ 08/15/22    127-13  BGN  4.838 1.1285   46.0  2.09       4.12  26.9
  5) T 7 ⅝ 11/15/22    132-00+ BGN  4.835 1.1687   49.9  2.07       4.12  28.0
  6) T 7 ⅛ 02/15/23    126-15+ BGN  4.838 1.1177   55.1  1.31       4.12  36.8
  7) T 6 ¼ 08/15/23    116-19+ BGN  4.841 1.0265   64.8  -.12       4.12  51.2
  8) T 7 ½ 11/15/24    132-24  BGN  4.840 1.1663   82.0  -.37       4.12  61.6
  9) T 7 ⅝ 02/15/25    134-17  BGN  4.841 1.1813   85.4  -.57       4.12  65.5
 10) T 6 ⅞ 08/15/25    125-19  BGN  4.843 1.0990   93.4  -1.81      4.12  77.3
 11) T 6 ¾ 08/15/26    124-23+ BGN  4.843 1.0871  108.4  -3.08      4.12  93.2
 12) T 6   02/15/26    114-26+ BGN  4.840  .9999  102.9  -3.52      4.12  91.0
 13) T 6 ½ 11/15/26    121-21  BGN  4.843 1.0585  112.0  -3.61      4.12  97.2
 14) T 6 ⅝ 02/15/27    123-16  BGN  4.839 1.0735  117.5  -3.92      4.12 103.0
 15) T 6 ⅜ 08/15/27    120-15+ BGN  4.839 1.0446  124.2  -4.76      4.12 111.0
 16) T 6 ⅛ 11/15/27    117-09+ BGN  4.837 1.0150  127.9  -5.37      4.12 115.1

Australia 61 2 9777 8600      Brazil 5511 3048 4500      Europe 44 20 7330 7500      Germany 49 69 920410
Hong Kong 852 2977 6000 Japan 81 3 3201 8900 Singapore 65 6212 1000 U.S. 1 212 318 2000 Copyright 2005 Bloomberg L.P.
                                                                    0 02-Dec-05 14:19:29
```

Figure 11.19 Bloomberg page DLV for March 2006 ('H6') Treasury long-bond contract, as at 2 December 2005.

© Bloomberg L.P. Used with permission. Visit *www.bloomberg.com*

discontinued in the early 1990s). This trades a notional 5-year gilt, with eligible gilts being those of 4 to 7 years maturity.

Figure 11.20 shows Bloomberg page DES for the 'front month' long-gilt futures contract as at December 2005, while Figure 11.21 shows page DLV for this contract. We see that there are fewer eligible bonds for this contract, partly explained by the fact that there are fewer gilts in issue than Treasuries.

Futures pricing

Although it may not appear so on first sight, a futures exchange is probably as close as it is to get to an example of the economist's perfect and efficient market. The immediacy and liquidity of the market will ensure that at virtually all times the price of any futures contract reflects fair value. In essence, because a futures contract represents an underlying asset – albeit a synthetic one – its price cannot differ from the actual cash market price of the asset itself.

Table 11.6 LIFFE long gilt future contract description.

Unit of trading	UK gilt bond having a face value of £100,000 and a coupon of 6% and a *notional* maturity of 10 years (changed from contract value of £50,000 from the September 1998 contract)
Deliverable grades	UK gilts with a maturity ranging from $8\frac{3}{4}$ to 13 years from the first day of the delivery month (changed from 10–15 years from the December 1998 contract)
Delivery months	March, June, September, December
Delivery date	Any business day during the delivery month
Last trading day	11:00 hours two business days before last business day of delivery month
Quotation	Percent of par expressed as points and hundredths of a point – e.g., 114.56 (changed from points and 1/32nds of a point, as in 114-17 meaning 114 17/32 or 114.53125, from the June 1998 contract)
Minimum price movement	0.01 of one point (one tick)
Tick value	£10
Trading hours	08:00–16:15 hours 16:22–18:00 hours (automated pit trading on screen)

This is because the market sets futures prices such that they are arbitrage-free. We can illustrate this with an hypothetical example.

Let us say that the benchmark 10-year bond, with a coupon of 8%, is trading at par. This bond is the underlying asset represented by the long bond futures contract; the front month contract expires in precisely 3 months. If we also say that the 3-month Libor rate (the repo rate) is 6%, what is fair value for the front month futures contract?

For the purpose of illustration let us start by assuming the futures price to be 105. We could carry out the following arbitrage-type trade:

- buy the bond for £100;
- simultaneously sell the future at £105;
- borrow £100 for 3 months at the repo rate of 6%.

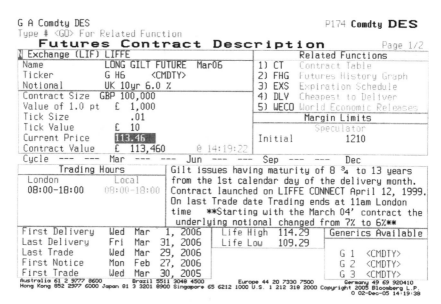

Figure 11.20 Bloomberg page DES for March 2006 ('H6') long-gilt contract.

© Bloomberg L.P. Used with permission. Visit *www.bloomberg.com*

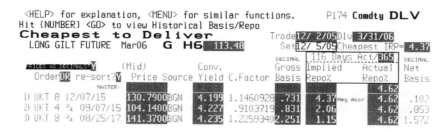

Figure 11.21 Bloomberg page DLV for March 2006 ('H6') long-gilt contract as at 2 December 2005.

© Bloomberg L.P. Used with permission. Visit *www.bloomberg.com*

As this is a leveraged trade we have borrowed the funds with which to buy the bond, and the loan is fixed at 3 months because we will hold the position to the futures contract expiry, which is in exactly 3 months' time. At expiry, as we are short futures we will deliver the underlying bond to the futures clearing house and close out the loan. This strategy will result in cash flows for us as shown below:

- *Futures settlement cash flows*: Price received for bond = 105.00
  Bond accrued = 2.00
    (8% coupon for 3 months)
  Total proceeds = 107.00

- *Loan cash flows*: Repayment of principal = 100.00
  Loan interest = 1.500
    (6% repo rate for 3 months)
  Total outlay = 101.50

The trade has resulted in a profit of £5.50, and this profit is guaranteed as we have traded the two positions simultaneously and held them both to maturity. We are not affected by subsequent market movements. The trade is an example of a pure arbitrage, which is risk-free. There is no cash outflow at the start of the trade because we borrowed the funds used to buy the bond. In essence, we have locked in the forward price of the bond by trading the future today, so that the final settlement price of the futures contract is irrelevant. If the situation described above were to occur in practice it would be very short-lived, precisely because arbitrageurs would buy the bond and sell the future to make this profit. This activity would force changes in the prices of both bond and future until the profit opportunity was removed.

So, in our illustration the price of the future was too high (and possibly the price of the bond was too low as well) and not reflecting fair value because the price of the synthetic asset was out of line with the cash asset.

What if the price of the future was too low? Let us imagine that the futures contract is trading at 95.00. We could then carry out the following trade:

- sell the bond at 100;
- simultaneously buy the future for 95;
- lend the proceeds of the short sale (100) for 3 months at 6%.

This trade has the same procedure as the first one with no initial cash outflow, except that we have to cover the short position in the repo market, through which we invest the sale proceeds at the repo rate of 6%. After 3 months we are delivered a bond as part of the futures settlement, and this is used to close out our short position. How has our strategy fared?

- *Futures settlement*   Clean price of bond = 95.00
  cash flows   Bond accrued = 2.00
                           Total cash outflow = 97.00

- *Loan cash flows*   Principal on loan maturity = 100.00
                           Interest from loan = 1.500
                           Total cash inflow = 101.500

The profit of £4.50 is again a risk-free arbitrage profit. Of course, our hypothetical world has ignored considerations such as bid–offer spreads for the bond, future and repo rates, which would apply in the real world and impact on any trading strategy. Yet again, however, the futures price is out of line with the cash market and has provided opportunity for arbitrage profit.

Given the terms and conditions that apply in our example, there is one price for the futures contract at which no arbitrage profit opportunity is available. If we set the future price at 99.5, we would see that both trading strategies, buying the bond and selling the future or selling the bond and buying the future, yield a net cash flow of 0. There is no profit to be made from either strategy. So, at 99.5 the futures price is in line with the cash market, and it will only move as the cash market price moves; any other price will result in an arbitrage profit opportunity.

Arbitrage-free futures pricing

The previous section demonstrated how we can arrive at the fair value for a bond futures contract provided we have certain market information. The market mechanism and continuous trading will ensure that the fair price *is* achieved, as arbitrage profit opportunities are eliminated. We can determine the bond future's price given:

- the coupon of the underlying bond, and its price in the cash market;
- the interest rate for borrowing or lending funds, from the trade date to the maturity date of the futures contract. This is known as the *repo* rate.

For the purpose of deriving this pricing model we can ignore bid–offer spreads and borrowing and lending spreads. If we set the following:

r is the repo rate;
rc is the bond's running yield;
P_{bond} is the price of the cash bond;
P_{fut} is the price of the futures contract;
t is the time to expiry of the futures contract.

We can substitute these symbols into the cash flow profile for our first trade strategy, that of buying the bond and selling the future. This gives us:

- *Futures settlement cash flows*   Clean price for bond $= P_{fut}$
  Bond accrued $= rc \times t \times P_{bond}$
  Total proceeds $= P_{fut} + (rc \times t \times P_{bond})$

- *Loan cash flows*   Repayment of loan principal $= P_{bond}$
  Loan interest $= r \times t \times P_{bond}$
  Total outlay $= P_{bond} + (r \times t \times P_{bond})$

The profit from the trade would be the difference between the proceeds and outlay, which we can set as follows:

$$\text{Profit} = P_{fut} + rc \times t \times P_{bond} - (P_{bond} + r \times t \times P_{bond})$$

We have seen how the futures price is at fair value when there is no profit to be gained from carrying out this trade, so if we set profit at 0, we get the following:

$$0 = P_{fut} + rc \times t \times P_{bond} - (P_{bond} + r \times t \times P_{bond})$$

Solving this expression for the futures price P_{fut} gives us:

$$P_{fut} = P_{bond} + P_{bond}t(r - rc)$$

Re-arranging this we get:

$$P_{fut} = P_{bond}(1 + t[r - rc]) \tag{11.3}$$

If we repeat the procedure for the other strategy, that of selling the bond and simultaneously buying the future and set the profit to 0, we will obtain the same expression for the futures price as given in (11.3) above.

It is the level of the repo rate in the market, compared with the running yield on the underlying bond, that sets the price for the futures contract. From the examples used at the start of this section we can see that it is the cost of funding compared with the repo rate that determines if the trade strategy results in a profit. The expression $[r - rc]$ from (11.3) is the net financing cost in the arbitrage trade, and is known as the *cost of carry*. If the running yield on the bond is higher than the funding cost (the repo rate) this is positive funding or *positive carry*. Negative funding (*negative carry*) is when the repo rate is higher than the running yield. The level of $[r - rc]$ will determine whether the futures price is trading above the cash market price or below it. If we have positive carry (when $rc > r$) then the futures price will trade below the cash market price, known as trading at a *discount*. Where $r > rc$ and we have negative carry then the futures price will be at a premium over the cash market price. If the net funding cost was 0, such that we had neither positive or negative carry, then the futures price would be equal to the underlying bond price.

The cost of carry related to a bond futures contract is a function of the yield curve. In a positive yield curve environment the 3-month repo rate is likely to be lower than the running yield on a bond so that the cost of carry is likely to be positive. As there is generally only a liquid market in long bond futures out to contracts that mature up to 1 year from the trade date, with a positive yield curve it would be unusual to have a short-term repo rate higher than the running yield on the long bond. So, in such an environment we would have the future trading at a discount to the underlying cash bond. If there is a negative sloping yield curve the futures price will trade at a premium to the cash price. It is in circumstances of changes in the shape of the yield curve that opportunities for relative value and arbitrage trading arise, especially as the bond that is cheapest-to-deliver for the futures contract may change with large changes in the curve.

Hedging using futures

Bond futures are used for a variety of purposes. Much of one day's trading in futures will be speculative – that is, a punt on the direction of the market. Another main use of futures is to hedge bond positions. In theory, when hedging a cash bond position with a bond futures contract, if cash and futures prices move together then any loss from one position will be offset by a gain from the other. When prices move exactly in lockstep with each other, the hedge is considered perfect. In practice, the price of even the cheapest-to-deliver bond (which one can view as being the bond being traded – implicitly – when one is trading the bond future) and the bond future will not move exactly in line with each other over a period of time. The difference between the cash price and the futures price is called the *basis*. The risk that the basis will change in an unpredictable way is known as *basis risk*. The term *basis* is also used to describe the difference in price between the future and the deliverable cash bond. The basis is of considerable significance. It is often used to establish the fair value of a futures contract, as it is a function of the cost of carry. The *gross basis* is defined (for deliverable bonds only) as follows:

$$\text{Gross basis} = \text{Clean bond price} - (\text{Futures price} \times \text{Conversion factor})$$

Futures are a liquid and straightforward way of hedging a bond position. By hedging a bond position the trader or fund manager is hoping to balance the loss on the cash position by the profit gained from the hedge. However, the hedge will not be exact for all bonds except the CTD bond, which we can assume is the futures contract underlying bond. The basis risk in a hedge position arises because the bond being hedged is not identical to the CTD bond. The basic principle is that if the trader is long (or net long, where the desk is running long and short positions in different bonds) in the cash market, an equivalent number of futures contracts will be sold to set up the hedge. If the cash position is short the trader will buy futures. The hedging requirement can arise for different reasons. A market maker will wish to hedge positions arising out of client business, when she is unsure when the resulting bond positions will be unwound. A fund manager may, for example, know that she needs to realise a cash sum at a specific time in the future to meet fund liabilities, and sell bonds at that time. The market maker will want to hedge against a drop in value of positions during the time the bonds are held. The fund manager will want to hedge against a rise in interest rates between now and the bond sale date, to protect the value of the portfolio.

When putting on the hedge position the key is to trade the correct number of futures contracts. This is determined by using the *hedge ratio* of the bond and the future, which is a function of the volatilities of the two instruments. The amount of contracts to trade is calculated using the hedge ratio, which is given by:

$$\text{Hedge ratio} = \frac{\text{Volatility of bond to be hedged}}{\text{Volatility of hedging instrument}}$$

Therefore, one needs to use the volatility values of each instrument. We can see from the calculation that if the bond is more volatile than the hedging instrument, then a greater amount of the hedging instrument will be required. Let us now look in greater detail at the hedge ratio.

THE HEDGE RATIO

There are different methods available to calculate hedge ratios. The most common ones are the conversion factor method, which can be used for deliverable bonds (also known as the *price factor* method) and the modified duration method (also known as the *basis point value* method).

Where a hedge is put on against a bond that is in the futures delivery basket it is common for the conversion factor to be used to calculate the hedge ratio. A conversion factor hedge ratio is more useful as it is transparent and remains constant, irrespective of any changes in the price of the cash bond or the futures contract. The number of futures contracts required to hedge a deliverable bond using the conversion factor hedge ratio is determined using the following equation:

$$\frac{\text{Number of}}{\text{futures lots}} = \frac{\text{Nominal value of cash bond} \times \text{Bond conversion factor}}{\text{Nominal value of the futures contract}}$$

(11.4)

Unlike the conversion factor method, the modified duration hedge ratio may be used for all bonds, both deliverable and non-deliverable. In calculating this hedge ratio the modified duration is multiplied by the dirty price of the cash bond to obtain the BPV. As we discovered in Chapter 5, the BPV represents the actual impact of a change in the yield on the price of a specific bond. The BPV allows the trader to calculate the hedge ratio to reflect the different price sensitivity of the chosen bond (compared with the CTD bond) to IR movements. The hedge ratio calculated using BPVs must be constantly updated, because it will change if the price of the bond and/or the futures contract changes. This may necessitate periodic adjustments to the number of lots used in the hedge. The number of futures contracts required to hedge a bond using the BPV method is calculated using the following:

$$\frac{\text{Number of}}{\text{futures lots}} = \frac{\text{Nominal value of bond}}{\text{Nominal value of futures contract}} \times \frac{\text{BPV bond}}{\text{BPV future}}$$

(11.5)

where the BPV of a futures contract is defined with respect to the BPV of its CTD bond as given below:

$$\text{BPV futures contract} = \frac{\text{BPV CTD bond}}{\text{Conversion factor CTD bond}}$$

INTEREST-RATE OPTIONS

As with the other instruments described in this chapter, there is a large and diverse literature available on options and option products. We introduce the subject here – interested readers may wish to look up the further reading highlighted in the Bibliography.

Introduction

Options have unique characteristics that make them stand apart from other classes of derivatives. Because they confer a right to conduct a certain transaction, but not an obligation, their payoff profile is different from other financial assets, both cash and off-balance sheet. The advance in financial engineering since the early 1980s is demonstrated most spectacularly in the growth of options, which are very flexible and versatile financial instruments. Options contracts were originally introduced on agricultural commodities over 200 years ago, financial options date from the 1970s. A seminal paper by Black and Scholes, which appeared in the *Journal of Political Economy* in 1973, was the essential catalyst, since as a result of this research the market now had a straightforward way to price options. There are now several other option pricing models used in the markets in addition to Black–Scholes, some developed specifically for the new exotic option structures that have been introduced. When originally traded they were essentially vanilla instruments; however, the flexibility of options was such that they were soon combined into exotic structures. The range of combinations of options that can be dealt today, and the complex structured products that they form part of is constrained only by imagination and customer requirements. Virtually all participants in capital markets will have some requirement that is met by the use of options. Options are a big subject, and there is a large selection of specialist texts devoted to them. In this section we provide an introductory overview of bond options, some basic terminology and one or two uses that they might be put to. Interested readers are directed to the texts listed in the Bibliography.

Definition

An option is a contract in which the buyer has the right, but not the obligation, to buy or sell an underlying asset at a predetermined price during a specified period of time. The seller of the option, known as the *writer*, grants this right to the buyer in return for receiving the price of the option, known as the *premium*. An option that grants the right to buy an asset is a *call option*, while the corresponding right to sell an asset is a *put option*. The option buyer has a long position in the option and the option seller has a short position in the option.

Before looking at the other terms that define an option contract, we'll discuss the main feature that differentiates an option from all other derivative instruments, and from cash assets. Because options confer on a buyer the right to effect a transaction, but not the obligation (and correspondingly on a seller the obligation, if requested by the buyer, to effect a transaction), their risk/reward characteristics are different from other financial products. The payoff profile from holding an option is unlike that of any other instrument. Let us consider the payoff profiles for a vanilla call option and a gilt futures contract. Suppose that a trader buys one lot of the gilt futures contract at 114.00 and holds it for 1 month before selling it. On closing the position the profit made will depend on the contract sale price: if it is above 114 the trader will have made a profit and if below 114.00 she will have made a loss. On one lot this represents a £1,000 gain for each point above 114.00. The same applies to someone who had a short position in the contract and closed it out: if the contract is bought back at any price below 114.00 the trader will realise a profit. The profile is shown in Figure 11.22.

This profile is the same for other OBS instruments such as FRAs and swaps, and of course for cash instruments such as bonds or equity. The payoff profile therefore has a *linear* characteristic, and it is linear whether one has bought or sold the contract.

The profile for an option contract differs from the conventional one. Because options confer a right to one party but not an obligation (the buyer), and an obligation but not a right to the seller, the profile will differ according to the position. Suppose now that our trader buys a call option that grants the right to buy a gilt futures contract at a price of 114.00 at some point during the life of the option, her resulting payoff profile will be like that shown in Figure 11.23. If during the life of the option the price of the futures contract rises above 114.00, the trader will exercise her right to buy the future, under the terms of the option contract. This is known as *exercising* the option. If, on the other hand, the price of the future falls below 114.00, the trader will not exercise the option and, unless there is a reversal in price of the future, it will eventually expire worthless. In this respect it is exactly

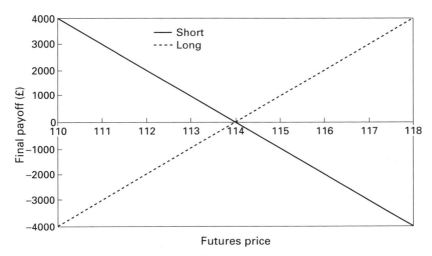

Figure 11.22   Payoff profile for a bond futures contract.

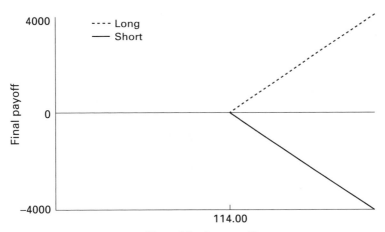

Figure 11.23   Payoff profile for a call option contract.

like an equity or bond warrant. The seller of this particular option has a very different payout profile. If the price of the future rises above 114.00 and the option is exercised, the seller will bear the loss that the buyer is now enjoying. The seller's payoff profile is also shown in Figure 11.23. If the option is not exercised and expires, the seller will have pocketed her premium, and this makes her a profit.

This illustrates how – unlike every other financial instrument – the holders of long and short positions in options do not have the same symmetrical payoff profile. The buyer of the call option will benefit if the price of the underlying asset rises, but will not lose if the price falls (except the funds paid for purchasing the rights under the option). The seller of the call option will suffer loss if the price of the underlying asset rises, but will not benefit if it falls (except realising the funds received for writing the option). The buyer has a right but not an obligation, while the seller has an obligation. The premium charged for the option is the seller's compensation for granting such a right to the buyer.

Let us recap on the basic features of the call option. A call option is the right to buy, without any obligation, a specified quantity of the underlying asset at a given price on or before the expiry date of the option. A long position in a call option allows the holder, as shown in Figure 11.23, to benefit from a rise in the market price of the underlying asset. If our trader wanted to benefit from a fall in the market level, but did not want to short the market, she would buy a *put* option. A put option is the right to sell, again without any obligation, a specified quantity of the underlying asset at a given price on or before the expiry date of the option. Put options have the same payoff profile as call options, but in the opposite direction!

Originally, options were written on commodities such as wheat and sugar. Nowadays, these are referred to as *options on physicals*. Today, one is able to buy or sell an option on a wide range of underlying instruments, including financial products such as foreign exchange, bonds, equities, and commodities, and derivatives such as futures, swaps, equity indices and other options.

Option terminology

Let us now consider the main terminology used in the options markets.

- *Call* – the right to buy the underlying asset.
- *Put* – the right to sell the underlying asset.
- *Strike price* – the price at which the option may be exercised, also known as the *exercise* price.
- *Expiry date* – the last date on which the option can be exercised, also known as the maturity date.

- *American* – the style of option; an American option can be exercised at any time until expiry.
- *European* – an option which may be exercised on the maturity date only, and not before.
- *Premium* – the price of the option, paid by the buyer to the seller.

The *strike price* describes the price at which an option is exercised. For example, a call option to buy ordinary shares of a listed company might have a strike price of £10.00. This means that if the option is exercised the buyer will pay £10 per share. Options are generally either *American* or *European* style, which defines the times during the option's life when it can be exercised. There is no geographic relevance to these terms, as both styles can be traded in any market. There is also another type, *Bermudan*-style options, which can be exercised at pre-set dates.

The payoff profiles for bought and sold calls and puts are shown at *Figure 11.24.*

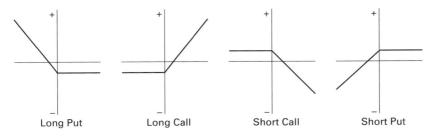

Figure 11.24 Basic option profiles.

Option premium

The *premium* of an option is the price at which the option is sold. Option premium is made up of two constituents, *intrinsic value* and *time value*.

The intrinsic value of an option is the value of the option if it is exercised immediately, and it represents the difference between the strike price and the current underlying asset price. If a call option on a bond futures contract has a strike price of £100 and the future is currently trading at £105, the intrinsic value of the option is £5, as this would be the immediate profit gain to the option holder if it were exercised. Since an option will only be exercised if there is benefit to the holder from so doing, its intrinsic value will never be less than 0. So, in our example if the bond future was trading at £95 the intrinsic value of the call option would be 0. For a put option the intrinsic value is the amount by which the current underlying price is below the strike price. When an option has intrinsic value it is described as being *in-the-money*. When the strike price for a call option is higher than the underlying price (or for a put option is lower than the underlying price) and has no intrinsic value it is said to be *out-of-the-money*. An option for which the strike price is equal to the current underlying price is said to be *at-the-money*. This term is normally used at the time the option is first traded, in cases where the strike price is set to the current price of the underlying asset.

The time value of an option is the amount by which the option value exceeds the intrinsic value. An option writer will almost always demand a premium that is higher than the option's intrinsic value, because of the risk that the writer is taking on. This reflects the fact that over time the price of the underlying asset may change sufficiently to produce a much higher intrinsic value. During the life of an option, the option seller has nothing more to gain over the initial premium at which the option was sold; however, until expiry there is a chance that the writer will lose if the markets move against her. The value of an option that is out-of-the-money is composed entirely of time value.

Pricing options

When we have discussed all the IR products described in this book so far, both cash and derivatives, it has been possible to determine pricing because of rigid mathematical principles, and also because on maturity of the instrument there is a defined procedure that takes place such that one is able to calculate fair value. This does not apply to options because there is uncertainty as to what the outcome will be on expiry; an option seller does not know whether the option will be exercised or not. This factor makes options more difficult to price than other market instruments.

The original pricing model for options was the Black–Scholes (B-S) model, published by Fischer Black and Myron Scholes in 1973. Banks use this model or variations of this model, as well as another pricing model known as the *binomial* method. Deriving the B-S model is outside the scope of this book and involves some frighteningly complex mathematics, so we will not attempt it here. Interested readers are recommended to study the subject further via some of the texts in the Bibliography. However, to give an idea of the principles involved we will briefly restate the B-S model here.

If we accept that the fair price of any financial asset is its expected value, the fair value of an option at expiry would be the sum of all its possible values, multiplied by the probability of that value occurring. Because options can end up being virtually any value, the probability distribution that we need to use is a continuous rather than a discrete one. One of the assumptions of the B-S model is that prices in the market follow a normal distribution (see the author's book *Introduction to Value-at-Risk* in this series), or strictly speaking a *lognormal* distribution, meaning that the logarithm of the prices follows a normal distribution. The B-S model for the fair value of a call option is:

$$C = SN(d_1) - Xe^{-rt}N(d_2) \qquad (11.6)$$

with

$$d_1 = \frac{\ln\left(\frac{S}{X}\right) + \left(r + \frac{\sigma^2}{2}\right)t}{\sigma\sqrt{t}} \quad \text{and} \quad d_2 = d_1 - \sigma\sqrt{t}$$

where
$C =$ Value of a call option;
$S =$ Current price of the underlying asset;
$X =$ Strike price;
$r =$ Risk-free market rate of interest;
$t =$ Time to maturity;
$N(\cdot) =$ Cumulative normal distribution function;
$\sigma =$ Volatility of the underlying asset returns.

The B-S model can be set up as a computer or spreadsheet model to enable the fair value of a call option to be calculated. It can be viewed as measuring the expected present value of the option based on the assumption that market prices follow a lognormal distribution. Statisticians often point out that in practice the distribution of market prices has 'fatter tails' than that observed in a standard normal distribution, and the term for this feature is *leptokurtosis*. This is not something we need to consider here. The B-S model is widely used in the markets, although as we have noted other pricing models also exist that are used – often to price non-vanilla *exotic* options. As well as the assumption of normal distribution of prices the model makes certain other assumptions, including the existence of a liquid market, ability to sell short, no bid–offer IR spreads, the option is European style and zero transaction costs. The model is often modified to allow for when these assumptions do not apply.

Table 11.7 Black–Scholes model reproduced in Excel spreadsheet, showing required cell formulae – Black–Scholes calculator.

Cell	C	D	
8	**Underlying price, S**	100	
9	Volatility %	0.0691	
10	Option maturity years	0.25	
11	**Strike price, X**	99.50	
12	Risk-free interest rate %	0.05	
13			
14			
15			**Cell formulae:**
16	ln (S/X)	0.005 012 542	= LN (D8/D11)
17	Adjusted return	0.000 045 601 250 0	= ((D12 − D9)^2/2)*D10
18	Time-adjusted volatility	0.131 434 394	= (D9*D10)$^{0.5}$
19	d_2	0.038 484 166	= (D16 + D17)/D18
20	$N(d_2)$	0.515 349 172	= NORMSDIST(D19)
21			
22	d_1	0.169 918 56	= D19 + D18
23	$N(d_1)$	0.567 462 908	= NORMSDIST(D22)
24	e^{-rt}	0.987 577 8	= EXP(−D10*D12)
25			
26	**CALL**	6.106 024 296	= D8*D23 − D11*D20*D24
27	**PUT**	4.370 015 446*	= D26 − D8 + D11*D24

* By put–call parity, $P = C - S \times Xe^{-rt}$.

Table 11.7 shows an Excel spreadsheet set up with the B-S model to price an option on a bond with the following terms:

- *Underlying price, S*   100
  Volatility (%) = 0.0691
  Option maturity (years) = 0.25

- *Strike price, X*   99.50
  Risk-free interest rate (%) = 0.05

We can see the cell formulae required in Table 11.5.

The B-S model – as we have reproduced it – calculates the fair value for a call option. What if we need to price a put option? In fact, the model can be used in the same manner to price put options as well, as a result of the relationship between the price of a call option and a put option with the same terms. This relationship is known as the *put–call parity*. Essentially, this states that the principle of arbitrage-free pricing demands that call and put option prices for options of otherwise similar terms must be equal.

Note that one of the inputs to the model is the asset's *volatility*. Of the inputs to the B-S model, the variability of the underlying asset, or its volatility, is the most problematic. The distribution of asset prices is assumed to follow a lognormal distribution, because the logarithm of the prices is normally distributed (we assume lognormal rather than normal distribution to allow for the fact that prices cannot – as could be the case in a normal distribution – have negative values): the range of possible prices starts at 0 and cannot assume a negative value. Volatility is defined as the annualised standard deviation of returns (prices).

However, calculating volatility using the standard statistical method gives us a figure for *historic volatility*. What is required is a figure for *future* volatility, since this is relevant for pricing an option expiring in the future. Future volatility cannot be measured directly, by definition. Market makers get around this by using an option pricing model 'backwards', as shown in Figure 11.25.

An option pricing model calculates the option price from volatility and other parameters. Used in reverse the model can calculate the volatility implied by the option price. Volatility measured in this way is called *implied volatility*. Evaluating implied volatility is straightforward using this method and generally more appropriate than using historic volatility, as it provides a clearer measure of an option's fair value. Implied volatilities of deeply in-the-money or out-of-the-money options tend to be relatively high.

Bond options will also be a function of the coupon on a bond. Coupons sometimes lower the price of a call option because a coupon makes it more attractive to hold a bond rather than an option on the bond. Call options on bonds are often priced at a lower level than similar options on, say, zero-coupon bonds.

Figure 11.25 Option-implied volatility and pricing model.

Certain options cannot be priced using the B-S model and in such cases other modes, such as the binomial pricing model, are used.

Behaviour of option prices

We can see by examining the components of the B-S model that the price of an option will vary not only with the price of the underlying instrument but also with other factors such as volatility, time to expiry and interest rates. This makes it unique amongst derivatives, whose prices (options apart) generally move in line with the underlying rate. For example, the value of an IR swap will move with the swap rate, while a bond future generally moves tick-for-tick with the price of the CTD bond. Options differ and as a result the relationship between option price and the price of the underlying is not always linear. The market therefore uses four quantities to measure the movement in the price of an option, known as the 'Greeks'. Some of these are defined below:

- *delta* – the change in option premium (price) for a unit change in the underlying asset price;
- *theta* – the change in premium for a unit change in the time to expiry;
- *rho* – the change in premium for a unit change in interest rates;
- *vega* – the change in premium for a unit change in volatility;
- *lambda* – the percentage change in premium for a percentage change in the underlying asset price;
- *gamma* – the change in *delta* for a unit change in the underlying asset price.

To calculate *delta*, therefore, the expression is:

$$\delta = \frac{\text{Change in option premium}}{\text{Change in underlying price}}$$

This is also known as the *hedge ratio*. All these units of measurement are used to manage whole option books rather than one option position, as they allow the option trader to observe the impact of market moves on the entire book. By taking a weighted aggregate of all the Greeks, it is possible to summarise the position and exposure of the option portfolio. As an example, if there is a change in market volatility, the combined effect on the book can be calculated, obviating the need to re-price all the options individually. This is why we referred to the delta of an options book as its hedge ratio. To hedge an option book against changes in the underlying asset price, the option trader would manage the book so that the portfolio delta has a sum of 0, which would make it *delta neutral*. If the delta is kept at 0 the book will be effectively hedged.

Using options in bond markets

Long call strategy

A strategy of buying call options is a simple and straightforward way to put on a position where one is anticipating a fall in interest rates and a rise in the price of bonds. The trader will buy an option on an underlying bond. For example, say that a trader buys a 3-month call option on a 10-year government bond with a strike price of £100 per cent. The premium for the option is £5. On the expiry date, if the bond is trading at above 100 the option will be exercised; if the bond is trading below 100 the option will not be exercised and will expire worthless. The trader will then have lost the premium paid for the option. We can see that for the strategy to break even the bond must be trading at £105 or above, otherwise the net profit/loss will be eaten away by the premium paid for the option.

What if the underlying bond trades at above £105 before the expiry of the option? If the option is European it can only be exercised on maturity, so this fact is not relevant. But what if the option is American style? Should the trader exercise? Remember that the value of an option is comprised of intrinsic value and time value. If an option is exercised before expiry, the holder will receive the intrinsic value of the option but not the time option (as it is being exercised there is no time value to allow for). However, if the option itself is sold, rather than exercised, then the holder will receive the full worth of the option, both intrinsic value and time value. So, in practice, American options are rarely exercised ahead of maturity and trade in a similar fashion to European options.

Short call strategy

If a trader's view is that interest rates will rise or remain stable she can sell or *write* a call option. The income from such a trade is finite and limited to the premium received for selling the option. The risk

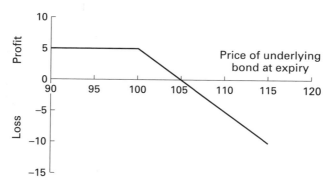

Figure 11.26   Profit/loss profile for short call strategy.

profile for this strategy is the mirror image of the long call profile that would apply in our first example. If we consider a short call option with the same terms as above, the strike price is £100 and the writer will realise profit if the underlying bond does not rise above £105. This is why a trader may write the option either because her view of bond prices is bearish, or because she expects interest rates to remain where they are. The p/l resulting is the same for both outcomes, and is illustrated in Figure 11.26.

Long put strategy

This position to put on in anticipation of a rise in increase in interest rates and fall in bond prices, the opposite to the long call position. The p/l profile is shown in Figure 11.27.

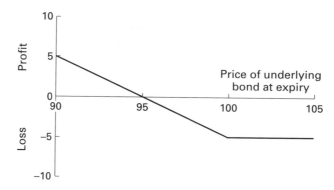

Figure 11.27   Profit/loss profile for a long put strategy.

The opposite position for someone who is expecting rates to decrease or remain stable is a *short put* position.

For simplicity, we have ignored the time value factor of options, as well as other considerations such as the time value of money (funds used to purchase options must be borrowed at a rate of interest, or forego interest if not invested and used to buy the option) and whether a coupon is paid on the underlying bond during the life of the option. These would all impact on the analysis of an option position; however, this section has illustrated the principles involved.

Hedging using bond options

Earlier in this chapter we discussed how bond trading desks can use swaps or futures to hedge their books. Options are also used frequently to hedge bond positions. Using futures will hedge against downside risk for a bond, although of course it will also preclude any possible upside gain if the market moves in the trader's favour. A hedge using options can be used to protect against IR risk while still allowing for upside gains. The two most popular hedging strategies are the *covered call* and the *protective put*.

Covered call hedge

If a trader or investor is long a bond, she can hedge the position by writing a call option on the bonds. The result is a short position in a call option and a long position in the underlying asset. If the price of the bond falls the investor will suffer a loss; however, this will be offset by the premium income received for writing the option. The bond position is hedged therefore by the amount of premium received, which may or may not offset the total loss on the bond position. The p/l profile is identical in shape to a short put strategy. This hedge has provided some downside protection against a fall in the price of the bond; however, there is still upside gain available, and any profit resulting from a rise in the underlying bond price will be enhanced by the amount of premium income.

Protective put hedge

The protective put is a more complete hedge of a long bond position. If a trader or investor buys a put option, she is locking in receipt of the strike price of the bond at any time during the option life, minus the

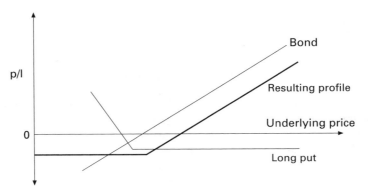

Figure 11.28   Protective put strategy.

premium paid for buying the option. The trader has protection if interest rates rise and the value of the bond falls, because the put option will be in-the-money. At the same time the trader will benefit if the bond price rises, although her resulting profit will be minus the cost of the put option. Effectively, the trader has formed a long call position. The option strike price sets the minimum price that is being locked in for the long bond position and the level of the downside protection. Therefore, the higher the strike price is, the more the option will cost (other things being equal). The option premium that the trader is willing to pay will need to be evaluated, and is the trade-off between greater risk protection and the option cost. The p/l profile for a protective put is shown in Figure 11.28.

Exotic options

The great versatility and flexibility of options has resulted in the creation of many different types of variation on the plain-vanilla options that we have described in this chapter. Options with one or more of their terms that differ from the basic type are known as *exotic options*. The capital markets trade structured products that often include exotic option components.

An *Asian* option is one where the payout on expiry compares the average level of the underlying asset – during a certain time period in the option's life – with the strike price, rather than the level of the underlying on expiry. A *basket* option is one whose payout is dependent on the value of a portfolio of assets – that is, it is an option on an underlying basket of assets rather than one asset. A *cliquet* option is a periodic rest option with multiple payouts, also known as a *ratchet* option. Therefore, during the life of the option the strike will reset at set dates, and there is a payout if the option is in-the-money at each of these dates. All these options may be *forward starting* which means that the option becomes active at some point in the future after its terms have been agreed. A *quanto* option is one in which the underlying asset is in a different currency from the payout currency – for example, an option on gilts that paid out on expiry in US dollars.

As one can imagine, the subject matter is immense and the interested reader may wish to consult a specialist options market text, such as Kolb (2000).

Example 11.4 Options on CBOT US T-bond future.

This is an exchange-traded option with standardised terms:

Nominal value	$100,000
Notional coupon	8%
Maturity	20 years
Premium	Quoted in 64ths of % of face value
Tick value	$15.625

An extract from a trading screen is given below, showing the increase in time value for longer-dated options and the decrease in intrinsic value as the strike price approaches the underlying price.

Strike	Calls		Puts	
	December	March	December	March
94	4-07	4-19	0-25	1-21
95	3-18	3-42	0-36	1-44
96	2-35	3-05	0-53	2-07
97	1-60	3-36	1-14	2-38
98	1-25	2-07	1-43	3-09
99	0-62	1-46	2-16	3-48
100	0-41	1-24	2-59	4-26
101	0-26	1-06	3-44	5-08

BIBLIOGRAPHY

Black, F. and Scholes, M. (1973). The pricing of options and corporate liabilities. *Journal of Political Economy.*

Bodie, Z. and Taggart, R. (1978). Future investment opportunities and the value of the call provision on a Bond. *Journal of Finance*, **33**, 1187–2000.

Choudhry, M. (2001). *The Bond and Money Markets.* Butterworth-Heinemann, Oxford, UK.

Choudhry, M. (2006). *The Futures Bond Basis.* John Wiley & Sons, Chichester, UK.

Fabozzi, F. J. (1997). *Fixed Income Mathematics: Analytical and Statistical Techniques* (3rd edn). McGraw-Hill, Princeton, NJ, ch. 16.

Kalotay, A., Williams, G. O. and Fabozzi, F. J. (1993). A model for the valuation of bonds and embedded options. *Financial Analysts Journal*, May–June, 35–46.

Kish, R. and Livingstone, M. (1992). The determinants of the call feature on corporate bonds. *Journal of Banking and Finance*, **16**, 687–703.

Kolb, R. (2000). *Futures, Options and Swaps.* Blackwell, Oxford, UK.

Livingstone, M. (1993). *Money and Capital Markets* (2nd edn). New York Institute of Finance, New York.

Mitchell, K. (1991). The call, sinking fund, and term-to-maturity features of corporate bonds: An empirical investigation. *Journal of Financial and Quantitative Analysis*, **26**, June, 201–222.

Narayanan, M. P. and Lim, S. P. (1989). On the call provision on corporate zero-coupon bonds. *Journal of Financial and Quantitative Analysis*, **24**, March, 91–103.

Questa, G. (1999). *Fixed Income Analysis for the Global Financial Market.* John Wiley & Sons, Chichester, UK, ch. 8.

Van Horne, J. C. (1986). *Financial Management and Policy.* Prentice Hall, Englewood Cliffs, NJ.

Windas, T. (1994). *An Introduction to Option-adjusted Spread Analysis.* Bloomberg Publications, Princeton, NJ.

Chapter

12

....

INTRODUCTION TO CREDIT DERIVATIVES

Perhaps the most significant development to have taken place in debt capital markets since the first edition of this book was published is the growth in use of credit derivative instruments. At the time of writing of the first edition, these products had been introduced in both the US and London markets; however, they were not a liquid product and were viewed as more of a risk management tool for banks than a brand new investment product in their own right. They should now be viewed in a more important light.

Credit derivatives are set to make the same impact on global capital markets as interest-rate derivatives did when the latter were first introduced in the early 1980s. Then, as now, market participants benefited from improved liquidity, transparency and accessibility in the cash market directly as a result of developments in the derivative market. The increasingly wide use of credit derivatives suggests that we are in the process of a transformation in credit markets in the same way that use of derivatives transformed interest-rate markets a generation earlier.

An article in the 15 March 2003 issue of *The Economist* reported that credit derivatives were used by just 0.2% of American banks. This implies that they are not vital or important instruments in the financial markets. In a way, this would be a reasonable conclusion to make. However, while this figure is undoubtedly higher now, its absolute value is not really relevant. The importance of credit derivatives lies in the potential they generate for greater transparency and disintermediation for the market *as a whole*: transparency with regard to asset valuation, liquidity and accessibility. Greater transparency and liquidity for just a small percentage of the market – typically, the largest banks and securities houses that take on and manage credit risk – works through into better trading conditions for all market participants. This then is the new paradigm shift currently taking place in credit markets, brought about by the isolation of credit as an asset class: greater transparency in evaluating fair value, and increased opportunity to speculate and hedge in credit.

The universe of credit derivatives includes credit default swaps (*CDSs*), total return swaps, credit-linked notes (*CLNs*) and structured credit products such as synthetic structured finance securities. Market notional volumes as a whole, of which the CDS is the most frequently traded, are shown at Figure 12.1. This illustrates the steady rise in use of these products.

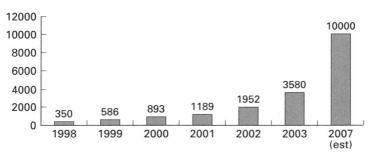

Figure 12.1 Credit derivatives volumes, $bn notional.
Source: British Bankers Association.

Recent occurrences would seem to imply a growing maturity in the credit derivatives market. High-profile credit events – such as the Parmalat default in 2003 or the Ford and GM downgrades in 2005 – have not seen market liquidity dry up; rather the opposite, as dealers sought to make two-way prices continuously available. The revised International Swap Dealers Association (*ISDA*) definitions from 2003 means we have a standard legal agreement to cover all trades, significantly reducing translation risk. And widely available pricing platforms – such as those from CreditTrade and Mark-It – provide an independent third-party price for investors. All this serves to make the synthetic market more of a driver of the cash market than the other way around – in other words, the 'tail wagging the dog' scenario that exists now in interest-rate markets since the introduction of derivatives there.

In this chapter we provide an overview of the main elements of the market. We describe credit derivatives, instruments that are used to invest in and trade credit synthetically. They are also used to manage credit risk in banking and portfolio management. Credit derivatives exist in a number of forms. We classify these into two main types, *funded* and *unfunded* credit derivatives, and give a description of each type. We then discuss the main uses of these instruments by banks and portfolio managers. We also consider the main credit events that act as triggering events under which payouts are made on credit derivative contracts.

Readers should note we do not cover credit derivative pricing, which is beyond the scope of this book. This is covered in the author's book *Structured Credit Products: Credit Derivatives and Synthetic Securitisation* (Choudhry, 2004a).

INTRODUCTION

Credit derivatives are financial contracts designed to enable traders and investors to access specific credit-risky investments in synthetic (i.e., non-cash) form. They can also be used to hedge credit risk exposure by providing insurance against losses suffered due to credit events. Credit derivatives allow investors to manage the credit risk exposure of their portfolios or asset holdings, essentially by providing insurance against deterioration in the credit quality of the borrowing entity. The simplest credit derivative works exactly like an insurance policy, with regular premiums paid by the protection buyer to the protection seller, and a payout in the event of a specified credit event.

The principle behind credit derivatives is straightforward. Investors desire exposure to debt that has a risk of defaulting because of the higher returns this offers. However, such exposure brings with it concomitant credit risk. This can be managed with credit derivatives. At the same time, the exposure itself can be taken on synthetically if, for instance, there are compelling reasons why a cash market position cannot be established. The flexibility of credit derivatives provides users a number of advantages, and as they are over-the-counter products they can be designed to meet specific user requirements.

What constitutes a credit event is defined specifically in the legal documents that describe the credit derivative contract. A number of events may be defined as credit events that fall short of full bankruptcy, administration or liquidation of a company. For instance, credit derivatives contracts may be required to pay out under both technical as well as actual default.

A *technical default* is a delay in timely payment of an obligation, or a non-payment altogether. If an obligor misses a payment, by even 1 day, it is said to be in technical default. This delay may be for operational reasons (and so not really a great worry) or it may reflect a short-term cash flow crisis, such as the Argentina debt default for 3 months. But, if the obligor states it intends to pay the obligation as soon as it can, and specifies a time-span that is within, say, 1–3 months, then while it is in technical default it is not in actual default. If an obligor is in *actual default*, it is in default and declared as being in default. This does not mean a mere delay of payment. If an obligor does not pay, and does not declare an intention to pay an obligation, it may then be classified by the ratings agencies as being in 'default' and rated 'D'.

If there is a technical or actual default by the borrower so that, for instance, a bond is marked down in price, the losses suffered by the investor can be recouped in part or in full through the payout made by the credit derivative. A payout under a credit derivative is triggered by a *credit event*. As banks define default in different ways, the terms under which a credit derivative is executed usually include a specification of what constitutes a credit event.

Why use credit derivatives?

Credit derivative instruments enable participants in the financial market to trade in credit as an asset, as they isolate and transfer credit risk. They also enable the market to separate funding considerations from credit risk.

Credit derivatives have three main types of application:

- *Diversifying the credit portfolio* – a bank or portfolio manager may wish to take on credit exposure by providing credit protection in return for a fee. This enhances income on their portfolio. They may sell credit derivatives to enable non-financial counterparties to gain credit exposures, if these clients are unable or unwilling to purchase the assets directly. In this respect the bank or asset manager performs a credit intermediation role.
- *Reducing credit exposure* – a bank can reduce credit exposure either for an individual loan or a sectoral concentration by buying a CDS. This may be desirable for assets that cannot be sold for client relationship or tax reasons. For fixed-income managers a particular asset or collection of assets may be viewed as an attractive holding in the long term, but at risk from short-term downward price movement. In this instance a sale would not fit in with long-term objectives; however, short-term credit protection can be obtained via a credit swap. For instance, a bank can buy credit protection on a BB-rated entity from an AA-rated bank. It then has eliminated its credit risk to the BB entity, and substituted it for AA-rated counterparty risk. Notice that as the bank retains a counterparty risk to the credit default swap issuer one could argue that its credit risk exposure is never completely removed. In practice, this is not a serious problem since the bank can manage counterparty risk through

careful selection and diversification of counterparties. In fact, in the interest-rate swap market, AA (interbank) quality is now considered a proxy for the government benchmark.

- *Accessing illiquid credits* – investors can use credit derivatives to gain synthetic exposure to assets that, for one reason or another, they cannot or will not access in the cash market. By transacting in a credit derivative with a market making bank, the investor can gain an exposure that replicates the exposure that would be obtained if he had purchased the asset in the cash market. An example of this is the structured finance market, where the demand for certain mortgage-backed and asset-backed securities outstrips supply; where there is a shortage of paper, investors trade in credit derivatives to obtain the exposure they require.

The intense competition amongst commercial banks, combined with rapid disintermediation, has meant that banks have been forced to evaluate their lending policy with a view to improving profitability and return on capital. The use of credit derivatives assists banks with restructuring their businesses, because they allow banks to repackage and parcel out credit risk, while retaining assets on balance sheet (when required) and thus maintaining client relationships. As the instruments isolate certain aspects of credit risk from the underlying loan or bond and transfer them to another entity, it becomes possible to separate the ownership and management of credit risk from the other features of ownership of the assets in question. This means that illiquid assets such as bank loans and illiquid bonds can have their credit risk exposures transferred; the bank owning the assets can protect against credit loss even if it cannot transfer the assets themselves.

The same principles carry over to the credit risk exposures of portfolio managers. For fixed-income portfolio managers some of the advantages of credit derivatives include the following:

- They can be tailor-made to meet the specific requirements of the entity buying the risk protection, as opposed to the liquidity or term of the underlying reference asset.
- They can be 'sold short' without risk of a liquidity or delivery squeeze, as it is a specific credit risk that is being traded. In the cash market it is not possible to 'sell short' a bank loan, for example, but a credit derivative can be used to establish synthetically the same economic effect.

- As they theoretically isolate credit risk from other factors such as client relationships and interest-rate risk, credit derivatives introduce a formal pricing mechanism to price credit issues only. This means a market can develop in credit only, allowing more efficient pricing; it even becomes possible to model a term structure of credit rates.
- When credit derivatives are embedded in certain fixed-income products, such as structured notes and credit-linked notes, they are then off-balance-sheet instruments (albeit part of a structure that may have on-balance-sheet elements) and as such incorporate tremendous flexibility and leverage, exactly like other financial derivatives. For instance, bank loans are not particularly attractive investments for certain investors because of the administration required in managing and servicing a loan portfolio. However, an exposure to bank loans and their associated return can be achieved by a total return swap, for instance, while simultaneously avoiding the administrative costs of actually owning the assets. Hence, credit derivatives allow investors access to specific credits while allowing banks access to further distribution for bank loan credit risk.
- They enable institutions to take a view on credit positions to take advantage of perceived anomalies in the price of secondary market loans and bonds, and the price of credit risk.

Thus, credit derivatives can be an important instrument for bond portfolio managers as well as commercial banks wishing to increase the liquidity of their portfolios, gain from the relative value arising from credit pricing anomalies and enhance portfolio returns.

Classification of credit derivative instruments

A number of instruments come under the category of credit derivatives. Irrespective of the particular instrument under consideration, all credit derivatives can be described with respect to the following characteristics:

- the *reference entity*, which is the asset or name on which credit protection is being bought and sold;
- the *credit event*, or events, which indicate that the reference entity is experiencing or about to experience financial difficulty and which act as trigger events for payments under the credit derivative contract;

- the *settlement mechanism* for the contract, whether cash settled or physically settled; and
- the *deliverable obligation* that the protection buyer delivers (under physical settlement) to the protection seller on the occurrence of a trigger event.

Credit derivatives are grouped into *funded* and *unfunded* instruments. In a funded credit derivative, typified by a CLN, the investor in the note is the credit-protection seller and is making an upfront payment to the protection buyer when it buys the note. Thus, the protection buyer is the issuer of the note. If no credit event occurs during the life of the note, the redemption value of the note is paid to the investor on maturity. If a credit event does occur, then on maturity a value less than par will be paid out to the investor. This value will be reduced by the nominal value of the reference asset that the CLN is linked to. The exact process will differ according to whether *cash settlement* or *physical settlement* has been specified for the note.

In an unfunded credit derivative, typified by a CDS, the protection seller does not make an upfront payment to the protection buyer. Instead, the protection seller will pay the nominal value of the contract (the amount insured, in effect), on occurrence of a credit event, minus the current market value of the asset or its recovery value.

Definition of a credit event

The occurrence of a specified credit event will trigger the default payment by the protection seller to the protection buyer. Contracts specify physical or cash settlement. In physical settlement, the protection buyer transfers to the protection seller the deliverable obligation (usually the reference asset or assets), with the total principal outstanding equal to the nominal value specified in the default swap contract. The protection seller simultaneously pays to the buyer 100% of the nominal value. In cash settlement, the protection seller hands to the buyer the difference between the nominal amount of the default swap and the final value for the same nominal amount of the reference asset. This final value is usually determined by means of a poll of dealer banks.

The following may be specified as credit events in the legal documentation between counterparties:

- downgrade in Standard & Poor's (*S&P*) and/or Moody's credit rating below a specified minimum level;
- financial or debt restructuring – for example, occasioned under administration or as required under US bankruptcy protection;
- bankruptcy or insolvency of the reference asset obligor;
- default on payment obligations such as bond coupon and continued non-payment after a specified time period;
- technical default – for example, the non-payment of interest or coupon when it falls due;
- a change in credit spread payable by the obligor above a specified maximum level.

The 1999 ISDA credit default swap documentation specifies bankruptcy, failure to pay, obligation default, debt moratorium and 'restructuring' to be credit events. Note that it does not specify a rating downgrade to be a credit event.[1]

The precise definition of 'restructuring' is open to debate and has resulted in legal disputes between protection buyers and sellers. Prior to issuing its 1999 definitions, ISDA had specified restructuring as an event or events that resulted in making the terms of the reference obligation 'materially less favourable' to the creditor (or protection seller) from an economic perspective. This definition is open to more than one interpretation and caused controversy when determining if a credit event had occurred. The 2001 definitions specified more precise conditions, including any action that resulted in a reduction in the amount of principal. In the European market restructuring is generally retained as a credit event in contract documentation, but in the US market it is less common to see it included. Instead, US contract documentation tends to include as a credit event a form of modified restructuring, the impact of which is to limit the options available to the protection buyer as to the type of assets it could deliver in a physically settled contract.

ASSET SWAPS

Asset swaps pre-date the introduction of the other instruments we discuss in this chapter and so, strictly speaking, are not credit

---

[1] The ISDA definitions from 1999 and restructuring supplement from 2001 are available at *www.ISDA.org*

derivatives. However, they are used for similar purposes and there is considerable interplay between the cash and synthetic markets using asset swaps – hence the need to discuss them here.

Asset swaps are used to alter the cash flow profile of a bond. The asset swap market is an important segment of the credit derivatives market since it explicitly sets out the price of credit as a spread over the London Interbank Offer Rate (*Libor*). Pricing a bond by reference to Libor is commonly used and the spread over Libor is a measure of credit risk in the cash flow of the underlying bond. Asset swaps can be used to transform the cash flow characteristics of reference assets, so that investors can hedge the currency, credit and interest-rate risks to create synthetic investments with more suitable cash flow characteristics. An asset swap package involves transactions in which the investor acquires a bond position and then enters into an interest-rate swap with the bank that sold him the bond. The investor pays fixed and receives floating. This transforms the fixed coupon of the bond into a Libor-based floating coupon.

An example would be that the protection buyer holding a risky bond wishes to hedge the credit risk of this position. By means of an asset swap the protection seller will agree to pay the protection buyer Libor ± a spread in return for the cash flows of the risky bond (there is no exchange of notional at any point). In the event of default the protection buyer will continue to receive the Libor ± a spread from the protection seller. In this way the protection buyer has transformed its original risk profile by changing both its interest rate and credit risk exposure.

The generic structure is shown at Figure 12.2.

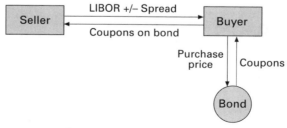

Figure 12.2   Asset swap.

Example 12.1   Asset swap.

Assume that an investor holds a bond and enters into an asset swap with a bank. Then the value of an asset swap is the spread the bank pays over or under Libor. This is based on the following components:

(i)   value of the coupons of the underlying asset compared with the market swap rate;
(ii) the accrued interest and the clean price premium or discount compared with par value.

Thus, when pricing the asset swap it is necessary to compare the par value and the underlying bond price.

The spread above or below Libor reflects the credit spread difference between the bond and the swap rate.

The Bloomberg asset swap calculator pricing screen at Figure 12.3 shows these components in the analysis of the swapped spread details.

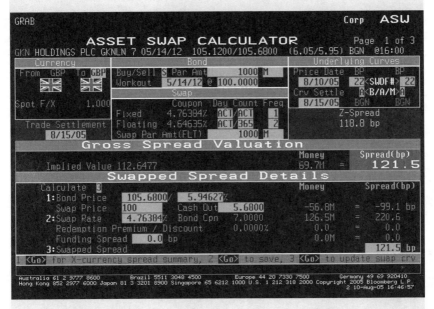

Figure 12.3   Bloomberg example of asset swap calculator screen.

© Bloomberg L.P. Used with permission. Visit *www.bloomberg.com*

Example 12.2   Asset swap terms.

Let us assume that we have a credit risky bond with the following details:

Currency:	EUR
Issue date:	31 March 2000
Maturity:	31 March 2007
Coupon:	5.5% per annum
Price (dirty):	105.3%
Price (clean):	101.2%
Yield:	5%
Accrued interest:	4.1%
Rating:	A1

To buy this bond the investor would pay 105.3% of par value. The investor would receive the fixed coupons of 5.5% of par value. Let us assume that the swap rate is 5%. The investor in this bond enters into an asset swap with a bank in which the investor pays the fixed coupon and receives Libor ± a spread.

The asset swap price (i.e., spread) on this bond has the following components:

(i) The value of the excess value of the fixed coupons over the market swap rate is paid to the investor. Let us assume that in this case that this is approximately 0.5% when spread into payments over the life of the asset swap.

(ii) The difference between the bond price and par value is another factor in the pricing of an asset swap. In this case the price premium which is expressed in present value terms should be spread over the term of the swap and treated as a payment by the investor to the bank (if a dirty price is at a discount to the par value then the payment is made from the bank to the investor). For example, in this case let us assume that this results in a payment from the investor to the bank of approximately 0.23% when spread over the term of the swap.

These two elements result in a net spread of 0.5% − 0.23% = 0.27%. Therefore, the asset swap would be quoted as Libor + 0.27% (or Libor + 27 basis points).

CREDIT DEFAULT SWAPS

The most common credit derivative is the *credit default swap*. This is sometimes abbreviated to *credit swap* or *default swap*. A CDS is a bilateral contract in which a periodic fixed fee or a one-off premium is paid to a protection seller, in return for which the seller will make a payment on the occurrence of a specified credit event. The fee is usually quoted as a basis point multiplier of the nominal value. It is usually paid quarterly in arrears.

The swap can refer to a single asset, known as the *reference asset* or *underlying asset*, or a basket of assets. The default payment can be paid in whatever way suits the protection buyer or both counter-parties. For example, it may be linked to the change in price of the reference asset or another specified asset, it may be fixed at a pre-determined recovery rate or it may be in the form of actual delivery of the reference asset at a specified price. The basic structure is illustrated in Figure 12.4.

The maturity of the credit swap does not have to match the maturity of the reference asset and often does not. On occurrence of a credit event, the swap contract is terminated and a settlement payment made by the protection seller or guarantor to the protection buyer. This termination value is calculated at the time of the credit event, and the exact procedure that is followed to calculate the termination value will depend on the settlement terms specified in the contract. This will be either cash settlement or physical settlement:

- *Cash settlement* – the contract may specify a predetermined payout value on occurrence of a credit event. This may be the nominal value of the swap contract. Such a swap is known in some markets as a *digital credit derivative*. Alternatively, the

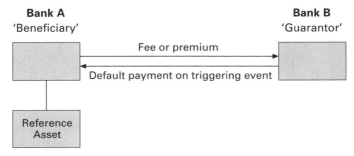

Figure 12.4 Credit default swap.

termination payment is calculated as the difference between the nominal value of the reference asset and its market value at the time of the credit event. This arrangement is more common with cash-settled contracts.[2]

- *Physical settlement* – on occurrence of a credit event, the buyer delivers the reference asset to the seller, in return for which the seller pays the face value of the delivered asset to the buyer. The contract may specify a number of alternative assets that the buyer can deliver; these are known as *deliverable obligations*. This may apply when a swap has been entered into on a reference name rather than a specific obligation (such as a particular bond) issued by that name. Where more than one deliverable obligation is specified, the protection buyer will invariably deliver the asset that is the cheapest on the list of eligible assets. This gives rise to the concept of the *cheapest to deliver*, as encountered with government bond futures contracts, and is in effect an embedded option afforded the protection buyer.

In theory, the value of protection is identical irrespective of which settlement option is selected. However, under physical settlement the protection seller can gain if there is a recovery value that can be extracted from the defaulted asset; or its value may rise as the fortunes of the issuer improve. Despite this, swap market-making banks often prefer cash settlement as there is less administration associated with it. It is also more suitable when the swap is used as part of a synthetic structured product, because such vehicles may not be set up to take delivery of physical assets. Another advantage of cash settlement is that it does not expose the protection buyer to any risks should there not be any deliverable assets in the market – for instance, due to shortage of liquidity in the market. Were this to happen, the buyer may find the value of its settlement payment reduced. Nevertheless, physical settlement is widely used because counterparties wish to avoid the difficulties associated with determining the market value of the reference asset under cash settlement. Physical settlement also permits the protection seller to take part in the creditor negotiations with the reference entity's administrators, which may result in improved terms for them as holders of the asset.

---

[2] Determining the market value of the reference asset at the time of the credit event may be a little problematic as the issuer of the asset may well be in default or administration. An independent third-party *calculation agent* is usually employed to make the termination payment calculation.

Example 12.3

XYZ plc credit spreads are currently trading at 120 basis points (bps) relative to government-issued securities for 5-year maturities and 195 bps for 10-year maturities. A portfolio manager hedges a $10m holding of 10-year paper by purchasing the following CDS, written on the 5-year bond. This hedge protects for the first 5 years of the holding, and in the event of XYZ's credit spread widening will increase in value and may be sold on or before expiry at profit. The 10-year bond holding also earns 75 bps over the shorter-term paper for the portfolio manager

Term	5 years
Reference credit	XYZ plc 5-year bond
Credit event payout date	The business day following occurrence of specified credit event
Default payment	Nominal value of bond × [100 − Price of bond after credit event]
Swap premium	3.35%

Assume now that midway into the life of the swap there is a technical default on the XYZ plc 5-year bond, such that its price now stands at $28. Under the terms of the swap the protection buyer delivers the bond to the seller, who pays out $7.2m to the buyer.

The CDS enables one party to transfer its credit risk exposure to another party. Banks may use default swaps to trade sovereign and corporate credit spreads without trading the actual assets themselves; for example, someone who has gone long a default swap (the protection buyer) will gain if the reference asset obligor suffers a rating downgrade or defaults, and can sell the default swap at a profit if he can find a buyer counterparty.[3] This is because the cost of

---

[3] Be careful with terminology here. To 'go long' of an instrument generally is to purchase it. In the cash market, going long of the bond means one is buying the bond and so receiving coupon; the buyer has therefore taken on credit risk exposure to the issuer. In a CDS, to go long is to buy the swap, but the buyer is purchasing protection and therefore paying premium; the buyer has no credit exposure on the name and has in effect 'gone short' on the reference name (the equivalent of shorting a bond in the cash market and paying coupon). So, buying a CDS is frequently referred to in the market as 'shorting' the reference entity.

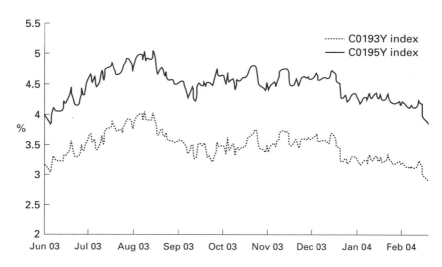

Figure 12.5 Investment-grade credit default swap levels.

Rates source: Bloomberg L.P.

protection on the reference asset will have increased as a result of the credit event. The original buyer of the default swap need never have owned a bond issued by the reference asset obligor. CDSs are used extensively for flow trading (i.e., the daily customer buy and sell business) of single reference name credit risks or, in *portfolio swap* form, for trading a basket of reference credits. CDSs and CLNs are also used in structured products, in various combinations, and their flexibility has been behind the growth and wide application of the synthetic collateralised debt obligation and other credit hybrid products.

Figure 12.5 shows US dollar CDS price levels (in basis points) during 2003 and 2004 for BBB-rated reference entities, for 3- and 5-year CDS contracts. The graph shows the level of fluctuation in CDS prices. It also shows clearly the term structure of credit rates, as the 5-year CDS price lies above the 3-year rate at all times.

Figure 12.6 shows Bloomberg screen WCDS, which contains CDS prices for a wide range of reference names, grouped according to industry category. Our example, from 1 December 2005, shows a selection of industrial corporate names.

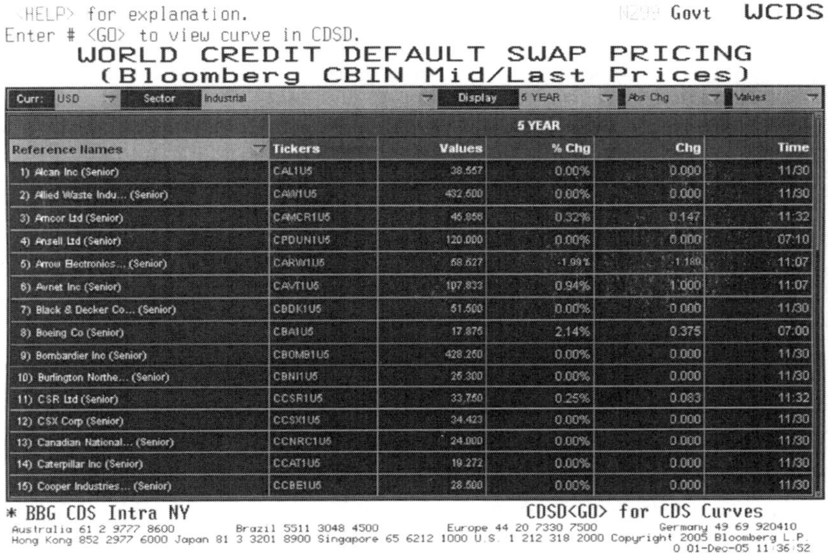

HELP> for explanation. M289 Govt **WCDS**
Enter # <GO> to view curve in CDSD.
WORLD CREDIT DEFAULT SWAP PRICING
(Bloomberg CBIN Mid/Last Prices)

Curr: USD ▾ Sector Industrial ▾ Display 5 YEAR ▾ Abs Chg ▾ Values ▾

Reference Names	Tickers	Values	% Chg	Chg	Time
1) Alcan Inc (Senior)	CALI1U5	38.557	0.00%	0.000	11:30
2) Allied Waste Indu... (Senior)	CAWI1U5	432.500	0.00%	0.000	11:30
3) Amcor Ltd (Senior)	CAMCR1U5	45.956	0.32%	0.147	11:32
4) Ansell Ltd (Senior)	CPDUN1U6	120.000	0.00%	0.000	07:10
5) Arrow Electronics... (Senior)	CARW1U5	58.527	-1.99%	-1.180	11:07
6) Avnet Inc (Senior)	CAVT1U5	107.833	0.94%	1.000	11:07
7) Black & Decker Co... (Senior)	CBDK1U5	51.500	0.00%	0.000	11:30
8) Boeing Co (Senior)	CBAI U5	17.875	2.14%	0.375	07:00
9) Bombardier Inc (Senior)	CBOMB1U5	428.250	0.00%	0.000	11:30
10) Burlington Northe... (Senior)	CBNI1U5	26.300	0.00%	0.000	11:30
11) CSR Ltd (Senior)	CCSR1U5	33.750	0.25%	0.083	11:32
12) CSX Corp (Senior)	CCSX1U5	34.423	0.00%	0.000	11:30
13) Canadian National... (Senior)	CCNRC1U6	24.000	0.00%	0.000	11:30
14) Caterpillar Inc (Senior)	CCAT1U5	19.272	0.00%	0.000	11:30
15) Cooper Industries... (Senior)	CCBE1U5	28.500	0.00%	0.000	11:30

* BBG CDS Intra NY CDSD<GO> for CDS Curves
Australia 61 2 9777 8600 Brazil 5511 3048 4500 Europe 44 20 7330 7500 Germany 49 69 920410
Hong Kong 852 2977 6000 Japan 81 3 3201 8900 Singapore 65 6212 1000 U.S. 1 212 318 2000 Copyright 2005 Bloomberg L.P.
0 01-Dec-05 11:36:52

Figure 12.6 Bloomberg screen WCDS showing extract of world CDS prices, as at 1 December 2005.

© Bloomberg L.P. Used with permission. Visit *www.bloomberg.com*

CREDIT-LINKED NOTES

A standard *credit-linked note* is a security, usually issued by an investment-grade entity, that has an interest payment and fixed maturity structure similar to a vanilla bond. The performance of the note, however, including the maturity value, is linked to the performance of a specified underlying asset or assets, as well as to that of the issuing entity. Notes are usually issued at par. The notes are often used by borrowers to hedge against credit risk, and by investors to enhance the yield received on their holdings. Hence, the issuer of the note is the protection buyer and the buyer of the note is the protection seller.

CLNs are essentially hybrid instruments that combine a credit derivative with a vanilla bond. The CLN pays regular coupons; however, the credit derivative element is usually set to allow the issuer to decrease the principal amount if a credit event occurs. For example, consider an issuer of credit cards that wants to fund its (credit card) loan portfolio via an issue of debt. In order to hedge the credit risk of the portfolio, it issues a 2-year CLN. The principal amount of the bond is 100% as usual, and it pays a coupon of 7.50%, which is 200 basis points above the 2-year benchmark. If, however, the incidence of bad debt amongst credit-card holders exceeds 10% then the terms state that note holders will only receive back £85 per £100 nominal. The credit-card issuer has in effect purchased a credit option that lowers its liability in the event that it suffers from a specified credit event, which in this case is an above-expected incidence of bad debts. The credit-card bank has issued the CLN to reduce its credit exposure, in the form of this particular type of credit insurance. If the incidence of bad debts is low, the note is redeemed at par. However, if there a high incidence of such debt, the bank will only have to repay a part of its loan liability.

Figure 12.7 depicts the cash flows associated with a CLN. CLNs exist in a number of forms, but all of them contain a link between the return they pay and the credit-related performance of the underlying asset. Investors may wish to purchase the CLN because the coupon paid on it will be above what the same bank would pay on a vanilla bond it issued, and higher than other comparable investments in the market. In addition, such notes are usually priced below par on issue. Assuming the notes are eventually redeemed at par, investors will also have realised a substantial capital gain.

As with CDSs, CLNs may be specified under cash settlement or physical settlement. Specifically, under:

- *cash settlement* – if a credit event has occurred, on maturity the protection seller receives the difference between the value of the initial purchase proceeds and the value of the reference asset at the time of the credit event;
- *physical settlement* – on occurrence of a credit event, at maturity the protection buyer delivers the reference asset or an asset among a list of deliverable assets, and the protection seller receives the value of the original purchase proceeds minus the value of the asset that has been delivered.

Structured products may combine both CLNs and CDSs to meet issuer and investor requirements. For instance, Figure 12.8 shows a credit structure designed to provide a higher return for an investor on comparable risk to the cash market. An issuing entity is set up in the form of a *special-purpose vehicle* (SPV) which issues CLNs to the market. The structure is engineered so that the SPV has a neutral

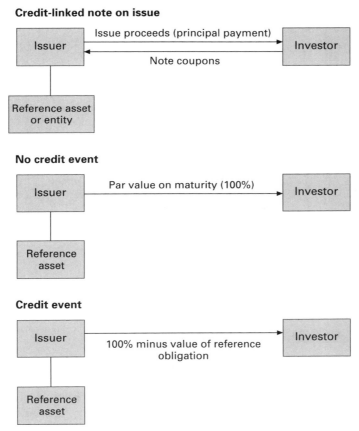

Figure 12.7   Cash-settled credit-linked note.

position on a reference asset. It has bought protection on a single reference name by issuing a funded credit derivative, the CLN, and simultaneously sold protection by selling a CDS on this name.

The proceeds of the CLN are invested in risk-free collateral such as T-bills or a Treasury bank account. The coupon on the CLN will be a spread over Libor. It is backed by the collateral account and the fee generated by the SPV in selling protection with the CDS. Investors in the CLN will have exposure to the reference asset or entity, and the repayment of the note is linked to the performance of the reference entity. If a credit event occurs, the maturity date of the CLN is brought forward and the note is settled at par minus the value of the reference asset or entity.

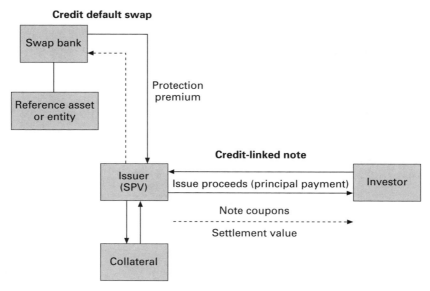

Figure 12.8   CLN and CDS structure on single reference name.

TOTAL RETURN SWAPS

A *total return swap* (TRS), sometimes known as a *total rate of return swap* or *TR swap*, is an agreement between two parties to exchange the total returns from financial assets. This is designed to transfer the credit risk from one party to the other. It is one of the principal instruments used by banks and other financial instruments to manage their credit risk exposure, and as such is a credit derivative. One definition of a TRS is given in Francis *et al.* (1999), which states that a TRS is a swap agreement in which the *total return* of a bank loan or credit-sensitive security is exchanged for some other cash flow, usually tied to Libor or some other loan or credit-sensitive security.

In some versions of a TRS the actual underlying asset is sold to the counterparty, with a corresponding swap transaction agreed alongside; in other versions there is no physical change of ownership of the underlying asset. The TRS trade itself can be to any maturity term – that is, it need not match the maturity of the underlying security. In a TRS the total return from the underlying asset is paid over to the counterparty in return for a fixed or floating cash flow. This makes it slightly different from other credit derivatives, as the payments

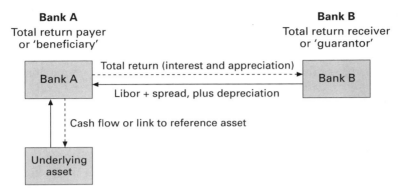

Figure 12.9   Total return swap.

between counterparties to a TRS are connected to changes in the market value of the underlying asset, as well as changes resulting from the occurrence of a credit event.

Figure 12.9 illustrates a generic TR swap. The two counterparties are labelled as banks, but the party termed 'Bank A' can be another financial institution, including insurance companies and hedge funds that often hold fixed-income portfolios. In Figure 12.9, Bank A has contracted to pay the 'total return' on a specified reference asset, while simultaneously receiving a Libor-based return from Bank B. The reference or underlying asset can be a bank loan such as a corporate loan or a sovereign or corporate bond. The total return payments from Bank A include the interest payments on the under-lying loan as well as any appreciation in the market value of the asset. Bank B will pay the Libor-based return; it will also pay any difference if there is a depreciation in the price of the asset. The economic effect is as if Bank B owned the underlying asset, as such TR swaps are synthetic loans or securities. A significant feature is that Bank A will usually hold the underlying asset on its balance sheet, so that if this asset was originally on Bank B's balance sheet, this is a means by which the latter can have the asset removed from its balance sheet for the term of the TR swap.[4] If we assume Bank A has access to Libor funding, it will receive a spread on this from Bank B. Under the terms of the swap, Bank B will pay the difference

---

[4] Although it is common for the receiver of the Libor-based payments to have the reference asset on its balance sheet, this is not always the case.

between the initial market value and any depreciation, so it is some-times termed the 'guarantor', while Bank A is the 'beneficiary'.

The total return on the underlying asset is the interest payments and any change in the market value if there is capital appreciation. The value of an appreciation may be cash settled, or alternatively there may be physical delivery of the reference asset on maturity of the swap, in return for a payment of the initial asset value by the total return 'receiver'. The maturity of the TR swap need not be identical to that of the reference asset, and in fact it is rare for it to be so.

The swap element of the trade will usually pay on a quarterly or semiannual basis, with the underlying asset being revalued or marked-to-market on the refixing dates. The asset price is usually obtained from an independent third-party source such as Bloomberg or Reuters, or as the average of a range of market quotes. If the obligor of the reference asset defaults, the swap may be terminated immediately, with a net present value payment changing hands according to what this value is, or it may be continued with each party making appreciation or depreciation payments as appropriate. This second option is only available if there is a market for the asset, which is unlikely in the case of a bank loan. If the swap is termin-ated, each counterparty will be liable to the other for accrued interest plus any appreciation or depreciation of the asset. Commonly, under the terms of the trade the guarantor bank has the option to purchase the underlying asset from the beneficiary bank, and then deal directly with the loan defaulter.

With a TRS the basic concept is that one party 'funds' an underlying asset and transfers the total return of the asset to another party, in return for a (usually) floating return that is a spread to Libor. This spread is a function of:

- the credit rating of the swap counterparty;
- the amount and value of the reference asset;
- the credit quality of the reference asset;
- the funding costs of the beneficiary bank;
- any required profit margin;
- the capital charge associated with the TR swap.

The TRS counterparties must therefore consider a number of risk factors associated with the transaction, which include:

- the probability that the TR beneficiary may default while the reference asset has declined in value;
- the reference asset obligor defaults, followed by default of the TR

swap receiver before payment of the depreciation has been made to the payer or 'provider'.

The first risk measure is a function of the probability of default by the TRS receiver and the market volatility of the reference asset, while the second risk is related to the joint probability of default of both factors as well as the recovery probability of the asset.

TRS contracts are used in a variety of applications by banks, other financial institutions and corporates. They can be written as pure exchanges of cash flow differences – rather like an interest-rate swap – or the reference asset can be actually transferred to the total return payer, which would then make the TRS akin to a 'synthetic repo' contract:[5]

- *As pure exchanges of cash flow differences* – using TRSs as a credit derivative instrument, a party can remove exposure to an asset without having to sell it. This is conceptually similar to interest-rate swaps, which enable banks and other financial institutions to trade interest-rate risk without borrowing or lending cash funds. A TRS agreement entered into as a credit derivative is a means by which banks can take on unfunded off-balance-sheet credit exposure. Higher-rated banks that have access to LIBID funding can benefit by funding on-balance-sheet assets that are credit protected through a credit derivative such as a TRS, assuming the net spread of asset income over credit protection premium is positive.
- *Reference asset transferred to the total return payer* – in a vanilla TRS the total return payer retains rights to the reference asset, although in some cases servicing and voting rights may be transferred. The total return receiver gains an exposure to the reference asset without having to pay out the cash proceeds that would be required to purchase it. As the maturity of the swap rarely matches that of the asset, the swap receiver may gain from the positive funding or *carry* that derives from being able to roll over short-term funding of a longer-term asset.[6] The total return

---

[5] When a bank sells stock short, it must borrow the stock to deliver it to its customer, in return for a fee (called a 'stock loan'), or it may lend cash against the stock which it then delivers to the customer (called a 'sale and repurchase agreement' or *repo*). The counterparty is 'selling and buying back' while the bank that is short the stock is 'buying and selling back'. A TRS is a synthetic form of repo, as the bond is sold to the TRS payer.

[6] This assumes a positively sloping yield curve.

payer, on the other hand, benefits from protection against market and credit risk for a specified period of time, without having to liquidate the asset itself. On maturity of the swap the total return payer may reinvest the asset if it continues to own it, or it may sell the asset in the open market. Thus, the instrument may be considered a *synthetic repo*.

The economic effect of the two applications may be the same, but they are considered different instruments:

- The TRS as a credit derivative instrument actually takes the assets off the balance sheet, whereas the tax and accounting authorities treat repo as if the assets remain on the balance sheet.
- A TRS trade is conducted under the ISDA standard legal agreement, while repo is conducted under a standard legal agreement called the Global Master Repurchase Agreement (GMRA).

It is these differences that, under certain circumstances, make the TRS funding route a more favourable one.

We now explain in more detail the main uses of TRSs.

Synthetic repo

A portfolio manager believes that a particular bond (which she does not hold) is about to decline in price. To reflect this view she may do one of the following:

- *Sell the bond in the market and cover the resulting short position in repo* – the cash flow out is the coupon on the bond, with capital gain if the bond falls in price. Assume that the repo rate is floating – say, Libor + a spread. The manager must be aware of the funding costs of the trade, so that unless the bond can be covered in repo at *general collateral* rates,[7] the funding will be at a loss. The yield on the bond must also be lower than the Libor + a spread received in the repo.
- *As an alternative, enter into a TRS* – the portfolio manager pays the total return on the bond and receives Libor + a spread. If the bond yield exceeds the Libor spread, the funding will be negative;

---

[7] That is, the bond cannot be *special*. A bond is special when the repo rate payable on it is significantly (say, 20–30 basis points or more) below the *general collateral* repo rate, so that covering a short position in the bond entails paying a substantial funding premium.

however, the trade will gain if the trader's view is proved correct and the bond falls in price by a sufficient amount. If the break-even funding cost (which the bond must exceed as it falls in value) is lower in the TRS, this method will be used rather than the repo approach. This is more likely if the bond is special.

Reduction in credit risk

A TRS conducted as a synthetic repo is usually undertaken to effect the temporary removal of assets from the balance sheet. This can be done by entering into a short-term TRS with, say, a 2-week term that straddles the reporting date. Bonds are removed from the balance sheet if they are part of a sale plus TRS transaction. This is because legally the bank selling the asset is not required to repurchase bonds from the swap counterparty, nor is the total return payer obliged to sell the bonds back to the counterparty (or indeed sell the bonds at all on maturity of the TRS).

Hence, under a TRS an asset such as a bond position may be removed from the balance sheet. This may be desired for a number of reasons: for example, if the institution is due to be analysed by credit rating agencies or if the annual external audit is due shortly. Another reason why a bank may wish to temporarily remove lower credit-quality assets from its balance sheet is if it is in danger of breaching capital limits in between the quarterly return periods. In this case, as the return period approaches, lower-quality assets may be removed from the balance sheet by means of a TRS, which is set to mature after the return period has passed. In summary, to avoid adverse impact on regular internal and external capital and credit exposure reporting, a bank may use TRSs to reduce the number of lower-quality assets on the balance sheet.

Capital structure arbitrage

A capital structure arbitrage describes an arrangement whereby investors exploit mis-pricing between the yields received on two different loans by the same issuer. Assume that the reference entity has both a commercial bank loan and a subordinated bond issue outstanding, but that the former pays Libor + 330 basis points while the latter pays Libor + 230 basis points. An investor enters into a TRS in which it is effectively purchasing the bank loan and

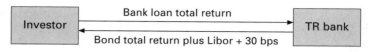

Figure 12.10   Total return swap in capital structure arbitrage.

selling short the bond. The nominal amounts will be at a ratio of, say, 2 : 1, as the bonds will be more price-sensitive to changes in credit status than the loans.

The trade is illustrated in Figure 12.10. The investor receives the 'total return' on the bank loan, while simultaneously paying the return on the bond in addition to Libor + 30 basis points, which is the price of the TRS. The swap generates a net spread of $(100 \text{ bps} \times \frac{1}{2}) + (250 \text{ bps} \times \frac{1}{2}) = 175$ basis points.

The TRS as a funding instrument

A TRS can be regarded as a funding instrument – in other words, as a substitute for a repo trade. There may be legal, administrative, operational or other reasons why a repo trade is not entered into to begin with. In these cases, provided that a counterparty can be found and the funding rate is not prohibitive, a TRS may be just as suitable.

Consider a financial institution such as a regulated broker-dealer that has a portfolio of assets on its balance sheet that it needs to obtain funding for. These assets are investment-grade structured finance bonds such as credit-card asset-backed securities, residential mortgage-backed securities and collateralised debt obligation notes, and investment-grade convertible bonds. In the repo market, it is able to fund these at Libor + 6 basis points – that is, it can repo the bonds out to a bank counterparty, and will pay Libor + 6 basis points on the funds it receives.

Assume that for operational reasons the bank can no longer fund these assets using repo. It can fund them using a basket TRS instead, providing a suitable counterparty can be found. Under this contract, the portfolio of assets is swapped out to the TRS counterparty, and cash received from the counterparty. The assets are therefore sold off the balance sheet to the counterparty, an investment bank. The investment bank will need to fund this itself, it may have a line of credit from a parent bank or it may swap the bonds out itself. The funding rate it charges the broker-dealer will depend on the rate at which it can fund the assets itself. Assume this is Libor + 12 basis points – the higher rate reflects the lower liquidity in the basket TRS market for non-vanilla bonds.

The broker-dealer enters into a 3-month TRS with the investment bank counterparty, with a 1-week interest-rate reset. This means that at each week interval the basket is revalued. The difference in value from the last valuation is paid (if higher) or received (if lower) by the investment bank to the broker-dealer; in return, the broker-dealer also pays 1-week interest on the funds it received at the start of the trade. In practice, these two cash flows are netted off and only one payment changes hands, just as in an interest-rate swap. The terms of the trade are shown below:

- *Trade date*: 22 December 2003;
- *Value date*: 24 December 2003;
- *Maturity date*: 24 March 2004;
- *Rate reset*: 31 December 2003;
- *Interest rate*: 1.198 75% (this is the 1-week USD Libor fix of 1.078 75 + 12 basis points).

The swap is a 3-month TRS with 1-week reset, which means that the swap can be broken at 1-week intervals and bonds in the reference basket can be returned, added to or substituted.

Assume that the portfolio basket contains five bonds, all US dollar denominated. Assume further that these are all investment-grade, credit-card, asset-backed securities with prices available on Bloomberg. The combined market value of the entire portfolio is taken to be $151,080,951.00.

At the start of the trade, the five bonds are swapped out to the investment bank, which pays the portfolio value for them. On the first reset date, the portfolio is revalued and the following calculations confirmed:

- *Old portfolio value*: $151,080,951.00;
- *Interest rate*: 1.198 75%;
- *Interest payable by broker-dealer*: $35,215.50;
- *New portfolio value*: $152,156,228.00;
- *Portfolio performance*: +$1,075,277
- *Net payment – broker-dealer receives*: $1,040,061.50.

The rate is reset for value 31 December 2003 for the period to 7 January 2004. The rate is 12 basis points over the 1-week USD Libor fix on 29 December 2003, which is 1.157 50 + 0.12 or 1.2775%.

This interest rate is payable on the new 'loan' amount of $152,156,228.00.

The TRS trade has become a means by which the broker-dealer can obtain collateralised funding for its portfolio. Like a repo, the bonds are taken off the broker-dealer's balance sheet, but unlike a repo the tax and accounting treatment also assumes they have been permanently taken off the balance sheet. In addition, the TRS is traded under the ISDA legal definitions, compared with a repo which is traded under the GMRA standard repo legal agreement.

CREDIT OPTIONS

Credit options are also bilateral over-the-counter financial contracts. A credit option is a contract designed to meet specific hedging or speculative requirements of an entity, which may purchase or sell the option to meet its objectives. A credit call option gives the buyer the right – without the obligation – to purchase the underlying credit-sensitive asset, or a credit spread, at a specified price and specified time (or period of time). A credit put option gives the buyer the right – without the obligation – to sell the underlying credit-sensitive asset or credit spread. By purchasing credit options, banks and other institutions can take a view on credit spread movements for the cost of the option premium only, without recourse to actual loans issued by an obligor. The writer of credit options seeks to earn premium income.

Credit option terms are similar to those used for conventional equity options. A *call* option written on a stock grants the purchaser the right but not the obligation to purchase a specified amount of the stock at a set price and time. A credit option can be used by bond investors to hedge against a decline in the price of specified bonds, in the event of a credit event such as a ratings downgrade. The investor would purchase an option whose payoff profile is a function of the credit quality of the bond, so that a loss on the bond position is offset by the payout from the option.

As with conventional options, there are both vanilla credit options and exotic credit options. The vanilla credit option grants the purchaser the right, but not the obligation, to buy (or sell if a *put* option) an asset or credit spread at a specified price (the *strike* price) for a specified period of time up to the maturity of the option. A credit option allows a market participant to take a view on credit only, and no other exposure such as interest rates. As an example, consider an investor who believes that a particular credit spread, which can be that of a specific entity or the average for a sector (such as 'all AA-rated sterling corporates'), will widen over the next 6 months. She can buy a 6-month call option on the relevant credit spread, for which a one-off premium (the price of the option) is paid. If the credit spread indeed does widen beyond the strike during the 6 months, the option will be in the money and the investor will gain. If not, the investor's loss is limited to the premium paid. Depending on whether the option is American or European, the option may be exercised before its expiry date or on its expiry date only.

Exotic credit options are options that have one or more of their parameters changed from the vanilla norm; the same terms are used as in other option markets. Examples include the barrier credit option, which specifies a credit event that would trigger (activate) the option or inactivate it. A digital credit option would have a payout profile that would be fixed, irrespective of how much in the money it was on expiry, and a zero payout if out of the money.

GENERAL APPLICATIONS OF CREDIT DERIVATIVES

Credit derivatives have allowed market participants to separate and disaggregate credit risk, and thence to trade this risk in a secondary market (see, for example, Das, 2000). Initially, portfolio managers used them to reduce credit exposure; subsequently, they have been used in the management of portfolios, to enhance portfolio yields and in the structuring of synthetic collateralised debt obligations (CDOs). Banks use credit derivatives to transfer the credit risk of their loan and other asset portfolios, and to take on credit exposure based on their views on the credit market. In this regard they also act as credit derivatives market makers, running mis-matched books in long- and short-position CDSs and TRSs. This is exactly how they operate in the interest-rate market, using interest-rate swaps. Now that the market in CDSs is very liquid, they act more as synthetic investment products in their own right, rather than simply as risk management tools. The market in CDSs of ABS is an example of credit derivatives being used to invest synthetically in assets that are not available in the cash market (in this case, ABS bonds), by investors who wish to hold certain asset classes but cannot source them directly.

Use of credit derivatives by portfolio managers

Enhancing portfolio returns

Asset managers can derive premium income by trading credit exposures in the form of derivatives issued with synthetic structured notes. This would be part of a structured credit product. A pool of risky assets can be split into specific tranches of risk, with the most risky portion given the lowest credit rating in the structure. This is known as 'multi-tranching'. The multi-tranching aspect of structured products enables specific credit exposures (credit spreads and outright default), and their expectations, to be sold to meet specific areas of demand. By using structured notes such as CLNs, tied to the assets in the reference pool of the portfolio manager, the trading of credit exposures is crystallised as added yield on the asset manager's fixed-income portfolio. In this way the portfolio manager enables other market participants to gain an exposure to the credit risk of a pool of assets but not to any other aspects of the portfolio, and without the need to hold the assets themselves.

Reducing credit exposure

Consider a portfolio manager who holds a large portfolio of bonds issued by a particular sector (say, utilities) and believes that spreads in this sector will widen in the short term. Previously, in order to reduce her credit exposure she would have to sell bonds; however, this may crystallise a mark-to-market loss and may conflict with her long-term investment strategy. An alternative approach would be to enter into a CDS, purchasing protection for the short term; if spreads do widen, these swaps will increase in value and may be sold at a profit in the secondary market. Alternatively, the portfolio manager may enter into TRSs on the desired credits. She pays the counterparty the total return on the reference assets, in return for Libor. This transfers the credit exposure of the bonds to the counterparty for the term of the swap, in return for the credit exposure of the counterparty.

Consider now the case of a portfolio manager wishing to mitigate credit risk from a growing portfolio (say, one that has just been launched). Figure 12.11 shows an example of an unhedged credit

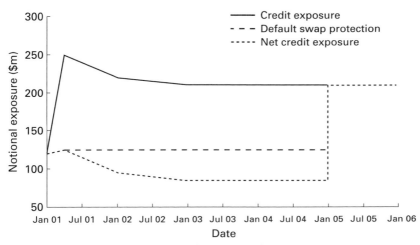

Figure 12.11 Reducing credit exposure.

exposure to a hypothetical credit-risky portfolio. It illustrates the manager's expectation of credit risk building up to $250m as assets are purchased, and then reducing to a more stable level as the credits become more established.[8] A 3-year CDS entered into shortly after provides protection on half of the notional exposure, shown as the broken line. The net exposure to credit events has been reduced by a significant margin.

Credit switches and zero-cost credit exposure

Protection buyers utilising CDSs must pay premium in return for laying off their credit risk exposure. An alternative approach for an asset manager involves the use of credit switches for specific sectors of the portfolio. In a credit switch the portfolio manager purchases credit protection on one reference asset or pool of assets, and simultaneously sells protection on another asset or pool of assets.[9] So, for example, the portfolio manager would purchase protection for a particular fund and sell protection on another. Typically, the entire

---

[8] For instance, the fund may be invested in new companies. As the names become more familiar to the market the credits become more 'established' because the perception of how much credit risk they represent falls.

[9] A pool of assets would be concentrated on one sector, such as utility company bonds.

transaction would be undertaken with one investment bank, which would price the structure so that the net cash flows would be 0. This has the effect of synthetically diversifying the credit exposure of the portfolio manager, enabling her to gain and/or reduce exposure to sectors as desired.

Exposure to market sectors

Investors can use credit derivatives to gain exposure to sectors for which they do not wish a cash market exposure. This can be achieved with an *index* swap, which is similar to a TRS, with one counterparty paying a total return that is linked to an external reference index. The other party pays a Libor-linked coupon or the total return of another index. Indices that are used might include the government bond index, a high-yield index or a technology stocks index. Assume that an investor believes that the bank loan market will outperform the mortgage-backed bond sector; to reflect this view he enters into an index swap in which he pays the total return of the mortgage index and receives the total return of the bank loan index.

Another possibility is synthetic exposure to foreign currency and money markets. Again we assume that an investor has a particular view on an emerging market currency. If he wishes he can purchase a short-term (say, 1-year) domestic coupon-bearing note, whose principal redemption is linked to a currency factor. This factor is based on the ratio of the spot value of the foreign currency on issue of the note to the spot value on maturity. Such currency-linked notes can also be structured so that they provide an exposure to sovereign credit risk. The downside of currency-linked notes is that if the exchange rate goes the other way the note will have a zero return – in effect, a negative return once the investor's funding costs have been taken into account.

Trading credit spreads

Assume that an investor has negative views on a certain emerging-market government bond credit spread relative to UK gilts. The simplest way to reflect this view would be to go long a CDS on the sovereign, paying X basis points. Assuming that the investor's view is correct and the sovereign bonds decrease in price as their credit spread widens, the premium payable on the credit swap will increase. The investor's swap can then be sold into the market at this higher premium.

SUPPLY AND DEMAND AND THE CREDIT DEFAULT SWAP BASIS

The credit default swap (CDS) basis is the difference between the price of a CDS and the yield spread of the same reference asset in the cash markets, generally given by the asset-swap price (ASW). In Choudhry (2001b) we noted that, while the theoretical case can be made as to why the CDS price should be equal to the ASW price, market observation tells us that this is not the case. The difference in pricing between the cash and synthetic markets results from the impact of a combination of factors, noted in Choudhry (2004b). In essence, it is because credit derivatives isolate and trade credit as their sole asset – separately from any funding consideration – that they are priced at a different level than the asset swap on the same reference asset. There are also other important factors, including the impact of supply and demand, and we make an observation in this regard in this article.

A negative basis

The difference between the CDS and the ASW price is the CDS *basis*. The basis is given by:

Credit default spread (D) – Asset swap spread (S)[10]

Where $D - S > 0$ we have a *positive basis*. A positive basis occurs when the credit derivative trades higher than the asset swap price, and is the norm. Where $D - S < 0$ we have a *negative basis*. This describes where the credit derivative trades tighter than the cash bond asset swap spread. It is more unusual to see this for any length of time. On balance, the net impact of all the factors that drive the basis serves to make it positive. In essence, this is because the seller of protection on a standard CDS contract is affording a greater level of protection on the reference name than a cash investor in a bond issued by that reference name.[11]

---

[10] We may state the formal definition of the credit default swap–bond basis as being the difference between the credit default spread and the par bond floating-rate spread of the same reference asset, the latter as expressed for an asset swap on the bond.

[11] For further detail on the basis see Choudhry (2004b) and Choudhry (2006a, b).

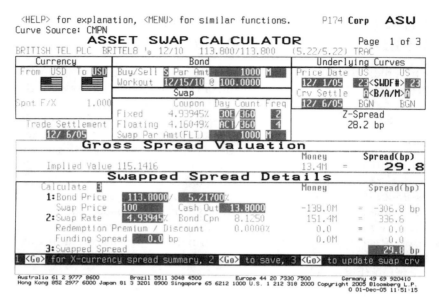

Figure 12.12   Bloomberg screen ASW, asset swap spread for British Telecom bond as at 1 December 2005.

© Bloomberg L.P. Used with permission. Visit *www.bloomberg.com*

Figure 12.12 shows Bloomberg screen ASW for the British Telecom 8.125% 2010 bond. This indicates an asset swap spread of 29.8 basis points. Figure 12.13 shows screen CRVD, which lists the ASW spread as well as the CDS price for that reference name. We see that the price for this bond in the CDS market is 43.60 basis points; this is the 5-year CDS price for British Telecom, and is the best price to compare because the bond in question is a 5-year bond. From these two values it is a simple calculation to determine the basis, which is shown on Figure 12.13 as 15.7 basis points. Note that the asset swap spread or the Z-spread can be used in the basis calculation, although it is more common for market practitioners to use the latter.[12]

One of the factors that impacts the basis is supply and demand, in

---

[12] For an accessible explanation of the Z-spread see the article on this that can be downloaded free from the 'Learning Curve' section of *www.yield-curve.com*. A fuller account of bond spreads and relative value analysis, including asset–swap spreads and Z-spreads, is given in the author's book *Corporate Bond Markets* (John Wiley & Sons 2005).

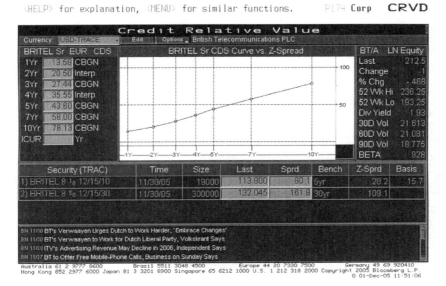

Figure 12.13 Bloomberg screen CRVD, CDS curve versus Z-spread for British Telecom bond as at 1 December 2005.

© Bloomberg L.P. Used with permission. Visit *www.bloomberg.com*

both cash and synthetic markets. For many reference names there is greater liquidity in the synthetic market than in the cash market, which would tend to influence the basis into negative territory, but other factors push the basis the other way (see Choudhry 2004b). With structured finance assets such as asset-backed securities (ABSs) though, supply in the cash market is a key factor, and has been responsible for negative basis over a longer time period than observed in conventional bond markets.

Supply and demand

The bonds we will consider in this illustration are all examples of residential mortgage-backed securities (RMBS) – in fact, a special class of RMBS known as Home Equity.[13] We show three of these bonds in Table 12.1.

All three bonds were part of new issues, for first settlement in September 2004. The mezzanine tranches were in high demand at

---

[13] For further information on Home Equity securities see Fabozzi (2004).

Table 12.1   Securities used in illustration, showing CDS and cash market prices, 21 September 2004.

Bond	Amount issued ($m)	CDS spread	Libor spread on note	CUSIP number	Interest frequency
ACCR 2004–3 2M7	7.665	335	350	004375BX8	Monthly on 25th
CWL 2004–6 B	46.0	340	375	126673BL5	Monthly on 25th
NCHET 2004–2 M9	19.374	345	400	64352VGJ4	Monthly on 25th

Bond terms source: Bloomberg L.P.
CDS price source: KBC Financial Products.

time of issue. Under conventional circumstances the CDS price for these securities would be expected to lie above the note yield. But, in fact, the opposite is true, as the market quotes shown in Table 12.1 indicate. This reflects the lack of supply of these bonds in the market, such that investors are forced to access them in the synthetic market.

The small size of these note tranches is a key reason behind the low availability of paper. We see that only $7.6 million of the ACCR bond is available, a very low figure in any securitisation. The entire securitisation itself is a large issue, as we see from Figure 12.14. This shows the Bloomberg DES page for the transaction, which is called Accredited Mortgage Loan Trust. From this we see that a total of $766.43 million of notes was issued as part of this deal, but the tranche in question – the Baa3/BBB-rated 2M7 piece – made up less than 1% of this total. Given this paucity of supply, the bond can be sourced more easily in the CDS market, but this carries with it a reduction in yield spread, associated with the greater demand over supply.[14]

We observe similar characteristics for the two other bonds in our sample. The Countrywide Asset-Backed Certificates transaction is made up of a total of $4.426 billion in 12 different tranches; the mezzanine tranche rated Baa3/BBB was issued in size of only $46 million. The total size of the New Century Home Equity Loan Trust

---

[14] In effect, the cash market note yield of 350 basis points for this bond is a theoretical construct. As the bond in effect cannot be purchased, as no paper is available, the cash market yield for this name cannot actually be earned by any investor.

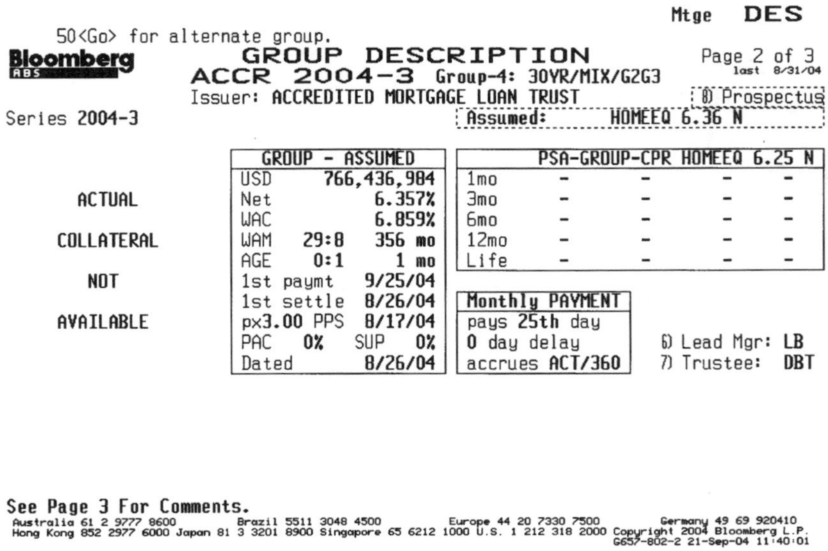

Figure 12.14 Bloomberg screen DES for ACCR Home Equity securitisation transaction.

deal was $1.937 billion, while the particular mezzanine tranche we are interested in was issued in size of only 1% of this total. This bond exhibits the widest spread in our small group, with the CDS trading at a premium of 55 basis points to the theoretical cash price.

CDS mechanics

The CDS contracts written on these structured finance securities have minor differences in their terms compared with vanilla single-name CDS instruments. This includes the following:

- A premium payment set to match the payment date of the cash bond, in this case a monthly payment on the 25th of each month – the standard CDS payment terms are quarterly in arrears.
- In practice, an un-fixed maturity date. The CDS written on these bonds is set to match their maturity. From Figure 12.15 we see that the ACCR 2M7 tranche has a weighted-average life

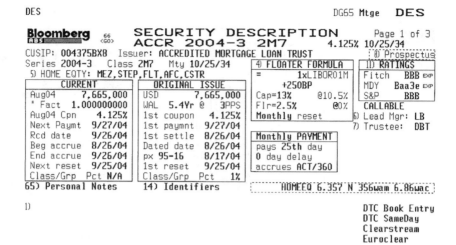

Figure 12.15 Bloomberg screen DES for 2M7 tranche of ACCR transaction, 21 September 2004.

© Bloomberg L.P. Used with permission. Visit *www.bloomberg.com*

of 5.4 years. This is of course an estimate based on a specified pre-payment rate, which is standard practice for all RMBS bonds. In reality, the bond may well pay off before or after 5.4 years. The CDS contract language specifies that the contract expires when the cash bond itself is fully paid off.

- The transaction undertaken by the investor for the CDS that references the ACCR 2M7 tranche was for a notional of $10 million. This is more than the actual amount in existence of the physical bond. Hence, it is standard practice for all structured finance CDS contracts to always be cash-settled instruments.

By setting the terms in this way, investors are able to access these types of names and asset classes where the cash market bond is no longer available to them, by selling protection on the bond tranches using a CDS.

The CDS market maker that is the counterparty to the CDS investor may gain from acting in this business in the following ways:

- buying protection on this class of assets releases economic capital that can be invested in higher-yielding assets elsewhere;

- it may be able to find similar assets in the cash market that yield a higher spread than the CDS protection it is paying for;
- it can treat this business as trading activity – CDS market making – and seek to gain a trading profit.

Irrespective of the motivation of the investor and the CDS counterparty to these trades, this business illustrates the contribution to market liquidity of credit derivatives, as well as the impact of supply and demand on reversing the market convention of a positive basis.

BIBLIOGRAPHY

Choudhry, M. (2001a) *The Bond and Money Markets: Strategy, Trading, Analysis.* Butterworth-Heinemann, Oxford, UK.

Choudhry, M. (2001b). Some issues in the asset-swap pricing of credit default swaps. *Derivatives Week*, Euromoney Publications, 2 December 2001.

Choudhry, M. (2003). Some Issues in the asset-swap pricing of credit default swaps. In: F. Fabozzi (ed.), *Professional Perspectives on Fixed Income Portfolio Management* (Vol. 4). John Wiley & Sons, New York.

Choudhry, M. (2004a). *Structured Credit Products: Credit Derivatives and Synthetic Securitisation.* John Wiley & Sons, Singapore.

Choudhry, M. (2004b). The credit default swap basis: Analysing the relationship between cash and synthetic markets. *Journal of Derivatives Use, Trading and Regulation*, June, 9–26.

Choudhry, M. (2006a). Further observations on the CDS basis. *Journal of Structured Finance*, Winter.

Choudhry, M. (2006b). *The Credit Default Swap Basis.* Bloomberg Publishing, New York.

Das, S. (2004). *Credit Derivatives and Credit Linked Notes* (2nd edn). John Wiley & Sons, Singapore, chs 2–4.

Duffie, D. and Huang, M. (1996). Swap rates and credit quality. *Journal of Finance*, **51**(3), July.

Fabozzi, F. J. (2004). *Handbook of Fixed Income Securities* (5th edn). McGraw-Hill, New York.

Francis, J., Frost J. and Whittaker, G. (1999). *Handbook of Credit Derivatives.* Richard D. Irwin, New York.

Hogg, R. and Craig, A. (1970). *Introduction to Mathematical Statistics* (3rd edn). Macmillan, New York.

Hull, J. and White, A. (2000). Valuing credit default swaps, I: No counterparty default risk. *Journal of Derivatives*, **8**(1), Fall.

Jarrow, R. A. and Turnbull, S. M. (1995). Pricing options on derivative securities subject to credit risk. *Journal of Finance*, **50**, 53–58.

Tolk, J. (2001). Understanding the risks in credit default swaps. *Moody's Investors Service Special Report*, 16 March.

Chapter

13

....

APPROACHES TO GOVERNMENT BOND TRADING AND YIELD ANALYSIS[1]

---

[1] This chapter was first published in *Professional Perspectives on Fixed Income Portfolio Management*, Volume 3, edited by Frank J. Fabozzi (John Wiley & Sons) 2002. It was revised and updated and subsequently appeared in the author's book *Fixed Income Analysis* (John Wiley & Sons Asia) 2004. It appears in this book with new Bloomberg screens added.

In this chapter we consider some approaches to government bond trading from first principles, based on the author's experience in the UK gilt market. It is based on a series of internal papers written by the author during 1995–1997, and while the observations date from some time ago the techniques described can be applied to any government market and are still in widespread use. We also incorporate for this edition a look at some useful Bloomberg screens that can be used as part of the analysis.

INTRODUCTION

Portfolio managers who do not wish to put on a naked directional position, but rather believe that the yield curve will change shape and flatten or widen between two selected points, put on relative value trades to reflect their view. Such trades involve simultaneous positions in bonds of different maturity. Other relative value trades may position high-coupon bonds against low-coupon bonds of the same maturity, as a tax-related transaction. These trades are concerned with the change in yield spread between two or more bonds rather than a change in absolute interest-rate level. The key factor is that changes in spread are not conditional upon directional change in interest-rate levels; that is, yield spreads may narrow or widen whether interest rates themselves are rising or falling.

Typically, spread trades will be constructed as a long position in one bond against a short position in another bond. If it is set up correctly, the trade will only incur a profit or loss if there is change in the shape of the yield curve. This is regarded as being *first-order risk-neutral*, which means that there is no interest-rate risk in the event of change in the general level of market interest rates, provided the yield curve experiences essentially a parallel shift. In this chapter we examine some common yield spread trades.

The determinants of yield

The yield at which a fixed-interest security is traded is market-determined. This market determination is a function of three factors: the term-to-maturity of the bond, the liquidity of the bond and its credit quality. Government securities such as gilts are default-free and so this factor drops out of the analysis. Under 'normal' circumstances the yield on a bond is higher the greater its maturity, this reflecting both the expectations hypothesis and liquidity preference theories. Intuitively, we associate higher risk with longer-dated instruments, for which investors must be compensated in the form of higher yield. This higher risk reflects greater uncertainty with longer-dated bonds, both in terms of default and future inflation and interest-rate levels. However, for a number of reasons the yield curve assumes an inverted shape and long-dated yields become lower than short-dated ones.[2] Long-dated yields, generally, are expected to be less volatile over time compared with short-dated yields. This is mainly because incremental changes to economic circumstances or other technical considerations generally have an impact for only short periods of time, which affects the shorter end of the yield curve to a greater extent.

The liquidity of a bond also influences its yield level. The liquidity may be measured by the size of the bid–offer spread, the ease with which the stock may be transacted in size and the impact of large-size bargains on the market. It is also measured by the extent of any *specialness* in its repo rate. Supply and demand for an individual stock and the amount of stock available to trade are the main drivers of liquidity.[3] The general rule is that there is a yield premium for transacting business in lower-liquidity bonds.

In the analysis that follows we assume satisfactory levels of liquidity – that is, it is straightforward to deal in large sizes without adversely moving the market.

Spread trade risk weighting

A relative value trade usually involves a long position set up against a short position in a bond of different maturity. The trade must be weighted so that the two positions are first-order neutral, which means the risk exposure of each position nets out when considered as a single trade, but only with respect to a general

---

[2] For a summary of term structure theories see Choudhry (2001).

[3] The amount of stock issued and the amount of stock available to trade are not the same thing. If a large amount of a particular issue has been locked away by institutional investors, this may impede liquidity. However, the existence of a large amount at least means that some of the paper may be made available for lending in the stock loan and repo markets. A small issue size is a good indicator of low liquidity.

Term	Bond	Price	Accrued	Dirty price	Yield (%)	Modified duration	BPV	Per £1m nominal
2-yr	6% 10/8/1999	98-17	127	100.62	6.753	1.689	0.016642	166.42
5-yr	7% 7/6/2002	100-10	10	100.50	6.922	3.999	0.040115	401.15
10-yr	7.25% 7/12/2007	101-14	10	101.64	7.052	6.911	0.070103	701.03
25-yr	8% 7/6/2021	110-01	10	110.25	7.120	11.179	0.123004	1230.04

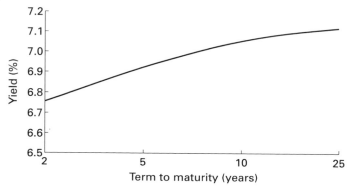

Figure 13.1   Gilt prices and yields for value 17 June 1997.

Source: Williams de Broe and Hambros Bank Limited; author's notes.

change in interest-rate levels. If there is a change in yield spread, a profit or loss will be generated.

A common approach to weighting spread trades is to use the *basis point value (BPV)* of each bond.[4] Figure 13.1 shows price and yield data for a set of benchmark gilts for value date 17 June 1997.[5] The BPV for each bond is also shown, per £100 of stock. For the purposes of this discussion we quote mid-prices only and assume that the investor is able to trade at these prices. The yield curve at that date is shown in Figure 13.2.

The yield spread history between these two stocks over the previous 3 months and up to yesterday's closing yields is shown in Figure 13.3. An investor believes that the yield curve will flatten between the 2-year and 10-year sectors of the curve and that the spread between

---

[4] This is also known as *dollar value of a basis point (DVBP)* or *present value of a basis point (PVBP)*.

[5] Gilts settle on a $T + 1$ basis.

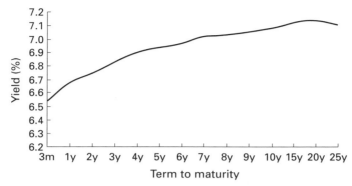

Figure 13.2 Benchmark gilt yield curve, 16 June 1997.

Source: Hambros Bank Limited; author's notes.

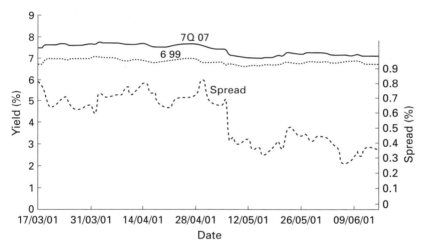

Figure 13.3 6% Treasury 1999 and $7\frac{1}{4}$% 2007 3 months' yield spread history as at 16 June 1997.

Note: yield values are shown on the left axis, spread values on the right – which uses a larger scale for clarity.

the 6% 1999 and the 7.25% 2007 will narrow further from its present value of 0.299%.

To reflect this view the investor buys the 10-year bond and sells short the 2-year bond, in amounts that leave the trade first-order risk-neutral. If we assume the investor buys £1 million nominal of the 7.25% 2007 gilt, this represents an exposure of £1,230.04 loss (profit) if there is a 1-basis-point increase (decrease) in yields. Therefore, the nominal amount of the short position in the 6% 1999 gilt must equate this risk exposure. The BPV per £1 million nominal of the 2-year bond is £166.42, which means that the investor must sell (1230.04/166.42) or £7.3912 million of this bond, given by a simple ratio of the two BPVs. We expect to sell a greater nominal amount of the shorter-dated gilt because its risk exposure is lower. This trade generates cash because the short sale proceeds exceed the long buy purchase funds, which are, respectively:

- Buy £1m 7.25% 2007:   −£1,102,500;
- Sell £7.39m 6% 1999:   +£7,437,025.

What are the possible outcomes of this trade? If there is a parallel shift in the yield curve, the trade neither gains or loses. If the yield spread narrows by, say, 15 basis points, the trade will gain either from a drop in yield on the long side or a gain in yield in the short side, or a combination of both. Conversely, a widening of the spread will result in a loss. Any narrowing spread is positive for the trade, while any widening is harmful.

The trade would be put on the same ratio if the amounts were higher, which is *scaling* the trade. So, for example, if the investor had bought £100 million of the 7.25% 2007, he would need to sell short £739 million of the 2-year bonds. However, the risk exposure is greater by the same amount, so that in this case the trade would generate 100 times the risk. As can be imagined, there is a greater potential reward but at the same time a greater amount of stress in managing the position.

Using BPVs to risk-weight a relative value trade is common but suffers from any traditional duration-based measure because of the assumptions used in the analysis. Note that when using this method the ratio of the nominal amount of the bonds must equate the reciprocal of the bonds' BPV ratio. So, in this case the BPV ratio is (166.42/1,230.04) or 0.1353, which has a reciprocal of 7.3912. This means that the nominal values of the two bonds must always be in the ratio of 7.39 : 1. This weighting is not static, however; we know that duration measures are a static (snapshot) estimation of dynamic properties such as yield and term to maturity. Therefore, for anything but very short-term trades the relative values may need to be adjusted as the BPVs alter over time, so-called *dynamic adjustment* of the portfolio.

Another method to weight trades is by duration-weighting, which involves weighting in terms of market values. This compares with the BPV approach which provides a weighting ratio in terms of nominal values. In practice, the duration approach does not produce any more accurate risk weighting.

A key element of any relative value trade is the financing cost of each position. This is where the repo market in each bond becomes important. In the example just described, the financing requirement is: repo out the 7.25% 2007, for which £1.1 million of cash must be borrowed to finance the purchase; the trader pays the repo rate on this stock; and reverse repo the 6% 1999 bond, which must be borrowed in repo to cover the short sale; the trader earns the repo rate on this stock.

If the repo rate on both stocks is close to the general repo rate in the market, there will be a bid–offer spread to pay but the greater amount of funds lent out against the 6% 1999 bond will result in a net financing gain on the trade whatever happens to the yield spread. If the 7.25% 2007 gilt is special, because the stock is in excessive demand in the market (for whatever reason), the financing gain will be greater still. If the 6% 1999 is *special*, the trade will suffer a financing loss.

In this case, however, the cash sums involved for each bond make the financing rates academic, as the amount paid in interest in the 7.25% 2007 repo is far outweighed by the interest earned on cash lent out when undertaking reverse repo in the 6% 1999 bond. Therefore, this trade will not be impacted by repo rate bid–offer spreads or specific rates, unless the rate on the borrowed bond is excessively special.[6] The repo financing cash flows for the 6% 1999 and 7.25% 2007 are shown in Figures 13.4 and 13.5, respectively, the Bloomberg repo/reverse repo screen RRRA. They show that at the time of the trade the investor had anticipated a 14-day term for the position before reviewing it and/or unwinding it.

A detailed account of the issues involved in financing a spread trade is contained in Choudhry (2002b).[7]

---

[6] In fact, the 6% 1999 did experience very special rates at certain times, briefly reaching negative rates at the start of 1998. However, the author had unwound the position long before then!

[7] And just so you know, this trade was profitable as the yield spread between the 6% 1999 and 7.25% 2007 did indeed narrow, prior to the entire curve inverting just over 1 month later.

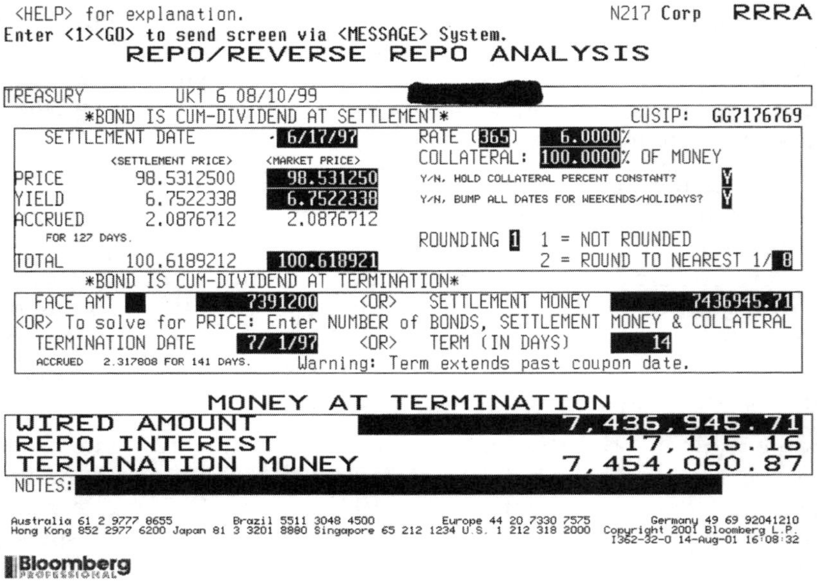

<HELP> for explanation.   N217 Corp   **RRRA**
Enter <1><GO> to send screen via <MESSAGE> System.
        REPO/REVERSE REPO ANALYSIS

TREASURY   UKT 6 08/10/99
        BOND IS CUM-DIVIDEND AT SETTLEMENT   CUSIP: GG7176769
    SETTLEMENT DATE   - 6/17/97   RATE (365)   6.0000%
        <SETTLEMENT PRICE> <MARKET PRICE> COLLATERAL: 100.0000% OF MONEY
PRICE   98.5312500   98.531250   Y/N, HOLD COLLATERAL PERCENT CONSTANT?   Y
YIELD   6.7522338   6.7522338   Y/N, BUMP ALL DATES FOR WEEKENDS/HOLIDAYS? Y
ACCRUED   2.0876712   2.0876712
    FOR 127 DAYS.   ROUNDING 1 1 = NOT ROUNDED
TOTAL   100.6189212   100.618921   2 = ROUND TO NEAREST 1/ 8
        BOND IS CUM-DIVIDEND AT TERMINATION
    FACE AMT   7391200   <OR>   SETTLEMENT MONEY   7436945.71
<OR> To solve for PRICE: Enter NUMBER of BONDS, SETTLEMENT MONEY & COLLATERAL
    TERMINATION DATE   7/ 1/97   <OR>   TERM (IN DAYS)   14
    ACCRUED 2.317808 FOR 141 DAYS.   Warning: Term extends past coupon date.

        MONEY AT TERMINATION
WIRED AMOUNT   7,436,945.71
REPO INTEREST   17,115.16
TERMINATION MONEY   7,454,060.87
NOTES:

Australia 61 2 9777 8655   Brazil 5511 3048 4500   Europe 44 20 7330 7575   Germany 49 69 92041210
Hong Kong 852 2977 6200 Japan 81 3 3201 8880 Singapore 65 212 1234 U.S. 1 212 318 2000 Copyright 2001 Bloomberg L.P.
                                                                    I362-32-0 14-Aug-01 16°08:32

Bloomberg

Figure 13.4   Bloomberg screen RRRA showing repo cash flows for
6% 1999, 17 June to 1 July 1997.

© Bloomberg L.P. Used with permission. Visit *www.bloomberg.com*

<HELP> for explanation.   N217 Corp   **RRRA**
Enter <1><GO> to send screen via <MESSAGE> System.
        REPO/REVERSE REPO ANALYSIS

TREASURY   UKT7 ¼ 12/07/07   111.7093/111.7093   (5.06/5.06) BFV @16:09
        BOND IS CUM-DIVIDEND AT SETTLEMENT   CUSIP: GG7303389
    SETTLEMENT DATE   6/17/97   RATE (365)   6.1250%
        <SETTLEMENT PRICE> <MARKET PRICE> COLLATERAL: 100.0000% OF MONEY
PRICE   101.4375000   101.437500   Y/N, HOLD COLLATERAL PERCENT CONSTANT?   Y
YIELD   7.0478043   7.0478043   Y/N, BUMP ALL DATES FOR WEEKENDS/HOLIDAYS? Y
ACCRUED   0.1986301   0.1986301
    FOR 10 DAYS.   ROUNDING 1 1 = NOT ROUNDED
TOTAL   101.6361301   101.636130   2 = ROUND TO NEAREST 1/ 8
        BOND IS CUM-DIVIDEND AT TERMINATION
    FACE AMT   1000000   <OR>   SETTLEMENT MONEY   1016361.30
<OR> To solve for PRICE: Enter NUMBER of BONDS, SETTLEMENT MONEY & COLLATERAL
    TERMINATION DATE   7/ 1/97   <OR>   TERM (IN DAYS)   14
    ACCRUED 0.476712 FOR 24 DAYS.

        MONEY AT TERMINATION
WIRED AMOUNT   1,016,361.30
REPO INTEREST   2,387.75
TERMINATION MONEY   1,018,749.05
NOTES:

Australia 61 2 9777 8655   Brazil 5511 3048 4500   Europe 44 20 7330 7575   Germany 49 69 92041210
Hong Kong 852 2977 6200 Japan 81 3 3201 8880 Singapore 65 212 1234 U.S. 1 212 318 2000 Copyright 2001 Bloomberg L.P.
                                                                    I362-32-0 14-Aug-01 16°10:02

Bloomberg

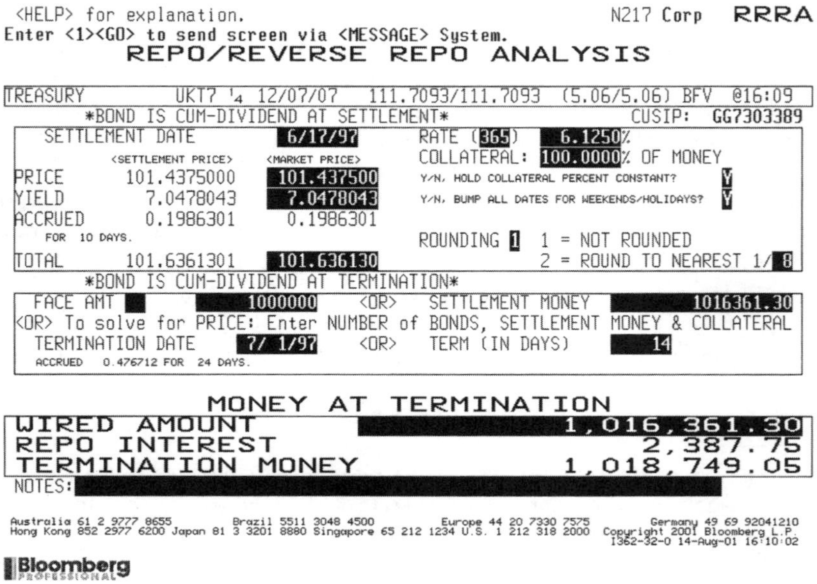

Figure 13.5   Bloomberg screen RRRA showing repo cash flows for
7.25% 2007, 17 June to 1 July 1997.

© Bloomberg L.P. Used with permission. Visit *www.bloomberg.com*

Identifying yield spread trades

Yield spread trades are a type of relative value position that a trader can construct when the objective is to gain from a change in the spread between two points on the yield curve. The decision on which sectors of the curve to target is an important one and is based on a number of factors. An investor may naturally target, say, the 5- and 10-year areas of the yield curve to meet investment objectives and have a view on these maturities. Or a trader may draw conclusions from studying the historical spread between two sectors.

Yield spreads do not move in parallel, however, and there is not a perfect correlation between the changes of short-, medium- and long-term sectors of the curve. The money market yield curve can sometimes act independently of the bond curve. Table 13.1 shows the change in benchmark yields during 1996/1997. There is no set pattern in the change in both yield levels and spreads. It is apparent that one segment of the curve can flatten while another is steepening, or remains unchanged.

Another type of trade is where an investor has a view on one part of the curve relative to two other parts of the curve. This can be

Table 13.1   Yield levels and yield spreads during November 1996 to November 1997.

			Changes in yield levels			
	3-month	**1-year**	**2-year**	**5-year**	**10-year**	**25-year**
10/11/1996	6.06	6.71	6.83	7.31	7.67	7.91
10/07/1997	6.42	6.96	7.057	7.156	7.025	6.921
Change	0.36	0.25	0.227	−0.154	−0.645	−0.989
10/11/1997	7.15	7.3	7.09	6.8	6.69	6.47
Change	0.73	0.34	0.033	−0.356	−0.335	−0.451
			Changes in yield spread			
	3m/1y	**1y/2y**	**2y/5y**	**5y/10y**	**5y/25y**	**10y/25y**
10/11/1996	−0.65	−0.12	−0.48	−0.36	−0.6	−0.24
10/07/1997	−0.54	−0.457	−0.099	0.131	0.235	0.104
Change	0.11	−0.337	0.381	0.491	0.835	0.344
10/11/1997	−0.15	0.21	0.29	0.11	0.33	0.22
Change	0.39	0.667	0.389	−0.021	0.095	0.116

Source: ABN Amro Hoare Govett Sterling Bonds Ltd, Hambros Bank Limited; Tullett & Tokyo; author's notes.

reflected in a number of ways, one of which is the butterfly trade, which is considered below.

COUPON SPREADS[8]

Coupon spreads are becoming less common in the gilt market because of the disappearance of high-coupon or other exotic gilts and the concentration on liquid benchmark issues. However, they are genuine spread trades. The US Treasury market presents greater opportunity for coupon spreads due to the larger number of similar-maturity issues. The basic principle behind the trade is a spread of two bonds that have similar maturity or similar duration but different coupons.

Figure 13.6 shows the yields for a set of high-coupon and low(er)-coupon gilts for a specified date in May 1993 and the yields for the same gilts 6 months later. From the yield curves we see that general yield levels decline by approximately 80–130 basis points. The last column in the table shows that, apart from the earliest pair of gilts (which do not have strictly comparable maturity dates), the perform-ance of the lower-coupon gilt exceeded that of the higher-coupon gilt in every instance. Therefore, buying the spread of the low-coupon versus the high-coupon should, in theory, generate a trading gain in an environment of falling yields. One explanation for this is that the lower-coupon bonds are often the benchmark, which means the demand for them is higher. In addition, during a bull market, more bonds are considered to be 'high' coupon as overall yield levels decrease.

The exception noted in Figure 13.6 is the outperformance of the 14% Treasury 1996 compared with the lower-coupon $10\frac{1}{4}$% 1995 stock. This is not necessarily conclusive, because the bonds are 6 months apart in maturity, which is a significant amount for short-dated stock. However, in an environment of low or falling interest rates, shorter-dated investors such as banks and insurance companies often prefer to hold very high-coupon bonds because of the high income levels they generate. This may explain the demand for

---

[8] First presented by the author as an internal paper to the head of Treasury at ABN Amro Hoare Govett Sterling Bonds Limited in April 1995; subsequently incorporated into this article.

Gilt	Maturity	10/05/1993 Yield (%)	12/11/1993 Yield (%)	Yield change (%)
10Q 95	21-Jul-95	6.393	5.390	−1.003
14 96	10-Jan-96	6.608	5.576	−1.032
15Q 96	3-May-96	6.851	5.796	−1.055
13Q 96	15-May-96	6.847	5.769	−1.078
13Q 97	22-Jan-97	7.142	5.999	−1.143
10H 97	21-Feb-97	7.131	5.974	1.157
7 97	6-Aug-97	7.219	6.037	−1.182
8T 97	1-Sep-97	7.223	6.055	−1.168
15 97	27-Oct-97	7.294	6.113	−1.161
9T 98	19-Jan-98	7.315	6.102	−1.213
7Q 98	30-Mar-98	7.362	6.144	−1.218
6 99	10-Aug-99	7.724	6.536	−1.188
10Q 99	22-Nov-99	7.731	6.552	−1.179
8 03	10-Jun-03	8.075	6.854	−1.221
10 03	8-Sep-03	8.137	6.922	−1.215

Stock	Term	10-May-93	12-Nov-93
Gilt	1	5.45	5.19
10Q 95	2	6.39	5.39
10 96	3	6.94	5.82
10H 97	4	7.13	5.97
9T 98 and 7Q 98	5	7.31	6.14
10Q 99	6	7.73	6.55
9 00	7	7.67	6.54
10 01	8	8.01	6.82
9T 02	9	8.13	6.95
8 03	10	8.07	6.85
9 08	15	8.45	7.18
9 12	20	8.55	7.23
8T 17	30	8.6	7.22

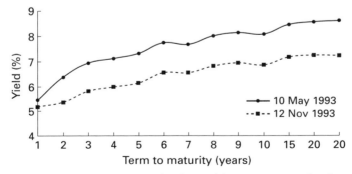

Figure 13.6 Yield changes on high- and low-coupon gilts from May 1993 to November 1993.

Source: ABN Amro Hoare Govett Sterling Bonds Ltd; Bloomberg; author's notes.

the 14% 1996 stock[9] although the evidence at the time was only anecdotal.

BUTTERFLY TRADES[10]

Butterfly trades are another method by which traders can reflect a view on changing yield levels without resorting to a naked punt on interest rates. They are another form of relative value trade; amongst portfolio managers they are viewed as a means of enhancing returns. In essence, a butterfly trade is a short position in one bond against a long position of two bonds, one of shorter maturity and the other of longer maturity than the short-sold bond. Duration-weighting is used so that the net position is first-order risk-neutral, and nominal values are calculated such that the short sale and long purchase cash flows net to 0, or very closely to 0.

This section reviews some of the aspects of butterfly trades.

Basic concepts

A butterfly trade is *par excellence* a yield curve trade. If the average return on the combined long position is greater than the return on the short position (which is a cost) during the time the trade is maintained, the strategy will generate a profit. It reflects a view that the short-end of the curve will steepen relative to the 'middle' of the curve while the long-end will flatten. For this reason higher convexity stocks are usually preferred for the long positions, even if this entails a loss in yield. However, the trade is not 'risk-free', for the same reasons that a conventional two-bond yield spread is not. Although, in theory, a butterfly is risk-neutral with respect to parallel changes in the yield curve, changes in the shape of the curve can result in losses. For this reason the position must be managed dynamically and monitored for changes in risk relative to changes in the shape of the yield curve.

---

[9] This stock also has a special place in the author's heart, although he was No. 2 on the desk when the Treasury head put on a very large position in it ...!

[10] Revised and updated version of a paper first presented internally at Hambros Bank Limited in June 1997. Incorporated into this chapter.

In a butterfly trade the trader is long a short-dated and long-dated bond, and short a bond of a maturity that falls in between these two maturities. A portfolio manager with a constraint on running short positions may consider this trade as a switch out of a long position in the medium-dated bond and into duration-weighted amounts of the short-dated and long-dated bond. However, it is not strictly correct to view the combined long position to be an exact substitute for the short position – due to liquidity (and other reasons) the two positions will behave differently for given changes in the yield curve. In addition, one must be careful to compare like for like, as the yield change in the short position must be analysed against yield changes in *two* bonds. This raises the issue of portfolio yield.

Putting on the trade

We begin by considering the calculation of the nominal amounts of the long positions, assuming a user-specified starting amount in the short position. In Table 13.2 we show three gilts as at 27 June 1997. The trade we wish to put on is a short position in the 5-year bond, the 7% Treasury 2002, against long positions in the 2-year bond, the 6% Treasury 1999 and the 10-year bond, the $7\frac{1}{4}$% Treasury 2007. Assuming £10 million nominal of the 5-year bond, the nominal values of the long positions can be calculated using duration, modified duration or BPVs (the last two, unsurprisingly, will generate identical results). The more common approach is to use BPVs.

Table 13.2 Bond values for butterfly strategy.

	2-year bond	**5-year bond**	**10-year bond**
Gilt	6% 1999	7% 2002	$7\frac{1}{4}$% 2007
Maturity date	10 Aug 1999	07 Jun 2002	07 Dec 2007
Price	98–08	99–27	101–06
Accrued interest	2.30137	0.44110	0.45685
Dirty price	100.551	100.285	101.644
Gross redemption yield (%)	6.913	7.034	7.085
Duration	1.969	4.243	7.489
Modified duration	1.904	4.099	7.233
Basis point value	0.01914	0.0411	0.07352
Convexity	0.047	0.204	0.676

Source: Author's notes.

In a butterfly trade the net cash flow should be as close to 0 as possible, and the trade must be BPV-neutral. Let us use the following notation:

P_1 Dirty price of the short position;
P_2 Dirty price of the long position in the 2-year bond;
P_3 Dirty price of the long position in the 10-year bond;
M_1 Nominal value of short-position bond, with M_2 and M_3 the long-position bonds;
BPV_1 Basis point value of the short-position bond.

Now, if applying BPVs, the amounts required for each stock are given by:

$$M_1 P_1 = M_2 P_2 + M_3 P_3 \tag{13.1}$$

while the risk-neutral calculation is given by:

$$M_1 BPV_1 = M_2 BPV_2 + M_3 BPV_3 \tag{13.2}$$

The value of M_1 is not unknown, as we have set it at £10 million. The equations can be rearranged to solve for the remaining two bonds, which are:

$$\left. \begin{aligned} M_2 &= \frac{P_1 BPV_3 - P_3 BPV_1}{P_2 BPV_3 - P_3 BPV_2} M_1 \\ M_3 &= \frac{P_2 BPV_1 - P_1 BPV_2}{P_2 BPV_3 - P_3 BPV_2} M_1 \end{aligned} \right\} \tag{13.3}$$

Using the dirty prices and BPVs from Table 13.2, we obtain the following values for the long positions. The position required is short £10 million 7% 2002 and long £5.347 million of the 6% 1999 and £4.576 million of the $7\frac{1}{4}$% 2007. With these values the trade results in a zero net cash flow and a first-order, risk-neutral, interest-rate exposure. Identical results would be obtained using the modified duration values, and similar results using the duration measures. If using Macaulay duration the nominal values are calculated using:

$$D_1 = \frac{MV_2 D_2 + MV_3 D_3}{MV_2 + MV_3} \tag{13.4}$$

where D = Duration for each respective stock;
           MV = Market value for each respective stock.

Yield gain

We know that the gross redemption yield for a vanilla bond is that rate r where:

$$P_d = \sum_{i=1}^{N} C_i e^{-rn} \tag{13.5}$$

The right-hand side of equation (13.5) is simply the present value of the cash flow payments C to be made by the bond in its remaining lifetime. Equation (13.5) gives the continuously compounded yields to maturity; in practice, users define a yield with compounding interval m, that is:

$$r = \frac{e^{rmn} - 1}{m} \tag{13.6}$$

Treasuries and gilts compound on a semiannual basis.

In principle, we may compute the yield on a portfolio of bonds exactly as for a single bond, using equation (13.5) to give the yield for a set of cash flows which are purchased today at their present value. In practice, the market calculates portfolio yield as a weighted average of the individual yields on each of the bonds in the portfolio. This is described, for example, in Fabozzi (1993), and this description points out the weakness of this method. An alternative approach is to weight individual yields using bonds' BPVs, which we illustrate here in the context of the earlier butterfly trade. In this trade we have:

- short £10 million 7% 2002;
- long £5.347 million 6% 1999 and £4.576 million $7\frac{1}{4}$% 2007.

Using the semiannual adjusted form of equation (13.5) the true yield of the long position is 7.033%. To calculate the portfolio yield of the long position using market value weighting, we may use:

$$r_{port} = \left(\frac{MV_2}{MV_{port}}\right)r_2 + \left(\frac{MV_3}{MV_{port}}\right)r_3 \tag{13.7}$$

which results in a portfolio yield for the long position of 6.993%. If we weight the yield with BPVs we use:

$$r_{port} = \frac{BPV_2 M_2 r_2 + BPV_3 M_3 r_3}{BPV_2 M_2 + BPV_3 M_3} \tag{13.8}$$

Substituting the values from Table 13.2 we obtain:

$$r_{port} = \frac{(1,914)(5.347)(6.913) + (7,352)(4.576)(7.085)}{(1,914)(5.347) + (7,352)(4.576)}$$

$$= 7.045\%$$

We see that using BPVs produces a seemingly more accurate weighted yield, closer to the true yield computed using the expression above. In addition, using this measure a portfolio manager switching into the long butterfly position from a position in the 7% 2002 would pick up a yield gain of 1.2 basis points, compared with the 4 basis points that an analyst would conclude had been lost using the first yield measure.[11]

The butterfly trade therefore produces a yield gain in addition to the capital gain expected if the yield curve changes in the anticipated way.

Convexity gain

In addition to yield pick-up, the butterfly trade provides, in theory, a convexity gain which will outperform the short position irrespective of which direction interest rates move in, provided we have a parallel shift. This is illustrated in Table 13.3. This shows the changes in value of the 7% 2002 as interest rates rise and fall, together with the change in value of the combined portfolio.

We observe from Table 13.3 that whatever the change in interest rates, up to a point, the portfolio value will be higher than the value of the short position, although the effect is progressively reduced as yields rise. The butterfly will always gain if yields fall, and protects against downside risk if yields rise to a certain extent. This is the effect of convexity; when interest rates rise the portfolio value

---

[11] The actual income gained on the spread will depend on the funding costs for all three bonds, a function of the specific repo rates available for each bond. Shortly after the time of writing, the 6% Treasury 1999 went special, so the funding gain on a long position in this stock would have been excessive. However, buying the stock outright would have necessitated paying a yield premium, as demand for it increased as a result of it going special. In the event, the premium was deemed high, an alternative stock was nominated: the $10\frac{1}{4}\%$ Conversion 1999, a bond with near-identical modified duration value.

Table 13.3   Changes in bond values with changes in yield levels.

Yield change (bps)	7% 2002 value (£)	Portfolio value* (£)	Difference (£)	BPV 7% 2002 (5-year)	BPV 6% 1999 (2-year)	BPV 7.25% 2007 (10-year)
+250	9,062,370	9,057,175	−5,195	0.0363	0.0180	0.0584
+200	9,246,170	9,243,200	−2,970	0.0372	0.0182	0.0611
+150	9,434,560	9,435,200	640	0.0381	0.0184	0.0640
+100	9,627,650	9,629,530	1,880	0.0391	0.0187	0.0670
+50	9,825,600	9,828,540	2,940	0.0401	0.0189	0.0702
0	10,028,500	10,028,500	0	0.0411	0.0191	0.0735
−50	10,236,560	10,251,300	14,740	0.0421	0.0194	0.0770
−100	10,450,000	10,483,800	33,800	0.0432	0.0196	0.0808
−150	10,668,600	10,725,700	57,100	0.0443	0.0199	0.0847
−200	10,893,000	10,977,300	84,300	0.0454	0.0201	0.0888
−250	11,123,000	11,240,435	117,435	0.0466	0.0204	0.0931

*Combined value of long positions in 6% 1999 and 7.25% 2007. Values rounded. Yield change is parallel shift.

declines by less than the short position value, and when rates fall the portfolio value increases by more. Essentially, the combined long position exhibits greater convexity than the short position. The effect is greater if yields fall, while there is an element of downside protection as yields rise, up to the +150-basis-point parallel shift.

Portfolio managers may seek greater convexity whether or not there is a yield pick-up available from a switch. However, the convexity effect is only material for large changes in yield, and so if there was not a corresponding yield gain from the switch, the trade may not perform positively. As we noted, this depends partly on the funding position for each stock. The price/yield profile for each stock is shown in Figure 13.7.

Essentially, by putting on a butterfly as opposed to a two-bond spread or a straight directional play, the trader limits the downside risk if interest rates fall, while preserving the upside gain if yields fall.

To conclude the discussion of butterfly trade strategy, we describe the analysis using the BBA screen on Bloomberg. The trade is illustrated in Figure 13.8.

Using this approach, the nominal values of the two long positions are calculated using BPV ratios only. This is shown under the column 'Risk Weight', and we note that the difference is 0. However, the

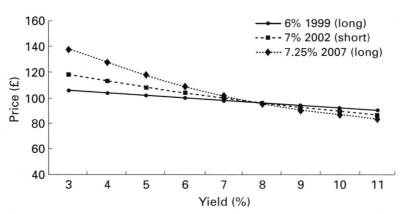

Figure 13.7 Illustration of convexity for each stock in butterfly trade, 27 June 1997.

Analysis using Bloomberg screen BBA.

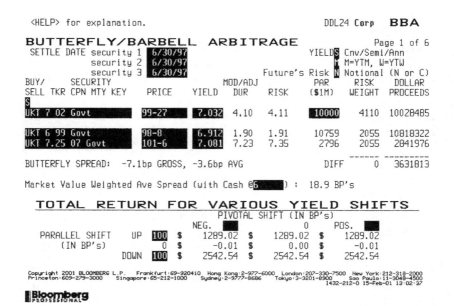

Figure 13.8 Butterfly trade analysis on 27 June 1997, on screen BBA.

© Bloomberg L.P. Used with permission. Visit *www.bloomberg.com*

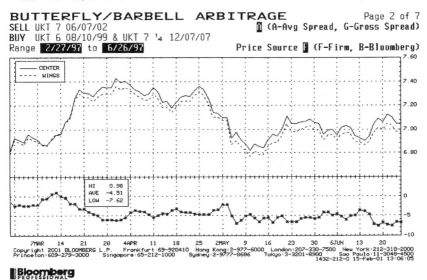

BUTTERFLY/BARBELL ARBITRAGE   Page 2 of 7
SELL UKT 7 06/07/02   🄰 (A-Avg Spread, G-Gross Spread)
BUY UKT 6 08/10/99 & UKT 7 ¼ 12/07/07
Range █2/27/97█ to █6/26/97█   Price Source 🄵 (F-Firm, B-Bloomberg)

Figure 13.9   Butterfly trade spread history.

© Bloomberg L.P. Used with permission. Visit *www.bloomberg.com*

nominal value required for the 2-year bond is much greater at £10.76 million, and for the 10-year bond much lower at £2.8 million. This results in a cash outflow of £3.632 million. The profit profile is, in theory, much improved; at the bottom of the screen we observe the results of a 100-basis-point parallel shift in either direction, which is a profit. Positive results were also seen for 200- and 300-basis-point parallel shifts in either direction. This screen incorporates the effect of a (uniform) funding rate, input on this occasion as 6.00%.[12] Note that the screen allows the user to see the results of a pivotal shift; however, in this example a 0-basis-point pivotal shift is selected.

This trade therefore created a profit whatever direction interest rates moved in, assuming a parallel shift.

The spread history for the position up to the day before the trade is shown in Figure 13.9, a reproduction of the graph on Bloomberg screen BBA.

---

[12] In reality the repo rate will be slightly different for each stock, and there will be a bid-offer spread to pay, but as long as none of the stocks are special the calculations should be reasonably close.

BLOOMBERG SCREENS

We illustrate two recent Bloomberg screens that can be used for both government and corporate bonds analysis here. The first is BQ which is a combination of a number of analytics and metrics.

To call up the screen we type the specific followed by <BQ>. So in this case for the 5% 2012 gilt we type:

UKT 5 12 <GOVT> <BQ> GO

Figure 13.10 is a page of the screen BQ and shows the bond price, plus a number of yield spreads. The G-spread is the yield below the government benchmark, which as we expect, given that this is a government bond, is very small. The I-spread is the spread to the interest-rate swap curve, in this case negative because it is a risk-free government bond. The three other spreads are:

- *ASW* – the asset swap spread, which is the spread payable above (or below) Libor if constructing an asset swap for this bond using an interest-rate swap to convert its coupon from fixed rate to floating rate.

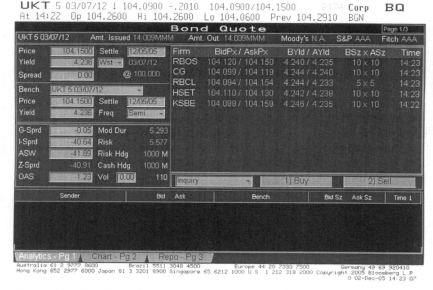

Figure 13.10 Bloomberg screen BQ, page 1, for UK gilt 5% 2012, as at 2 December 2005.

© Bloomberg L.P. Used with permission. Visit *www.bloomberg.com*

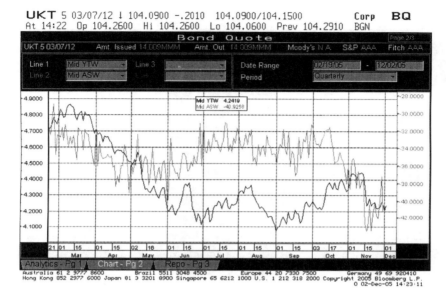

Figure 13.11   Bloomberg screen BQ, page 2, for UK gilt 5% 2012, as at 2 December 2005.

© Bloomberg L.P. Used with permission. Visit *www.bloomberg.com*

- *Z-spread* – the spread to the swap curve but using appropriate zero-coupon rates to discount each bond's cash flow rather than the uniform swap rate for the bond's maturity.
- *OAS* – the option-adjusted spread, the spread required to equate the bond's cash flows to its current price after adjusting for the effect of any embedded options (e.g., early redemption as with a callable bond); this is minimal with a bullet maturity gilt.

The right-hand side of page 1 of screen BQ shows some contributing prices from five banks or brokers.

For a full explanation of the use of these spread measures in corporate bond relative value analysis see Choudhry (2005).

Page 2 of the same screen at Figure 13.11 shows historical yield spreads, in this case the yield to maturity against the asset swap spread. The time period shown is user-selected.

Page 3 of the screen is a funding calculator, shown at Figure 13.12. We see here that for this holding of the bond the term is overnight and the nominal amount is £1 million.

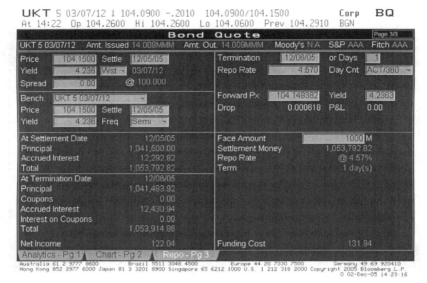

Figure 13.12   Bloomberg screen BQ, page 3, for UK gilt 5% 2012, as at 2 December 2005.

© Bloomberg L.P. Used with permission. Visit *www.bloomberg.com*

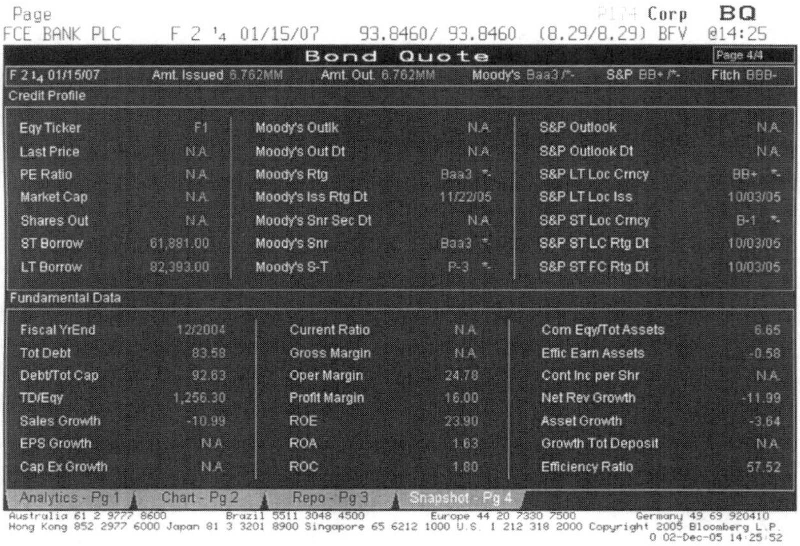

Figure 13.13   Bloomberg screen BQ, page 4, for the Ford 2.25% 2007 MTN, as at 2 December 2005.

© Bloomberg L.P. Used with permission. Visit *www.bloomberg.com*

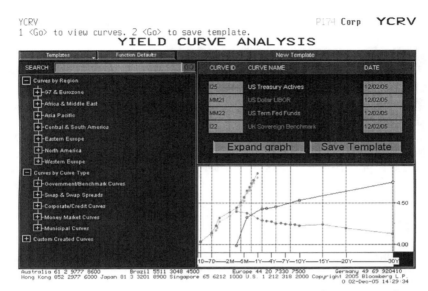

Figure 13.14 Bloomberg screen YCRV showing four US and UK curves, as at 2 December 2005.

© Bloomberg L.P. Used with permission. Visit *www.bloomberg.com*

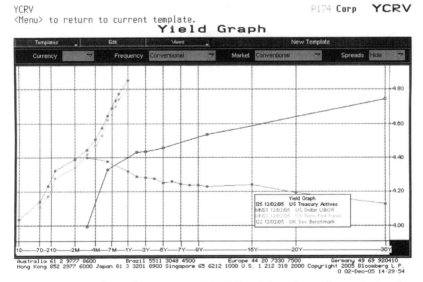

Figure 13.15 Bloomberg screen YCRV with enlarged graph display, as at 2 December 2005.

© Bloomberg L.P. Used with permission. Visit *www.bloomberg.com*

Page 4 of the screen is a credit ratings related page. Such a page is not shown for a gilt because it is seen as risk-free, so we illustrate it using the Ford 2.25% 2007 bond we introduced in Chapter 1. This is shown at Figure 13.13. We see the Moody's and S&P's ratings as well as ratings analyst fundamental data on the bond.

The screen YCRV shows a number of yield curve screens. For example, the user can select up to four different curves for historical comparison. We show this at Figure 13.14, which is screen YCRV selected with the US Treasury, USD Libor, US Term Fed Funds and the UK government benchmark shown. This is as at 2 December 2005. The large-size graph is shown at Figure 13.15.

BIBLIOGRAPHY

Choudhry, M. (2001). *The Bond and Money Markets: Strategy, Trading, Analysis*. Butterworth-Heinemann, Oxford, UK, ch. 6.

Choudhry, M. (2002a). *Professional Perspectives on Fixed Income Portfolio Management* (Vol. 3, edited by Frank J. Fabozzi). John Wiley & Sons, Chichester, UK.

Choudhry, M. (2002b). *The Repo Handbook*. Butterworth-Heinemann, Oxford, UK.

Choudhry, M. (2005). *Corporate Bond Markets: Instruments and Applications*. John Wiley & Sons, Singapore, ch. 15.

Fabozzi, F. (1996). *Bond Portfolio Management*. FJF Associates, chs 10–14.

Chapter

14

....

RISK MANAGEMENT

In this chapter we will consider aspects of the risks to which participants in the capital markets are exposed, and the risk management function to which banks and securities houses now devote a significant part of their resources. The profile of the risk management function and risk measurement tools such as Value-at-Risk was raised during the 1990s, following bank collapses such as that of Baring's and other trading losses suffered by banks such as Daiwa and Sumitomo. It was widely rumoured that one of the driving forces behind the merger of the old UBS with Swiss Bank (in reality, a takeover of UBS by Swiss Bank; the merged entity was named UBS) was the discovery of a multi-million loss on UBS's currency options trading book, which senior management had been unaware of right up until its discovery. In any case, shareholders of banks now demand greater comfort that senior executives are aware of the trading risks that their bank is exposed to, and that robust procedures exist to deal with these risks. For this reason it is now essential for all staff to be familiar with the risk management function in a bank.

CHARACTERISING RISK

The types of risk that a bank or securities house is exposed to as part of its operations in the bond and capital markets are broadly characterised as follows:

- *Market risk* – risk arising from movements in prices in financial markets. Examples include foreign exchange (*FX*) risk, interest-rate risk and basis risk.
- *Credit risk* – this refers to the risk that an issuer of debt will default. *Counterparty risk* refers to the risk that a counterparty from whom one has dealt with will cease trading, making recovery of funds owed difficult. Examples include sovereign risk, marginal risk and *force majeure* risk.
- *Liquidity risk* – the risk that a bank has insufficient funding to meet commitments as they arise. For a securities house, it is the risk that the market for its assets becomes too thin to enable fair and efficient trading to take place.
- *Operational risk* – risk of loss associated with non-financial matters such as fraud, system failure, accidents and ethics.

We can look at some of these risk types in some more detail:

- *Market risk* – this risk reflects uncertainty as to an asset's price when it is sold. Market risk is the risk arising from movements in financial market prices; for bondholders it is the risk arising from movement in interest rates, and this is specifically referred to as *interest-rate risk*.
- *Currency risk* – this arises from exposure to movements in FX rates. Currency risk is often sub-divided into *transaction* risk, where currency fluctuations affect the proceeds from day-to-day transactions, and *translation* risk, which affects the value of assets and liabilities on a balance sheet.
- *Other market risks* – there are residual market risks which fall in this category. Among these are *volatility* risk, which affects option traders, and *basis* risk, which has a wider impact. Basis risk arises whenever one kind of risk exposure is hedged with an instrument that behaves in a similar, but not necessarily identical manner. One example would be a company using 3-month interest-rate futures to hedge its commercial paper (*CP*) programme. Although Eurocurrency rates, to which futures prices respond, are well correlated with commercial paper rates, they do not invariably move in lockstep. If CP rates moved up by 50 basis points but futures prices dropped by only 35 basis points, the 15-basis-point gap would be the basis risk in this case.
- *Liquidity risk* – this is the potential risk arising when an entity cannot meet payments when they fall due. It may involve borrowing at an excessive rate of interest, facing penalty payments under contractual terms or selling assets at below market prices (*forced sale* risk). It also refers to an inability to trade or obtain a price when desired, due to lack of supply or demand or a shortage of market makers.
- *Concentration risk* – any organisation with too great a proportion of its assets invested in one type of instrument, or in one specific geographical or industrial sector, is exposed to concentration risk. Banks will seek to limit this type of risk exposure by diversifying across investment types and geographical and country boundaries.
- *Reinvestment risk* – if an asset makes any payments before the investor's horizon, whether it matures or not, the cash flows will have to be reinvested until the horizon date. Since the reinvestment rate is unknown when the asset is purchased, the final cash flow is uncertain.

- *Sovereign risk* – this is a type of credit risk specific to a government bond. There is minimal risk of default by an industrialised country. A developing country may default on its obligation (or declare a debt 'moratorium') if debt payments relative to domestic product reach unsustainable levels.
- *Pre-payment risk* – this is specific to mortgage-backed and asset-backed bonds. For example, mortgage lenders allow the home-owner to repay outstanding debt before the stated maturity. If interest rates fall pre-payment will occur, which forces re-investment at rates lower than the initial yield.
- *Model risk* – some of the latest financial instruments such as exotic options are heavily dependent on complex mathematical models for pricing and hedging. If the model is incorrectly specified, is based on questionable assumptions or does not accurately reflect the true behaviour of the market, banks trading these instruments could suffer extensive losses.

RISK MANAGEMENT

The risk management function has grown steadily in size and importance within commercial and investment banks over the last 20 years. The development of the risk management function and risk management departments was not instituted from a desire to eliminate the possibility of all unexpected losses, should such an outcome indeed be feasible; rather from a wish to control the frequency, extent and size of trading losses in such a way as to provide the minimum surprise to senior management and shareholders.

Risk exists in all competitive business although the balance between financial risks of the types described above and general and management risk varies with the type of business engaged in. The key objective of the risk management function within a financial institution is to allow for a clear understanding of the risks and exposures the firm is engaged in, such that any monetary loss is deemed acceptable by the firm. The acceptability of any loss should be on the basis that such (occasional) loss is to be expected as a result of the firm being engaged in a particular business activity. If the bank's risk management function is effective, there will be no over-reaction to any unexpected losses, which may increase eventual costs to many times the original loss amount.

The risk management function

While there is no one agreed organisation structure for the risk management function, the following may be taken as being reflective of the typical bank set-up:

- an independent, 'middle office' department responsible for drawing up and explicitly stating the bank's approach to risk, and defining trading limits and the areas of the market that the firm can have exposure to;
- the head of the risk function reporting to an independent senior manager, who is a member of the executive board;
- monitoring the separation of duties between front, middle and back office, often in conjunction with an internal audit function;
- reporting to senior management, including firm's overall exposure and adherence of the front office to the firm's overall risk strategy;
- communication of risks and risk strategy to shareholders;
- where leading edge systems are in use, employment of the risk management function to generate competitive advantage in the market as well as control.

The risk management function is more likely to deliver effective results when there are clear lines of responsibility and accountability. It is also imperative that the department interacts closely with other areas of the front and back office. In addition to the above, the following are often accepted as ingredients of a risk management framework in an institution engaged in investment banking and trading activity:

- daily overview of risk exposure profile and profit & loss (*p&l*) reports;
- *Value-at-Risk* as a common measure of risk exposure, in addition to other measures including 'jump risk' to allow for market corrections;
- independent daily monitoring of risk utilisation by the middle-office risk management function;
- independent production of daily p&l, and independent review of front-office closing prices on a daily basis.

INTEREST-RATE RISK

A bank's trading book will have an interest-rate exposure arising from its net position. For example, an interest-rate swap desk will have exposure for each point of the term structure, out to the longest-dated swap that it holds on the book. A first-order measure of risk would be to calculate the effect of a 1-basis-point (1 b.p. = 0.01%) change in interest rates, along the entire yield curve, on the value of the net swaps position. This measures the effect of a *parallel shift* in interest rates. For large moves in interest rates, a bank's risk management department will also monitor the effect of a large parallel shift in interest rates – say, 1% or 5%. This is known as the bank's *jump risk*.

Derivatives desks often produce reports for trading books showing the effect on portfolio value of a 1-basis-point move, along each part of the term structure of interest rates. For example, such a report would show that a change of 1 basis point in 3-month rates would result in a change in value of £x – this measure is often referred to as a price variation per basis point, or sometimes as present value of a basis point (*PVBP*).

Jump risk refers to the effect on value of an upward move of 100 basis points for all interest rates – that is, for all points of the term structure. Each selected point on the term structure is called an *interest-rate bucket* or *grid point*. The jump risk figure is therefore the change in the value of the portfolio for a 1% parallel shift in the yield curve.

Table 14.1 shows an extract from the swap book risk report of a UK bank with the PVBP for selected points along the term structure. The jump risk report will show the effect of a 1% interest-rate move across all grid points; the sum of all the value changes is the jump risk.

As banks deal in a large number of currencies their jump risk reports will amalgamate the risk exposures from all parts of the bank. Table 14.2 shows an extract from the risk report for a currency options book of a major investment bank, dated before the introduction of the euro. It lists both value-at-risk exposure and jump risk exposure.

Table 14.1   Grid-point PVBPs.

Grid point (days)	PVBP (£)
1	1
7	5
91	−1,658
183	928
365	500
730	−1,839
1,643	−944
3,650	1,365
7,300	0
9,125	0

Table 14.2   Sample VaR units.

	Limits	Total VaR	Jump risk
AUD	3,500	1,312	−9,674
CHF	1,750	663	−7,802
DEM	5,000	3,969	−57,246
GBP	7,500	5,695	−74,215
JPY	150,000	49,563	−536,199
USD	4,500	3,339	−33,289
Total	172,250	64,541	−718,425

VALUE-AT-RISK

The advent of Value-at-Risk (*VaR*) as an accepted methodology for quantifying market risk and its adoption by bank regulators is part of the evolution of risk management. The application of VaR has been extended from its initial use in securities houses to commercial banks and corporates, following its introduction in October 1994 when JP Morgan launched RiskMetrics™ free over the Internet.

Definition

VaR is a measure of market risk. It is the maximum loss which can occur with X% confidence over a holding period of t days.

VaR is the expected loss of a portfolio over a specified time period for a set level of probability. For example, if a daily VaR is stated as £100,000 to a 95% level of confidence, this means that during the day there is a only a 5% chance that the loss will be *greater* than £100,000. VaR measures the potential loss in market value of a portfolio using estimated volatility and correlation. The 'correlation' referred to is the correlation that exists between the market prices of different instruments in a bank's portfolio. VaR is calculated within a given confidence interval, typically 95% or 99%; it seeks to measure the possible losses from a position or portfolio under 'normal' circumstances. The definition of normality is critical and is essentially a statistical concept that varies by firm and by risk management system. Put simply, however, the most commonly used VaR models assume that the prices of assets in the financial markets follow a normal distribution. To implement VaR, all of a firm's positions data must be gathered into one centralised database. Once this is complete, the overall risk has to be calculated by aggregating the risks from individual instruments across the entire portfolio. The potential move in each instrument (i.e., each risk factor) has to be inferred from past daily price movements over a given observation period. For regulatory purposes this period is at least 1 year. Hence, the data on which VaR estimates are based should capture all relevant daily market moves over the previous year.

The main assumption underpinning VaR – and which in turn may be seen as its major weakness – is that the distribution of future price and rate changes will follow past variations. Therefore, the potential portfolio loss calculations for VaR are worked out using distributions from historic price data in the observation period.

For a discussion of the normal distribution, refer to the author's book *An Introduction to Value-at-Risk*, part of this series.

Calculation methods

There are three main methods for calculating VaR. As with all statistical models, they depend on certain assumptions. The methods are:

- the correlation method (or variance/covariance method);
- historical simulation;
- Monte Carlo simulation.

Correlation method
(also known as the variance/covariance method)

This method assumes the returns on risk factors are normally distributed, the correlations between risk factors are constant and the delta (or price sensitivity to changes in a risk factor) of each portfolio constituent is constant. Using the correlation method, the volatility of each risk factor is extracted from the historical observation period. Historical data on investment returns are therefore required. The potential effect of each component of the portfolio on the overall portfolio value is then worked out from the component's delta (with respect to a particular risk factor) and that risk factor's volatility.

There are different methods of calculating the relevant risk factor volatilities and correlations. We consider two alternatives below:

(i)   Simple *historic volatility* (correlation). This is the most straightforward method, but the effects of a large one-off market move can significantly distort volatilities over the required forecasting period. For example, if using 30-day historic volatility, a market shock will stay in the volatility figure for 30 days until it drops out of the sample range and correspondingly causes a sharp drop in (historic) volatility 30 days *after* the event. This is because each past observation is equally weighted in the volatility calculation.

(ii) A more sophisticated approach is to weight past observations unequally. This is done to give more weight to recent observations so that large jumps in volatility are not caused by events that occurred some time ago. One method is to use exponentially-weighted moving averages.

Historic simulation method

The historic simulation method for calculating VaR is the simplest and avoids some of the pitfalls of the correlation method. Specifically, the three main assumptions behind correlation (normally distributed returns, constant correlations, constant deltas) are not needed in this case. For historic simulation the model calculates potential losses using actual historic returns in the risk factors and so captures the non-normal distribution of risk factor returns. This means rare events and crashes can be included in the results. As the risk factor returns used for revaluing the portfolio are actual past movements, the correlations in the calculation are also actual past correlations. They capture the dynamic nature of correlation as well as scenarios when the usual correlation relationships break down.

Monte Carlo simulation method

The third method, Monte Carlo simulation, is more flexible than the previous two. As with historic simulation, Monte Carlo simulation allows the risk manager to use actual historic distributions for risk factor returns rather than having to assume normal returns. A large number of randomly generated simulations are run forward in time using volatility and correlation estimates chosen by the risk manager. Each simulation will be different, but in total the simulations will aggregate to the chosen statistical parameters (i.e., historic distributions and volatility and correlation estimates). This method is more realistic than the previous two models and therefore is more likely to estimate VaR more accurately. However, its implementation requires powerful computers and there is also a trade-off in that the time to perform calculations is longer.

Validity of the variance-covariance (correlation) VaR estimate

The level of confidence in the VaR estimation process is selected by the number of standard deviations of variance applied to the probability distribution. Figure 14.1 shows a 98% confidence level

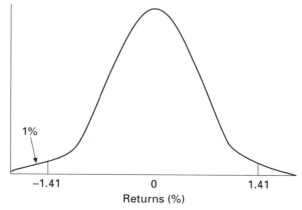

Figure 14.1 Measuring value-at-risk; a 98% confidence interval (1.41 standard deviations).

interval for the normal distribution. A standard deviation selection of 1.645 provides a 95% confidence level (in a one-tailed test) that the potential, estimated price movement will not be more than a given amount based on the correlation of market factors to the position's price sensitivity. This confidence level is used by the RiskMetrics™ version of correlation VaR.

Assessment of VaR tool

Although the methodology behind VaR is based on well-established statistical techniques, it is a more complex exercise to apply VaR in practice. Applying VaR to the whole firm can result in problems hindering the calculation, including unstable market data, issues in synchronising trading book positions across the bank and across global trading books, and the issues presented by the differing characteristics of different instruments. As one might expect, a VaR calculation can be undertaken more easily (and is likely to be proved inaccurate on fewer occasions) for an FX trading book than an exotic option trading book, due to the different behaviour of the prices of those two instruments in practice. Often banks will use a correlation method VaR model for some of their trading books and a Monte Carlo simulation approach for books holding exotic option instruments.

It is important to remember that VaR is a tool that attempts to quantify the size of a firm's risk exposure to the market. It can be viewed as a management information tool, useful for managing the business. It is conceptually straightforward to grasp because it encompasses the *market* risk of a firm into one single number; however, it is based on a statistical model of that firm's risks, and it does not capture – nor does it attempt to capture – all the risks that the firm is faced with. In the real world, the statistical assumptions used in VaR calculation will sometimes not apply – for example, in times of extreme market movements, such as market crashes or periods of high volatility, as experienced recently with the turmoil in Asian currency markets. For example, VaR makes no allowance for *liquidity* risk. In times of market correction and/or high market volatility, the inability of a bank to trade out of its positions (possibly because all of the other market participants have the same positions, and wish to trade out of them at the same time) will result in higher losses than normal, losses that a VaR model is unlikely to have catered for. In such a case, it would have been a combination of market and liquidity risk that the bank was exposed to and which resulted in trading losses. In addition, it has been argued that the normal distribution underestimates the risks of large market movements (as experienced in market crashes) and, therefore, is not an accurate representation of real market conditions. Banks may need to allow for this when calculating their VaR estimate – for example, by building in a compensating factor into their model.

Our discussion needs to be borne in mind at senior management level, so that it is clearly understood what the VaR figure means to a bank. It is important not to be over-reliant on VaR as the only measure of a firm's risk exposure, but rather as a tool forming part of an integrated and independent risk management function operating within the firm.

VaR METHODOLOGY FOR CREDIT RISK

Credit risk has emerged as a significant risk management issue this decade. As returns and interest spreads in developed markets have been reducing over time, in increasingly competitive markets banks and securities houses are taking on more forms of credit risk, in a bid to boost returns. This has led to both retail and investment banks being exposed to higher levels of *credit risk*. There are two main types of credit risk:

- credit spread risk;
- credit default risk.

Credit spread is the excess premium required by the market for taking on a certain assumed credit exposure. Credit spread risk is the risk of financial loss resulting from changes in the level of credit spreads used in the marking-to-market of a product. It is exhibited by a portfolio for which the credit spread is traded and marked. Changes in observed credit spreads affect the value of the portfolio. Credit default risk is the risk that an issuer of debt (*obligor*) is unable to meet its financial obligations. Where an obligor defaults a firm generally incurs a loss equal to the amount owed by the obligor less any recovery amount which the firm receives as a result of foreclosure, liquidation or restructuring of the defaulted obligor. By definition, all portfolios of exposures, except those of developed country government bonds, exhibit an element of credit default risk.

Modelling VaR for credit risk

After its initial introduction as a measurement tool for market risk, practitioners have recently begun to apply VaR methodology in the estimation of credit risk exposure. For example, JP Morgan's CreditMetrics™ applies the same methodology that is used in its RiskMetrics™ VaR model. CreditMetrics™ calculates probabilities of loss on a portfolio due both to default of any issuer, or due to any change in credit rating of an issuer. The investment bank CSFB has introduced its own credit risk VaR model that calculates the probability of loss due solely to instances of default of any issuer; their system is known as CreditRisk+. The main credit risk VaR methodologies take a *portfolio* approach to credit risk analysis. This means that:

- credit risks to each obligor across the portfolio are re-stated on an equivalent basis and aggregated in order to be treated consistently, regardless of the underlying asset class;
- correlations of credit quality moves across obligors are taken into account.

This allows portfolio effects – the benefits of diversification and risks of concentration – to be quantified.

The *portfolio* risk of an exposure is determined by four factors:

- size of the exposure;
- maturity of the exposure;
- probability of default of the obligor;
- systematic or concentration risk of the obligor.

All of these elements need to be accounted for when attempting to quantify credit risk exposure.

Credit VaR, like market risk VaR, considers (credit) risk in a mark-to-market framework. That is, it views credit risk exposure to arise because of changes in portfolio value that result from credit events, which are changes in obligor credit quality that include defaults, credit rating upgrades and rating downgrades. Nevertheless, credit risk is different in nature from market risk. Typically, market return distributions are assumed to be relatively symmetrical and approximated by normal distributions, for the purposes of VaR calculations. (In fact, the occurrence of extreme market movements, such as stock market crashes, is more frequent than would be predicted by pure normal distributions. If we were to model the frequency of actual

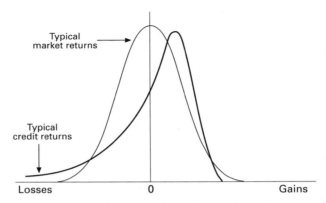

Figure 14.2　Distribution of market and credit returns.

market returns, our resulting distribution would exhibit fatter tails than the conventional normal curve, a phenomenon referred to as *leptokurtosis*.) In credit portfolios, value changes will be relatively small as a result of minor credit rating upgrades or downgrades, but can be substantial upon actual default of a firm. This remote probability of large losses produces skewed distributions with heavy downside tails that differ from the more normally distributed returns assumed for market VaR models. We illustrate the different curves in Figure 14.2.

This difference in risk profiles does not prevent us from assessing risk on a comparable basis. Analytical method market VaR models consider a time horizon and estimate value-at-risk across a distribution of estimated market outcomes. Credit VaR models similarly look to a horizon and construct a distribution of values given different estimated credit outcomes.

When modelling credit risk the two main measures of risk are:

- *Distribution of loss* – obtaining distributions of loss that may arise from the current portfolio. This considers the question of what the expected loss is for a given confidence level.
- *Identifying extreme or catastrophic outcomes* – this is addressed through the use of scenario analysis and concentration limits.

To simplify modelling no assumptions are made about the causes of default. Mathematical techniques used in the insurance industry are used to model the event of an obligor default.

Time horizon

The choice of time horizon will not be shorter than the time frame over which 'risk-mitigating' actions can be taken – that is, the time to run down a book or offload the exposure. In practice, this can be a fairly time-consuming and costly process. CSFB (who introduced the CreditRisk+ model) suggests two alternatives:

- a constant time horizon, such as 1 year;
- a hold-to-maturity time horizon.

Modelling credit risk requires certain data inputs – for example, CreditRisk+ uses the following:

- credit exposures;
- obligor default rates;
- obligor default rate volatilities;
- recovery rates.

These data requirements present some difficulties. There is a lack of comprehensive default and correlation data, and assumptions need to be made at certain times, which will affect the usefulness of any final calculation. For more liquid bond issuers there is obviously more data available. In addition, rating agencies such as Moody's have published data on, for example, the default probabilities of bonds of each category. We illustrate the 1-year default rates for rated bonds, as quoted by Moody's in 1997, at Table 14.3.

The annual probability of default of each obligor can be determined by its credit rating and then mapping between default rates and credit ratings. A default rate can then be assigned to each obligor.

Table 14.3   1-year default rates (%).

Credit rating	1-year default rate (%)
Aaa	0.00
Aa	0.03
A	0.01
Baa	0.12
Ba	1.36
B	7.27

Source: CSFB.

Default-rate volatilities can be observed from the historic volatilities of such rates.

Applications of credit VaR

A risk manager will often tell you that one purpose of a risk management system is to direct and prioritise actions, with a view to minimising the level of loss or expected loss. If we are looking at firm's credit exposure, when considering risk-mitigating actions there are various features of risk worth targeting, including obligors having:

- the largest absolute exposure;
- the largest percentage level of risk (volatility);
- the largest absolute amount of risk.

In theory, a credit VaR methodology helps to identify these areas and allows the risk manager to prioritise risk-mitigating action. This is clearly relevant in a bond dealing environment – for example, in times of market volatility or economic recession – when banks will seek to limit the extent of their loan book. Bond desks will seek to limit the extent of their exposure to obligors.

Another application that applies in a bond dealing environment is in the area of exposure limits. Within bank dealing desks, credit risk limits are often based on intuitive, but arbitrary, exposure amounts. It can be argued that this is not a logical approach because resulting decisions are not risk-driven. Risk statistics used as the basis of VaR methodology can be applied to credit limit setting, in conjunction with the standard qualitative analysis that is normally used. For this reason the limit setting departments of banks may wish to make use of a credit VaR model to assist them with their limit setting.

BIBLIOGRAPHY

Butler, C. (1999). *Mastering Value-at-Risk*. FT Prentice Hall, London.

GLOSSARY

. . . .

All-in price   *See* **Dirty price**.

Accrued interest   Interest which has been earned on a bond but not yet paid. An investor buying a bond must pay accrued interest to the seller, and this forms part of the final purchase price.

Arbitrage   The process of buying securities in one country, currency or market, and selling identical securities in another to take advantage of price differences. When this is carried out simultaneously, it is in theory a risk-free transaction. There are many forms of arbitrage transactions. For instance, in the cash market a bank might issue a money market instrument in one money centre and invest the same amount in another centre at a higher rate, such as an issue of 3-month US dollar CDs in the US at 5.5% and a purchase of 3-month Eurodollar CDs at 5.6%. In the futures market, arbitrage might involve buying 3-month contracts and selling forward 6-month contracts.

Auction   A method of issue where institutions submit bids to the issuer on a price or yield basis. Auction rules vary considerably across markets.

Basis risk   A form of market risk that arises whenever one kind of risk exposure is hedged with an instrument that behaves in a similar, but not necessarily identical way. For instance, a bank trading desk may use 3-month interest-rate futures to hedge its commercial paper or Euronote programme. Although Eurocurrency rates, to which futures prices respond, are well correlated with commercial paper rates they do not always move in lockstep. If, therefore, commercial paper rates move by 10 basis points but futures prices drop by only 7 basis points, the 3-basis-point gap would be the basis risk.

Bearer bond   A bond for which physical possession of the certificate is proof of ownership. The issuer does not know the identity of the bondholder. Traditionally, the bond carries detachable coupons, one for each interest payment date, which are posted to the issuer when payment is due. At maturity the bond is redeemed by sending in the certificate for repayment. These days bearer bonds are usually settled electronically, and while no register of ownership is kept by the issuer, coupon payments may be made electronically.

Benchmark A bond whose terms set a standard for the market. The benchmark usually has the greatest liquidity, the highest turnover and is usually the most frequently quoted.

Bid The price at which a market maker will buy bonds. A tight bid–offer spread is indicative of a liquid and competitive market.

Bid–Offer The two-way price at which a market will buy and sell stock.

Bill A *bill of exchange* is a payment order written by one person (the drawer) to another, directing the latter (drawee) to pay a certain amount of money at a future date to a third party. A bill of exchange is a bank draft when drawn on a bank. By accepting the draft, a bank agrees to pay the face value of the obligation if the drawer fails to pay, hence the term *banker's acceptance*. A *Treasury bill* is short-term government paper of up to 1 year's maturity, sold at a discount to principal value and redeemed at par.

Bulldog Sterling domestic bonds issued by non-UK domiciled borrowers. These bonds trade under a similar arrangement to gilts and are settled via the CGO.

Bullet A single redemption payment on maturity.

Callable bond A bond which provides the borrower with an option to redeem the issue before the original maturity date. In most cases certain terms are set before the issue, such as the date after which the bond is callable and the price at which the issuer may redeem the bond.

CBOT The Chicago Board of Trade, one of the two futures exchanges in Chicago, and one of the largest in the world.

Cedel *Centrale de Livraison de Valeurs Mobilières*, a clearing system for Eurocurrency and international bonds. Cedel is located in Luxembourg and is jointly owned by a number of European banks.

Central Gilts Office (CGO) The office of the Bank of England which runs the computer-based settlement system for gilt-edged securities and certain other securities (mostly bulldogs) for which the Bank acts as Registrar.

Certificate of deposit (CDs) A money market instrument of up to 1 year's maturity (although CDs of up to 5 years have been issued) that pays a bullet interest payment on maturity. After issue, CDs can trade freely in the secondary market, the ease of which is a function of the credit quality of the issuer.

CGO reference prices Daily prices of gilt-edged and other securities held in CGO which are used by CGO in various processes, including revaluing stock loan transactions, calculating total consideration in a repo transaction, and DBV assembly.

Credit derivative An OTC derivative contract whose payoff is linked to the credit quality performance of a named reference asset. Typified by the credit default swap contract.

CREST The paperless share settlement system through which trades conducted on the London Stock Exchange can be settled. The system is operated by CRESTCo and was introduced in 1996.

Cum-dividend Literally 'with dividend'; stock that is traded with interest or dividend accrued included in the price.

Day count The convention used to calculate accrued interest on bonds and interest on cash. For UK gilts the convention changed to actual/actual from actual/365 on 1 November 1998. For cash the convention in sterling markets is actual/365.

DBV (delivery by value) A mechanism whereby a CGO member may borrow from or lend money to another CGO member against overnight gilt collateral. The CGO system automatically selects and delivers securities to a specified aggregate value on the basis of the previous night's CGO reference prices; equivalent securities are returned the following day. The DBV functionality allows the giver and taker of collateral to specify the classes of security to include within the DBV. The options are: all classes of security held within CGO, including strips and bulldogs; coupon bearing gilts and bulldogs; coupon bearing gilts and strips; only coupon bearing gilts.

Delivery versus payment (DVP) The simultaneous exchange of securities and cash. The assured payment mechanism of the CGO achieves the same protection.

Dirty price The price of a bond including accrued interest. Also known as the **All-in price**.

Debt Management Office (DMO) An executive arm of the UK Treasury, responsible for cash management of the government's borrowing requirement. This includes responsibility for issuing government bonds (gilts), a function previously carried out by the Bank of England. The DMO began operations in April 1998.

Duration weighting The process of using the modified duration value for bonds to calculate the exact nominal holdings in a spread position. This is necessary because £1 million nominal of a 2-year bond is not equivalent to £1 million of, say, a 5-year bond. The modified duration value of the 5-year bond will be higher, indicating that its basis point value (*BPV*) will be greater, and that therefore £1 million worth of this bond represents greater sensitivity to a move in interest rates (risk). As another example, consider a fund manager holding £10 million of 5-year bonds. The fund manager wishes to switch into a holding of 2-year bonds with the same overall risk position. The basis point values of the bonds are 0.041 583 and 0.022 898, respectively. The ratio of the BPVs are 0.041 583/0.022 898 = 1.816. The fund manager therefore needs to switch into £10m × 1.816 = £18.160 million of the 2-year bond.

Euroclear   An international clearing system for Eurocurrency and international securities. Euroclear is based in Brussels and managed by Morgan Guaranty Trust Company.

Ex-dividend (xd) date   A bond's record date for the payment of coupons. The coupon payment will be made to the person who is the registered holder of the stock on the xd date. For UK gilts this is seven working days before the coupon date.

FSA   The Financial Services Authority, the body responsible for the regulation of investment business, and the supervision of banks and money market institutions in the UK. The FSA took over these duties from nine 'self-regulatory organisations' that had previously carried out this function, including the Securities and Futures Authority (*SFA*), which had been responsible for regulation of professional investment business in the City of London. The FSA commenced its duties in 1998.

Future   A futures contract is a contract to buy or sell securities or other goods at a future date at a predetermined price. Futures contracts are usually standardised and traded on an exchange.

GEMM   A gilt-edged market maker, a bank or securities house registered with the Bank of England as a market maker in gilts. A GEMM is required to meet certain obligations as part of its function as a registered market maker, including making two-way price quotes at all times in all gilts and taking part in gilt auctions. The DMO now makes a distinction between conventional gilt GEMMs and index-linked GEMMs, known as IG GEMMs.

General collateral (GC)   Securities, which are not 'special', used as collateral against cash borrowing. A repo buyer will accept GC at any time that a specific stock is not quoted as required in the transaction. In the gilts market GC includes DBVs.

Immunisation   This is the process by which a bond portfolio is created that has an assured return for a specific time horizon irrespective of changes in interest rates. The mechanism underlying immunisation is a portfolio structure that balances the change in the value of a portfolio at the end of the investment horizon (time period) with the return gained from the reinvestment of cash flows from the portfolio. As such, immunisation requires the portfolio manager to offset interest-rate risk and reinvestment risk.

Initial margin   The excess either of cash over the value of securities, or of the value of securities over cash in a repo transaction at the time it is executed and subsequently, after margin calls.

ISMA   The International Securities Market Association. This association drew up with the PSA (now renamed the Bond Market Association) the PSA/ISMA Global Master Repurchase Agreement. Now known as the International Capital Markets Association (ICMA).

Libid   The London Interbank Bid Rate, the rate at which banks will pay for funds in the interbank market.

Libor   The London Interbank Offered Rate, the rate for all major currencies up to 1 year set at 11:00 hours each day by the BBA.

Libor fixing   The Libor rate 'fixed' by the BBA at 11:00 hours each day, for maturities up to 1 year.

LIFFE   The London International Financial Futures and Options Exchange.

Limean   The arithmetic average of Libor and Libid rates.

Liquidity   A word describing the ease with which one can undertake transactions in a particular market or instrument. A market where there are always ready buyers and sellers willing to transact at competitive prices is regarded as liquid. In banking, the term is also used to describe the requirement that a portion of a bank's assets be held in short-term risk-free instruments, such as government bonds, T-Bills and high-quality CDs.

Margin call   A request following marking-to-market of a repo transaction for the initial margin to be reinstated or, where no initial margin has been taken, to restore the cash/securities ratio to parity.

Mark-to-market   The act of revaluing securities to current market values. Such revaluations should include both coupon accrued on the securities outstanding and interest accrued on the cash.

Matched book   This refers to the matching by a repo trader of securities repoed in and out. It carries no implications that the trader's position is 'matched' in terms of exposure – for example, to short-term interest rates.

Offer   The price at which a market maker will sell bonds.

Opening leg   The first half of a repo transaction. *See* **Closing leg**.

Option   The right (but not the obligation) to buy or sell securities at a fixed price within a specified period.

OTC   Over the counter. Strictly speaking any transaction not conducted on a registered stock exchange. Trades conducted via the telephone between banks, and contracts such as FRAs and (non-exchange traded) options are said to be OTC instruments. OTC also refers to non-standard instruments or contracts traded between two parties; for example, a client with a requirement for a specific risk to be hedged with a tailor-made instrument may enter into an OTC-structured option trade with a bank that makes markets in such products.

Preference shares   These are a form of corporate financing. They are normally fixed-interest shares whose holders have the right to receive dividends ahead of ordinary shareholders. If a company were to go into liquidation, preference shareholders would rank above ordinary shareholders for the repayment of their investment in the company. Preference shares (*prefs*) are normally traded within the fixed-interest division of a bank or securities house.

Primary market   The market for new debt, into which new bonds are issued. The primary market is made up of borrowers, investors and the investment banks which place new debt into the market, usually with their clients. Bonds that trade after they have been issued are said to be part of the secondary market.

Refer   The practice whereby a trader instructs a broker to put 'under reference' any prices or rates he has quoted to him, meaning that they are no longer 'firm' and the broker must refer to the trader before he can trade on the price initially quoted.

Registered bond   A bond for which the issuer keeps a record (register) of its owners. Transfer of ownership must be notified and recorded in the register. Interest payments are posted (more usually electronically transferred) to the bondholder.

Repo rate   The return earned on a repo transaction expressed as an interest rate on the cash side of the transaction.

Secondary market   The market in instruments after they have been issued. Bonds are bought and sold after their initial issue by the borrower, and the market place for this buying and selling is referred to as the secondary market. The new issues market is the *primary* market.

Securities and Exchange Commission   The central regulatory authority in the US, responsible for policing the financial markets including the bond markets.

Settlement The process of transferring stock from seller to buyer and arranging the corresponding movement of funds between the two parties.

Special A security which for any reason is sought after in the repo market, thereby enabling any holder of the security to earn incremental income (in excess of the GC rate) through lending them via a repo transaction. The repo rate for a special will be below the GC rate, as this is the rate the borrower of the cash is paying in return for supplying the special bond as collateral. An individual security can be in high demand for a variety of reasons: for instance, if there is sudden heavy investor demand for it, or (if it is a benchmark issue) it is required as a hedge against a new issue of similar maturity paper.

Strip A zero-coupon bond which is produced by separating a standard coupon-bearing bond into its constituent principal and interest components.

Tranche One of a series of two or more issues with the same coupon rate and maturity date. The tranches become fungible at a future date, usually just after the first coupon date.

Underwriting An arrangement by which a company is guaranteed that an issue of debt (bonds) will raise a given amount of cash. Underwriting is carried out by investment banks, who undertake to purchase any part of the debt issue not taken up by the public. A commission is charged for this service.

Variation margin The band agreed between the parties to a repo transaction at the outset within which the value of the collateral may fluctuate before triggering a right to call for cash or securities to reinstate the initial margin on the repo transaction.

Warrant A security giving the holder a right to subscribe to a share or bond at a given price and from a certain date. If this right is not exercised before the maturity date, the warrant will expire worthless.

When-issued trading Trading a bond before the issue date; no interest is accrued during this period. Also known as the 'grey market'.

Zero-coupon bond A bond issued at discount to par and which redeems at par. It carries no coupon during its life.

ABBREVIATIONS

....

ABS	Asset Backed Securities
ALM	Asset Liability Management
ASW	Bloomberg term for Asset SWap
BBA	British Bankers Association
BIS	Bank for International Settlements
BoE	Bank of England
BPV	Basis Point Value
B-S	Black–Scholes
CBOT	Chicago Board of Trade
CDs	Certificates of Deposit
CDO	Collateralised Debt Obligation
CDS	Credit Default Swap
Cedel	*Centrale de Livraison de Valeurs Mobilières*
CGO	Central Gilts Office
CLN	Credit Linked Note
CMO	Collateralised Mortgage Obligation
CP	Commercial Paper
CPI-U	Consumer Price Index (US)
CSFB	Credit Suisse First Boston
CTD	Cheapest To Deliver
CUSIP	The bond identification number for US securities
DBV	Delivery By Value
D&P	Duff & Phelps Credit Rating Co.
DES	DEScription (Bloomberg screen)
DMO	Debt Management Office
DVBP	Dollar Value of a Basis Point
DVP	Delivery Versus Payment
ECB	European Central Bank
EIB	European Investment Bank
EMTN	Euro Medium Term Note,

EURIBOR, Euribor	EURo InterBank Offered Rate
Fitch	Fitch Investors Service, Inc.
FRA	Forward Rate Agreement
FRN	Floating Rate Note
FSA	Financial Services Authority
FX	Foreign eXchange
GC	General Collateral
GEMM	Gilt Edged Market Maker
GMRA	Global Master Repurchase Agreement
GNMA	Government National Mortgage Association
GDP	Gross Domestic Product
GRY	Gross Redemption Yield
HP	Hewlett Packard
IAN	Indexed Amortising Note
ICMA	International Capital Market Association
IDN	Interest Differential Note
IG-GEMM	Index-linked Gilt Edged Market Maker
IMF	International Monetary Fund
IR	Interest Rate
IRR	Internal Rate of Return
ISIN	International Securities Identification Number
ISDA	International Swap Dealers Association
ISMA	The International Securities Market Association
IT	Information Technology
LCH	London Clearing House
LIBID, Libid	London Interbank BID Rate
LIBOR, Libor	London InterBank Offer Rate
LIFFE	London International Financial Futures Exchange
LOC	Letter Of Credit
MBS	Mortgage Backed Securities
Moody's	Moody's Investors Service, Inc.
MTN	Medium Term Note
OBS	Off Balance Sheet
O/N	OverNight rate
OTC	Over The Counter
P/L, p/l	Profit and Loss
Prefs	Preference shares
PSA	Public Securities Association
PVBP	Present Value of a Basis Point
RMBS	Residential Mortgage Backed Securities

ROE	Return On Equity
S&P	Standard & Poor's Corporation
SEC	Securities and Exchange Commission
SEDOL	Stock Exchange Daily Official List
SFA	Securities and Futures Authority
Sibor	Singapore InterBank Offer Rate
SPC	Special Purpose Company
SPE	Special Purpose Entity
SPV	Special Purpose Vehicle
T-bill	Treasury bill
TIIS	Treasury Inflation Indexed Securities
TIPS	Treasury Inflation Protected Securities
T/N	Tom-Next or Tomorrow-to-the-Next
TR	Total Return
TRS	Total Return Swap
VaR	Value-at-Risk
WAL	Weighted Average Life
xd	Ex-dividend
YTM	Yield To Maturity

INDEX

Other titles by the author

....

Corporate Bond Markets: Instruments and Applications, John Wiley & Sons, 2005.

The Money Markets Handbook: A Practitioner's Guide, John Wiley & Sons, 2005.

Structured Credit Products: Credit Derivatives and Synthetic Securitisation, John Wiley & Sons, 2004.

Advanced Fixed Income Analysis, Elsevier, 2004.

Handbook of European Fixed Income Securities (editor, with Frank Fabozzi), John Wiley & Sons, 2004.

Analysing and Interpreting the Yield Curve, John Wiley & Sons, 2004.

The Gilt-edged Market, Butterworth-Heinemann, 2003.

Derivative Instruments (with Brian Eales), Butterworth-Heinemann, 2003.

The Repo Handbook, Butterworth Heinemann 2002.

Capital Market Instruments: Analysis and Valuation, FT Prentice Hall, 2001.

Bond Market Securities, FT Prentice Hall, 2001.

The Bond and Money Markets: Strategy, Trading, Analysis, Butterworth-Heinemann, 2001.